Contents

W0009612

Figures

Contributors

John Beebe trained as a psychiatrist at Stanford University Medical Center, where he was Chief Resident in 1970–1971. Since 1971, he has been in the private practice of psychotherapy in San Francisco. Trained at the C.G. Jung Institute of San Francisco, he became an analyst in 1978. A past president of the San Francisco Institute, he is active in its training program and is a frequent lecturer internationally on topics related to analytical psychology. He founded the *San Francisco Jung Institute Library Journal* in 1979, and was the first American co-editor of the *Journal of Analytical Psychology* from 1990 to 1997. He is the author of *Integrity in Depth* (1992) and the editor of several books, including C.G. Jung's *Aspects of the Masculine* (1989) and *Terror, Violence and the Impulse to Destroy* (2003).

Joseph Cambray, PhD is the Honorary Secretary of the International Association for Analytical Psychology, co-editor-in-chief of the *Journal of Analytical Psychology*, and the author of various articles on the theory and practice of Jungian analysis. He is a member of the New England Society of Jungian Analysts, past president of the C.G. Jung Institute, Boston, and is on the faculty of the Center for Psychoanalytic Studies at Massachusetts General Hospital, Harvard University. He maintains private psychotherapy practices in Boston, MA and Providence, RI.

Linda Carter, MSN, CS graduated from Georgetown and Yale Universities. She is a graduate of the C.G. Jung Institute of Boston where she is on the faculty, supervising and teaching analysts in training. She has presented papers at national and international conferences including explorations of night terrors. She has private practices in Boston, MA and Providence, RI.

George B. Hogenson, PhD is a training analyst in the Chicago Society of Jungian Analysts. He is the author of *Jung's Struggle with Freud*, and numerous articles on the history and theory of analytical psychology. He holds advanced degrees from Yale University (philosophy) and the

University of Chicago (clinical social work) and is a leading exponent of the dynamic systems or emergentist interpretation of Jung's system of psychology.

Samuel L. Kimbles, PhD is a clinical psychologist, Jungian analyst, and organizational consultant. He is an Associate Clinical Professor of Family and Community Medicine at the University of California, San Francisco, and maintains a private practice in Santa Rosa and San Francisco, CA.

Thomas B. Kirsch, MD is a Jungian analyst in private practice in Palo Alto, CA. He is Past President, C.G. Jung Institute, San Francisco, Past President of the International Association for Analytical Psychology, and member of the Academy of Psychoanalysis. He is also the author of numerous articles and book reviews on analytical psychology, and *The Jungians*, published by Routledge (2000).

Jean Knox, PhD, MBBS, MRCPsych is a psychiatrist and Jungian analyst in private practice in Oxford, and co-editor-in-chief of the *Journal of Analytical Psychology*. She has published a number of papers exploring the links between analytical psychology and cognitive neuroscience and attachment theory, and her book *Archetype, Attachment, Analysis: Jungian Psychology and the Emergent Mind* was published by Brunner-Routledge in 2003.

Hester McFarland Solomon is Vice President of the IAAP, with past responsibility as Chair of the Ethics Procedures Sub-Committee and Ethics Liaison, and is currently Chair of the Grants and Research Sub-Committee. She is a training analyst and supervisor for the Jungian Section of the British Association of Psychotherapists. She has been Chair of the BAP's Council, its Training Committee, and its Ethics Committee, and is a Fellow of the Association. She has published widely and has co-edited three books: *Jungian Thought in the Modern World*, *Contemporary Jungian Clinical Practice*, and most recently *The Ethical Attitude in Analytic Practice*.

Thomas Singer, MD is a psychiatrist and Jungian analyst in San Francisco. He is on the faculty of UCSF Medical Center and a Medical Expert for the Federal Social Security system. A member of the San Francisco C.G. Jung Institute, Dr Singer has written *Who's the Patient Here? Portraits of the Young Psychotherapist* and *A Fan's Guide to Baseball Fever: The Official Medical Reference*. He has edited *The Vision Thing: Myth, Politics and Psyche in the World* and has recently co-edited *The Cultural Complex: Contemporary Jungian Perspectives on Psyche and Society*.

Murray Stein, PhD is the President of the International Association for Analytical Psychology. He has lectured widely and has written several papers and a book (*Jung's Treatment of Christianity*) on the subject of analytical psychology and spirituality. After living and practising as a Jungian Analyst for 25 years in Chicago, he now resides in Switzerland.

Jan Wiener is a training analyst and supervisor for the Society of Analytical Psychology (SAP) and the British Association of Psychotherapists. She is at present Director of Training at the SAP. She works part-time in an out-patient psychotherapy clinic in Thorpe Coombe Hospital, Walthamstow and in private practice. For the past 10 years she has visited St Petersburg, Russia, teaching and supervising students interested in analytical psych-ology. She is co-liaison officer for the IAAP of the St Petersburg Develop-ing Group in Analytical Psychology. She is author of a number of papers on analytical psychology and of *Counselling and Psychotherapy in Primary Health Care: A Psychodynamic Approach* (1998), written with Mannie Sher and published by Palgrave/Macmillan. More recently, together with Richard Mizen and Jenny Duckham, she has edited *Supervising and Being Supervised: A Practice in Search of a Theory* (2003), published by Palgrave/ Macmillan.

Beverley Zabriskie, a Jungian analyst in private practice in New York City, is an Assistant Editor of the *Journal of Analytical Psychology*. She has been a member of the faculties of the C.G. Jung Institute of New York and the C.G. Jung Center of Mexico City. Publications include "A meeting of rare minds", Preface to *Atom and Archetype: The Pauli-Jung Correspondence*, Princeton University Press, 2001 and "The psyche as process", *Psycho-analytic Dialogues*, **10**(3), 2000. She is a past president of the National Association for the Advancement of Psychoanalysis.

Series preface

This series focuses on advanced and advancing theory in psychotherapy. Its aims are: to present theory and practice within a specific theoretical orientation or approach at an advanced, postgraduate level; to advance theory by presenting and evaluating new ideas and their relation to the approach; to locate the orientation and its applications within cultural contexts both historically in terms of the origins of the approach, and contemporarily in terms of current debates about philosophy, theory, society and therapy; and, finally, to present and develop a critical view of theory and practice, especially in the context of debates about power, organisation and the increasing professionalisation of therapy.

As editors of this volume, Joe Cambray and Linda Carter have commissioned chapters of high academic quality from respected practitioners and theorists in the field of analytical psychology. They have, with great thought and care, constructed a book which takes the reader through a number of contemporary debates concerning key concepts and developments in this field, including archetypes, human development, consciousness, personality types, and synchronicity. The whole volume works on what the editors refer to as (two) axes: the *intellectual/historical* – which not only forms the cultural matrix for Jung's model of the psyche but also acts as a frame for the subsequent intellectual and organisational development of analytical psychology; and the *developmental* – which encompasses the reconsideration and reworking of core concepts of theory and method. From its first chapter, which considers the history of analytical psychology, the book holds and combines a focus on past, present and future. The contributors draw on Jung's own body of work, focus on and, to a certain extent, shape the current state of analytical psychology, and point to future areas for exploration. Drawing on developments in neuroscientific, evolutionary, psychoanalytic, philosophical and historical studies, both authors and editors fulfill the brief of the series, inviting the reader into important interdisciplinary territory. Notwithstanding its advancing nature and the sophistication of the ideas it contains, this volume stands as readable, accessible and stimulating to a general, professional audience as well as to those in the field of analytical pyschology.

Keith Tudor

Introduction

Joseph Cambray and Linda Carter

This volume calls attention to recent developments in analytical psychology along several axes, the first being the intellectual, historical background which in part formed the cultural matrix for Jung's articulation of his model of the psyche. This perspective has been emerging in recent years with numerous journal articles on Jung's ideas as well as a number of new biographies that have shed light on various aspects of his background, the most definitive being the recently published biography by Deirdre Bair, *Jung: A Biography* (2003); and the first large-scale intellectual history, *Jung and the Making of Modern Psychology: The Dream of a Science* by the historian of analytical psychology Sonu Shamdasani. The second axis includes reconsideration of core concepts and practices in the Jungian tradition, which can be corroborated, elaborated and enhanced by the influx of innovative ideas from diverse fields such as cognitive science and neuroscience, attachment theory, psychoanalysis, and complexity theory. These approaches have been increasingly employed in the recent literature; they have been the focus of multidisciplinary conferences including the international Congress of the International Association for Analytical Psychology (IAAP) in Barcelona, Spain, August 2004. Similarly, these viewpoints are variously threaded throughout the chapters. Integration of this new information offered in the present volume serves to deepen and strengthen as well as modify the Jungian position and identity while offering dialogue with psychotherapists from other schools, psychoanalysts, scientists, and scholars.

The present text assumes a basic familiarity with core Jungian concepts. For a good contemporary introduction to Jung's work see Ann Casement's *Carl Gustav Jung* (2001); a concise, readily accessible presentation of numerous concepts can be found in Andrew Samuels, *et. al.*'s *A Critical Dictionary of Jungian Analysis* (1986). Patient permission and protection of confidentiality have been maintained throughout the text.

Chapter 1 deals with the history of analytical psychology written by Thomas B. Kirsch, past-president of the IAAP and author on various aspects of Jungian history including his *The Jungians: A Comparative and Historical Perspective*, a detailed account which chronicles the history of the Jungian movement in its transition from an oral to a written tradition. Here he skill-fully weaves together biography with social history, giving a background and frame for the following chapters. Wide interest in multiple facets of historical studies on Jung, his ideas, and the movement that derives from his work has become evident from the three well-attended Jungian history symposia spearheaded by Tom in collaboration with one of the editors of this book (JC), co-sponsored by the C.G. Jung Institute of San Francisco and the *Journal of Analytical Psychology*, in addition to the abovementioned recent biographies and intellectual histories.

Author, analyst and scholar George Hogenson examines the intellectual history behind one of Jung's signature concepts, the archetype, in Chapter 2. After introducing various views on the "archetype" he explores uses of the term in the history of the biological sciences. Following his tracing of Jung's development of the concept, he elaborates the emergentist model that he presented in his 2001 *Journal of Analytical Psychology* paper "The Baldwin Effect revisited." While free-standing, this chapter also fits well into the cor-pus of his other works in the area of the history of ideas with a special interest in the scientific roots of Jung's major concepts. These studies have included a careful look at Jung's philosophical and scientific sources and differentiated them from Freud's.

In Chapter 3, analyst Jean Knox, the UK co-editor-in-chief of the *Journal of Analytical Psychology* and author of the recent book *Archetype, Attach-ment, Analysis: Jungian Psychology and the Emergent Mind* (2003), presents a contemporary Jungian developmental model combining attachment theory, psychoanalysis, and Jungian theory. Her views and use of the concept of archetype differ in subtle but crucial ways from Hogenson yet remain within the larger emergentist paradigm.

The author of Chapter 4, John Beebe, analyst, past co-editor-in-chief of the *Journal of Analytical Psychology* and dean of American studies in typol-ogy, previously has discussed Jung's first full-length book after his break with Freud, *Psychological Types* (CW 6), in terms of its being one of the first postmodern presentations of the human psyche. This is based on the book's articulation of a non-pathological view of the multiplicity of consciousness. In the present chapter, John provides additional intellectual background to Jung's system of types. He then guides the reader through his own extension of the model to ground it more securely in archetypal theory. He does this with a detailed personal account which doubles as a case history exemplifying theoretical ideas in conjunction with lived experience.

The co-editors of this volume jointly authored Chapter 5, bringing emer-gentist models of the mind that are informing recent reformulations of Jungian theory to the subject of analytical methods. Reassessing Jung's innovative clinical methodology that stems from his formulation of the transcendent function, we argue that amplification, active imagination, and work with dreams can all be enhanced by incorporation of research findings from multiple perspectives, including from cognitive science and neuroscience as well as attachment and complexity theories in conjunction with the narrative traditions associated with mythology and story-telling.

Another dimension of analytic methods is given in Chapter 6, a study of transference and countertransference written by Jan Wiener, an analyst with the Society of Analytical Psychology in London. She draws on a wealth of personal experience as an analyst, supervisor, and teacher to deal with this complicated subject with its long history both within analytical psychology and in psychoanalysis. Due to the controversial nature of analytical psychology's varying approaches to transference and countertransference, the editors chose to devote a chapter specifically to this topic rather than attempt to reduce it to a single subject area in Chapter 4. Jan graciously agreed to this task and explicates the history and contemporary developments in this area with a lively and cogent synthesis of a tremendous quantity of information.

Chapter 7 was co-written by analyst–authors Tom Singer and Sam Kimbles, both from San Francisco. They link Joseph Henderson's ideas about the cultural unconscious with Jung's complex theory to develop their own model of cultural complexes. Through Singer's and Kimbles' work, an emergentist perspective on the psychology at play between the personal and the collective layers of the psyche has been conceived within a wholly Jungian framework. This is nicely illustrated with clinical experiences from Sam's practice and from Tom's depiction of the cultural complex operative in James Carroll's *Constantine's Sword*. They also expand Donald Kalsched's views on trauma, demonstrating the relevance of cultural complexes within and between groups.

International Association for Analytical Psychology President, Murray Stein, who has published numerous books and articles on Jungian psychology, authored Chapter 8. This chapter discusses a central concern of most therapists who find value in a Jungian approach, the religious or spiritual dimension of clinical work. A concise orientation to Jung's thought in this area is followed by case studies that should help the professional therapist and student more immediately grasp the relevance of the spiritual dimension in practice, especially in the context of long-term, ongoing Jungian analysis.

One of the editors of this volume, Joe Cambray, authored Chapter 9, in which he re-examines another of Jung's signature concepts, synchronicity. This is elaborated first in terms of selected aspects of the intellectual and cultural backgrounds from which the idea emerged. This is followed by a reassessment of synchronicity in terms of the concept of emergence from complexity theory. One of Jung's clinical examples of synchronicity is re-examined from this vantage and a set of clinical vignettes from the author's practice is put forward. This chapter highlights the value of a theory of emergence in identifying, including, and working with synchronistic experience in general psychotherapeutic practice.

Chapter 10, written by International Association for Analytical Psychology Vice President Hester Solomon, brings forward the importance of ethics in clinical practice, a significant topic for all helping professionals. Hester, who has extensive experience in dealing with ethics matters in multiple venues, presents a theory about the origins of the ethical attitude in early development. She goes on to emphasize and demonstrate the centrality of this for modern adult analytic and psychotherapeutic practice.

Beverley Zabriskie, analyst, author and Assistant Editor of the *Journal of Analytical Psychology*, concludes the book with endnotes wherein she gives her thoughts on the chapters with the intention of deepening the reader's understanding and synthesizing an overall perspective with relevant linkages. She adds an assessment of the book's strengths and weaknesses, and offers recommendations that go beyond the current scope of this work.

References

Casement, A. (2001) *Carl Gustav Jung*, London: Sage.
Samuels, A., Shorter, B. and Plaut, F. (1986) *A Critical Dictionary of Jungian Analysis*, London: Routledge.

Chapter 1

History of analytical psychology

Thomas B. Kirsch

The history of analytical psychology is part of the larger history of depth psychology and psychoanalysis, with which it is intertwined and yet separate. Due to the painful and bitter parting between the founders of psychoanalysis and analytical psychology, Sigmund Freud and Carl Gustav Jung, a reliable early history has been difficult to ascertain. In a profound way the cleavage between the two founders has both promoted and at the same time inhibited the growth of the two fields. It is not my intention to rehash the Freud/Jung controversy, because it is so fraught with factional disputes that any objective view is hard to establish. However, it is necessary that it be mentioned as a baseline problem that has had a long-term and defining imprint on both schools.

Through study of the history of these two movements, one can develop a deeper understanding of why the founders had to separate and travel their own pathways. Beyond the personal clash between the two men, there was a wide cultural divergence. Simply put, Freud's training was in biology, and his theories of the unconscious developed out of a neurophysiological background. Jung, on the other hand, was deeply influenced by continental philosophy, especially Leibniz's "unconscious perceptions," Kant's "dark representations" and *ding-an-sich*, Schopenhauer's "tendency of the unconscious material to flow into quite definite molds," and finally Nietzsche's ideas from *Thus Spake Zarathustra*.

Any history of analytical psychology must begin with its founder, C.G. Jung. It is not the intent to give extensive biographical material on Jung, but there are salient facts about his life which have influenced the development of analytical psychology.

Jung was born on 26 July 1875, in a small Swiss village, Kesswil, along the Rhine River. He came from a long line of Protestant ministers, including his father. His mother's ancestors had mediumistic experiences, as did she. Jung had powerful dreams at a very young age, which he describes in his autobiography, *Memories, Dreams, and Reflections*.[1] As mentioned above, he had a strong interest in philosophy, but he went to medical school in Basel, Switzerland, graduating in 1900.

He then moved to Zurich, where he worked at the Burghölzli clinic under Professor Eugen Bleuler. Jung became Bleuler's first assistant and remained at the Burghölzli until 1909 when he left to enter private practice, which he continued with some interruptions until his death in 1961.

In 1903 he married Emma Rauschenbach, the daughter of a wealthy industrialist from Schaffhausen, and they had five children, four girls and one boy. In 1909 they built a house on Lake Zurich in Kusnacht where they lived the rest of their lives. Jung also developed a very important relationship in 1912 with a former patient of his, Toni Wolff. She was the other woman in Jung's life, and she became his assistant. These circumstances were known to Jung's family as well as to his patients and disciples, and the three parties involved appeared to be comfortable with the arrangement. In recent years this situation has received much attention, and has given rise to the belief that Jung was a womanizer.[2]

In 1924 Jung built the tower in Bollingen, mostly with his own hands; he continued working on it for the rest of his life. The tower was also on Lake Zurich, but it was in a very secluded part, and here Jung could live in a simple and introverted way. He spent many weeks at a time in Bollingen.

Jung's work on word association experiments at the Burghölzli led him to contact Freud, since he realized that Freud's observations on the unconscious were crucial to an explanation of his own research results. This led to Jung writing to Freud in 1906, and in 1907 the Jungs, along with Ludwig Binswanger, travelled to Vienna, where the first conversation between Jung and Freud lasted for 13 hours. Freud recognized Jung's talents and later referred to the younger man as his "crown prince." For the next six years, Jung was a leading adherent of Freud's, and he represented psychoanalysis both in Europe and in the United States, becoming the first president of the International Psychoanalytic Association, and editor of the major psychoanalytic journal and various books. The bitter breakup of their relationship is dramatically chronicled through the letters they exchanged (see McGuire 1974 on the Freud/Jung Letters).

Sabina Spielrein is mentioned over 30 times in the letters and I would like to draw attention to her, as a great deal of new material has come out recently. Consulting Freud as supervisor, she was Jung's first patient with whom he used psychoanalytic techniques. Sabina Spielrein was a 19-year-old Russian Jewish woman who was brought in on an emergency basis on the evening of 17 August 1904 with a diagnosis of hysteria. Jung became her doctor and psychotherapist, and an extremely strong transference/countertransference situation developed. By the following spring she was well enough to attend medical school in Zurich, and was able to leave the hospital. She continued to see Jung as a patient over the next few years, and a strong love relationship developed between the two of them. The exact nature of what happened in their interaction is unknown, but some, including Bruno Bettelheim, are convinced that they had a complete sexual relationship. After graduating from medical school in Zurich she moved to Vienna, where she became a part of the Viennese psychoanalytic circle and became a psychoanalyst. She married and had a daughter, and after moving around for several years, she returned to Russia where she became a leader in psychoanalysis. She opened a psychoanalytic kindergarten in Moscow in 1925, but as Stalin gained control of the country psychoanalysis was outlawed and she returned to Rostov; little is known of what she did there. She was killed by the Nazis in 1942 along with other Jews of the city. Much of this material has become available only in the past 14 years with the breakdown of the Soviet empire. Also, her hospital records at the Burghölzli have been released by surviving family members, so we have a much better idea of her state of being in the hospital. Her story is very dramatic, and recently she has become the object of many new books, movies, and theatrical plays. She is no longer just a footnote in psychoanalytic history and her papers linking sexuality, destruction, and creativity have become better known. Freud included a footnote on her when he first wrote about the "death instinct" in *Beyond the Pleasure Principle* in 1922.

Let us return to what happened to Jung after the breakup of his relationship to Freud. Jung underwent a profound introversion where images from the unconscious flooded him. He spent much time alone and went through periods of disorientation. At the conclusion of the First World War and this period of what he called "confrontation with the unconscious," he felt much more secure and had developed the basic elements of what he was to call his new psychology – analytical psychology. The first use of this term is in his *Psychology of the Unconscious*, written in 1912–1913. Although Jung coined the term "analytical psychology," it has often been used interchangeably with the term "Jungian." Many modern-day analysts refer to themselves as Jungian analysts, others as analytical psychologists, and still others as Jungian psychoanalysts. These different identities refer to various levels of commitment, allegiance, and identification with both Jung and analytical psychology. It seems that as we move further away from the life and work of Jung, terms other than "Jungian analyst" are coming more into common usage.

In 1921 Jung published a major work, *Psychological Types*, where he described the now well-known typology introversion/extraversion, along with the feeling/thinking and intuitive/sensation functions. These terms have come into common usage in many languages, and the psychological type theory is used extensively in business applications.

By the 1920s, Jung's reputation and psychology had become well established and his interest in the creative process led him to attract many writers and artists. His psychology particularly attracted students from England and the United States along with others from around the world. He gave seminars during the academic year to his English-speaking students in Zurich, and he lectured and traveled widely throughout Europe and United States, along with trips to Africa and India. In 1934 he became president of the

International Medical Society of Psychotherapy and in that capacity he worked closely with colleagues strongly identified with the political leadership of Nazi Germany. His reputation has been marred by that association, which I will discuss in more detail below with the history of analytical psychology in Germany.

In 1928 he received a manuscript from Richard Wilhelm, a renowned sinologist, who had translated an ancient Chinese alchemical text, *The Secret of the Golden Flower* (1929). Through this book Jung became interested in the subject of alchemy, and for the remainder of his life he studied and wrote about alchemy texts (mainly European). Through the language of alchemy he saw the expression of the unconscious in its symbolic form and could then draw parallels between the dreams of twentieth-century individuals and the imaginings of medieval alchemists.

In the wake of a broken leg, he suffered a heart attack in 1944, and was in semi-retirement until his death in 1961. In 1948 he inaugurated the founding of the C.G. Jung Institute in Zurich with a lecture there, and each year until his death he met with the students from the Institute. Jung was not interested in promoting organizations, because he was concerned that they tend to stifle the creativity of the individual. This impression seemed to result from his leadership experience in the International Psychoanalytic Association and the International Medical Society of Psychotherapy, which had not gone well.

By the time of Jung's 80th birthday he had sufficiently overcome his aversion to organizations, and the International Association for Analytical Psychology was founded. The IAAP has become the accrediting body for all Jungian analysts in the world, and has put on an international congress every three years where new research in the field can be presented. In the same year (1955) the *Journal of Analytical Psychology* was founded in London, and it has become the leading Jungian journal in the English language – more about both outgrowths later on.

Jung received many honors during his lifetime, including honorary degrees from Harvard, Yale, Oxford, Calcutta, Clark University, and many others. His books have been translated into many languages, and his ideas on the nature of the psyche including theory of archetypes, the collective unconscious, extraversion/introversion, complex, Self, individuation, and synchronicity have coined terms that have come into common usage.

Analytical psychology has had different patterns of development from country to country. It has had a continual presence since the early 1920s in Switzerland, the United States, the United Kingdom, and Germany. There has been a long-standing interest in analytical psychology in other places such as France, Italy, and Israel. The last quarter of the twentieth century saw a rapid expansion of interest in Jung's psychology, including Australia, New Zealand, Brazil, South Korea, Japan, South Africa, Austria, Scandinavia, and more recently the Baltic countries, the Czech Republic, Hungary,

Bulgaria, Russia, Poland, China, Mexico, and Venezuela. At this point in time, analytical psychology has become a truly worldwide phenomenon.

Switzerland

The history of analytical psychology begins in Switzerland, where Jung lived and worked. Zurich naturally provided fertile soil for psychoanalysis and by 1912 a well-functioning psychoanalytical association connected to the Burghölzli and the University of Zurich was in place. However, in 1912 the Zurich Psychoanalytical Association separated from the Burghölzli and became an independent organization with no academic affiliation, which contributed to psychoanalysis and analytical psychology developing their own independent institutions.

A further separation took place on 10 July 1914 when Alphonse Maeder led the Zurich psychoanalytic group to an almost unanimous decision to resign *en masse* from the International Psychoanalytic Association and the Zurich Psychoanalytic Association. This happened after Freud's denunciation of Jung and the Zurich school in his *On the History of the Psychoanalytic Movement* (1914:70), where Freud had established an orthodoxy that did not allow for free and unimpeded research.

On 30 October of the same year it was decided to rename the society the Association for Analytical Psychology on the suggestion of Professor Messmer (Muser 1984). This group, consisting mainly of medical doctors, met on a regular basis every other week until 1918, when it became absorbed into the newly formed Analytical Psychology Club. During the period between 1912 and 1918 Jung reformulated his major theories of the psyche, the collective unconscious, archetypes, individuation, and psychological types, and the meetings at the Club must have been significant.

Shamdasani's recent research (1998) has shown that between 1916 and 1918 there were two separate Jungian groups; a professional one, the *Verein* and a lay group, the Analytical Psychology Club, which became a model for similar clubs in other cities and countries. The two groups merged in 1918 under the name of the Analytical Psychology Club, and this was the meeting place for both analysts and analysands.

Following the First World War, Jung emerged from his "confrontation with the unconscious" (Jung 1963) and his fame spread, especially in the English-speaking countries and Europe. Individuals would write to Jung asking to see him in analysis and, if accepted, they would come to Zurich for varying lengths of time. In those days analyses were usually much shorter for many reasons, not least financial considerations which prevented protracted stays. Most foreigners' analyses were less than a year, and many lasted only weeks or a few months.

In 1925 Jung began to give seminars in English in Zurich (McGuire 1989), and from 1928 to 1939 he gave a seminar in English each academic semester.

Originally the transcripts of these seminars were distributed only selectively, but in recent years many of them have been edited and published. Individuals who were in analysis with Jung were invited to attend seminars, as well as Zurich analysts. In his role as professor at the Eidgenossische Technische Hocschule, Jung gave a weekly lecture on basic aspects of analytical psychology to the general student body, and analysands who could understand German were invited to attend. These lectures were quickly translated into English by these analysands.

The combination of analysis and seminars provided the training for the first generation of Jungian analysts. The analysis was usually done with Jung and Toni Wolff. The analysand would see Jung one day and Toni Wolff either later the same day or the following day. This type of analysis, of seeing more than one analyst at a time, has been called "multiple analyses" (Kirsch 1976) and became an accepted and usual pattern in Zurich, and in other countries following the Zurich model. It was sharply criticized by Michael Fordham (1976) in London because he claimed that the transference/countertransference implications were not being analyzed and interpreted. Fordham and his followers believed that the "multiple analyses" model allowed for too much acting out by both the patient and the analyst, fostering avoidance and splitting. On the other hand, the input of two analysts of different psychological types and genders could be helpful, at times, to the patient. Jo Wheelwright, one of those who experienced multiple analyses in Zurich, stated that Jung was excellent for archetypal interpretations while Toni Wolff was more experienced at working on personal issues and overall he found her to be a better practical analyst than Jung (Wheelwright 1974). This pattern of multiple analyses has continued into subsequent generations of analysts in Zurich and other places. The increasing importance of analyzing the transference has lessened its practice considerably.

In the early days the path to becoming a Jungian analyst was fluid. Jung would write a letter stating that the person had studied his methods and was ready to practice as an analyst. However, seeing Jung was no guarantee that an individual would receive a letter of accreditation. Many people who expected such a letter never received one, whereas others who did not plan to become analysts received Jung's blessing. In some instances Jung recommended further academic training to an analysand, e.g. Jo Wheelwright, while others were accepted with very little academic training, for instance Hilde Kirsch.

During the 1930s, Jung did not seem very interested in forming his own school of psychology and psychotherapy. As president of the International General Medical Society for Psychotherapy, he was more interested in finding points of commonality among the different schools of psychotherapy. In 1938, he signed a statement produced by the International General Medical Society for Psychotherapy, which outlined points of agreement among the various psychotherapeutic schools. In Switzerland, he became president of the Swiss Society for Practical Psychology where he was again attempting to form a common, non-sectarian basis for psychotherapy. However, some of his closest associates during that period recognized the need to form an institute in Zurich where Jung's psychology could be studied. Due to the Second World War, the plan had to be put on hold until 1948.

After the war, a small institute for the study of Jung's psychology was founded at Gemeindestrasse 27 in Zurich, the same building where the Analytical Psychology Club was housed. There was much discussion about the choice of its name. Toni Wolff favored "Institute for Complex Psychology," while Jung's chief concern was the omission of his name in the title. Jung's followers won out, and it became the C.G. Jung Institute. Jung gave the inaugural speech on 24 April 1948 on the subject of the history of "Complex Psychology," and he suggested areas for research, such as: further experiments with the word-association test and family structure; more fully elaborated clinical case histories; research on dreams in relationship to physical illness, death, catastrophes; research on the normal family in terms of psychic structure; the compensatory nature of marriage; and finally, much more work on symbolism – triadic and tetradic forms and their historical development in relationship to philosophy, religion, and the new field of microphysics. At the end of the speech he recognized that much of the list was "mere desideratum" and "not all of it will be fulfilled" (Jung 1948: para. 475–476).

The establishment of the Jung Institute changed the way one became a Jungian analyst. It was no longer strictly a personal matter between the individual and Jung. At the Institute, training became part of a larger educational experience where the individual's analysis was still paramount, but where academic criteria had to be fulfilled and formal structures began to play a significant role. However, the Jung Institute was not an international accrediting body, so that individuals still could become analysts by having personal analysis with Jung and receiving a letter of recommendation from him. It was only with the founding of the International Association for Analytical Psychology (IAAP) in 1955 that the authority for accreditation was definitively transferred from Jung personally to a professional association.

The Institute was set up along the lines of a European university with many classes, non-compulsory attendance, and the only requirement being that students pass a test in a given subject at the end of the year. Admissions requirements included the minimum of a master's degree in any field, along with a personal biography and interviews. The lack of specificity in a clinical discipline went along with Jung's idea that a non-clinical background could be an appropriate foundation for becoming an analyst. The profession of Jungian analyst was seen as a separate discipline and one could become an analyst via theology, economics, or philosophy just as readily as through the traditional disciplines of medicine, psychology, and social work. Such liberal admission requirements have allowed individuals, for instance, to make a midlife change and become analysts by studying in Zurich. In the meantime, clinical requirements to practice any kind of therapy have tightened world-wide, but the Zurich Institute remained, until recently, a training center where non-clinically trained people could become analysts. However, the tightening of requirements clinically has affected the Zurich Institute. The basic tracks include the following subjects: Fundamentals of Analytical Psychology, Psychology of Dreams, Association Experiments, General History of Religion, Fairy Tales, Mythology, General Psychopathology. After taking the required courses, students have to pass a test, the *propaedeuticum*, in each of the given subjects. After passing the test they attend case colloquia, where patient material is discussed, and further courses to deepen their knowledge of analytical psychology.

In the early years, symbolic understanding was emphasized over clinical training. In order to graduate from the Institute, students then had to pass another set of examinations, write and defend a thesis, and write up analytic cases demonstrating Jungian methods. The Institute offered tracks in German, English, French, and Italian. The vast majority of the early students were American, British, or Swiss. For many years the number of students hovered around 30 at any given time; the atmosphere was lively and intimate and the discussions intense. Jung would visit the Institute from time to time to meet with the students and he often attended the yearly students' party. Although the Institute in Zurich was not the first Jungian training center in the world (London and San Francisco having started in 1946), it was by far the most organized and the largest. With the presence of Jung in the background and many of the first generation of analysts providing the bulk of the teaching and analysis, Zurich was the center for analytical psychology.

During the first 20 years of its operation, the Institute was a very creative place to be; there was an intimacy and an intensity which the students attending there really enjoyed. Jung and the first generation of analysts around him were the primary teachers and there was an atmosphere of congeniality. Then there was an episode of a sexual transgression by the director of studies at the time, which involved the entire Institute as well as governmental structures in both the United States and Switzerland. The affair produced a heated division within the Institute community and, as a consequence, the director of studies was forced out. This event was a harbinger of change in the Jungian world as the question of boundary violations was at issue in many other Jungian training programs at the time. Clinical boundaries were to assume greater importance in the future of all training programs, including Zurich. Perhaps change happened more slowly in Zurich because the influence of Jung's own interest in archetypal symbolism and mythological amplification of dreams held sway over clinical traditions more dominant in other training centers, as well as Jung's relationship to Toni Wolff.

The Jung Institute was the central cohesive structure for analytical psychology in Zurich as it provided the training and the exchange of intellectual ideas. However, there was a need for a professional organization in Switzerland which could deal with the political, administrative, and professional issues that faced the growing number of graduates working there. Another important development was the establishment of the Klinik am Zurichberg, an inpatient facility utilizing Jungian theory and practice. Many students from the Jung Institute did part of their clinical training at this facility and, at the time, it was the only Jungian-oriented hospital in the world. When the founders of the Klinik retired, the divisions within the remaining staff resulted in the hospital philosophy reverting to a more traditional one.

As Jung's ideas became more popular, the Jung Institute in Zurich could no longer accommodate all the students. In 1973 an old mansion, which was owned by the community in Kusnacht on the Lake of Zurich, became available, and Adolf Guggenbühl-Craig, as the president of the Institute, was able to arrange a favorable lease agreement. Located close to Jung's home, the building seemed ideal to house the growing Institute. Student enrollment increased steadily and by the end of the 1980s, out of a total of 400 students, over 100 were American. At the same time, the Institute had widened its international character with the addition of students from Asia, Africa, and the smaller European countries. As geographical boundaries expanded, so did the curriculum. Clinical issues had greater emphasis and the number of required clinical colloquia, as well as individual supervisory hours for students, increased. This broadening of analytic theory was anathema to some of the first-generation analysts, especially Marie-Louise von Franz, who felt that Jung's contributions were being diluted by the addition of psychoanalytic theory and practice. These changes within the Institute curriculum demonstrated to von Franz that not enough attention was being paid to the individuation process going on in the unconscious. Honoring her strong beliefs about the nature of Jung's work, she withdrew from teaching at the Institute in the early 1980s. Other analysts and candidates joined her, and they began to meet informally on a regular basis.

This resulted in the "von Franz group" eventually forming their own institute, the Research and Training Centre in Depth Psychology, which came into being on 8 May 1994 and was incorporated as a foundation the following day. On the surface, the programs of the Jung Institute and the Centre seem very similar. However, as one probes more deeply into the heart and soul of this new program, meaningful differences emerge. In the Centre, the collective unconscious, or objective psyche, becomes the most central guide for each individual and the value of the outer collective is minimized. Students at the original Jung Institute have more concern for the collective values and the persona than do their Centre counterparts. Former members of the Jung Institute whose allegiance moved to the new Centre have given up their membership in both the IAAP and the SGfAP (the Swiss society for analytical psychology). Candidates graduating from the Centre will not be eligible to become members in the IAAP as their training will not be with IAAP members. The Centre has much the feeling of the old Institute during the 1950s and 1960s, when the number of students was small and the courses were similar in nature to the curriculum at the Centre.

At this time we have two trainings going on in Zurich. Those who want to study mainly von Franz and Jung go to the Research Centre, whereas those wishing a more traditional Jungian training attend the Jung Institute in Kusnacht.

I have gone into much greater detail with Switzerland than I will with the other training institutes because of its long history and the centrality of its position. It is also the only Institute that is run on a university model; all the other Institutes are part-time and additional to other professional activities such as private practice, hospital practice, or working in a clinic.

The United States

The next country where analytical psychology developed was the United States. Jung made his first visit there in 1909 when he, along with Freud, gave lectures at Clark University in Worcester, Massachusetts, where they received honorary doctorates. This was the first of many visits for Jung but it was Freud's only trip to America.

Analytical psychology first took root in New York, and two decades later it was established in San Francisco and Los Angeles. These three centers developed relatively independently of one another and have unique histories. They developed during Jung's lifetime, and he had contact with individuals of each center. Other Jungian groups did not develop in the United States until the early 1970s.

Jung made three trips to the United States between 1909 and 1912 as an adherent of psychoanalysis and a colleague of Freud. These visits were mainly to the eastern seaboard, centered on Boston and New York. Both Freud and Jung were widely acclaimed on their first visit and were enthusiastically greeted by the medical elite and the intellectual establishment. When Jung returned for the third time in 1912 to deliver a series of lectures on psychoanalysis at the medical school of Fordham University in New York, he publicly expressed his differences with Freud for the first time. Although we know from the Freud–Jung correspondence and Jung's publication of the *Wandlungen und Symbole der Libido* in the *Jahrbuch* (English translation: *Psychology of the Unconscious* (1916/1991)) that differences in viewpoints were emerging, it was only in the Fordham lectures that Jung made these differences explicit and public. While accepting Freud's view of infantile sexuality, he relativized its importance and began to state that a neurosis develops out of a conflict in the present and that one must analyze the here and now to rid the person of suffering. Furthermore, Jung expanded the concept of libido beyond Freud's conception which primarily focused on sexual and aggressive drives. Jung defined libido as psychic energy in general including sex and aggression but also consisting of other primary drives such as the nutritive or the spiritual.

The first Jungian in the United States was Beatrice Hinkle, a physician who made the first English translation of *Wandlungen und Symbole der Libido* as *Psychology of the Unconscious* in 1916. Beatrice Hinkle has the further distinction of having set up the first psychotherapy clinic of any kind in the United States at the Cornell Medical College in New York in 1908. She studied and analyzed with Jung in 1911 and then returned to New York, where she joined Constance Long, a British physician who had also analyzed with Jung, and two American physicians, Eleanor Bertine and Kristine Mann. The four physicians formed a small study group. The two younger women, Bertine and Mann, had met as medical students at Cornell Medical College where Hinkle held a position in the Neurology Department. In 1919 Bertine arranged for Drs Hinkle and Long, established analysts, to speak before an International Conference of Medical Women. Dr Mann was also a participant at that conference. Following the conference Mann and Bertine went to Zurich for analysis with Jung. While there, they met Esther Harding, an English physician, who was also in analysis with Jung. Harding and Bertine developed a close relationship which was to continue for the next 40 years. In 1924 they decided to relocate to New York. They returned to Zurich for analysis two months each year and spent summers at their residence on Bailey Island, Maine where they also saw analysands. In 1936, after Jung received an honorary degree from Harvard University, he gave a seminar on Bailey Island where many of his students at the time came to hear him.

Beginning in the 1920s, other Jungian analysts began to practice in New York who were not so closely aligned with Drs Mann, Bertine, and Harding. The most influential individual was Frances Wickes, a lay analyst, whose book *The Inner World of Childhood* (1927) became a best seller, followed by *The Inner World of Man* (1938) and *The Inner World of Choice* (1963). Henderson (1982) describes her work as being inspirational rather than analytical. There was a tension between Frances Wickes and the three women doctors. Wickes, as a lay person, had a different perspective from the three single professional women and there was a distant but respectful relationship between them.

Following the model of Zurich and London, New York started its own Analytical Psychology Club in 1936. The format was similar to that of other clubs with monthly meetings and papers presented by analysts, lay members of the Club, and guest speakers. An enduring achievement of the Analytical Psychological Club was the establishment of the Kristine Mann Library. When Mann died of cancer in 1945, the Club library was named in her honor. The library has assembled a press archive of Jung and his work starting in the early 1900s and has amassed a large collection of related material on mythology, comparative anthropology, psychology, and religion. Many unpublished manuscripts can be found there.

During Jung's 1937 visit to New York, Paul and Mary Mellon consulted him and the following year, they attended the Eranos conference in Ascona, Switzerland.³ They remained in Zurich until the the fall of 1939 in analysis with Jung. Prior to leaving Zurich, Mary Mellon discussed her idea of having Jung's Collected Works translated and published in English. Before the Mellons were able to return to Zurich and finalize the negotiations, Mary Mellon died tragically in *status asthmaticus* in the spring of 1946. In her memory, Paul Mellon created the Bollingen Foundation, named after Jung's tower. The first volume of the Collected Works to be published in English was *Psychology and Alchemy* in 1953. The Bollingen Foundation subsidized the publication of Jung's writings in order to make them available to the general reader. The Foundation dissolved in the early 1980s, and at that time Princeton University Press took over the publication of the Collected Works.

At the conclusion of the Second World War the Medical Society for Analytical Psychology was formed and in 1954, a division of psychologists was formed. Realizing that they had more in common than divided them, they combined to form the New York Association for Analytical Psychology in 1957 which became one of the founding members of the IAAP at its inaugural meeting in Zurich in 1958.

C.G. Jung Foundation

Interest in Jung's psychology continued to grow, and the Analytical Psychology Club had neither the financial resources nor the personnel to meet the growing need. The analysts in New York, spearheaded by Esther Harding, decided to form a foundation which would serve as a central point for all activities concerning Jung's analytical psychology. Initially the scope of the foundation was national, and it included analytical training, a clinic, book publishing, a library, and an information center. It became operational in 1963. The New York Foundation is basically a lay organization with membership open to any individual regardless of prior experience, either academic or analytic. For financial reasons it has ceased publishing books, and it no longer has a clinic. It has lost its national character, but it remains a valuable resource for those living in the Greater New York area.

A significant event was the establishment of the Archive for Research in Archetypal Symbolism (ARAS), a large collection of pictures and commentary on their archetypal significance from numerous cultures and ages. The collection was begun by Olge Froebe-Kapteyn in Ascona at the behest of Jung in the 1930s and had been supported by the Bollingen Foundation. When the Bollingen Foundation was phasing out its operations, the New York Jung Foundation was offered the ARAS collection if it would provide housing and continued care for its development. Mrs Jane Pratt agreed to underwrite and guarantee the costs for the first ten years of its existence so that ARAS became an integral part of the Foundation in the late 1960s. Paul Mellon also lent support to ARAS with a generous grant which has helped to put ARAS on firm financial ground. Eventually, ARAS separated from the Foundation and formed its own national board and administration. It continues to thrive today with an ever-growing collection and wider distribution.

Although a New York professional association was formed in 1946, the training program was informal until the establishment of the Foundation. When the Foundation was formed, the New York Institute became a part of it. The training center developed its own board which has governed policies with regard to training and which has been separate from the Foundation board.

The first candidates graduated in 1963. Before the Foundation existed, training consisted of a long period of personal analysis and supervision of cases with another analyst, after which the prospective analyst would be invited to join the professional group. There was no special requirement for admission beyond a degree in psychology or medicine. One of the unique features of training in New York has been the requirement of all candidates attending a two-year, once-a-week group therapy. This developed out of a two-year, leaderless group therapy experience of six senior analysts from 1960 to 1962 who found it so useful personally that they made it a requirement of the training program. Christopher Whitmont, one of those six original senior analyst members, recognized how much conflict there was between members and how individual analysis did not prepare one for dealing with professional conflict. Personal analysis helped with the intrapsychic and some interpersonal issues but it did not necessarily help the individual to relate within a group.

Theoretically, analytical psychology in New York has stayed close to its roots in Jung's theory. The founders, Esther Harding, Eleanor Bertine, Kristine Mann, and Frances Wickes, all had close ties to Jung, and this connection has continued. The professional group numbers over 100 members. Over the years there have been numerous personal tensions within the membership, with some members changing their voting membership to other professional societies. At present, approximately 15 members of the New York society have applied to form their own new society with their own view of training. This has produced a great deal of tension and, at the time of writing, the situation has not yet been resolved.

San Francisco

The second region in the United States to develop an interest in Jung's psychology was the San Francisco Bay Area. Elizabeth and James Whitney, Sr spent time in Zurich in the early 1920s and returned to Berkeley to become the first psychoanalysts of any persuasion west of the Mississippi River. James, Sr died shortly after returning but Elizabeth had a long and illustrious career as a Jungian analyst. By 1940 Joseph and Jane Wheelwright had returned from Zurich and Joseph Henderson had returned as well with an intermediate stop in New York. An Analytical Psychology Club was formed, and several doctors and psychologists wished to begin training. During the Second World War, Drs Henderson and Wheelwright worked at a rehabilitation clinic examining returning military personnel from the South Pacific. Here they worked alongside their Freudian counterparts and a collegiality developed which was highly unusual at that time.

In 1943, the Medical Society for Analytical Psychology (MSAP) (same name but separate from New York) was formed and the professional group differentiated from the Analytical Psychology Club. Joseph Wheelwright became a founding member of the Langley Porter Neuropsychiatric Institute in 1941 and was a professor there for the next 30 years. Joseph Henderson began teaching at the Stanford University Medical Center in San Francisco and remained there until 1959 when the complex moved to Palo Alto. Through these positions, many young doctors were attracted to Jungian training and the early composition of the San Francisco Jung Society had a predominance of medically trained analysts. This was different from New York, where there was little contact with the medical and psychotherapeutic communities. Also, there was relatively little contact between the New York group and the San Francisco one.

In 1948, four psychologists, who had their analyses with the medical analysts, were accepted as trainees within the professional group. These four immediately formed the Association of Analytical Clinical Psychologists as a counterpart to the medical group. In those days the rivalry in the United States between medicine and psychology was acute and each discipline felt the need to have its own organization. However, both groups quickly realized that analysis should not be restricted to a single discipline and they formed the Northern California Society of Jungian Analysts.

Two psychologists, Elizabeth Howes and Sheila Moon, had analysis with Elizabeth Whitney and also had seen Dr and Mrs Jung in Zurich. Drs Howes and Moon and their professional work were strongly influenced by a Christian viewpoint. In 1944 a decision had to be made as to whether they should be a part of the newly forming professional group. The two women elected to go their own way and in 1955 formed the Guild for Psychological Studies, of which Mrs Emma Jung was a founding sponsor. To this day, the Guild has functioned as a separate organization, presenting lectures and workshops to interested participants. This early cleavage was significant because it established analytical psychology in Northern California as a clinical discipline, and individuals with a predominantly Christian orientation found a niche in the Guild. The separation of the Guild from the MSAP, as well as the fact that most of the professional members were physicians, led to criticism that the San Francisco Jungians were more interested in their medical persona than in the deeper values of analytical psychology.

On 13 July 1964 the C.G. Jung Institute was created as a non-profit organization; subsequently the training was restructured, a low-fee outpatient clinic was formed, and a building to house these activities was purchased. In 1972 a most significant event occurred for the San Francisco Institute. On her eightieth birthday, friends and former analysands established a foundation in Frances Wickes' name. Over the years, the foundation distributed small grants, but in 1972 the board decided to dissolve the foundation and to make a terminal grant of $1,500,000 to the C.G. Jung Institute of San Francisco. With the grant, the San Francisco group bought its present residence for $150,000 and with the remainder established an endowment. For the following several years the financial stability of the Institute was assured by the earnings from the endowment as well as by contributions from interested lay public. The existing programs of the Institute grew rapidly and new ones were developed. New staff members were employed to manage the library, public programs, the clinic, and overall administration.

The training of analysts has been the core activity of the Institute. The evaluation of candidates, for many years, was conducted by an equal number of San Francisco and Los Angeles analysts. When the joint evaluating committees were instituted, it was unique in the Jungian world. No other Jungian group included outside evaluators passing judgment on its candidates. The initial reason was the small size of both societies, but over time it was recognized that sharing was beneficial for both the candidates and the analysts doing the evaluations. In spite of major differences in outlook, the joint board had worked well until recently. The joint board and the yearly California North–South Jungian Conference also promoted a general working relationship between the two societies.

Because of its large size and endowment, the San Francisco Institute has numerous programs, a large library, an active ARAS collection, its own journal, the *San Francisco Library Journal*, and an active clinic.

Changes have occurred in the make-up of the San Francisco Jung Institute as fewer medical doctors have applied for training with the general movement in psychiatry away from psychotherapy to a biological-pharmacological approach. Currently applicants come from the fields of psychology or social work, with the occasional psychiatric nurse practitioner or marriage and family counselor. Women predominate among the present applicants and candidates, representing a shift away from the early days when applicants were mainly male medical doctors. The San Francisco Jung Institute has approximately 125 active members and 50 candidates in various stages of training.

The San Francisco Jung Institute has long been considered one of the most well established and respected Jungian institutes in the world. From the very beginning it established good relations with psychoanalysis. The Wheelwrights, Joseph Henderson, and Elizabeth Whitney worked well together to found the early professional group. At the time of writing there have been no serious splits within the professional group, and an air of respect generally prevails among the membership. From the outset there have been monthly dinner meetings of the membership so that there is ample opportunity for members to get to know each other in a less structured setting.

Los Angeles

The third area where analytical psychology developed was Los Angeles. German Jewish refugees, James and Hilde Kirsch, and Max and Lore Zeller, arrived in 1940 and 1941 respectively. None of them had the proper credentials to practice as psychotherapists or analysts, so that the development of analytical psychology occurred outside the mainstream of psychotherapeutic and analytic training. Nevertheless, many people were attracted to analytical psychology and an Analytical Psychology Club was formed. There was a strong connection between Zurich and Los Angeles, and in 1950 20 individuals from Los Angeles were in analysis in Zurich. A fund was developed to bring Zurich lecturers to Los Angeles and there has continued to be a connection between the two Jungian centers.

In 1952 the San Francisco and Los Angeles groups cautiously planned a joint meeting in Santa Barbara, California to explore areas of mutual interest. They hoped that a meeting between the two societies could lessen mutual projections. The initial meeting proved to be fruitful, and the two societies decided to get together on a yearly basis from then on. The annual event became known as the North–South Conference, and it was the first-ever meeting between two Jungian societies.

In the mid-1970s, Edward Edinger arrived in Los Angeles from New York. Although Edinger brought with him the knowledge and experience of a classical Jungian, he did not have a personal analysis with Jung. Edinger's intellectual focus was on the works of C.G. Jung and Marie-Louise von Franz and his published books reworked Jung's ideas into a language which seemed easier to grasp than Jung's. For over 20 years, Edinger influenced many Los Angeles analysts who have shared this point of view. On the other hand, many candidates were interested in the new developments in psychoanalysis which had relevance for analytical psychology and this led to an enormous tension within the Los Angeles Jungian community. In the 1990s, the division between those who adhered closely to the words of Jung and von Franz and those who wished to incorporate psychoanalytic concepts into Jungian practice widened. Finally, after the death of Edinger in 1998, a second professional society was formed which has been closely aligned to Edinger's point of view.

Analytical psychology has developed in Los Angeles from a small German Jewish émigré enclave to a substantial professional Jungian community. Currently the Society of Jungian Analysts of Southern California includes approximately 70 members (the majority having been certified within the past six years) and 50 candidates. The Institute, founded in 1967 without an endowment, has managed to survive and grow throughout this period. The Institute components include its own ARAS collection, the Hilde Kirsch Children's Center, the Max and Lore Zeller Book Store, the James Kirsch Lecture Room, the Kieffer Frantz Clinic, the journal *Psychological Perspectives*, and numerous ongoing projects. There is an active training program with many candidates. A second professional society has recently formed in which classical works of Jung and Marie Louise von Franz are emphasized.

Later developments of analytical psychology in the United States

I have presented the development of New York and the two California societies in some detail, firstly because they all were formed while Jung was still alive, and there was communication with him about their formation. Secondly, there were no new Jungian groups for another 30 years, until the early 1970s, in the United States. Thirdly, the United States has been the only country within which independent Jungian societies have developed. In all other countries the development of groups has been on a national level.

By the early 1970s, there were Americans who had trained in Zurich and returned to different areas in the United States. In order to lessen the isolation of these individuals and to promote a broader training program, these individuals came together to form the Inter-Regional Society of Jungian Analysts (IRSJA). The analysts and their respective candidates have continued to meet twice a year for seminars and examinations, and when enough analysts from a particular area have been certified, the group has separated and become an autonomous society. This has been partially successful, but often a large enough group has not wished to disaffiliate. As the Inter-Regional group has become larger, it has accepted candidates from areas where there is an existing society. This has caused some tension within the different American groups, as this was not part of the original intent of the IRSJA.

At the time of writing there are groups in most parts of the country, including Chicago, Texas, New England, and the Pacific Northwest, as well as parts of Canada. Space does not permit me to follow the development of these various groups, but they all have evolved out of a combination of the Inter-Regional training and graduates from the Zurich Institute returning to the United States or Canada. In New England, all the founders were Zurich graduates, and there were no IRSJA members for a long time.

As the Inter-Regional grew, there was concern from the existing societies about territorial issues. As there was no national American group, the existing societies at that time – Boston, New York, San Francisco, and Los Angeles – met with representatives from Inter-Regional and formed the Council of American Societies of Jungian Analysts (CASJA). As new societies have formed, they have all become members of CASJA, now broadened to North America and called CNASJA. CNASJA has no official position or authority, but it does host a regular meeting and provide a forum for issues which emerge among the societies. It has proved to be effective for airing disputes.

The newer societies have a range of attitudes with respect to analytical psychology, from largely developmental to highly symbolic. How long the societies can remain separate and not form a national organization remains to be seen. If one adds up the membership of all the American societies, it presents close to one quarter of the total membership of the IAAP. Analytical psychology in the United States is vibrant and it takes on many shapes and forms.

United Kingdom

The United Kingdom provided fertile soil for the development of psychoanalysis and analytical psychology. The early followers of Jung did not conform to an intellectual orthodoxy; it was only when H.G. Baynes, an extraverted English physician, went for analysis to Jung after the First World War that a firm foundation for Jung's psychology was established (Jansen 2003). Jung gave his first professional talk in England in 1914, and his last visit was in 1938 when he received an honorary doctorate from Oxford. In between, he made numerous professional trips, held seminars for his students, and gave a series of five lectures at the Tavistock clinic in 1935 which were attended by many prominent British physicians and psychotherapists.

An Analytical Psychology Club, modeled on the Club in Zurich, was formed and held its first meeting on 15 September 1922 at the home of Esther Harding, then living in London before she moved to the United States in 1924. The Analytical Psychology Club quickly grew from the initial five in 1922 to approximately 25 members. In the beginning, in order to qualify for membership, all the members had to be analyzed by either Jung or Toni Wolff, but this requirement was quickly changed, and analysis and recommendation by any qualified Jungian analyst became acceptable. Regular lectures, discussion groups on a variety of subjects, and a large library became the main aspects of the Club. As with the Zurich Club, important and ongoing issues were: how to relate as a group; the relationship of the individuation process to group process; and the purpose of the group – whether to focus on inner archetypal issues or on social and political questions. H.G. Baynes, later known as Peter, was the leader of the Jungians in England until his untimely death in 1943. He became Jung's assistant in Zurich in the early 1920s and in 1925 he arranged the safari to Africa for himself and Jung. He returned to England in 1929 and practiced there until his death. By the late 1930s there was both a medical and a lay group of analysts.

One of Baynes's leading students was Michael Fordham, who, at that time, was still beginning as a child psychiatrist. Fordham was not able to have analysis with Jung, and instead saw a neophyte Jungian in London. Fordham became the leader of the Jungians after Baynes's death, and he initiated the founding of a professional society, the Society of Analytical Psychology (SAP), as well as inaugurating a clinical Jungian publication, the *Journal of Analytical Psychology*. Fordham's interest in child analysis led him to have both professional and personal contact with Melanie Klein and Donald Winnicott. He was strongly influenced by both of them, and he incorporated many of their theories into the classical Jungian model. This led in the 1960s to the evolution of what became known as the "London developmental school" versus the "Zurich classical school." The London school emphasized infancy and early child development, whereas the Zurich school focused primarily on archetypal imagery and amplification of those images.

As the developmental approach within the SAP became more firmly established, the analysts and candidates who adhered to a more classical Jungian approach became uncomfortable. The tension between the two perspectives has often been described as a personal conflict between Michael Fordham and Gerhard Adler, which Fordham denied, claiming that the differences were theoretical. Adler complained that his trainees were not acceptable at the SAP, and that his seminars were badly attended. By 1975 Adler and his colleagues were ready to form their own group, where the more traditional Jungian positions could be expressed; this resulted in the formation of the Association of Jungian Analysts (AJA). However, AJA began to have its own internal conflicts when analysts arrived from Zurich and were asked to do further training in London. This split the group once again into those analysts who trained in Zurich and the ones who trained in the UK. Consequently, more Zurich oriented analysts founded the Independent Group of Analytical Psychologists (IGAP). To have two more classically oriented Jungian societies was politically untenable for the SAP, which was the original group and the one with the longest history. The SAP members had long been active in the British Association for Psychotherapy (BAP), which had a Jungian section. A compromise was worked out so that the Jungian section of BAP would become another UK-based group, with the result that there would be two "developmentally oriented societies" and two "classically oriented societies." That decision was reached in 1986, and in the following years each of the four societies evolved on its own path.

Two much larger umbrella organizations have been founded in Great Britain, the United Kingdom Council for Psychotherapy (UKCP) and the British Confederation of Psychotherapists (BCP). The UKCP is the true umbrella organization for all psychotherapists in the UK, and numbers over 3,000 psychotherapists of all persuasions. All the Jungian organizations were members of this umbrella organization. In 1992 the BCP was formed to be an umbrella organization for all psychoanalytic organizations. The members of the BCP were not comfortable having the broad spectrum of psychotherapists representing psychoanalytic issues. Both SAP and BAP, and more recently AJA, have become members of the BCP, but IGAP has not been invited to join the BCP. Standards are the issue, and this is expressed in terms of the frequency of sessions per week for analytic candidates and the frequency with which clinic patients are seen by the candidates.

It was in this atmosphere of *Sturm und Drang* (storm and stress) in London that Andrew Samuels published his classic book, *Jung and the Post-Jungians* (1985), wherein he developed a classification of analytical psychologists which included a classical, a developmental, and an archetypal school. Briefly summarized, the classical school, consciously working in Jung's tradition, focuses on self and individuation. The developmental school has a specific focus on the importance of infancy in the evolution of the adult personality, and an equally important emphasis on the analysis of the transference and countertransference. The developmental school has a close relationship to psychoanalysis, although influence in the opposite direction is not as significant. The archetypal school focuses on imagery in therapy with little emphasis on overt transference and countertransference. When Samuels' book came out in 1985, most analysts did not like being labeled in this way, as it went against the grain of individuality and authenticity.

Since the book's publication, there has been a continual evolution of the tripartite division. The classical and developmental schools still exist, but the archetypal school as a clinical discipline never gained acceptance as a separate entity in the UK. The archetypal school has either been integrated or eliminated, probably a bit of both. Further evolutions in the classical and developmental schools respectively have led to additional philosophical and theoretical divisions which stretch the limits on both ends. On the classical side, a new (ultra-classical) group has emerged which emphasizes the original works of Jung and Marie-Louise von Franz. This view is championed by the Research Centre in Zurich and the second society in Los Angeles. At the other end of the spectrum are those analysts who have become primarily psychoanalytic but originally trained at Jungian Institutes. These analysts have adopted the rules of abstinence and neutrality in a psychoanalytic way, valuing the psychoanalytic frame over the working alliance and valuing transference/countertransference exploration over explicit fantasy and dream images. The enthusiasm for psychoanalysis has come about through Jungian analysts who were not satisfied with either their classical or developmental Jungian analyses. They have not coalesced to form any definite professional societies.

Analytical psychology in the UK has been heavily influenced by psychoanalytic thinking, but formal contacts between the two have been minimal. Michael Fordham was an exception since in 1945, through his friendship with the psychoanalyst John Rickman, he began a forum between psychoanalysts and analytical psychologists in the Medical Section of the British Psychological Society (Astor 1995). In 1962, Fordham was elected chairman of the Royal-Medico Psychological Association, which later became the Royal College of Psychiatrists. However, in spite of these important positions, analytical psychologists have not been able to obtain formal recognition from the British psychoanalytic community, which is something they have very much wanted.

In 1993, a Centre for Psychoanalytic Studies at the University of Essex was founded. It offers a range of postgraduate degree courses, public lectures, short specialist courses, and opportunities for research (Papadopoulos 1996). Subsequently, the Society of Analytical Psychology established a Chair in Analytical Psychology for that Center. Since the fall of 1995 Renos Papadopoulos and Andrew Samuels have been sharing the half-time position equally. The placement of the Center structurally in the midst of a university has been a positive opening for analytical psychology. There is contact with other departments within the university, and the students participate in a rich and varied psychoanalytic curriculum.

Currently, most analytical psychologists in England practice some hybrid of analytical psychology and object-relations psychoanalysis, with those of a more classical Jungian persuasion in the minority. The political issue of an umbrella organization of all analytical psychologists in England has not been settled. It is important to emphasize that the historical developments in the UK have foreshadowed similar events in other countries. As a result of Fordham's individual relationship to psychoanalysts and his particular relationship to Jung, these events occurred in the UK decades earlier than in other countries.

Germany

The story of Jung and analytical psychology in Germany is intimately connected with the general history of Germany in the twentieth century, and the spectres of Nazism and Hitler are a persistent presence. Jung personally, and analytical psychology in general, were closely connected to the Nationalist Socialist regime; much has been written about this period in Jung's life. Both Jung's detractors and his apologists have argued for over half a century as to whether Jung was a Nazi and/or anti-Semitic. (A brief discussion of this important issue will follow; for a more detailed elucidation the reader is referred to Samuels 1993; Kirsch 2000; Maidenbaum and Martin 2002; Bair 2003.)

There has been a Jungian presence in Germany since the early 1920s when Richard Gustav Heyer and Kathe Bugler returned from Zurich to Munich having had analysis with Jung. Several individuals from Berlin also had analysis with Jung, and in 1931 they formed the C.G. Jung Society of Berlin. What was called a "Society" in Berlin was equivalent to an Analytical Psychology Club elsewhere; it included both analysands and analysts. When the Nazi's came to power in 1933, those of Jewish descent were removed from the official membership. Jung gave several workshops to the Berlin Jungian Society during the 1930s.

The story becomes more complicated after the Nazis come into power. There are two overlapping structures with which both Jung and Jungians became involved. The first is the General Medical Society for Psychotherapy, which had been founded in 1926 for psychotherapeutically oriented physicians. It had yearly meetings with participants from all of Europe and the United States. Jung was made honorary Vice President of this organization in 1931. When Ernst Kretchmer, the president, resigned in 1933 for political reasons, Jung was asked to take over the organization. He insisted that the name be changed to the International Medical Society for Psychotherapy and that Jewish members from Germany be allowed to be individual members. Jews had been banned from the Nazified German section and he wanted them to remain as individual members of the International Society. He also made a statement comparing Aryan psychology and Jewish psychology, which was quite unfortunate and which has been the basis for attacking Jung as an anti-Semite as well as a Nazi. Jung remained president of this organization until 1940, when he finally resigned and gave up trying to keep the organization out of the political fire.

The man who headed up the Nazified German section was named Matthias Goering, a self-styled Adlerian psychiatry professor who was also a distant cousin of Hermann Goering. Professor Goering, through his cousin, had close connections with the Nazi hierarchy and in 1936 became head of a psychotherapy institute called the Goering Institute. This became the main training center for psychotherapists until the end of the Nazi regime. Analytical psychology was one of the subjects taught at the Goering Institute by Jungians who were members of the Nazi party (Cocks 1997). Although Jung himself had nothing to do with this, his psychology was perpetuated by Dr Heyer and others in this system throughout the war. Heyer protected Bugler, who was half Jewish. Bugler, although not a physician, had been the first German to be analyzed by Jung in the early 1920s.

After the Second World War, all the different schools of psychotherapy and analysis had to rise from the ashes. As a consequence of his Nazi affiliation, Jung discredited Heyer, who then returned to Munich. Kathe Bugler did not like the direction that Jungian psychology was taking in Berlin; she disaffiliated herself from the analytic organizations that were forming but continued to practice as a Jungian analyst. Many of the early Jungians after the war went to her for analysis. Harald Schultz-Henke, a neo-Freudian who attempted to bring together all the psychoanalytic theoretical perspectives, founded a neo-Freudian institute which those interested in Jungian psychology also attended. By graduating from this program, the Jungians gradually formed their own section from within. Candidates from the two schools took the same seminars but then branched out to study and analyze with their own respective teachers and analysts. These conditions continue to the present day. The Berlin Jungians have one of the largest groups in the world.

During this same period after the war, Wilhelm Bitter in Stuttgart founded a Jung Institute much more closely aligned to Zurich. Professor Bitter had been in Switzerland during the war, and he was not politically associated with the Nazis. In 1958 these two groups combined to form the German Association of Jungian Analysts. Over time, satellite institutes have developed in other cities in Germany such as Munich, Cologne, and Bremen. The Stuttgart group has remained more closely aligned to Zurich whereas the Berlin group has been much influenced by psychoanalysis.

Germany was also one of the first countries where government health insurance paid for psychoanalytic treatment, so that a large number of psychoanalytically oriented therapists have had economic support. Since East and West Germany combined, the economic support for psychoanalysis has had to be modified. Germany and other European countries are struggling with the issue of financial reimbursement by the government, which requires that psychoanalysts be accredited in some standard way. Thus, who is and who is not a Jungian analyst according to governmental policy has profound economic ramifications.

IAAP

Jung had a decidedly ambivalent relationship with organizations. The only Jungian organizations which existed prior to the formation of the Institute in Zurich were the Analytical Psychology Clubs in some of the major cities of Europe and the United States. Even there, Jung kept his distance and was never closely involved with the administration of any of the clubs (including the one in Zurich); however, he did lend support by giving lectures and seminars.

In 1955, Jung celebrated his eightieth birthday and some of his Zurich followers urged him to consider the formation of an international professional organization (Meier 1992, personal communication). Thus, the IAAP was founded in Switzerland in 1955 and was structured according to Swiss law.

At its inception the aims of the IAAP were (1) to promote analytical psychology, (2) to accredit professional groups, and individual members where no group existed, and (3) to hold congresses on a regular basis. In order to accredit analysts, minimum standards of training were stipulated in the Constitution.

The work of the IAAP has increased markedly since its founding and the leaders have many duties, including: resolving conflict between groups and individuals; evaluating new groups and individuals; reaching out to new areas of the world seeking development, such as Russia and Asia; organizing congresses; and publishing congress proceedings, an annual newsletter, and a membership list. Politically, the association has broadened from its Northern European roots to encompass the rest of Europe, the Americas, and parts of

Asia and Africa. The IAAP, with its many functions, has played an increasingly prominent role in the growth of analytical psychology with a primary mandate to accredit analysts and offering an organizational identification.

Analytical psychology in the rest of the world

In this chapter I have focused on Switzerland, the United States, the United Kingdom, and Germany because they have all had a continued Jungian presence from the time that Jung first established his independent psychology in the early 1920s. Furthermore, these Jungian professional groups were established during Jung's lifetime, which meant that he knew and influenced them to some degree. However, there are other countries where analytical psychology developed and that were within Jung's purview.

One example is Israel. Erich and Julie Neumann originally established residence in Palestine in 1934. They began a small group in Tel Aviv, and it has grown slowly over the years. Erich Neumann was arguably Jung's most creative student and the themes of his books follow Jung's line of archetypal theory. The Neumanns taught both child and adult analysis, and Israel was a charter member of the IAAP. In recent years there have been many personality conflicts within the Israeli professional society, and now it has divided into three separate groups based on these personal alignments.

Italy is another country where there has been a Jungian presence since the mid-1930s. Ernst Bernhard, a German Jewish Jungian who saw Jung in 1933 for a spiritual crisis, settled in Rome in 1935. He was protected during the Second World War and began to practice again in 1944. At the present time there are two major Jungian associations in Italy, and the founders of both had their analyses with Bernhard. The conflict between the two groups began as a personality conflict but the two now work together on many projects of mutual interest.

France is another country with an early Jungian presence, which began in 1929. Before the Second World War, there was an active Analytical Psychology Club in Paris, which the Jungs visited and where both lectured, Jung in 1932 and Emma in the late 1930s. During the Second World War there was a cessation of Jungian activity, which did not begin again until well after its end. Elie Humbert, a Catholic priest, saw Jung in analysis during the late 1950s. He was probably one of Jung's last patients. Humbert returned to Paris, and through the force of his intellect and his personal dynamism, a group of individuals began to train to become Jungian analysts. This group has grown rapidly and is one of the largest and most active in the world today.

In the past 30 years there has been a tremendous increase in analytical psychology. Many countries in Europe have developed Jungian societies, including Belgium, Denmark, Sweden, Spain, and Austria, with individuals in the other European countries. Mexico, Venezuela and Brazil have developed strong Jungian groups, and other countries in Latin America have an emerging interest. Australia and New Zealand have formed a combined group which requires a lot of travel for its members. South Africa has its own Jungian society, as does Japan.

Since the fall of communism and the Soviet state, the countries of Eastern Europe and Russia have shown a strong interest in analytical psychology. It has been difficult for people from these areas to afford personal analysis, which is, of course, fundamental to becoming an analyst. Various scholarships and foundations have helped to support analytic training for a few individuals, and analysts from the West have committed themselves to teaching in these countries. The most prominent example of this is the work of Jan Wiener and Catherine Crowther who have gone on a regular basis to St Petersburg, where many of the students have graduated from a two-year course.

The end result is that analytical psychology has become a worldwide phenomenon. What began as Jung's psychology has truly developed into analytical psychology, with Jung as its founder but many others contributing to its body of literature and knowledge. As with any discipline which has such an inherent subjective factor, the theory and practice have undergone many revisions. Each individual analyst is somewhere on a continuum and is influenced by his/her analytic training and own individual nature.

Analytical psychology, along with other forms of depth psychology, has been under attack in recent years. New anti-depressants have changed the way many depressions are treated, and psychotherapy is no longer the first treatment of choice. Health insurance, private and governmental, no longer reimburses long-term psychotherapy, threatening the economic viability of many psychotherapists, who continue to increase in number. Conditions vary from country to country, but the trend is the same the world over. Fewer people enter psychoanalysis of any sort, including Jungian analysis.

Psychoanalysis is over 100 years old, and it is no longer the young and exciting discipline that it once was. It has failed to live up to its promises of healing the individual and of transforming society; in the 1950s it was seen by many as a panacea for the ills of the world. Although Freudian psychoanalysis bears the brunt of disillusionment, Jung and analytical psychology come in for their share of criticism. Yet many of Jung's ideas are now part of mainstream Western culture, and much of his specialized terminology is incorporated into everyday language.

One might ask: what is it that makes one Jungian? That is not an easy question to answer. For some, Jung may be like some distant relative in the past with whom they have some tenuous connection. For others the connection may be more immediate and personal. Whether it was his broad view of the unconscious, his thoughts on individuation, or his interest in the more esoteric aspects of the psyche, Jung spoke to us in some immediate and personal way. Maybe we have moved away from that initial experience, but we still hold on to it at some deep level. Jung emphasized the reality of the unconscious, especially as seen through one's dreams, and it seems that most

Jungians take this seriously. The reality of the dream, its potential for open-ing ever wider aspects of one's psyche, is something Jungians value above all.

Clearly, there is room for a clinical discipline of Jungian analysis. Jung, among others, has shown us that openness to forms of experience beyond everyday reality is essential to our humanness. Whether we call the level of the psyche that is in touch with that other reality the collective unconscious, the Self, the God-image, the objective psyche, or something else, it has always been, and will always be, part of us.

Notes

1   When *Memories, Dreams, and Reflections* was published in 1963, it was thought to be Jung's autobiography, but later it was found to be "edited" by Aniela Jaffe and that it actually had been written in part by her. There is much controversy about how much of the book Jung actually wrote.
2   In the early days of psychoanalysis, erotic attachment between analyst and analy-sand occurred in many instances and Jung's relationship to Toni Wolff is an example. Recent literature has emphasized the destructive aspects to the analysis when this occurs, and there are now much stricter rules relating to this phenomenon.
3   The *Eranos* conferences began in 1933 and were held on a yearly basis to facilitate communication among scholars involved in East–West studies. They included the fields of science, the humanities, mythology, psychology, and related disciplines. Jung spoke there 14 times and the conferences continue to this day, albeit in an altered form.

References

Astor, J. (1995) *Michael Fordham: Innovations in Analytical Psychology*, London: Routledge.
Bair, D. (2003) *Jung: A Biography*, Boston: Little Brown and Co.
Cocks, G. (1997) *Psychotherapy in the Third Reich: The Goering Institute*, 2nd edition, New Brunswick, NJ: Transaction Publishers.
Fordham, M. (1976) Discussion of T. Kirsch's article "The practice of multiple analyses", *Contemporary Psychoanalysis*, **12**(2):159–167.
Freud, S. (1914) *On the History of the Psychoanalytic Movement*, Standard Edition XIV, London: Hogarth Press.
—— (1961) *Beyond the Pleasure Principle*, New York: W.W. Norton & Co.
Henderson, J. (1982) "Reflections on the history and practice of Jungian analysis" in M. Stein (ed.) *Jungian Analysis*, La Salle, IL.: Open Court Publishing.
Jansen, D.B. (2003) *Jung's Apprentice*, Einsiedeln, Switzerland: Daimon Verlag.
Jung, C.G. (1916/1991) *Psychology of the Unconscious*, Princeton, NJ: Princeton Unversity Press.
—— (1921/1923/1964) *Psychological Types*, CW 6, Princeton, NJ: Princeton University Press.
—— (1948) *Symbolic Life*, CW 18, Princeton NJ: Princeton University Press.
—— (1953/1980) *Psychology and Alchemy*, CW 12, Princeton NJ: Princeton University Press.

—— (1963) *Memories, Dreams, Reflections*, New York: Pantheon Books.

Kirsch, T. (1976) "The practice of multiple analyses in analytical psychology", *Contemporary Psychoanalysis*, **12**(2):159–167.

Kirsch, T. (2000) *The Jungians*, London: Routledge.

McGuire, W. (1974) *Freud/Jung Letters*, Princeton, NJ: Princeton University Press.

McGuire, W. (ed.) (1989) *Analytical Psychology: Notes of the Seminar Given in 1925 by C. G. Jung*, Bollingen Series XCIX, Princeton, NJ: Princeton University Press.

Maidenbaum, A. and Martin, S. (eds) (2002) *Jung and the Shadow of Anti-Semitism*, Berwick, ME: Nicolas-Hays Publishing.

Muser, F.E. (1984) *Zur Geschichte des Psychologischen Clubs Zurich von den Anfangen bis 1928*, Zurich Analytical Psychology Club.

Papadopoulos, R. (ed.) (1996) Report on New Center, *IAAP Newsletter*, **16**: 94–97.

Samuels, A. (1985) *Jung and the Post-Jungians*, London: Routledge.

—— (1993) *The Political Psyche*, London: Routledge.

Shamdasani, S. (1998) *Cult Fictions*, London: Routledge.

Wheelwright, J. (1974) "Jung and Freud Speak to Each Other", *Psychological Perspectives*, **5**(2):171–176.

Chapter 2

Archetypes: emergence and the psyche's deep structure

George B. Hogenson

Among the concepts commonly associated with C.G. Jung, few are more widely recognized, nor more poorly understood, than the theory of archetypes. This state of affairs leads many, both within the Jungian community and among Jung's critics, to speak with confidence about this central concept while talking past one another. Leading Jungian and post-Jungian theorists such as Anthony Stevens, James Hillman and Jean Knox can thus assume radically divergent positions such as Stevens's deeply biological and evolutionary interpretation (Stevens 1982, 2003) of archetypes that stands in stark contrast to the essentially literary or intuitive use of the concept by Hillman and his followers (Hillman 1983, 1994). Similarly, Knox uses a sophisticated grasp of recent findings in developmental psychology and the cognitive sciences to present a picture of archetypes as developmentally derived properties within a more general theory of mind (Knox 2001, 2003). At some remove from these theories, one encounters an almost cosmically mystical view of the archetypes held by some of Jung's original followers, who draw heavily on Jung's correspondence with the physicist, Wolfgang Pauli for inspiration (Gieser 2004). In recent years the diversity of opinion on the nature of archetypes, combined with a variety of new discoveries and theories in the sciences concerned with the nature of mind, has led to still other interpretations of Jung's theory (Van Eenwyk 1997; Saunders and Skar 2001; Rosen, et al. 1991; Robertson 1987; Pietikainen 1998; Noll 1985; Jung and von Franz 1980). Once again, however, consensus eludes the commentary, and while a rich and instructive discourse has developed around the topic of archetypes, it is not clear that Jungian theory is any closer to realizing a unified point of view on this central organizing concept.

In this chapter I do not propose to resolve all of the issues that surround the theory of archetypes. However, I do believe that at least some of the confusion and debate that characterize this portion of Jung's system of psychology results from a failure to see Jung's own theoretical development in context and as an effort on the part of an unusually creative and innovative, but also determinedly rigorous, investigator to impose conceptual order on some very illusive phenomena. Put simply, a major reason for the lack of consensus regarding archetypes is that *Jung did not have a theory of archetypes*. Rather, I want to argue, Jung himself never really got beyond the pre-theoretical level of making observations to which he applied his powerful intuitive faculties to frame hypotheses. For example, in his 1925 seminar on analytical psychology the reader finds the following definitions of an archetype: "The archetypes are sources of energy. If people who have no views of life catch hold of an archetypal idea, say a religious idea, they become efficient" (Jung 1989:91). "There are certain general or collective ideas from which the thinker derives his judgment, and these we know as the logical modi, but these in turn are derived from some underlying idea; in other words, the logical modi go back to archetypal origins" (Jung 1989:123). And finally, "the archetypes are records of reactions to subjective sense-images" (Jung 1989:135).

Seen from this point of view, Jung's own project becomes one of searching for the appropriate framework within which to test his hypotheses. This approach to Jung's process of theory development, however, brings into focus a problem that helps explain much of the confusion that surrounds the theory of archetypes. In order to find a suitable scientific venue for his hypotheses, Jung was constrained to venture into the theoretical domains of other disciplines. But as Patricia Kitcher (Kitcher 1995) has argued in her study of Freud's interdisciplinary efforts, once a creative investigator in one discipline becomes dependent on the insights of another science, he or she is always vulnerable to the vicissitudes and changes taking place in that science. Thus both Freud and Jung made extensive use of Sir James Frazer's anthropological writings, but hardly any anthropologist would now take Frazer seriously. To some degree, Jung had the advantage on Freud in this case, because he was sufficiently younger to be able to take into account the dramatic changes taking place in all of the major sciences in the early twentieth century. To continue with the example of anthropology, Jung was able to shift his attention from Frazer to the more sophisticated theories of researchers such as Lucien Lévy-Bruhl, a move Freud could not make due to his commitment to mid-nineteenth century conclusions drawn from other sciences. In this chapter, therefore, I hope to shed light on the nature of Jung's thinking about archetypes, and their place in analytical psychology – both theoretical and clinical – by first coming to terms with Jung's own relationship to the problem. To do this, I will first sketch some historical background to the notion of archetypal structure, pointing to two distinct interpretations of the notion of an archetype that were current in the nineteenth century, each of which probably influenced Jung, but also set up a conflict even before he began to think seriously about the application of the term "archetype" to matters psychological. I will then review the ways in which Jung actually addresses the notion of the archetype.

The background for a concept

What is an archetype? In her critique of biological innatism, Susan Oyama (Oyama 2000) argues that a particular bias in the Western philosophical tradition, going at least as far back as Plato, assumes that the appearance of phenomena requires the pre-existence of a plan. This bias, Oyama argues, is one of the most entrenched habits of thought in the tradition, and gives shape to virtually every discussion of the workings of mind in particular. For Plato this was surely the case, as the doctrine of ideas makes clear. Plato saw the phenomenal world as little more than a shadowy illusion, only vaguely capturing the ontologically pure world of the forms or archetypes.

Oyama makes the case that in the Western tradition the Platonic model is an ontological constant, regardless of the level of analysis employed. One does not escape the commitment to a pre-existing plan by renouncing an idealized and transcendent domain of forms in favor of a genetic blueprint, or whatever other analogue one may choose. One could, however, make different uses of the notion of a plan. For late antique and early medieval neo-Platonists and theologians such as Dionysius the Areopagite, the theory of archetypes helped define the hierarchical structure of God's creation. Not even the rise of nominalism in the later Middle Ages could really dislodge the notion of the universal and hierarchical. In this sense, which would return in the two seminal interpretations of the archetype in the nineteenth century, those of Goethe and Owen, the notion of the archetype did not rely so much on the ontological status of the archetype as on its analytic and descriptive utility. Finally, with the rise of the natural sciences, the mathematical analysis of an archetype or plan came to play a crucial role. For Newton, to take the greatest of the classical instances, the idea that God had created an ordered universe led to the belief that His plan could be revealed through calculation, a belief that clearly bore fruit in the rise of modern science.

In Germany, however, resistance to Newton's theorizing was intense, and there is a way in which we can see in that conflict harbingers of the theoretical problems Jung confronted. The leading opponent of Newton in the early part of the eighteenth century was Leibniz, who rejected Newton's theory of gravitation because it implied the possibility of action at a distance in the absence of any medium of transmission. For Leibniz this was the height of occultism and could not be sustained. His alternative was to posit the doctrine of the monad, a theory in which the entire state of the universe was contained in each monadic entity, itself closed off from all other monads. In his theory, all of the lesser monads perceived the world as it was ordered by God, and interactions were, at the ontological level, ordered in a harmonious but not causal pattern. Relying heavily on Platonic, and neo-Platonic – as well as some Gnostic and Kabalistic – concepts, Leibniz viewed the processes of conscious development as movement to ever higher levels of clarity regarding the ordering of the harmonious world within each monad. Thus for him, the infinitesimal calculus became a means of representing and reflecting on the progressive approach to the image of creation contained in the mind of God, as much as it was a means of calculating approximations of reality.

By the end of the eighteenth century, the principal opponent of Newtonian science was the poet and polymath, Johann Wolfgang von Goethe. Goethe's approach to the sciences drew heavily on the work of Kant, himself an intellectual descendant of Leibniz, for whom an intimate relationship existed between the aesthetic and the scientific. Kant argued that in the case of living organisms, a purely mechanical understanding, as proposed by Newton, was insufficient. As Anne Harrington summarizes Kant's position, the philosopher proposed that "at least for heuristic purposes" it was necessary in the case of living organisms to posit a "natural purpose," a point of view that lead Goethe to view the study of nature as an "aesthetic–teleological" process (Harrington 1996:5). As Harrington characterizes Goethe's approach:

> Goethe's resulting aesthetic–teleological vision of living nature would subsequently function as one of the later generation's recurrent answers to the question of what it "meant" to be a holistic scientist in the grand German style. In contrast to the meaningless fragmentation of Newton's universe, Goethe had imagined a rich and colorful world shaped by aesthetic principles of order and patterning. The whole messy diversity of visible nature, he thought, could in fact be shown to be a product of a small number of fundamental forms or Gestalten. By observing and comparing the various metamorphoses of one or another form, he felt that the original or primal form of the type in question could be deduced using the pure judgments of the mind, in a manner akin to seeing the "form" of something in Plato's philosophy.
>
> (Harrington 1996:5)

Goethe's notion that a complete, or holistic, comprehension of a given natural state entailed an aesthetic as well as a teleological point of view, and that one approached the ur-form of a phenomenon by way of examining the changes or metamorphoses in a given form, anticipates the earliest efforts on Jung's part to delve into the imaginal structure of the mind, as we will see below when I take up Jung's seminal book, *Transformations and Symbols of the Libido*.

One result of Goethe's aesthetic–teleological view of nature was an interpretation of the foundations of order that brought back into focus the notion of the archetype. Leibniz had played with the idea of the archetype in his Kabalistic speculations, in the form of the Adam Kadmon, or primordial man, but Goethe took the concept into the realm of natural science as he conceived of it. Here again, we also encounter Goethe's fascination with the idea that perceived forms – phenomena – are permutations on some deeper pattern. As Robert J. Richards recounts Goethe's progress:

After he saw to the publication of his *Metamorphosis of Plants*, Goethe turned to consider animals. He wished to provide structural and development descriptions comparable to those he had offered for plants. In the first instance, these descriptions would be based on the conception of a dynamic type – which would later be dubbed an "archetype." The archetype would furnish a model by which to understand the structural and developmental features of all animals. But the archetype, as he gradually came to conceive it, would be more than a simple pattern useful for comparative zoology: it would be a dynamic force actually resident in nature, under whose power creatures would come to exist and develop.

(Richards 2002:440)

The fact that Goethe conceived of the archetype as something "more than a simple pattern useful for comparative zoology" would place his theory at variance with the rapidly developing discipline of comparative anatomy. Understanding the distinction that was about to arise in the history of science is important for understanding some of the confusion that persists around Jung's use of the concept of the archetype. Again, the distinction arises out of the different scientific traditions that developed in England and Germany. In the early nineteenth century, Romanticism was at its apogee, and thinkers in both England and Germany were pursuing their own versions of a holistic science. In England, however, even the Romantic tendency was subjected to a dose of practicality. The eminent anatomist, Richard Owen was an important figure in this movement, and he derived from the German romantics the notion of an archetype. For Owen, however, while the archetype was indeed a "kind of creative blueprint," as Adrian Desmond puts it, "in practical terms, it was simply a picture of a generalized or schematic vertebrate; but this in itself provided [Owen] with a standard by which to gauge the degree of specialization of fossil life." (Desmond 1982:43). For Owen, in other words, the archetype provided the means for establishing a taxonomy of vertebrate – or other – species. This was not, however, the real purpose behind Goethe's notion of the archetype. Again, to quote Richards:

Goethe's approach differed considerably from that of other anatomists of the period, who tended to focus their studies on particular vertebrate species (most often the human) and paid scant attention to elucidating a common form that might unite these various groups. His efforts would also differ from those later anatomists, like Richard Owen, who would pursue a general archetypal pattern but one that illustrated the least common denominator of the vertebrate class, describing the vertebrate archetype as essentially a string of vertebrae. By contrast, Goethe conceived the archetype as an *inclusive form*, a pattern that would contain all the parts really exhibited by the range of different vertebrate species. Since corresponding parts of various groups would vary considerably from one another (for instance, the limb of a horse and that of a human being), the archetypal form would not be representable to the external eye but only to the inward eye.

(Richards 2002:443; emphasis in original)

For Goethe, the combination of features attributed to the archetype – inclusive form, dynamic force, and interior or intuitive representation – resulted in an investigative strategy that emphasized the transformations through which a given natural phenomenon could be seen to progress. Peter Saunders and Patricia Skar, in their treatment of the dynamic nature of the archetype, to which I return below, cite Goethe himself on the need for a means of studying the process of metamorphosis, a need that was satisfied by Goethe's notion of the archetype (Saunders and Skar 2001:310). Saunders and Skar suggest that Jung derived his concept of the archetype from Goethe's dynamic understanding of the concept, and in this I concur with them. Nevertheless, there are moments in Jung's writings where he appears to be working out of the taxonomic approach to archetypes embraced by Owen. The same may be said in regard to many commentators on Jung. In these instances one gets the impression that a catalog of archetypes is available, and that the theoretician or the practicing analyst can inventory a set of dream images, or other psychic phenomena, measure the phenomenon against the archetypal catalog and confidently claim that a certain archetype is at work in the person's life. This is the approach to the archetypal that tends to result in the production of symbol books, and it is increasingly viewed with skepticism by contemporary Jungian theoreticians and clinicians.

I have pursued this historical discussion at some length in order to set the stage for understanding the fundamental premise of contemporary theorizing about the nature of the archetypes in Jung's system of psychology. The point of view that increasingly dominates discussions of archetypes emphasizes the dynamics of the psychic systems rather than the particularities of one or another archetype. Thus, in his exceptional study of the archetypal dimensions of trauma, Donald Kalsched (1996) focuses his clinical discussions on the dynamics of deep – archetypal – splitting and the emergence of imagery in the trauma victim that acts defensively but can become self-attacking as development progresses. But Kalsched has little interest in attaching labels to the imaginal figures that can emerge in these clinical moments. For him, the dynamic processes are the center of concern, although the particularities of the imaginal material are of great concern to the patient.

Development of a theory

Although there are intimations that Jung entertained some notion of archetypes fairly early in his career, and his familiarity with Goethe would have reinforced any intuitions he had, the term itself is not used by Jung until 1919 in a lecture titled "Instinct and the unconscious," delivered to a joint meeting of the Aristotelian Society, the Mind Association, and the British Psychological Society (Jung 1919). Despite the fact that the term itself does not appear in Jung's early writings, we can still see the path taken to arrive at the theory. I believe it is worthwhile briefly reviewing the development of Jung's thinking both because it sheds light on this central concept and because different theoreticians engage Jung's thinking at various points in the development of his understanding of archetypes.

Jung's earliest publication, the dissertation on "so-called occult phenomena" (Jung 1902) foreshadows a number of later developments in his thinking. Of particular importance are Jung's first intimations that he sees the workings of the psyche as teleological. In this case, a description of séances, or spirit encounters, actually undertaken by Jung's cousin Helene, the young somnambulist produced a series of increasingly fantastic visionary experiences while in a trance-like state. Jung interpreted these visions and spirit visitations as attempts on the part of the girl's adolescent psyche to find a form of self-expression suited to her process of maturation. We can, therefore, highlight two issues that would come to play decisive roles in Jung's theory of the psyche, and by extension in his theory of archetypes. First is the notion that the psyche is in some sense teleological. This notion gives a directionality to the workings of the unconscious mind, insofar as they can be seen as operating developmentally to move the individual into more mature – what Jung would later see as individuated – states. Secondly, Jung was clearly prepared, even as early as the dissertation, to take seriously the workings of images and fantasies, not in the negative or reductive manner that he would encounter with Freud, but rather as altogether appropriate instruments of development. In other words, the imaginal or fantasy world of the individual was not to be viewed as a deficient, or worse a purposefully deceptive, operation of the psyche but rather as an equal partner with what Jung would call directed thinking. What is lacking in the dissertation is a theory of what the underlying mechanisms that give rise to the kinds of fantasies Helene produced might be. Rather, Jung takes a largely phenomenological approach to the séances, and seeks only to deduce the function of the fantasies. In large measure, one can therefore trace the origins of Hillman's archetypal psychology all the way back to this earliest stage of Jung's own development. The focus is almost exclusively on the workings of the imaginal products of the psyche, with little attention or interest in what biological or cognitive mechanisms may be at work that give rise to the fantasies, and with the object of guiding a developmental process of individuation.

The next step in Jung's development was the formation of the theory of complexes. This phase in Jung's theory-building was largely the result of the prompting of his chief at the Burghölzli hospital, Eugen Bleuler, who guided Jung's work after he left the University of Basel. Bleuler's role in Jung's life is often occluded by the intensity of Jung's relationship with Freud, but it is a mistake to underestimate the influence Bleuler had on the neophyte psychiatrist. Several factors may be briefly mentioned in the present context. First of all, the Burghölzli practiced a form of treatment that we would now call milieu therapy. The physicians under Bleuler's leadership lived in the hospital – Jung's first children were born there – and thus were in constant contact with the most severe cases of psychosis. For Jung it was this intimate familiarity with psychotics that prepared the ground for his disagreements with Freud, almost from the moment they first made contact with one another. Second, Bleuler himself had an insatiable desire to learn all the most recent developments in psychology and psychopathology, and to that end pushed his staff to read and report on everything happening in the world of psychiatry and psychology. For Jung, again, this lead to a prodigious famil-iarity with the scientific literature in the field on which he was able to draw at will in his later work. Third, Bleuler's concern for the scientific basis of psychiatry prompted him to assign genuinely experimental projects to his staff. Jung's assigned project was the replication and development of the word association test as it was being used by Wilhelm Wundt and others. Finally, Bleuler sought to promote his subordinates by sponsoring them in further education. Jung was sent to Paris to attend the lectures of Pierre Janet, and also came to know Theodore Flournoy in Geneva. Both of these men would greatly influence Jung's thinking in ways that would have far greater, and more sustained influence than Freud would have (for a more detailed discussion of Jung's relationship to both Janet and Flournoy, see Shamdasani (2003)).

It was, however, in the work on the word association test that Jung first formulated the theory of the complex. Although the term did not originate with Jung, he gave it new meaning as he unpacked the results of the associ-ation test. Prior to Jung's work on the test, it had been used primarily as a means to study the "laws of association," a tradition in psychology stretching back to Aristotle.

Beginning with the fairly simple form of the association test used by Wundt and Gustav Aschaffenburg, which focused attention on the reaction time of a response, but most of all on the actual content of the response, Jung added a number of innovative measures to the test, including the first real use of galvanic skin response and cardio-pulmonary function to yield a more com-plete picture of the individual response process. He also, under the influence of Bleuler established base norms of response in various classes of people (normal versus psychologically disturbed, educated versus uneducated) and measured the impact of various external influences on the subjects of his studies – alcohol, distraction, fatigue (Jung and Riklin 1904). In addition to enlarging the scope of the test, however, Jung's innovations demonstrated that the psychological and the physiological were intimately implicated in one another. As he would argue, it was the feeling tone that defined the complex, not just the associative references and the cognitive delay in response. This insight would later lead Jung to posit the existence of what he called the psychoid nature of phenomena such as synchronicity, which seemed to transgress the assumed boundaries of material cause and effect. Nevertheless, at this point Jung used the association test to begin to define the deeper structure of the psyche. Although it was Freud to whom he turned for guidance, it was really more to Janet that he owed the insights that he used to make order of the theory of complexes. Specifically, it was Janet's notion that the psyche was fundamentally made up of partial personalities, his dissociative model, rather than Freud's repression model that carried Jung forward.

In the theory of the complex we again see the foundations of more contemporary theories of the archetypes. Jung maintained that as he observed the behavior of complexes he was able to discern what he referred to as a core or inner kernel to the complex. As he began to see these core qualities of the complexes he was increasingly able to segregate the complexes into groups or categories. This characteristic of the complex – that it exhibited a kind of typical core element – became the initial insight leading to the theory of archetypes. This aspect of the theory of complexes has provided the starting point for the provocative interpretation of archetypes developed by Saunders and Skar, who characterize the archetype as a class of complexes which are considered to fall into the same "category," as Jung put it. "In mathematical language," they continue, "we can say that an archetype is an equivalence class of complexes" (Saunders and Skar 2001:312). At the same time, Jung's recognition of the physiological aspects of the complex, as well as their typical character, has provided the basis for Anthony Stevens's evolutionary interpretation of the archetypes. In particular, Stevens has associated the physiology and the typicality of the complex with the biological aspects of John Bowlby's theories of attachment and attachment disorder. In the area of archetypes, by uniting Bowlby's notion that the infant has an innate need for attachment with the notion that the complex arises from a deficit in some innate need, Stevens establishes his argument that the archetype corresponds to a genetically defined need that must be fulfilled to develop successfully.

What is interesting here is that the position of Saunders and Skar and that of Stevens are almost diametrically opposed to one another, even though both make the claim that the theory of complexes, arising out of Jung's work on the word association test, forms the basis for their interpretations of the theory of archetypes. Both models certainly capture elements of Jung's thinking about archetypes, but it is also the case that both models have deficiencies that will have to be addressed. Part of the reason for the existence of deficiencies in almost all the proposed interpretations of the theory of archetypes, as I have already noted, was Jung's own lack of a single, grounded, understanding of just what a theory of archetypes should entail. With the conclusion of his work on the word association test, and the development of his relationship with Freud, the situation was, if possible, about to get worse.

It is worth noting that prior to Jung's meeting with Freud, and the development of their close collaboration, Jung expresses relatively little interest in mythology. Freud, on the other hand, had begun to use myth – or at least one myth – as a touchstone for the development of his theory of the psyche at least as early as 1897, when he wrote to Fliess to comment on the compelling power of the story of Oedipus in his self-analysis (Ferris 1997:150). Freud's case studies were shot through with literary references and allusions to the classical foundations of the culture. Indeed, Freud's anthropological explorations, largely in the form of reading Frazer's *Golden Bough* and some of Darwin's more speculative accounts of primitive society, clearly reflect the sometimes romantic, sometimes classicist bent of nineteenth-century armchair speculation on the nature of non-European peoples. Linguistic plays, arcane etymologies and a relentless comparative accumulation of materials were part of Freud's approach to demonstrating the validity of his theories that Jung adopted wholesale, albeit in the service of his own theory-building. But Freud was not the only influence on Jung. Jung's relationship with Flournoy in Geneva was also close, and towards the end of his relationship with Freud it appears that Jung turned increasingly to Flournoy both for personal support and for inspiration. Flournoy's study of a "somnambulist" in his book *From India to the Planet Mars* (Flournoy 1901/1994) was an explicit inspiration for Jung's *Wandlungen und Symbole der Libido* (*Transformations and Symbols of the Libido*) (Jung 1991), which Jung – correctly, I believe – credits with finally ending the relationship with Freud.

Wandlungen is a complex and often confused book that defies easy summarization. Flournoy had provided Jung with a series of fantasies produced by a young woman named Frank Miller. Until Sonu Shamdasani (1990) tracked down the true history of Ms Miller, Jung and his commentators had all worked on the assumption that Miller was on the verge of a schizophrenic breakdown when she wrote the fantasies. Nothing of the sort was in fact the case, but Jung proceeded nevertheless to use the material for a diagnostic analysis of the imminent collapse of the young woman's psyche. Beyond that, however, Jung pushed his analysis in the direction of a kind of elementary comparative mythology, relating the fantasies of Ms Miller to the song of Hiawatha and other mythic renderings of the tale of the hero. His erudition was clearly at least the equal of Freud's by this point, and one of the problems of the text, which would become characteristic of Jung's writings, was that his search for references and allusions in the fantasies ranges so widely that most readers are unable to keep up with his argument. The point of all this comparative myth analysis, however, was very much the same as Freud's simultaneous project in *Totem and Taboo* (Hogenson 1983). Both men were intent on demonstrating that their theories were sustained by their manifest ubiquity in human culture. A point that is often missed by critics of Jung is that by the end of *Totem and Taboo* Freud had developed at least as strong an argument for a "collective unconscious" as anything Jung proposed. And, as

Jung would maintain to the end of his life, Freud had also developed a theory of archetypes; only there was just one archetype in Freud's system and that was the Oedipus archetype (Jung 1977:288).

In the profusion of materials in *Wandlungen* one episode stands out, and has been singled out for perhaps as much commentary as any single remark in Jung's writings; the case of the "Solar Phallus Man." This case involved a severely schizophrenic patient in the Burghölzli who remarked that when he looked at the sun he saw what appeared to be a phallic extension hanging down from the disk, and, he went on, it was this tube-like protrusion that caused the wind to blow. The case was originally reported by Jung's subordinate, Johann Jakob Honegger, but Jung incorporated it into his text with a commentary connecting the man's vision to certain teachings of the ancient cult of Mithraism. For reasons that remain obscure, Jung developed, about this time, a fascination with Mithraism that persisted well into the 1920s. In this case Jung asserted that the psychotic patient could not have been familiar with the Mithraic myth because it had not yet been published, thus ruling out cryptomnesia as a source of the delusion. Jung was at least partially mistaken in this assertion; as it happened that he was working off the date of the 1910, second edition of Albrecht Dieterich's book *Ein Mithrasliturgie* which was originally published in 1903. However, we now know that the patient, one Emile Schwyzer (1862–1931), was hospitalized at the Burghölzli in 1901, i.e. before the publication of Dieterich's book (Bair 2003). Richard Noll, in his effort to discredit Jung's theory of archetypes and the collective unconscious, has speculated that even if Schwyzer had not seen Dieterich's book, there were several other potential sources of similar information (Noll 1994). However, as Deirdre Bair has now made clear, Schwyzer had been incarcerated in various mental institutions both in England and in Switzerland beginning in 1882 at the age of 20 (Bair 2003). In consequence, Noll's already speculative position becomes tenuous at best. It is nevertheless the case that the question of cryptomnesiac reproduction of myths is a sticking point for much of Jung's speculation on archetypes (Shamdasani 2003). One of the most compromising aspects of Jung's presentation of his theory, which was repeated by many of his original followers, was his frequent resort to the assurance that some patient "could not have had any familiarity with" a given myth or motif. To an unacceptable degree this assertion is as often based on class biases in Jung as it is on any evidence. Eventually, Jung backed away from the Solar Phallus Man as a test case, but the problems presented by that case continued to haunt his theory.

The dual nature of archetypal discourse, and the problem it presents

The Solar Phallus Man – and *Wandlungen* in general – presents a problem for Jung and for subsequent theorizing about archetypes. The problem has to do with the relationship between the brain or the mind or the psyche and the shared imaginal world of myths, fairy tales and, in fact, dreams and psychotic delusions and hallucinations. The argument of that book, really the first in which Jung attempted to develop the foundations for a more general theory of the psyche, was that under certain circumstances, such as the onset or presence of a psychosis, the human mind tends to produce typical patterns of ideation and representation. Thus, Ms Miller, who Jung believed was on the verge of a psychotic breakdown, produced fantasies that closely resembled the hero legends of Native Americans – as Jung had them from Longfellow – or other hero traditions. Squinting at the sun, the Solar Phallus Man spontaneously generates a story that closely resembles the mythology of an obscure Roman cult that ceased to exist almost 2000 years earlier. Once it became evident, however, that both the Solar Phallus Man and Ms Miller could be drawing on cryptomnesiac memories to generate their fantasies, the notion that there were patterns of mind that reproduced themselves over generations became increasingly questionable. Jung's solution to this problem rested, to a large degree, not on some mystical notion of the transcendent nature of myths, as critics from Freud on have alleged, but rather on his surprisingly deep commitment to an evolutionary theory of mind.

A crucial aspect of Jung's entire project was his commitment to linking depth psychology, to the extent possible, to the larger scientific program of the twentieth century. This desire clearly motivated his long association with the physicist Wolfgang Pauli, and it is evident in other places as well. In the case of the early work on archetypes, the most important influences appear to come from the first ethologists, and the emerging neo-Darwinian model in evolutionary theory, particularly as presented by James Mark Baldwin and Conway Lloyd Morgan (Hogenson 2001). As late as the 1940s, Jung insisted that if the human body was the result of evolution, there was no reason to think that the human psyche was anything other than the result of evolution as well. Jung was fond of simple animal-based examples and his reasoning throughout seems to have been along the lines that if weaver birds consistently produce the same basic form of nest without any instruction in how to do so, then one can argue that humans produce typical mythologems without any particular instruction. But it was also clear that instruction, in the form of such things as epic poems about Indian heroes, did exist. The question for Jung then becomes, why this particular set of images rather than any other?

At this point Jung introduces a distinction into the theory of archetypes that brings us back to the discussion of archetypes as developed by Goethe and Owen, and that has become the center of much contemporary debate regarding archetypes. The distinction Jung draws is between what he termed the archetype-as-such and the archetypal image. The archetypal image is the representation that we find in a given myth. Thus Beowulf, Heracles and Hiawatha are all images of the hero archetype, and Jung is emphatic that these particular representations are cultural in origin and show certain variations from culture to culture. However, evolution has in some manner equipped the human mind with the capacity and the tendency to form or otherwise engage images of just this sort. Unfortunately, Jung is extremely vague on just how he thinks this has taken place, or in what form the archetype-as-such is to be conceptualized. He tends to rely heavily on metaphors to explain what he means by the archetype-as-such; it is like a crystal lattice, implicit in a supersaturated solution, or it is like the instinct of the weaver bird, or it is somehow transmitted by "Mendelian particles."

It is at this point that I believe we can see the workings of Jung's own background – and the influence of Goethe in particular – in the development of his theory of archetypes. One can characterize the two models of the archetype proposed by Owen and Goethe respectively as a distinction between a fundamental structure and a fundamental process. For Owen, the vertebrate archetype defines the most fundamental structure of the vertebrate organism, i.e., the simple vertebrae. For Goethe, the archetype does not consist in a fundamental structure, but in the overall process that gives rise to the entirety of the organism – and that process cannot be narrowly defined and specified. Jung, in a sense, tries to have it both ways. He knows, as an early twentieth-century scientist, especially one trained as a medical doctor, that good science proceeds by defining fundamental structures in organisms. Therefore, one should be able to define categories of archetypal images, perhaps based on categories of complexes as proposed by Saunders and Skar (2001), and in so doing provide a kind of taxonomy or anatomy of the psyche in keeping with Owen's model. On the other hand, one could adopt the position that the archetypes are part of a dynamic system – whether in the Freudian sense of the dynamics of the topological models or in Jung's notion of the teleological functions of the psyche – which would align once more with Goethe, for whom nature was an altogether dynamic, process-based phenomenon, and for whom Owen's structural model has no resonance.

The emergence of emergence

As I noted above, I have reviewed this historical material at length because I believe that in order to understand contemporary theory and practice regarding archetypes it is important to understand the foundations of Jung's thinking on the subject and to recognize the ambiguities that attend the whole notion. The result of Jung's ambiguity is that each theoretician picks out that aspect of Jung's discussion of archetypes that best suits his or her established predisposition or training from some other field. Thus, to take two of the cases with which I began this chapter, Anthony Stevens, along with his collaborator, John Price, remarks that "Archetypes are conceived as neuropsychic units which evolved through natural selection and which are responsible for determining the behavioral characteristics as well as the affective and cognitive experiences typical of human beings" (Stevens and Price 1996:6).

On the other hand, James Hillman confidently claims that "The *datum* with which archetypal psychology begins is the image. The image was identified with the psyche by Jung ('image is psyche' – Jung 1966:para. 75), a maxim which archetypal psychology has elaborated to mean that the soul is consti- tuted of images, that the soul is primarily an imagining activity most natively and paradigmatically presented by the dream" (Hillman 1983:14). Slightly further along, Hillman elaborates his argument in a manner directly contrary to Stevens: "The 'poetic basis of mind' was a thesis Hillman (1975:xi) first set forth in his 1972 Terry Lectures at Yale University. It states that archetypal psychology 'starts neither in the physiology of the brain, the structure of language, the organization of society, nor the analysis of behavior, but in processes of imagination' " (Hillman 1983:19). So here we have two recog- nized authorities, both of whom can cite Jung as their inspiration, who are nevertheless diametrically opposed to one another. Stevens has, since his book *Archetypes: A Natural History of the Self* (1982) appeared, maintained a steadfast adherence to a largely biological, indeed genetic, interpretation of the theory of archetypes, while Hillman has, with equal steadfastness, maintained the imaginal position.

There are a host of issues that differentiate these positions, but a crucial difficulty rides on Jung's distinction between the archetype-as-such and the archetypal image. In the rest of this chapter I will argue that this distinction, which Jung used to defend himself against accusations that he was advocating the inheritance of cultural content, has become the critical point of differen- tiation among contemporary theoreticians trying to work out the meaning of the notion of archetypes. The reason for this is the rise of a point of view on the origin of phenomena that was unavailable to Jung. That point of view is widely referred to as "emergence."

The first detailed discussion of emergence in the Jungian literature was by David Tresan (Tresan 1996), who reviewed a range of literature on the con- cept. In essence, emergence is based on the notion that within certain kinds of system, phenomena can come into being without any precursor state predict- ing the appearance of those phenomena. Bruce Weber has characterized emergence in the following terms (but see as well discussions of emergence in Chapters 5 and 9 of this volume):

> Emergence occurs when new properties appear in a system that were not present in, and could not easily have been predictable from, the com- ponents of the system. Emergent phenomena obey laws that arise with the novel properties. Emergent phenomena impose conditions on their constituents that depend on the nature of the emergent phenomena.
>
> (Weber 2003:311)

A simple example is water. There are no particular characteristics of hydrogen and oxygen that would lead one to predict that in combination these two gasses would form a liquid at room temperature or that the liquid would have characteristics such as being heavier by volume just before it turns into a solid than it is after it has solidified. These properties of water are emergent properties of the combination of hydrogen and oxygen. Both Saunders and Skar (Saunders and Skar 2001) and Hogenson (Hogenson 2001) have argued that the key to understanding archetypes lies in their being entirely emergent phenomena. Critics of this radical position, such as Anthony Stevens and Jean Knox – who nevertheless does take a position that involves a less radical form of emergence – object to the strongly emergent position because it appears to eliminate Jung's concept of the archetype-in-itself. Thus, for example, Stevens writes in the revised edition of his book *Archetypes* that:

> Where I part company from Hogenson (Hogenson 2001) is over his insistence that archetypes can possess no place or location, being no more than "the emergent properties of the dynamic developmental system of brain, environment and narrative." This position is endorsed by Saunders and Skar (2001). The difference between their position and mine can be understood in terms of semantics. What do we mean when we use the term archetype? When I define archetype as "innate neuropsychic potential", I am talking about the *archetype-as-such* which is actualized in the form of the archetypal images, motifs, ideas, relationships and behaviors. In my view, Hogenson's definition of archetypes as "emergent properties" is describing the *actualized manifestations* of archetypes rather than archetypes-as-such.
>
> (Stevens 2003:284; emphasis in original)

In a similar vein, Jean Knox remarks that:

> The difficulty that arises with [the approach of Saunders and Skar (and by extension that of Hogenson) is that] archetypes . . . lose a key distinguishing characteristic, that of the archetype-as-such as a primitive sketch or Gestalt without information or representational content.
>
> (Knox 2003:64)

Stevens, to his credit, puts his finger on the problem that is at the center of this chapter: what do we mean when we use the term "archetype"? What did Jung mean when he used it? The difficulty is that both Stevens and Knox, despite otherwise divergent views on many aspects of the debate, embrace the notion, more characteristic of Owen than of Goethe, that at some level one must describe a template upon which archetypal phenomena rest. Additionally, this template must in some significant sense inhere in the individual, either as genetic coding or as the not quite *a priori*, but potentially prenatal, image schemas of developmental psychology. Thus Jean Knox writes regarding the image schema and the archetype-in-itself:

The image schema would therefore seem to be a model that, for the first time, offers a developmentally sound description of the archetype-as such and of the archetypal image. The abstract pattern itself, the image schema, is never experienced directly, but as a foundation or ground plan that can be likened to the concept of the archetype-as-such. This pro- vides the invisible scaffolding for a whole range of metaphorical exten- sions that can be expressed in conscious imagery that would therefore seem to correspond to the archetypal image. These metaphorical elabor- ations are always based on the Gestalt of the image schema from which they are derived.

(Knox 2003:62)

Let me be clear on the point that Knox does view the formation of the basis of the archetypal as in some sense emergent. Theories of emergent behavioral formation are increasingly common in developmental psychology (Thelen and Smith 1998; Thelen *et al.* 2001), and Knox is well aware that the image schema cannot come into being by innate genetic programming. Neverthe- less, as I read her work on image schemas, and their successor states, internal working models, she does argue for the need to have a "ground plan" or otherwise establish a template for the formation of archetypal phenomena, precisely the problem identified in Susan Oyama's critique of the Western philosophical tradition, and it is in many ways analogous to the view of the vertebrate archetype proposed by Richard Owen.

There is another problem that arises at this point in the effort to under- stand Jung's use of the term "archetype-as-such." Simply put, we must ask whether Jung himself actually conceived of the archetype-as-such as an endogenous structure of the developing brain, which is the position that is implicit in the position of Knox and Stevens, among others. This is a difficult point to tease out, because it involves us once again in the problematic inter- pretation of Jung's philosophical commitments. Why would this be the case? To answer this question it is necessary to go back to Jung's introduction of the notion of the archetype. At the conference in 1919 where Jung first used the term, he remarked:

In this "deeper" stratum we also find the *a priori*, inborn forms of "*intu- ition*," namely the *archetypes* of perception and apprehension, which are the necessary *a priori* determinants of all psychic processes. Just as his instincts compel man to a specifically human mode of existence, so the archetypes force his way of perception and apprehension into specifically human patterns.

(Jung 1919:para. 270)

What is notable in this passage is its deeply Kantian resonances. Jung was, as he repeatedly made clear, strongly influenced by Kant, and frequently referred to Kant's critical philosophy. In the *Critique of Pure Reason* (Kant 1787/1929), where the issue of the *a priori* nature of mind is central, Kant's project is to argue for the *logical* necessity of certain characteristics of human perception, such as the perception of all objects occurring in space and time, or that all events are perceived as having a cause. It was not Kant's intention to argue that there had to be something along the lines of what we would recognize as a genetic program for space and time or an image schema for space and time. Rather the contrary. Kant's argument, in effect, regresses, perhaps infinitely, behind such claims. In other words, to perceive the workings of the genes or the image schemas forming in the neonate, one must first perceive in space and time and in reference to causality. Thus the *a priori*, or as Kant would also have it, the transcendental status of space, time and causality cannot be proven by empirical research. All one really has, in what we would now call consciousness, are phenomena. Jung's explicit use of the Kantian language of the *a priori* in determining the universally human "way of perception and apprehension" appears to point us far more decisively in the direction of an infinitely regressing, transcendental archetype-as-such that leaves in its wake the phenomenal experience of the archetypal image, in which case the genetic blueprints or image schemas can be seen as archetypal images rather than instances of the archetype-in-itself.

This sense of the illusiveness of the archetype-as-such is captured by Jung much later in life. Writing in 1940, Jung stated flatly that:

> If we cannot deny the archetypes or otherwise neutralize them, we are confronted, at every new stage in the differentiation of consciousness to which civilization attains, with the task of finding a new *interpretation* appropriate to this stage, in order to connect the life of the past that still exists in us with the life of the present, which threatens to slip away from it.
>
> (Jung 1940/1969:para. 267)

The notion that any given interpretation of the true nature of the archetype is really only an attempt to link contemporary thinking back to the mode of expression – not the mode of perception, which Jung would argue is archetypally constant in a sense similar to Kant's argument – puts considerable strain on any argument that attempts finally to have grounded the archetype. In the same essay, Jung goes on to reinforce this sense:

> As to the *psychology* of our theme I must point out that every statement going beyond the purely phenomenal aspects of an archetype lays itself open to the criticism we have expressed above. Not for a moment dare we succumb to the illusion that an archetype can be finally explained and disposed of. Even the best attempts at explanation are only more or less successful translations into another metaphorical language. (Indeed,

language itself is only an image.) The most we can do is to *dream the myth onwards* and give it a modern dress.

(Jung 1940/1969:para. 271)

Indeed, in 1947 Jung was quite specific on this matter. It appeared to him at that point that "the real nature of the archetype is not capable of being made conscious, that it is transcendent, on which account I call it psychoid. More-over every archetype, when represented to the mind, is already conscious and therefore differs to an indeterminable extent from that which caused the rep-resentation" (Jung 1947/1969:para. 417).

Implications

Can we make sense of this understanding of the nature of the archetype in the clinical setting? In a recent paper on Ferenczi's work with a deeply trau-matized patient, Donald Kalsched provides a brief account of one of his own cases. A young woman, who was sexually abused by her father, was trying to reconstruct the events of the abuse. Kalsched recounts a point in the analysis when recognition of the archetypal dimensions of the abusive experience became evident:

> As these anxiety-saturated memories loomed into consciousness, her eye-sight would become clouded and the room would start to spin, so we could only explore a little at a time. As this process continued, we realized that these "memories" were all strangely "from above" – in other words, that a part of her had been dissociated, looking down at her violated body. One day, in a session I wondered out loud "where" she went during these dissociative episodes. She thought for a moment – then burst into tears and said very movingly, "I was in the arms of the Blessed Mother".
> (Kalsched 2003:479)

Kalsched goes on to recount how Ferenczi had encountered a very similar circumstance in his treatment of Elizabeth Severn, who was also sexually abused as a child. In the course of the treatment, a "supra-individual," given the name "Orpha," became a focal point in understanding the trauma. Kalsched narrates Severn's experience:

> "Orpha", otherwise known as the "organizing life instincts", was the name Ferenczi gave to what I would call a "daimonic" inner object that had come to the rescue of a patient named Elizabeth Severn, known in [Ferenczi's] Diary as "RN". Like my patient's "Blessed Mother", Orpha was Elizabeth Severn's "guardian angel", an inner, all-knowing, pre-cociously intellectual part of the self who seemed to have access to higher powers. Ferenczi and his patient were able to reconstruct the life-saving

activities of this remarkable inner object. At the moment of impossible suffering, Orpha would exit through an imaginary hole in the patient's head; ascend into the starry vault, and become an "Astral fragment", shining off in the distance like a star, full of compassion and understanding, while the patient's body was being tortured and abused. Then Orpha would descend again and help the shattered child assemble some kind of minimally functioning false self with which to go on existing.

(Kalsched 2003:480)

At the risk of detracting from Kalsched's remarkable insights into the nature of trauma, and archetypal dimensions of the experience, I believe it can be argued that he relies too heavily on the vocabulary of object relations to carry important parts of his argument. My reasons for being critical of this element, in what I otherwise consider to be perhaps the most important contribution to Jungian clinical thought in recent years, is that I believe the notion of the archetype as an emergent phenomenon can carry us well beyond the insights of object relations theory. How is this the case? The crucial element in both Kalsched's own case and the case of Elizabeth Severn is the role of the supra-individual figure to restore a sense of self to the abused child. It appears to me that in both accounts this function is central to the workings of the figure of the Blessed Mother or Orpha. However, from the standpoint of Jungian theory amalgamated with object relations theory these powerful figures run the risk of becoming mere substitutes for more conventional objects in the world of the child. As Kalsched writes in regard to his own patient, "Through a Jungian lens we would say that the Blessed Mother was an inner figure of 'daimonic' proportions – the Great 'archetypal' Mother, activated in the unconscious to compensate the regressing ego for the failure of reality-mediation by the personal mother" (2003:480). But is this an adequate interpretation of so singular a figure in so extraordinary an account of survival? Is the interpretation, we can ask, sufficient to the meaning of the symbolic intervention in the life of the child, and later in the life of the adult analysand?

It is at this point that it becomes essential to draw out Jung's relationship to the alternative points of view on the nature of the archetype with which this chapter began. The key to making this determination, I believe, lies in Jung's approach to the symbolic world to which the theory of archetypes gives rise. In the case of Kalsched's patient, for example, the figure of the Blessed Virgin Mary can be interpreted in ways that so transcend any reference to the personal mother that it is difficult to see how an analysis could stay within the frame provided by even a Jungian version of object relations. The immense variety of meanings and interpretations available within the symbolic ambit of the Blessed Virgin has been documented by Jaroslav Pelikan (Pelikan 1996) and one can see in his account how the image of the Blessed Mother – and, given the characteristics associated with Orpha, that figure as well – would carry the imaginal experience of the child far beyond a sense of the comforting qualities of the absent personal mother. Jung's approach to the archetypal symbol, which he emphasized was radically different from what he called Freud's "semiotic" approach, was clinically defined by Jung's method of amplification. Writing in 1947 of this methodological innovation, and its implementation in his approach by way of active imagination, Jung provides us with the key to his approach to the archetype in the form advocated by Goethe:

> The most remarkable thing about this method, I felt, was that it did not involve a *reductio in primam figuram*, but rather a synthesis – supported by an attitude voluntarily adopted, though for the rest wholly natural – of passive conscious material and unconscious influences, hence a kind of spontaneous amplification of the archetypes. The images are not to be thought of as a reduction of conscious contents to their simplest denominator, as this would be the direct road to the primordial images which I said previously was unimaginable; they make their appearance only in the course of amplification.
>
> (Jung 1947/1969:para. 403)

Recall Richards' distinction between the archetypal thinking of Owen and that of Goethe, where the former specifically sought the *"reductio in primam figuram"* while Goethe observed the transformations of the system in confidence that the inner eye would discern the deeper working of the entire ensemble of factors acting upon one another. Jung, of course, viewed his system of synthetic amplification as diametrically opposed to Freud's reductive method, and by highlighting this distinction we can see the two falling into the patterns of thought proposed by their predecessors.

With the return of this distinction, first highlighted by Owen and Goethe, between the archetype as the least common denominator or the basic form versus the dynamics of the metamorphosis of the system as a whole, we come back to the question of emergence. It is worth remembering that the title of Jung's first major attempt to deal with myth in an analytic manner was titled *Wandlungen und Symbole der Libido*. *Wandlungen*, usually translated as "transformations," shares a root sense with the more theological "transubstantiation" as in the Mass. Thus transformation and symbol are intimately connected in Jung's view of the workings of the psyche. But with the root sense of transubstantiation hidden in the background we can see that at some level Jung is not simply referring to the possibility of developmental change, but also of ontological change. The notion of ontological change captures the depth of the transformation evidently experienced by the young women who were able to find the counter-balance to their deep sense of violation by way of a transformative vision that gave way to a recovery of a lost sense of the sacred in the person of the Blessed Virgin Mary or in the essentially Gnostic Orpha. This understanding of the dimensions of change envisioned in Jung's understanding of the archetypal patterns of the psyche pushes us in the direction of the strong sense of emergence discussed in this chapter. The issue that is in question is whether or not one could plausibly deduce the probable course of development in the case material from the material as it is presented. The analogy here is to the ability to deduce plausibly the emergence of water from the combination of oxygen and hydrogen.

This question adumbrates a crucial next step in the development of analytical psychology's point of view on the archetype. Ironically, it appears to me that the course that will have to be taken will be by way of a return to the beginning of Jung's theorizing about the archetype. The issue is this: for Jung the inspiration for the theory of the archetype was his observation of the symbolic behavior of patients in the Burghölzli hospital and the work he did with the word association test. He saw patterns in both situations, but at first did not know what to do with them. Saunders and Skar have gone a great distance in examining the relationship of the theory of the complex, which derives from the word association test, to the theory of archetypes. Jean Knox, while perhaps overly emphasizing the actual formation of the archetype-as-such, has captured important issues in the development of the individual that dramatically advance our clinical understanding. Nevertheless, we remain in need of an account of the nature and workings of the symbol that is congruent with the theory of archetypes that Jung spent his life trying to work out.

Theories regarding the nature of the symbol underwent a decisive transformation in the early part of the twentieth century, particularly under the influence of the linguist, Ferdinand de Saussure whose examination of the nature of language categorically rejected the notion that reference in language was other than arbitrary. This was contrary to most thinking about language in the ancient and medieval periods when at least some linguistic forms, and certainly symbolic acts and representations, were considered to be grounded in their referents. However, it is no longer clear that de Saussure, and linguists who have followed him, captured all the characteristics of the symbol. Leading an alternative movement in the study of language, anthropologist and neuroscientist Terrence Deacon has challenged much of the received doctrine on the nature of the symbol. His objection to the notion of arbitrarity in the symbolic world is worth considering, as one can hear in it resonances with the position on the nature of the archetype as a deeply emergent phenomenon that has been developed here. Deacon remarks regarding the factors that might constrain the "evolution" of language:

> I have repeatedly argued that probably the most important of these constraints are those that arise from the semiotic infrastructure implicit in symbolic reference itself. This has almost entirely been ignored by linguists and cognitive scientists alike, largely because it has been assumed

that symbolic reference contributes no constraint on the form of language other than arbitrary. I believe that this is an unwarranted assumption based on the fallacy of generalization from individual symbol–object relationships to systems of symbols. As I will argue below, there are indeed constraints that are implicit in symbol use. The point I want to emphasize here, however, is that such semiotic constraints as involve symbol systems are neither located in brains nor in society, *per se.* They are a bit like the formal constraints that have shaped the development of mathematics (and yield such curious universal phenomena as prime numbers). Though I leave it to philosophers to argue over the nature of the "existence" of such formal constraints, I believe it cannot be denied that mathematics has had to evolve with respect to them. Similarly in the case of language, semiotic constraints have acted as selection pressures on the evolution of both language and brain structures.

(Deacon 2003:98)

A theory of archetypes must give rise to a viable theory of symbolization that satisfies the demands of the clinical setting, in which the amplification of a symbol is able to transform the psyche and the behavior of the analysand, and give an account of the range of phenomena that Jung tried to pull together under the rubric of the archetypes of the collective unconscious. The first rule of truly scientific investigation is to preserve the phenomena. Jung struggled to get the phenomena to be clear enough that theory-building could take place. At times he clearly missed the mark, as in the case of the Solar Phallus Man, but if one is to engage Jung at all, one must begin by taking seriously the effort he was engaged in to bring the symbol to life in the lives of his patients. His touchstone in this endeavor was the theory of the archetype, and its manifestation in the symbolic world of the human psyche. Returning to the interplay of these factors provides the key to further development in analytical psychology.

References

Bair, D. (2003) *Jung: A Biography*, Boston: Little Brown.

Deacon, T.W. (2003) "Multilevel selection in a complex adaptive system: the problem of language origin" in R.H. Weber and D.J. Depew (eds) *Evolution and Learning: The Baldwin Effect Reconsidered* (pp. 81–106), Cambridge, MA: The MIT Press.

Desmond, A. (1982) *Archetypes and Ancestors: Paleontology in Victorian London 1850–1875*, Chicago: University of Chicago Press.

Ferris, P. (1997) *Dr. Freud: A Life*. Washington, DC: Counterpoint.

Flournoy, T. (1901/1994) *From India to the Planet Mars: A Case of Multiple Personality with Imaginary Languages* (S. Shamdasani, ed.), Princeton, NJ: Princeton University Press.

Gieser, S. (2004) *The Innermost Kernel: Depth Psychology and Quantum Physics; Wolfgang Pauli's Dialogue with C.G. Jung*, New York: Springer.

Harrington, A. (1996) *Reenchanted Science*, Princeton, NJ: Princeton University Press.

Hillman, J. (1975) *Revisioning Psychology*, New York: Harper Colophon Books.

Hillman, J. (1983) *Archetypal Psychology: A Brief Account*, Woodstock, CT: Spring Publications.

Hillman, J. (1994) *Healing Fictions*, Woodstock, CT: Spring Publications.

Hogenson, G.B. (1983) *Jung's Struggle with Freud*, South Bend, IN: Notre Dame University Press.

Hogenson, G.B. (2001) "The Baldwin effect: a neglected influence on C.G. Jung's evolutionary thinking", *Journal of Analytical Psychology*, **46**(4), 591–611.

Jung, C. (1902) "On the psychology and pathology of so-called occult phenomena", CW 1, 3–88, Princeton, NJ: Princeton University Press.

Jung, C. (1919) "Instinct and the unconscious", *The British Journal of Psychology*, **X**(1), 15–23.

Jung, C. (1940/1969) "The psychology of the child archetype", CW 9i, 151–181, Princeton, NJ: Princeton University Press.

Jung, C.G. (1947/1969) "On the nature of the psyche", CW 8, 159–234, Princeton, NJ: Princeton University Press.

Jung, C.G. (1966) "Alchemical studies", CW 13, Princeton, NJ: Princeton University Press.

Jung, C.G. (1977) *C.G. Jung Speaking: Interviews and Encounters*, Princeton, NJ: Princeton University Press.

Jung, C.G. (1989) *Analytical Psychology: Notes of the Seminar given in 1925*, Princeton, NJ: Princeton University Press.

Jung, C.G. (1991) *The Collected Works of C.G. Jung. Supplementary Volume B: Psychology of the Unconscious: A Study of the Transformations and Symbolism of the Libido*, Princeton, NJ: Princeton University Press.

Jung, C.G. and Riklin, F. (1904) "The associations of normal subjects" (L. Stein, trans.) in H. Read, M. Fordham, G. Adler and W. McGuire (eds), *The Collected Works of C.G. Jung*, vol. 2 (pp. 3–196), Princeton, NJ: Princeton University Press.

Jung, E. and von Franz, M.-L. (1980) *The Grail Legend* (A. Dykes, trans.) Boston: Sigo Press.

Kalsched, D. (1996) *The Inner World of Trauma*, London: Routledge.

Kalsched, D. (2003) "Trauma and daimonic reality in Ferenczi's later work", *Journal of Analytical Psychology*, **48**, 479–489.

Kant, I. (1787/1929) *Critique of Pure Reason* (N. Kemp Smith, trans.) New York: St Martin's Press.

Kitcher, P. (1995) *Freud's Dream: A Complete Interdisciplinary Science of Mind*, Cambridge, MA: The MIT Press.

Knox, J.M. (2001) "Memories, fantasies, archetypes: an exploration of some connections between cognitive science and analytical psychology", *The Journal of Analytical Psychology*, **46**(4), 613–635.

Knox, J. (2003) *Archetype, attachment, analysis: Jungian psychology and the emergent mind*, Hove: Brunner-Routledge.

Noll, R. (1985) "Mental imagery cultivation as a cultural phenomenon: the role of visions in shamanism", *Current Anthropology*, **26**(4), 443–461.

Noll, R. (1994) *The Jung Cult: Origins of a Charismatic Movement*, Princeton, NJ: Princeton University Press.

Oyama, S. (2000) *The Ontogeny of Information: Developmental Systems and Evolution*, Raleigh, NC: Duke University Press.

Pelikan, J. (1996) *Mary through the Centuries; Her Place in the History of Culture*, New Haven, CT: Yale University Press.

Pietikainen, P. (1998) "Archetypes as symbolic forms", *Journal of Analytical Psychology*, **43**(3), 325–343.

Richards, R.J. (2002) *The Romantic Conception of life: Science and Philosophy in the Age of Goethe*, Chicago: University of Chicago Press.

Robertson, R. (1987) *C.G. Jung and the Archetypes of the Collective Unconscious*, New York: Peter Lang.

Rosen, D.H., Smith, S.M., Huston, H.L. and Gonzalez, G. (1991) "Emperical study of associations between symbols and their meanings: evidence of collective unconscious (archetypal) memory", *Journal of Analytical Psychology*, **36**, 211–228.

Saunders, P. and Skar, P. (2001) "Archetypes, complexes and self organization", *Journal of Analytical Psychology*, **46**(2), 305–323.

Shamdasani, S. (1990) "A woman called Frank", *Spring*, **50**, 26–56.

Shamdasani, S. (2003) *Jung and the Making of Modern Psychology: The Dream of a Science*, Cambridge: Cambridge University Press.

Stevens, A. (1982) *Archetypes: A Natural History of the Self*, New York: William Morrow & Co.

Stevens, A. (2003) *Archetype Revisited: An Updated Natural History of the Self*, Toronto: Inner City Books.

Stevens, A. and Price, J. (1996) *Evolutionary Psychiatry: A New Beginning*, London: Routledge.

Thelen, E., Schoner, G., Scheir, C. and Smith, L. (2001) "The dynamics of embodiment: a field theory of infant perseverative reaching", *Behavioral and Brain Sciences*, **24**(1), 1–86.

Thelen, E. and Smith, L.B. (1998) *A Dynamic Systems Approach to the Development of Cognition and Action*, Cambridge, MA: The MIT Press.

Tresan, D.I. (1996) "Jungian metapsychology and neurobiological theory", *Journal of Analytical Psychology*, **41**(3), 399–436.

Van Eenwyk, J.R. (1997) *Archetypes and Strange Attractors: The Chaotic World of Symbols*, Toronto: Inner City Books.

Weber, B.H. (2003) "Emergence of mind and the Baldwin effect" in B.H. Weber and D.J. Depew (eds) *Evolution and Learning: The Baldwin Effect Reconsidered* (pp. 309–326), Cambridge, MA: The MIT Press.

Chapter 3

Developmental aspects of analytical psychology: new perspectives from cognitive neuroscience and attachment theory

Jung's model of the mind

Jean Knox

In this chapter I shall examine the ways in which recent developments in cognitive neuroscience and attachment theory can shed new light on certain key features of Jung's model of the psyche. I will first give a brief summary of the central concepts of analytical psychology, highlighting the emergence of each key stage of the model as steps in the formation of an integrated theory.

Analytical psychology started to emerge as a separate discipline when Jung began to question the sexual nature of libido which remained the foundation stone of Freud's model of the psyche and on which psychoanalysis has been constructed. For Jung, this seemed too narrow a basis for the richness and complexity of psychic life; his view of libido as a neutral form of psychic energy that can be drawn on for a variety of purposes marked the point at which he abandoned his attempts to reconcile his model with that of Freud. Jung stated his rejection of sexuality as the source of psychic life quite clearly when he wrote: "I cannot see the real aetiology of neurosis in the various manifestations of infantile sexual development and the fantasies to which they give rise" (Jung 1916:para. 574).

Jung's repudiation of the basic premise of psychoanalysis caused great distress to both men and finally brought about the permanent rupture of their relationship (Freud and Jung 1961:534–540). It also opened up a fault line between the models of the mind they each constructed that persists to this day. For Freud, the unconscious was a "seething cauldron" of incestuous desires and wishes associated with the Oedipus complex, which are unacceptable to the conscious mind. Once Jung had rejected the sexual nature of libido it could really only be a matter of time before he developed a very different view of the nature of unconscious contents, which he was free to explore as both positive and negative. By 1930 he was able to describe his view of the unconscious as "the eternally living, creative, germinal layer in each of us" and to state that: "the unconscious contains not only the sources of instinct and the whole prehistoric nature of man right down to the animal level, but also, along with these, the creative seeds of the future and the roots of all constructive fantasies" (Jung 1961/1930:para. 760).

Jung's view that the unconscious is the source of creativity as well as destructiveness led him to conclude that the unconscious cannot be unified and then to the idea that dissociation, not repression, is the main mechanism keeping mental contents out of consciousness. Jung's interest in dissociation emerged out of his study of his cousin Helene Preiswerk, who entered trances during which she appeared to function as a medium for spirits, a phenomenon which contributed to Jung's ideas about sub-personalities (Hayman 1999:40–44).

James Astor makes the interesting point that Freud's response to this development in Jung's model was to conceptualize dissociation itself as pathological, in contrast to Jung's increasing confidence that different part selves coexist within the personality as a normal phenomenon and that the unconscious can often be a dissociated rather than a dynamically repressed unconscious (Astor 2002). Although Jung accepted that repression and dissociation are both mechanisms underpinning compartmentalization in the psyche, he rejected Freud's view that dissociation was always a defensive process, with the primary purpose of keeping unconscious instinctual wishes out of conscious awareness. Jung was familiar with the work of Janet and his clinical experience at the Burghölzli provided rich material for the evolution of his own distinctive understanding of the workings of the human mind, as Ellenberger highlights:

> Jung repeatedly referred to Janet (whose lectures he had attended in Paris during the winter semester (1902–1903)). The influence of *Psychological Automatism* can be seen from Jung's way of considering the human mind as comprising a number of sub-personalities (Janet's "simultaneous psychological existences"). What Jung called a "complex" was originally nothing but the equivalent of Janet's "subconscious fixed idea".
>
> (Ellenberger 1970:406)

Jung's study of Janet's ideas led on to the discovery of complexes. Jung conceived of these as fragmentary personalities or splinter psyches, within which there is perception, feeling, volition and intention, as though a subject were present which thinks and is goal-directed. The ego is only one complex among many, and consciousness is a consequence of the ego's capacity to appropriate as one's own and use effectively and freely the complexes that are already structuring one's existence. Without the ego's self-reflection, the complexes function automatically and have a compulsive quality (Brooke 1991:126).

Emotion and motivation are included in the functioning of complexes which function as dissociated parts of the mind. Jung was clear that the "feeling-tone", or emotion, holds clusters of memories together in an unconscious grouping which is dissociated from the rest of mental functioning; these clusters of emotionally based representations exist as a normal phenomenon as well as contributing to psychopathology, as Sandner and Beebe explain:

Jung thought that whatever its roots in previous experience, neurosis
consists of a refusal – or inability – in the here and now to bear legitimate
suffering. Instead this painful feeling or some representation of it is split
off from awareness and the initial wholeness – the primordial Self – is
broken. Such splitting "ultimately derives from the apparent impossibil-
ity of affirming the whole of one's nature" (Jung 1934:para. 980) and
gives rise to the whole range of dissociations and conflicts characteristic
of feeling-toned complexes. This splitting is a normal part of life. Initial
wholeness is meant to be broken, and it becomes pathological or diag-
nosable as illness, only when the splitting off of complexes becomes too
wide and deep and the conflict too intense. Then the painful symptoms
may lead to the conflicts of neurosis or to the shattered ego of psychosis.
(Sandner and Beebe 1984:298)

The profound implications of Jung's concept of the complex were fully recognized by Jolande Jacobi, who wrote that it was "[t]he revolutionary beginning which carried him beyond traditional psychology, paving the way for his
fundamental discovery of the 'dominants of the collective unconscious', or
archetypes" (Jacobi 1959:30). Jacobi stated unequivocally that "The notion
of the complex – if it is to be fully understood – calls, spontaneously as it
were, for an attempt to clarify the concept of the archetype" (ibid.). The
archetype is a fundamental feature of Jung's model, one that has become
most identified in popular culture with Jung's name.

  The concept of archetypes is many-layered, with several differing strands
that have become so interwoven that it has become extremely difficult to
distinguish them; these various, often contradictory, meanings have been
explored by a number of authors (Samuels 1985; Carrette 1994; Knox 2003;
see also Chapter 2). The ambiguity about archetypes can be traced directly
back to Jung's own writing, in which he drew on philosophy, religion, mythology, physics, biology, anthropology, psychology, psychiatry and psychoanalysis, and used these frames of reference to explore the concepts which
might help him in his struggle to understand the nature and functioning of
the human psyche. Each of these frameworks provided him with a perspective through which to view the idea of archetype and define its essential
features. Sometimes he wrote about archetypes as abstract organizing structures, sometimes as eternal realities, then again as core meanings; on other
occasions, he adopted a very sophisticated ethological viewpoint, in which he
identified archetypes as manifestations of instinct, a term which he used in a
much more biologically accurate way than Freud (Knox 2003).

  It is probably futile to trawl painstakingly through Jung's *Collected Works*,
finding evidence to suggest that one way of envisaging archetypes predomin-
ates over another in his writing. Neither Jung nor his early followers, such as
Jolande Jacobi, saw the need to distinguish between these ways of conceptualizing archetypes. Instead they seemed to feel that the fact that they found a

variety of models for inherent or innate structures within the cultural, religious, philosophical, psychological and biological frameworks which they studied provided cumulative evidence for the concept of the archetype (see also Chapter 2).

The essential point I want to make here is that Jung thought of archetypes as nuclei of meaning in the psyche, further elaborating his model of the psyche as compartmentalized. The idea that archetypes act as nuclei of unconscious meaning also underpins Jung's view that the unconscious is not merely an accumulation of all that is unacceptable to the conscious mind but plays an active role as a co-contributor to the construction of symbolic meaning in the human psyche. This led him to develop several key related ideas, those of self-regulation, compensation, individuation and the transcendent function.

Discussion of these processes takes us back once again to Jung's rejection of the sexual nature of libido as the fundamental organizing force in the human psyche. Freud's idea of instinctual drive subsumes mind to brain and body and decrees that the concreteness of the body, in the form of innate physiological processes and their associated drives, determines the symbolism of the mind. Jung's view was that this offered a closed model of the human mind, one in which the nature of mental content was pre-determined, an idea which he found unacceptable, writing:

> Unlike Freud, who after a proper psychological start reverted to the ancient assumption of the sovereignty of the physical constitution, trying to turn everything back in theory into instinctual processes conditioned by the body, I start with the sovereignty of the psyche.
>
> (Jung 1936:para. 968)

From this perspective, it was the mystery of the mind at work that also led to Jung's clear distinction between a symbol and a sign. He wrote:

> The symbol is not a sign that disguises something generally known – a disguise, that is, for the basic drive or elementary intention. Its meaning resides in the fact that it is an attempt to elucidate, by a more or less apt analogy, something that is still entirely unknown or still in the process of formation.
>
> (Jung 1966/1916:para. 492)

This rejection of bodily processes as direct determinants of psychic contents had profound implications; it led Jung to search for alternative mechanisms or processes that might control the organization of mental contents. It seems to me that discussion of Jung's mature model of the psyche focuses too often on the structural aspects, such as complexes, archetypes and the Self, to the neglect of his innovative and original understanding of the regulatory and organizing processes of the human mind. These processes are mechanisms for maintaining a psychic equilibrium and I shall explore later in this chapter the remarkable prescience shown by Jung when one examines these concepts in the light of contemporary neuroscience and attachment theory.

Jung developed the idea that self-regulation and compensation are the processes by which conscious biases are balanced by unconscious communications in the form of dreams, fantasies or even neurotic symptoms. Jung emphatically rejected the idea that analysis should consist solely of a one-way relationship between conscious and unconscious parts of the mind. "Individuation" is the term Jung coined to describe a separate process for bringing about psychological change, and he argued that it is in this process that the unconscious plays an active and creative role. Jung was quite specific that the purpose of analysis is to allow a person's sense of identity to enlarge to encompass unconscious material, a process which he named "individuation" and defined as:

> the process by which a person becomes a psychological "in-dividual", that is, a separate, indivisible unity or "whole". It is generally assumed that consciousness is the whole of the psychological individual. But knowledge of the phenomena that can only be explained on the hypothesis of unconscious psychic processes makes it doubtful whether the ego and its contents are in fact identical with the "whole".
>
> (Jung 1939:para. 490)

He made clear that the concept of "whole" must necessarily include not only consciousness but the illimitable field of unconscious occurrences as well. Later, in the same section, he wrote:

> Conscious and unconscious do not make a whole when one of them is suppressed and injured by the other. If they must contend, let it at least be a fair fight with equal rights on both sides. Both are aspects of life. Consciousness should defend its reason and protect itself and the chaotic life of the unconscious should be given the chance of having its way too – as much of it as we can stand ... This, roughly, is what I mean by the individuation process. As the name shows it is a process or course of development arising out of the conflict between the two fundamental psychic facts ... How the harmonising of conscious and unconscious data is to be undertaken cannot be indicated in the form of a recipe ... Out of this union emerge new situations and new conscious attitudes. I have therefore called the union of opposites "the transcendent function". This rounding out of the personality into a whole may well be the goal of any psychotherapy that claims to be more than a mere cure of symptoms.
>
> (Jung 1939:para. 522–524)

With statements such as this, Jung supported his view of the psyche as self-regulating, with neurotic symptoms and dreams operating as communications from the unconscious, to compensate for an unbalanced conscious attitude. Anthony Storr has pointed out that this concept runs through the whole of Jung's scheme of how the mind works, underpinning his classification of psychological types, and has summarized this with great clarity:

> In Western man, because of the achievements of his culture, there was an especial tendency towards intellectual hubris; an overvaluation of thinking which could alienate a man from his emotional roots. Neurotic symptoms, dreams and other manifestations of the unconscious were often expressions of the "other side" trying to assert itself. There was, therefore, within every individual, a striving towards unity in which divisions would be replaced by consistency, opposites equally balanced, consciousness in reciprocal relation with the unconscious.
>
> (Storr 1983:18)

This concept of self-regulation therefore lies at the heart of the individuation process and of the process of change in analysis, which can help to bring about a new synthesis between conscious and unconscious. Jung's views on self-regulation also led to the development of his classification of psychological types. The two main psychological types, introvert and extravert, are further modified by four main functions, thinking, feeling, sensation and intuition, any one of which may predominate in an individual's approach to life (this will be discussed at more length in Chapter 4).

Jung also developed the concept of the "transcendent function" as the process by which conscious and unconscious attitudes are compared and integrated with each other, reflecting his view of the unconscious as an active contributor to the meaning-making process. Jung stated unequivocally that in the process of symbol formation "the union of conscious and unconscious contents is consummated. Out of this union emerge new situations and new conscious attitudes. I have therefore called the union of opposites the transcendent function" (Jung 1939:para. 524).

However, this does not in itself resolve the dilemma as to what determines psychic imbalance – what is the organizing principle behind the process of self-regulation? Once Jung had so emphatically rejected instinctual drive as the bedrock on which psychic meaning is constructed, he needed to find an alternative process which governs the development and organization of the human psyche. His solution was the concept of the Self, which is both the centre and the totality of the psyche and which guides the process of individuation, suggesting that "the goal of psychic development is the self" (Jung 1963:188). Jung wrote:

> If the unconscious can be recognized as a co-determining factor along with consciousness, and if we can live in such a way that conscious and

unconscious demands are taken into account as far as possible, then the centre of gravity of the total personality shifts its position. It is no longer in the ego, which is merely the centre of consciousness, but in the hypothetical point between conscious and unconscious. This new centre might be called the self.

(Jung 1967:para. 67)

Jung fully realized the inconsistencies inherent in the concept of the Self and saw these as integral to the idea, writing: "The self, however, is absolutely paradoxical in that it represents in every respect thesis and antithesis and at the same time, synthesis" (Jung 1944:para. 22).

Jung's view of libido as neutral psychic energy and of the unconscious as an active co-contributor to meaning led him to see motivation teleologically, not just causally. He fully accepted that biological needs are powerful motivating factors and, indeed, he felt that Freud's view of the role of biology was too restricted in its focus on sexual drive to the exclusion of other biological forces. However, he felt that the psyche is also constantly searching for meaning, a spiritual and philosophical quest that is purposive. David Tresan (2004) identifies the explosive nature of an apparently innocuous phrase in "The psychology of the unconscious", where Jung writes about the mobility of the libido. Tresan recognizes that this concept of a detachable and mobile libido is the core of Jung's abandonment of Freud's sexual theory. Jung's later paper "On psychic energy" elaborates his view that libido can direct motivation not only towards a much wider range of biological gratifications than Freud envisaged, but also, in Tresan's words, "towards symbol formation, conceptualizing and cultural activity" (Tresan 2004:203). Jung's hypotheses about motivation have been left largely unexamined, at least in terms of his views on libido as reflections of his ideas about the factors that motivate human behaviour and mental functioning. In fact Jung identified several instinctual motivations; he saw hunger as the characteristic expression of the instinct of self-preservation, sexuality, the drive to activity which finds expression in the "urge to travel, love of change, restlessness, and the play-instinct". Jung also identified the reflective instinct, whereby "a natural process is transformed into a conscious content" and the creative instinct (Jung 1969/1937:para. 237–241).

Jung's mature model of the mind had important implications for his view of the process of change in analysis. He was adamant that the analyst is not merely a neutral observer and interpreter of the analysand's unconscious. He felt that Freud's approach led to a stereotyped process of analysis, in which the analyst knows beforehand what will emerge from the patient's unconscious. Jung was adamant that an effective analysis required the analyst to be affected and altered as well as the patient, and he viewed analysis as a dialectical process "in which the doctor, as a person, participates just as much as the patient" (Jung 1951:para. 239). This was the basis of Jung's view that the analyst must first have had a thorough training analysis himself, although he was under no illusion that this would be "an absolutely certain means of dispelling illusions and projections" (ibid.), but he argued that it would at least develop the capacity for self-criticism. He went on to suggest that "a good half of every treatment that probes at all deeply consists in the doctor's examining of himself, for only what he can put right in himself can he hope to put right in the patient", and proposed this as the true meaning of the concept of the "wounded physician" (ibid.). This view culminated in his diagram of the counter-crossing conscious and unconscious transference and countertransference relationships that he explored in alchemical terms and that emerge in analysis (Jung 1946:para. 422).

Post-Jungian psychologists have expanded many of Jung's ideas: the crucial role of personal experience forms the bedrock of the developmental school of analytical psychology. Michael Fordham was one of the pioneers of this approach and a major theoretical innovation he introduced into analytical psychology was the exploration of the application of Jung's model to child development. He introduced the concept of a primary or original self which deintegrates, giving rise to a cycle of deintegration–reintegration under the stimulation provided by the environment. This provides a more complete reconciliation of the apparent contradiction between the role of the archetype and that of interpersonal experience:

> [I]n essence deintegration and reintegration describe a fluctuating state of learning in which the infant opens itself to new experiences and then withdraws in order to reintegrate and consolidate those experiences. During a deintegrative activity, the infant maintains continuity with the main body of the self (or its centre) while venturing into the external world to accumulate experience in motor action and sensory stimulation.
>
> (Fordham 1988:64)

Gordon has clarified the developmental relationship between archetypal imagery and personal experience:

> [I]n the course of development the archetypal figures become tamed by being incarnated in and through actual relationships to actual persons; these persons come gradually to be perceived with more or less accuracy in terms of their actual nature and character. In other words, they become more humanized. Perceptions become more appropriate, less ruthless, more compassionate; the archetypal projections are withdrawn, and the capacity for truth emerges. And then both the paradisal and the terrifying worlds begin to recede.
>
> (Gordon 1993:303)

An exploration of analytical psychology from the perspectives of developmental neuroscience and attachment theory

How do these core concepts of Jungian analytical theory appear when examined through the lens of contemporary developmental neuroscience and attachment theory? Both Jung and Freud considered themselves to be scientists and their methods to be scientific, although Jung did ruefully acknowledge at times that he had to stray far from that path:

> I fancied I was working along the best scientific lines, establishing facts, observing, classifying, describing causal and functional relations, only to discover in the end that I had involved myself in a net of reflections which extend far beyond natural science and ramify into the fields of philosophy, theology, comparative religion and the humane sciences in general.
>
> (Jung 1954/1947:para. 421)

However, many of Jung's theories can now be seen to be remarkably consistent with the contemporary models of the psyche that are emerging in other, more empirically based psychological disciplines. In my brief summary of the key building blocks of Jung's model of the mind, I emphasized Jung's view that a divided or dissociated mind is a normal phenomenon, and this is a good place to start to examine the relationship between the key concepts of analytical psychology and those of other psychological disciplines.

Dissociation and complexes

Jung's view of the psyche as compartmentalized, both structurally and functionally, finds support from a wealth of theoretical and empirical studies undertaken by psychologists. Fred Bartlett (1932) introduced the concept of schemas, which he described as "an active organization of past reactions, or of past experiences, which must always be supposed to be operating in any well-adapted organic response". In 1943, Kenneth Craik published his major work *The Nature of Explanation* in which he argued that human beings translate external events into internal models and reason by manipulating these symbolic representations (Craik 1943). Johnson-Laird developed Craik's ideas and underlines the role of mental models as the determinants of our perception and experience, writing that "The limits of our models are the limits of our world" (Johnson-Laird 1989:471). He points out that mental models are internal symbols which, whether in relation to perception, reasoning or memory, provide a mental map of the situation that they represent. Peter Fonagy spells out the significance of Johnson-Laird's ideas for our understanding of the psyche, showing that we appraise the meaning of situations not on the basis of formal rules of logic, but on the basis of activation and manipulation of the particular mental model in operation. He writes:

> Mental model theory assumes that to understand is to construct mental models from knowledge and from perceptual or verbal evidence. To formulate a conclusion is to describe what is represented in the models. To test validity is to search for alternative models that refute the putative conclusion.
>
> (Fonagy 2001:120)

Another related line of enquiry is the study of memory and the recognition that there are multiple memory systems each with its own processes for recording, storing and accessing information. Daniel Schacter has extended the investigation of dissociation, showing that complex conceptual and semantic knowledge can be processed without conscious awareness, and has shown that memory for conceptual information can be demonstrated on testing without any conscious recollection by the subject of that information (Schacter 1996:189). A most dramatic example is given in an investigation of patients who have been anaesthetized; it shows that they may process auditory information during adequate anaesthesia; the presence of implicit memory for events which occurred during anaesthesia is shown by a change in test performance, showing that information has been taken in without the patient having conscious recollection of the event (Sebel 1995).

Daniel Schacter has developed the concept of implicit memory, whereby "past experiences unconsciously influence our perceptions, thoughts and actions" (Schacter 1996:9). Information may not only be encoded without awareness, it is also organized and stored in implicit memory in the form of abstract generalized patterns rather than as specific records of particular events; this information is not available to conscious recall. Unconscious meanings are gradually constructed through the process of the internalization of experience and its subsequent organization into generalized patterns in implicit memory.

John Bowlby's concept of the internal working model offers an evolutionary leap in our understanding of the human psyche and of the relationship between inner and outer reality. The internal working model is a concept which provides a synthesis of schema or mental model theory with implicit memory in the context of human relationships. Internal working models are the implicit, unconscious maps of our accumulated experience of past relationships with key attachment figures that we draw on to anticipate and understand new human encounters and relationships. The key features of internal working models demonstrate the ways in which experiences of key relationships are registered and then organized and stored in memory. In Bowlby's own words:

Starting, we may suppose, towards the end of his first year, and probably especially active during his second and third when he acquires the powerful and extraordinary gift of language, a child is busy constructing working models of how the physical world might be expected to behave, how his mother and other significant persons might be expected to behave, how he himself might be expected to behave, and how each interacts with the other. Within the framework of these working models he evaluates his situation and makes his plans. And within the framework of these working models of his mother and himself he evaluates special aspects of his situation and makes his attachment plans.

(Bowlby 1969:354)

The central features of internal working models therefore are that:

- experience of real relationships is "internalized";
- the representations of these relationships are stored as schemas, or working models and "the form these models take is in fact far more strongly determined by a child's actual experiences throughout childhood than was formerly supposed";
- whatever representational models of attachment figures and of self an individual builds during his childhood and adolescence, these tend to persist into and throughout adult life;
- as a result, any new person to whom an attachment is formed becomes assimilated into an existing model and perceptions of that person are organized by the existing model, even in the face of evidence that the model is inappropriate;
- the influence that existing working models have on current perceptions operates outside awareness;
- inappropriate but persistent representational models often coexist with more appropriate ones;
- the stronger the emotions aroused in a relationship, the more likely are the earlier and less conscious models to become dominant.

(Bowlby 1979:117, 141)

Indeed, the internal working model can be considered as the theoretical foundation stone of attachment theory in that it describes the infant's capacity for holding his mother (and others) in mind when she is not present and, hence, of creating mental models of relationships.

The theory of the complex can be shown to have much in common with that of the internal working model. Jung concluded from his careful and rigorous word-association studies that a complex consisted of:

the *image* of a certain psychic situation which is strongly accentuated emotionally and is, moreover incompatible with the habitual attitude of consciousness. This image has a powerful inner coherence, it has its own wholeness and, in addition, a relatively high degree of autonomy, so that it is subject to the control of the conscious mind only to a limited extent and therefore behaves like an animated foreign body in the sphere of consciousness.

(Jung 1934:para. 200–203)

In this passage, Jung also emphasized that the existence of complexes throws:

serious doubt on the naïve assumption of the unity of consciousness, which is equated with psyche, and on the supremacy of the will. Every constellation of a complex postulates a disturbed state of consciousness. The unity of consciousness is disrupted and the intentions of the will are impeded or made impossible. Even memory is often noticeably affected, as we have seen.

(ibid.)

Jung constantly emphasized the emotional basis of the complex. He also recognized that emotion is not merely a visceral or physiological experience, but is inextricably bound up with cognition, a view which has been independently elaborated within an information-processing framework by George Mandler (1975:47) and reinforced by neuroscientists such as Daniel Siegel who argues that "there are no discernible boundaries between our 'thoughts' and 'feelings' " (Siegel 1998:6).

Many of these ideas are strikingly compatible with the findings of contemporary research-based attachment theory in a way in which many original Freudian and Kleinian theoretical formulations, such as "drives", the "death instinct" and "unconscious fantasy", are not. Jung recognized the key role played by actual childhood experience, writing that:

More and more the neurologist of today realizes that the origin of the nervousness of his patients is very rarely of recent date but goes back to the early impressions and developments in childhood.

(Jung 1919:para. 1793)

Perhaps even more striking is his recognition of the unconscious nature of the parent's influence on the child, a key feature of the intergenerational transmission of attachment patterns. Jung wrote:

Parents too easily content themselves with the belief that a thing hidden from the child cannot influence it. They forget that infantile imitation is less concerned with action than with the parent's state of mind from which the action emanates. I have frequently observed children who were particularly influenced by certain unconscious tendencies in the parents and, in such cases, I have often advised the treatment of the mother rather than of the child.

(ibid.)

This remark resonates with Fraiberg's comment that there are ghosts from the unremembered past of the parents in every nursery and Alicia Lieberman's powerful exploration of the processes by which babies "become the carriers of the parents' unconscious fears, impulses, and other repressed or disowned parts of themselves" (Fraiberg *et al.* 1975; Lieberman 1999). Jung's description of the dissociated nature of consciousness, of the contribution of emotion and cognition to the complex and his awareness of the crucial part played by internalization and intergenerational transmission in the formation of unconscious contents have much in common with the contemporary view of attachment theorists about internal working models.

Archetypes

Although Jung fully acknowledged the crucial role that personal experience plays in the formation of the unconscious internal world, he struggled in his attempt to provide an integrated account of the interaction of real experience with innate psychic content and he did not offer any significant discussion of psychological development in infancy and childhood. Jung thought that the complex was organized around an innate core. He said that the complex is embedded in the material of the personal unconscious, but that its nucleus consists of an archetypal core, archetypes being systems of readiness for action, and at the same time images and emotions. Complexes are feeling-toned groups of representations in the unconscious and consist of "innate" (archetypal) patterns of expectation combined with external events which are internalized and given meaning by the "innate" pattern (Jacobi 1959).

The concept of the archetype seems to create a problem in Jungian theory, in terms of psychic innateness, similar to the problem that instinctual drive creates in psychoanalysis. Archetypes are often thought of as pre-formed innate packets of imagery and fantasy, waiting to pop out like butterflies from a chrysalis given the right environmental trigger, a model which suggests that something other than mind itself has created these mental contents. One of the main points of disagreement between different Jungian schools has centred on the nature of archetypes, their role in psychic functioning and their contribution to the process of change in analysis and therapy, a debate which parallels that of the psychoanalysts over the degree to which instinctual drive or actual experience shapes the internal world.

The wealth of research that has emerged in recent years in cognitive science and developmental psychology offers us new paradigms for understanding the relationship between genetic potential and environmental influence in the development of the human mind. The central theme here is that of self-organization of the human brain and the recognition that genes do not encode complex mental imagery and processes, but instead act as initial catalysts for developmental processes out of which early psychic structures reliably emerge. A developmental account of archetype lends considerable scientific support to the key role archetypes play in psychic functioning and as a crucial source of symbolic imagery, but at the same time identifies archetypes as emergent structures resulting from a developmental interaction between genes and environment that is unique for each person. Archetypes are not "hard-wired" collections of universal imagery waiting to be released by the right environmental trigger.

An alternative model for archetypes can be based on the evidence from developmental research which demonstrates the existence of Gestalt-type mental structures that are probably the earliest products emerging from the self-organization of the human brain, a process that continues from birth and probably starts even *in utero* (Piontelli 1992; Knox, 2003). In *The Body in the Mind*, Johnson (1987) suggests that the earliest form of mental organization, which provides a sense of embodied meaning, is the "image schema". These image schemas are early developmental mental structures which organize experience while themselves remaining without content and beyond the realm of conscious awareness.

It is crucial to emphasize here the bodily basis of the image schema – it is a mental Gestalt which develops out of bodily experience and forms the basis for abstract meanings, both in the physical and in the world of imagination and metaphor. One example might be the image schema of "containment". As Johnson writes:

> Our encounter with containment and boundedness is one of the most pervasive features of our bodily experience. We are intimately aware of our bodies as three-dimensional containers into which we put certain things (food, water, air) and out of which other things emerge (food and water wastes, air, blood etc.).
>
> (Johnson 1987:21)

For example, a child's experience of her mother as physically and psychologically containing is a metaphorical extension of this image schema, or archetype-as-such. The Gestalt of containment is simple but it can give rise to a wealth of meaning as it is expressed in the richness of physical intimacy and the parent's understanding and containment of her child's needs and emotions.

According to Lakoff (1987) and to Johnson, image schemas lie at the core of people's understanding, even as adults, of a wide variety of objects and events and of the metaphorical extensions of these concepts to more abstract realms. They form, in effect, a set of primitive meanings (Mandler 1992). Johnson (1987) investigates systematically this process whereby image schemas are metaphorically extended from the physical to the non-physical realm. Image schemas form the basis for "the extension of a central sense of a word to other senses by devices of the human imagination, such as metaphor" (Johnson 1987: xii). He suggests that metaphorical projections of this sort are one of the chief means for connecting up different senses of a term. For example, he says:

> [T]he OUT schema which applies to spatial orientation is metaphorically projected onto the cognitive domain where there are processes of choosing, rejecting, separating, differentiating abstract objects, and so forth. Numerous cases, such as *leave out, pick out, take out*, etc. . . . can be metaphorically orientated mental actions. What you *pick out* physically are spatially extended objects; what you *pick out* metaphorically are abstract mental or logical entities. But the relevant preconception schema is generally the same for both senses of *picking out*.
>
> (Johnson 1987:34; emphasis in original)

Image schemas would therefore seem to have certain key features that are similar to some of the ways in which Jung conceptualized archetypes. While image schemas are without symbolic content in themselves, they provide a reliable scaffolding on which meaningful imagery and thought are organized and constructed, thus meeting the need for a model that provides for the archetype-as-such and the archetypal image. The image schema would seem to correspond to the archetype-as-such, and the archetypal image can be equated with the innumerable metaphorical extensions that derive from image schemas. The metaphorical extensions of the image schema can provide a rich source of imagery and fantasy. The character of this imagery derives from the underlying image schema.

This developmental model for archetypes requires us to re-categorize them, removing them from the realm of innate mental content and acknowledging them as early products of mental development. In this way, analytical psychologists can avoid falling into the same trap as psychoanalysts who regard instinctual drives as the main source of unconscious fantasy. Any suggestion that the human mind contains innate pre-formed packets of imagery and fantasy, waiting to pop out given the right environmental trigger, is outdated and to be discredited.

There would therefore seem to be an image-schematic or archetypal quality to almost any experience, and this developmental model of the image schema would thus seem to strengthen the concept of the archetype but at the same time to identify the key features of an event, memory, dream or fantasy that justify us in using the term "archetypal". The image schema enables us to see clearly that it is the dynamic pattern of relationships of the objects of our inner world that is archetypal, rather than the specific characteristics of any particular object in inner or outer reality.

Recently, Vilayanur Ramachandran (2003: 58) has suggested a possible neurophysiological basis for the capacity for metaphor, basing this on studies of synesthesia, a phenomenon shown by a small number of people for whom, for example, looking at numbers or listening to tones evokes the experience of a particular colour. He suggests that, although synesthesia is strikingly evident in only a small percentage of the population, we all have some capacity for it and it reflects the functioning of the angular gyrus, the part of the brain where the occipital, parietal and temporal lobes meet and which is responsible for cross-modal synthesis. It is the brain region where information from touch, hearing and vision is thought to flow together to enable the construction of high-level perceptions. Ramachandran goes on to speculate that the role of the angular gyrus could have evolved so that the ability to engage in cross-modal abstraction could allow the emergence of other more abstract functions such as metaphors.

This capacity to reflect deep links between superficially dissimilar things is exactly the function performed by image schemas, which could therefore be the earliest representations formed as a result of the function of the angular gyrus in cross-modal synthesis. Image schemas reflect exactly the combination of information from different sensory modalities into a concept in which the common features from those differing sources of information are united into a mental Gestalt – what Jungians would call an archetype.

Self-regulation

Jung's ideas about the self-regulation of the psyche find support from contemporary attachment theory and neuroscience. Fundamental to self-regulation is the process of appraisal, a constant unconscious process by which experiences are constantly screened and evaluated to determine their meaning and significance. Bowlby himself wrote:

> Sensory inflow goes through many stages of selection, interpretation and appraisal before it can have any influence on behaviour, either immediately or later. This processing occurs in a succession of stages, all but the preliminary of which require that the inflow be related to matching information already stored in long-term memory.
>
> (Bowlby 1980:45)

New experience is therefore constantly being organized by unconscious internal working models, and unconscious implicit patterns are constantly being identified in conscious language. Jung's theories about self-regulation and compensation thus anticipated the contemporary concept of appraisal. It is rare for clinicians or research psychologists to recognize an active and constructive role for unconscious imagery, to accord it a compensatory symbolic function, and even Bowlby did not fully develop this idea, although he did touch briefly on the idea that "imaginary" fears may have a defensive function in the face of unknown dangers (Knox 2003:120). However, in her remarkable integration of cognitive science and psychoanalysis, Bucci develops the view that fantasy serves a compensatory function:

> [I]t is not that dreams or fantasies are symptoms in the sense of being regressive or pathological forms. Rather, somatic or psychic symptoms may carry out a progressive symbolizing function, in the same sense as dreams and fantasies, where other symbols are not available to be used. Symptoms, like dreams, are fundamentally attempts at symbolizing, healing in the psychic domain, although symptoms may then bring new problems of their own.
>
> (Bucci 1997:263)

Jung recognized how important it is to be able to evaluate experiences and to make judgements about them. He described this as the "feeling" function, which enables a person to decide on the value of an event or an experience, a concept that thus anticipated the contemporary concept of appraisal. Unfortunately, Jung's pioneering work in identifying the importance of this process goes largely unrecognized by those who now investigate appraisal from information-processing and neurophysiological perspectives. This may partly arise from the frequent misuse of the term "feeling function" by analytical psychologists themselves. Ann Casement points out that "in particular all kinds of fictions congregate around the *feeling* function. The latter, along with the *thinking* function, is a way of evaluating an experience" (Casement 2001:132; see also Chapter 4).

The emphasis Jung placed on the emotional tone of an experience can also find support in the work of neuroscientists and attachment theorists. Allan Schore (2000) draws on empirical research to support his view that the right hemisphere is predominant in "performing valence-dependent, automatic, pre-attentive appraisals of emotional facial expressions" and that the orbito-frontal system, in particular, is important in assembling and monitoring relevant past and current experiences, including their affective and social values. Joseph LeDoux highlights the crucial role of the hippocampus in the integration of conceptual information from different memory systems. He writes: "because the hippocampus and other convergence zones receive inputs from modulatory systems, during significant states of arousal, plasticity in these networks is coordinated with the plasticity occurring in other systems in the brain" (LeDoux 2002:318).

However, although convergence zones such as the hippocampus and the orbito-frontal system integrate information from different parts of the brain and so play a crucial role in appraisal, Cortina (2003) makes the important point that the whole brain is involved in the process of evaluating the meaning of experience. Siegel offers neuroscientific support for this view and for the central role of emotion in this process, suggesting that the limbic region has no clearly defined boundaries and that:

[T]he integration of a wide array of functionally segregated processes, such as perception, abstract thought and motor action, may be a fundamental role of the brain. Such an *integrative process* may be at the core of what emotion *does* and indeed what emotion *is*.

(Siegel 1998:7; emphasis in original)

Cortina links the processes by which the mind selects, sorts and stores information with Edelman's view of the neurological mechanisms which underpin them:

We constantly confront new information and new situations. How does the brain cope with this bewildering source of new information? Taking his cue from Darwinian selection, Edelman believes that the basic unit in the brain consists of groups or units of neuronal networks consisting of between 50 and 10,000 neurones. There are perhaps a hundred million of such groups. Experience that proves to be of value for the organism is "mapped" into these neuronal networks. A "map" is not a representation in the ordinary sense, but an interconnected series of neuronal networks that respond collectively to certain elemental categories or tendencies such as colors in the visual world or a particular situation that triggers a feeling in the emotional world. Edelman calls these categories "values" because they orient the developing organism toward selecting a limited amount of stimuli from an enormous array of possibilities.

(Cortina 2003:274–275)

Throughout development, the brain, in response to the selective stimulation created by experience, repeatedly increases some neural connections and prunes others, so that the surviving neural networks reflect the experiences that have created and repeatedly activated them. However, these surviving neural networks also have to be coordinated among themselves in order for us to develop a coherent and integrated view of the environment and of ourselves. This is achieved by the mechanism called "re-entrant signalling" which means that:

as groups of neurons are selected in a map, other groups in re-entrantly connected but different maps may also be selected at the same time. Correlation and coordination of such selection events are achieved by re-entrant signalling and by the strengthening of interconnections between the maps within a segment of time.

(Edelman 1994/1992:85)

Another crucial feature of self-regulation is that it is initially highly sensitive to and dependent on the interpersonal environment. Pioneering empirical research confirms this view. For example, Sander suggests that development depends on the:

> negotiation of a sequence of increasingly complex tasks of adaptation or "fitting together", between the infant and its caregiving environment over the first years of life. This is a sequence of negotiations of connectedness in the interactions between infant and mother that constructs the bridge to organization at the psychological level.
>
> (Sander 2002:13)

Sander argues that each living system, each organism, thus is seen as self-organizing, self-regulating, and self-correcting within its surround, its environment. Sander provides powerful support for this view with an experiment in which one group of neonates were fed on demand while another group were fed every four hours regardless of their state. The results were remarkable. Within a few days, the demand-fed sample began to show the emergence of one or two longer sleep periods in each 24 hours and, after a few more days, these longer sleep periods began to occur more frequently at night, in contrast to the neonates fed every four hours who showed no such change. In other words, the sleep rhythms of the demand-fed infants began to synchronize with the diurnal 24-hour day of the caregiver. Sander concludes:

> The emergence of a new and continuing 24-hour circadian rhythm in the demand-fed infant-caregiver system can be seen as an emergent property of a system in a state of stable regulation ... [t]he infant becomes a system within a larger system, held together by the capability of bio-rhythms to phase-shift, increase or decrease period length, moving in or out of synchrony with other rhythms.
>
> (Sander 2002:24)

The Self

Jung's concept of the Self is the one that offers most difficulty in terms of finding similar concepts in attachment theory and cognitive neuroscience. The idea of a pre-experiential innate organizing centre in the human psyche that determines the direction of psychic development is largely alien to contemporary neuroscience and attachment theory. Lichtenberg *et al.* (2002:81–82) state that our sense of who we are is derived from the integration of explicit and implicit autobiographical memories and suggest that when these are consonant a person experiences an increased sense of self-cohesion. Attachment theorists also propose that the sense of self is acquired through early attachment relationships (Cortina and Marrone 2003:12). Schore is explicit on this, writing: "The core of the self lies in patterns of affect regulation that integrate a sense of self across state transitions, thereby allowing for a continuity of inner experience" (Schore 1994:33). There is no suggestion of a pre-experiential self that guides this development.

Fonagy *et al.* provide a wealth of evidence underpinning the view that the sense of self as mental agent is not innately given but "arises out of the infant's perception of his presumed intentionality in the mind of the care-giver" (Fonagy *et al.* 2002:11). Just as archetypes can be re-formulated as emergent structures, the same process is therefore necessary in relation to the concept of the self, which needs to be re-conceptualized as a developmental achievement with identifiable stages – the self as physical agent, as social agent, as teleological agent and as representational agent (ibid.:205–206). This model echoes the work of Damasio, who also offers a developmental model of the self, the proto-self, the core self and the autobiographical self (Damasio 1999). However, Fonagy *et al.* offer a more precise and detailed account of the interpersonal and intra-psychic mechanisms that guide this developmental process.

The research evidence from contemporary neuroscience and attachment theory lends support to Fordham's model of an original self, which contains all the psychosomatic potential of the individual (see above), with the final development path emerging out of the ever-changing interaction between that potential and the environment.

Motivation

One of the fields that is developing most rapidly as the focus of research in developmental psychology is that of motivation. What are the forces that orient an infant's excitement and interest in key features of his or her environment? How does the infant select those aspects of the environment that will most enable survival and development? John Bowlby's answer was that the intense attachment of an infant to his or her primary caregiver is the foundation stone and that natural selection ensures that infants are intensely motivated to seek out and create loving relationships with those on whom their survival depends.

Lichtenberg *et al.* (2002:12) build on attachment theory to suggest that there are five motivational systems for humans; these are the need for (1) physio-logical regulation, (2) human attachment, (3) exploration, (4) avoidance and withdrawal in the face of conflict or danger, (5) sensual and sexual excitement.

These do not overlap directly with Jung's five instincts (described above – hunger, sexuality, the drive to activity, the reflective instinct and the creative instinct), but there are clearly some similarities between them, mainly in the recognition that there are multiple motivating forces, rather than the single motivating force of sexual drive that Freud proposed.

Cortina highlights how often emotion and motivation are confused and distinguishes them in relation to the search for a goal, which is the central characteristic of motivation. Emotions can act as psycho-physiological signals, telling us whether we are achieving our goals and activating a motivational system; for example, fear activates the attachment system in the face of danger. Significantly, Cortina (2003:282) also highlights "a new motivational system that is quintessentially human", the need to create meaning, which seems very close to Jung's view of a reflective instinct.

Unconscious fantasy

Bowlby was also quite clear that instinctual drives play no part in the formation of the internal world and that unconscious fantasy is not an expression of libido or the death instinct (Bowlby 1988:70). Although Bowlby was in analysis with Melanie Klein and later with Joan Riviere, he completely rejected his Kleinian heritage, describing Klein as "totally unaware of the scientific method" (Fonagy 1999:605). For Bowlby and for subsequent attachment theorists, an unbridgeable gulf exists between the psychoanalytic model in which instinctual drives give rise to unconscious fantasy and largely define the nature of internal objects, and an attachment theory view of the psyche, in which internal working models are gradually constructed from the wealth of accumulated experience of the real world and of actual relationships with key attachment figures.

I have suggested elsewhere that the internal working model offers us a new way of conceptualizing unconscious fantasy, which can, in essence, be considered to be the unconscious evaluation of experience and the imaginative exploration of its possible meanings and thus to play a key role in the process of compensation that Jung identified (Knox 2001). Eagle also draws important implications for the concept of fantasy from the idea of multiple and often conflicting internal working models. He suggests that "some working models may represent idealized representations that reflect the operations of defence and the fantasy of what the child would have liked the relationship with the caregiver to be, rather than the actual caregiving experience" (Eagle 1995:127). Accurate memories of past experience may coexist alongside both defensive and wish-fulfilling internal working models which offer a conflicting intrapsychic picture. The constant process of appraisal and comparison between these internal working models gives us a contemporary account of the transcendent function and of its contribution to unconscious fantasy. The roles of emotion and motivation are also fully recognized in this perspective on unconscious fantasy, since they play as important a role in the internal working model as cognitive content, a view endorsed by Lieberman who argues that the concept of internal working models needs to be expanded to "include aspects of impulse, drive and affect not usually associated with the set of rules and expectations that shape and forecast attachment relationships" (Lieberman 1999:754–755).

The concept of the archetype as image schema can also contribute significantly to the internal object world, in that the metaphorical extensions of image schemas can provide a rich source of unconscious imagery and fantasy, as Johnson (1987) proposes.

The analytic process

The unconscious meaning that we attribute to events plays a central role in the degree of emotion, pleasant or unpleasant, that those events arouse. Psychoanalytic psychotherapy of all orientations aims to bring about a gradual change in the unconscious meaning attributed to experiences and relationships, both past and present. Neurophysiologists such as Joseph LeDoux place appraisal at the heart of the effect of therapy, writing that "psychoanalysis, with emphasis on conscious insight and conscious appraisals, may involve the control of the amygdala by explicit knowledge through the temporal lobe memory system and other cortical areas involved in conscious awareness" (LeDoux 1998:265).

Margaret Wilkinson offers detailed clinical illustrations to support Allan Schore's view that the prefrontal limbic cortex retains the plastic capacities of early youth and that affectively focused treatment can literally alter the orbito-frontal system. The main vehicle for this is the non-verbal transference–countertransference dynamics which can be considered to be right hemisphere to right hemisphere communications (Wilkinson 2003). These repeated experiences of being with an analyst who is reliable, consistent and empathic are internalized, providing the basis for the gradual creation of new internal working models, which reflect the new patterns of sensitive responsiveness that gradually develop in an intense analytic relationship and store these in the form of "implicit relational knowledge" (Stern *et al.* 1998). This process reflects the rhythmic dialogue that Sander and others have described so clearly in infancy. Schore summarizes this succinctly:

> The attuned, intuitive clinician, from the first point of contact, is learning the nonverbal moment-to-moment rhythmic structures of the patient's internal states, and is relatively flexibly and fluidly modifying her own behaviour to *synchronize* with that structure, thereby creating a context for the organization of the therapeutic alliance.
>
> (Schore 2000:317)

The process of comparison is the fundamental process underlying the transcendent function and the essential feature of the process of symbolization, a view that also gains support from the recent work of neuroscientists. Daniel Siegel suggests that implicit and explicit representations are intertwined with each other and that the mental models of implicit memory help to organize the themes and ways in which the details of explicit autobiographical memory are expressed within a life story (Siegel 1999:42). Symbolic understanding is therefore a constant two-way process. Conscious explicit experience is internalized and rendered less conscious and more automatic and implicit — its patterns identified and stored as the internal working models of implicit memory; at the same time, unconscious implicit patterns are re-encoded and re-transcribed into ever more explicit representations which can eventually be expressed in conscious symbolic imagery and language. Jung captured this idea in his concept of the transcendent function, the process by which conscious and unconscious attitudes are compared and integrated with each other, reflecting his view of the unconscious as an active contributor to the meaning-making process. Jung stated unequivocally that in the process of symbol formation "the union of conscious and unconscious contents is consummated. Out of this union emerge new situations and new conscious attitudes. I have therefore called the union of opposites the 'transcendent function' " (Jung 1939:para. 524). The formation of new internal working models which underpin the emergence of secure attachments and reflective function would also seem to offer support for Jung's model of the transcendent function as a dialogue between conscious and unconscious processes of appraisal. In his essay on the transcendent function, Jung wrote:

> The present day shows with appalling clarity how little able people are to let the other man's argument count, although this capacity is a fundamental and indispensable condition for any human community. Everyone who proposes to come to terms with himself must reckon with this basic problem. For to the degree that he does not admit the validity of the other person, he denies the "other" within himself the right to exist and vice-versa. The capacity for inner dialogue is a touchstone for outer objectivity.
>
> (Jung 1957/1916:para. 187)

In this statement Jung describes the unconscious as the "other", recognizing that it may be projected onto another person and related to in that person rather than in oneself. However, Jung was using the term "transcendent function" to describe a person's ability to tolerate difference, an openness to alternative opinions and beliefs, not only in other people but also in oneself. Jung wrote: "the shuttling to and fro of arguments represents the transcendent function of opposites" (Jung 1957/1916: para. 189).

In attachment theory it is the development of this capacity which defines reflective function, in that reflective function depends on the awareness that other people have minds of their own with beliefs and judgements that may differ from one's own and that cannot be dismissed or treated as insignificant. Both transcendent function and reflective function are descriptions of the capacity to relate to other people as psychologically as well as physically separate. The concept of transcendent function would therefore seem to resonate with the aspects of reflective function that relate to psychological separateness – or individuation, which was Jung's own term for this process.

If we accept that a legitimate part of analytic work involves providing the setting and opportunities for the gradual creation of the patient's capacity for reflective function, then this also has profound implications for technique in clinical practice. Patients whose internal working models lack crucial representations of reflective function are unable to find meaning or symbolic significance in their own actions or those of others. With such patients, the nature of the analyst's interpretations may need to be modified and targeted towards demonstrating the analyst's own reflective function. This can be achieved by the analyst repeatedly showing his or her awareness that all the patient's behaviour is symbolic, that the analyst can find meaning in the patient's non-verbal communications. In other words, the analyst needs to show clearly that he or she relates to the patient as someone with a mind, even when the patient has no sense of his or her own mind at work. This "synthetic" or constructive method of analysis is very familiar to Jungians. Jung himself proposed that "The aim of the constructive method therefore is to elicit from the unconscious product a meaning that relates to the subject's future attitude", a statement that demonstrates his view of the unconscious as a creative contributor to change in analysis (Jung 1921:para. 702). This approach is beautifully exemplified by Michael Fordham in a passage in which he describes in detail his analytic work with a patient who frequently remained silent for long periods during sessions (Fordham 1996:193). Fordham's description shows how his interpretations demonstrate his awareness that there is meaningful communication in the patient's silent behaviour. The concept of reflective function has only become prominent in recent years, so it was not a term that Fordham used himself, but he used interpretations in a way that could facilitate the development of the patient's reflective function. Fordham described his approach as a modified version of the classical Jungian technique of amplification. It is modified in the sense that Fordham drew on his own countertransference responses in the form of his spontaneous thoughts and memories, using them as private amplifications which were not communicated to the patient but were drawn on to further his understanding of the patient's unconscious communications to him. These countertransference responses were the result of his own symbolizing capacity, his own reflective function in operation, which could attribute psychological intentionality to the patient's behaviour, when the patient could not see any such meaning himself.

Conclusions

I hope I have convinced the reader of this chapter that many of Jung's central concepts stand up well to scrutiny through the lens of cognitive neuroscience and attachment theory and can be reinvigorated when examined in this way, so that they become more potent as theoretical tools which can help us in our clinical practice. One of the fundamental themes in contemporary developmental psychology is that mind and meaning emerge out of developmental processes and the experience of interpersonal relationships rather than existing *a priori*. There is a constant tendency among Jungian analysts to reify unconscious structures such as archetypes or the Self and to see them as innate structures of the human mind, inherited with our genes. A developmental and attachment theory perspective provides a wealth of evidence that this is not the case, but instead that mind and meaning are constructed on the foundation stones of brain, instinct and perception, thus reconciling constructionism and biology in a model of the mind as self-organizing. From this perspective, understanding the way the mind works requires us to move from a search for structures to an understanding of the processes that underpin the emergence of symbolic meaning in the human mind. I hope that I have clarified some of the areas where Jung's interest in mental processes frequently anticipated later developments in attachment theory and cognitive neuroscience, and a Jungian model can be strengthened by studying them in the light of these new areas of discovery.

References

Astor, J. (2002) "Analytical psychology and its relation to psychoanalysis. A personal view", *Journal of Analytical Psychology*, **47**(4), 599–612.

Bartlett, F.C. (1932) *Remembering*, Cambridge: Cambridge University Press.

Bowlby, J. (1969) *Attachment and Loss, Vol. 1, Attachment*, London: Hogarth Press.

—— (1979) *The Making and Breaking of Affectional Bonds*, London: Tavistock Publications.

—— (1980) *Attachment and Loss, Vol. 3, Loss: Sadness and Depression*, London: Hogarth Press and the Institute of Psychoanalysis.

—— (1988) *A Secure Base: Clinical Applications of Attachment Theory*, London: Routledge.

Brooke, R. (1991) *Jung and Phenomenology*, London and New York: Routledge.

Bucci, W. (1997) *Psychoanalysis and Cognitive Science, A Multiple Code Theory*, New York and London: Guilford Press.

Carrette, J.R. (1994) "The language of archetypes: a conspiracy in psychological theory", *Harvest*, **40**, 168–193.

Casement, A. (2001) *Carl Gustav Jung*, London: Sage Publications.

Cortina, M. (2003) "Defensive processes, emotions and internal working models. A perspective from attachment theory and contemporary models of the mind", in M. Cortina and M. Marrone (eds), *Attachment Theory and the Psychoanalytic Process*, London: Whurr Publishers.

Cortina, M. and Marrone, M. (eds) (2003) *Attachment Theory and the Psychoanalytic Process*, London: Whurr Publishers.

Craik, K. (1943) *The Nature of Explanation*, Cambridge: Cambridge University Press.

Damasio, A. (1999) *The Feeling of What Happens: Body and Emotion in the Making of Consciousness*, New York: Harcourt Brace.

Eagle, M. (1995) "The developmental perspectives of attachment and psychoanalytic theory", in S. Goldberg, R. Muir and J. Kerr (eds), *Attachment Theory. Social, Developmental and Clinical Perspectives*, Hillsdale, NJ and London: Analytic Press.

Edelman, G. (1994/1992) *Bright Air, Brilliant Fire. On the Matter of the Mind*, London: Penguin Books. Originally published by Basic Books, New York.

Ellenberger, H.F. (1970) *The Discovery of the Unconscious. The History and Evolution of Dynamic Psychiatry*, London: Allen Lane/ Penguin Press.

Fonagy, P. (1999) "Psychoanalysis and attachment theory", in J. Cassidy and P. Shaver (eds), *Handbook of Attachment. Theory, Research and Clinical Applications*, New York and London: Guilford Press.

—— (2001) *Attachment Theory and Psychoanalysis*. New York: Other Press.

Fonagy, P., Gergely, G., Jurist, E. and Target, M. (2002) *Affect Regulation, Mentalization and the Development of the Self*, New York: Other Press.

Fordham, M. (1988) "The infant's reach", *Psychological Perspectives*, **21**, 59–76.

Fordham, M. (1996) "The supposed limits of interpretation", in Shamdasani, S. (ed.), *Analyst–Patient Interaction. Collected Papers on Technique*, London: Routledge.

Fraiberg, S., Adelson, E. and Shapiro, V. (1975) "Ghosts in the nursery: a psychoanalytic approach to the problem of impaired infant–mother relationships", *Journal of the American Academy of Child Psychiatry*, **14**, 387–422.

Freud, S., and Jung, C.G. (1961) *The Freud/Jung Letters*, (ed. W. McGuire), London: The Hogarth Press and Routledge & Kegan Paul.

Gordon, R. (1993) *Bridges. Metaphor for Psychic Processes*, London: Karnac Books.

Hayman, R. (1999) *A Life of Jung*, London: Bloomsbury.

Jacobi, J. (1959) *Complex/Archetype/Symbol in the Psychology of C.G. Jung*, New York: Bollingen Series, Pantheon Books.

Johnson, M. (1987) *The Body in the Mind. The Bodily Basis of Meaning, Imagination and Reason*, Chicago and London: Chicago University Press.

Johnson-Laird, P.N. (1989) "Mental models", in M.I. Posner (ed.), *Foundations in Cognitive Science*, Cambridge, MA and London: The MIT Press.

Jung, C.G. (1916) "Psychoanalysis and neurosis", CW 4, Princeton, NJ: Princeton University Press.

—— (1919) "Forward to Evans: 'The problem of the nervous child' ", CW 18.

—— (1921/1971) "Definitions", CW 6.

—— (1934) "A review of the complex theory", CW 8.

—— (1936) "Psychological typology", CW 6.

—— (1939) "Conscious, unconscious and individuation", CW 9i.

—— (1944) "Introduction to the religious and psychological problems of alchemy", CW 12.

—— (1946) "The psychology of the transference", CW 16.

—— (1951) "Fundamental questions of psychotherapy", CW 16.

—— (1954/1947) "On the nature of the psyche", CW 8.

—— (1957/1916) "The transcendent function", CW 8.

—— (1961/1930) "Introduction to Kranefeldt's 'Secret Ways of the Mind' ", CW 4.

—— (1963) *Memories, Dreams, Reflections*, London: Collins and Routledge & Kegan Paul.

—— (1966/1916) "The structure of the unconscious", CW 7.

—— (1967) "The detachment of consciousness from the object", CW 13.

—— (1969/1937) "Psychological factors in human behaviour", CW 8.

Knox, J. (2001) "Memories, fantasies, archetypes: an exploration of some connections between cognitive science and analytical psychology", *Journal of Analytical Psychology*, **46**(4), 613–636.

—— (2003) *Archetype, Attachment, Analysis. Jungian Psychology and the Emergent Mind*, Hove: Brunner-Routledge.

Lakoff, G. (1987) *Women, Fire and Dangerous Things: What Our Categories Reveal about the Mind*, Chicago: University of Chicago Press.

LeDoux, J. (1998) *The Emotional Brain*, London: Weidenfeld & Nicolson.

—— (2002) *The Synaptic Self*, New York: Viking Penguin; London: Macmillan.

Lichtenberg, J., Lachmann, F.M. and Fosshage, J.L. (2002) *A Spirit of Inquiry. Communication in Psychoanalysis*, Hillsdale, NJ: Analytic Press.

Lieberman, A. (1999) "Negative maternal attributions: effects on toddlers' sense of self", *Psychoanalytic Inquiry*, **19**(5), 737–754.

Mandler, G. (1975) *Mind and Body. Psychology of Emotion and Stress*, New York and London: W.W Norton & Co.

Mandler, J. (1992) " 'How to build a baby': II. Conceptual primitives", *Psychological Review*, **99**(4), 587–604.

Piontelli, A. (1992) *From Fetus to Child. An Observational and Psychoanalytic Study*, London and New York: Tavistock/Routledge.

Ramachandran, V.S. (2003) "Hearing colors, tasting shapes", *Scientific American*, **288**(5), 52–59.

Samuels, A. (1985) *Jung and the Post-Jungians*, London: Routledge & Kegan Paul.

Sander, L.W. (2002) "Thinking differently: principles of process in living systems and the specificity of being known", *Psychoanalytic Dialogues*, **12**(1), 11–42.

Sandner, D.F. and Beebe, J. (1984) "Psychopathology and analysis", in M. Stein (ed.) *Jungian Analysis*. Boulder, CO and London: Shambhala.

Schacter, D. (1996) *Searching for Memory. The Brain, the Mind and the Past*, New York: Basic Books.

Schore, A. (1994) *Affect Regulation and the Origins of the Self. The Neurobiology of Emotional Development*, Hillsdale, NJ: Lawrence Erlbaum.

Schore, A. (2000) "Minds in the making: attachment, the self-organizing brain and developmentally-orientated psychoanalytic psychotherapy", *British Journal of Psychotherapy*, **17**(3), 299–327.

Sebel, P. (1995) "Memory during anaesthesia: gone but not forgotten", *Anaesthesia and Analgesia*, **81**(4), 668.

Siegel, D. (1998) "The developing mind. Towards a neurobiology of interpersonal experience", *The Signal*, **6**(3–4), 1–11.

—— (1999) *The Developing Mind. Towards a Neurobiology of Interpersonal Experience*, New York and London: Guilford Press.

Stern, D., Bruschweiler-Stern, N., Harrison, A.M., Lyons-Ruth, K., Morgan, A.C., Nahum, J.P., Sander, L. and Tronick, E.Z. (1998) "The process of therapeutic change involving implicit knowledge: some implications of developmental observations for adult psychotherapy", *Infant Mental Health Journal*, **19**, 300–308.

Storr, A. (1983) *The Essential Jung. Selected Writings*, Princeton, NJ: Princeton University Press.

Tresan, D. (2004) "This new science of ours", *Journal of Analytical Psychology*, **49**(2), 195–218.

Wilkinson, M. (2003) "Undoing trauma. Contemporary neuroscience: a Jungian clinical perspective", *Journal of Analytical Psychology*, **48**(2), 235–254.

Chapter 4

Understanding consciousness through the theory of psychological types

John Beebe

This chapter will show how Jung's theory of psychological types, a corner-stone of his complex psychology, can be used by a practicing psycho-therapist to assess the development of consciousness in the course of individuation.

When Jung began to work on the psychological problem that he was attempt-ing to solve with his theory of types, he had an international reputation as an investigator of the unconscious. Early on, he had allied himself with the burgeoning psychoanalytic movement, which had made the idea of the unconscious, already topical by the end of the nineteenth century, a world preoccupation. So in 1921, when his book *Psychological Types* appeared with its description of various attitudes of consciousness, it looked to some as if Jung had turned away from the concerns he had embraced so boldly in the first part of his career. He seemed a bit like that other prewar trail-blazer, Picasso, who elected in the 1920s to abandon his cubist explorations of painterly depth for a conservative, neoclassical style that emphasized contour drawing in a conventional rendering of the human figure. Freud, who had long accused Jung of being in flight from the real unconscious because he could not accept the sexual theory, was able to crow to Ernest Jones:

> A new production by Jung of enormous size, seven hundred pages thick, inscribed "Psychological Types," the work of a snob and a mystic, no new idea in it. He clings to that escape he detected in 1913, denying objective truths in psychology on account of personal differences in the observer's constitution. No great harm to be expected from this quarter (Paskauskas 1993:424).[1]

Like Freud, most psychoanalysts assumed that Jung, in full retreat from the dynamic psychiatry the fathers of his early career had hoped he would help them build, had returned to the descriptive psychology that had informed Kraepelin. What he was no longer willing to deal with, according to these influential critics within the developing field of depth psychology in which Jung was still nominally a leading figure, was the unconscious.

This perception, which I would call a prejudice, has affected the reception of the subject of psychological type among depth psychologists ever since, including the majority of analytical psychologists working today. I well recall a friend in analytical training asking me some years ago when I mentioned that I was hard at work on understanding the type theory and its application to clinical work, "Is that a valid method of analysis?" To him, Jung's typology seemed, at best, an approach to conscious psychology, not very interesting or important to the training of a depth psychologist. Today, however, when academic spokesmen from the fields of cognitive psychology and neuroscience such as Howard Gardner,[2] Daniel Dennett, Antonio Damasio,[3] and Nicholas Humphrey have renewed public and professional interest in the nature of "consciousness," depth psychologists have been inspired to take up anew the question of how patients in analysis become "conscious." A contemporary definition of consciousness is offered by Corsini (2002:209):

> The distinguishing feature of mental life, variously characterized as the: (a) state of awareness as well as the content of the mind, that is, the ever-changing stream of immediate experience, comprising perceptions, feelings, sensations, images, and ideas; (b) central effect of neural reception; (c) capacity of having experience; (d) subjective aspect of brain activity; (e) relation of self to environment; and (f) totality of an individual's experience at any given moment.

Jung's pioneering emphasis on the "attitudes and functions of consciousness" has finally begun to seem less like a digression from the cutting edge of psychological understanding than a prescient anticipation of a direction in which depth psychology has found that it needs to go.

In relation to the exploration of the unconscious, Jung's turn to the topic of types of consciousness was not so much a regression as a repositioning. It involved what he described elsewhere as *reculer pour mieux sauter*, stepping backward in order to take a greater leap. The type theory was a contribution to the problem of the standpoint from which the individual experiences the unconscious. That the conscious standpoint of the patient could hardly be ignored Jung had already learned from his practical experience as a psychiatrist attempting to understand dreams and symptoms, for the patient's conscious stance often turned out to be what the unconscious was actually responding to.

By taking up the way consciousness is structured, Jung was engaging with the problem that Friedrich Nietzsche and William James had recognized a generation before, that consciousness cannot be taken for granted. Nietzsche had seriously questioned consciousness's identity as a unity, arguing that when we orient ourselves to reality it is not through a fixed standpoint but through a series of perspectives. And William James, even more deconstructively, had written in 1904:

> I believe that "consciousness," when once it has evaporated to this estate of pure diaphaneity, is on the point of disappearing altogether. It is the name of a nonentity, and has no right to a place among first principles. Those who still cling to it are clinging to a mere echo, the faint rumor left behind by the disappearing "soul" upon the air of philosophy. During the past year, I have read a number of articles whose authors seemed just on the point of abandoning the notion of consciousness . . . and substituting for it that of an absolute experience not due to two factors [such as "[t]houghts" and "things," "spirit and matter," "soul and body"]. But they were not quite radical enough, not quite daring enough in their negations. For twenty years past I have mistrusted "consciousness" as an entity; for seven or eight years past I have suggested its non-existence to my students, and tried to give them its pragmatic equivalent in realities of experience. It seems to me that the hour is ripe for it to be openly and universally discarded.
>
> To deny plumply that "consciousness" exists seems so absurd on the face of it – for undeniably "thoughts" do exist – that I fear some readers will follow me no farther. Let me then immediately explain that I mean only to deny that the word stands for an entity, but to insist most emphatically that it does stand for a function. There is, I mean, no aboriginal stuff or quality of being, contrasted with that of which material objects are made, out of which our thoughts of them are made; but there is a function in experience which thoughts perform, and for the performance of which this quality of being is invoked. That function is knowing. "Consciousness" is supposed necessary to explain the fact that things not only are, but get reported, are known. Whoever blots out the notion of consciousness from his list of first principles must still provide in some way for that function's being carried on.
>
> (James 1904:477)

By developing a theory that situates knowing within different types of psychological orientation, Jung found a way to incorporate both Nietzsche's emphasis on perspectives and James's insistence that consciousness can only be approached practically, through careful study of the way we actually "know" things. When in *Psychological Types* Jung sets out the case for basic "attitudes" of consciousness, we can feel the influence of Nietzsche's perspectivism, and when he writes of "functions of consciousness" we encounter language that reflects James's pragmatism.

But something else had been added, out of Jung's own experience, first, with the different understandings of the unconscious between Freud, Adler, and himself that had split up the early psychoanalytic movement into "schools," and second, with direct active imaginative encounters with the unconscious that drove home to him the reality of the psyche. Jung told the students in his 1925 English seminar that:

> Through the fact that I was worried about my difficulty with Freud, I came to study Adler carefully to see what was his case against Freud. I was struck at once by the difference in type. Both were treating neurosis and hysteria, and yet to the one man it looked so, and to the other it was quite different. I could find no solution. Then it dawned on me that possibly I was dealing with two different types, who were fated to approach the same set of facts from widely differing aspects. I began to see among my patients some who fit Adler's theories and others who fit Freud's, and thus I came to formulate the theory of extraversion and introversion.
>
> (Jung 1925/1989:31)

These terms for the basic attitudes of consciousness were apparently derived from words, *externospection* and *introspection*, that Binet had come up with to describe the different types of intelligence displayed by his own two infant daughters (Binet 1903, cited by Oliver Brachfeld 1954 in Ellenberger 1970:702–703). Jung's insistence on this differentiation would have been impossible had he not also come to the conviction, arrived at independently of any of his teachers and colleagues, that there was a reality that psychological consciousness was expected to construe whenever the unconscious was confronted. On the basis of his experience with the psyche, which Jung also shared with the members of his English seminar (Aniela Jaffe included this material in *Memories, Dreams, Reflections*), Jung had grasped that psychological consciousness was not just a knowing about, or a construction or reconstruction of, but (as the etymology of the word "consciousness" suggests) "a knowing with" unconscious reality. Edinger has noted that this etymology points to the "unconscious side of the term consciousness":

> *Conscious* derives from *con* or *cum*, meaning with or together, and *scire*, "to know" or "to see." It has the same derivation as conscience. Thus the root meaning of both consciousness and conscience is "knowing with" or "seeing with" an "other." In contrast, the word "science," which also derives from *scire*, means simple knowing, i.e. knowing without "withness." So etymology indicates that the phenomena of consciousness and conscience are somehow related and that the experience of consciousness is made up of two factors – "knowing" and "withness." In other words, consciousness is the experience of *knowing together with an other*, that is, in a setting of twoness.
>
> (Edinger 1984:36)

Something like what Jung means by consciousness is conveyed by Heinz Kohut's much later assertion that "introspection and empathy are essential ingredients of psychoanalytical observation and that the limits of psycho-analysis are defined by those of introspection and empathy" (Kohut 1959/ 1978). By the time Jung set out to write *Psychological Types*, consciousness had come to mean for him the way the reality of the psyche is both accessed and assessed, or what he sometimes called "understanding" (Jung 1972), which he made the basis of his entire approach to psychology. Consciousness, in this sense, was the indispensable investigative tool for all further work on the unconscious.

How this consciousness is achieved is the problem that Jung seeks to address in his book. As he put it, much later, "I considered it my scientific duty to examine first the condition of the human consciousness" (Jung 1957/ 1977:341).

The individuation of consciousness

What is not immediately apparent to those who try to approach Jung's psychology as if it were another science, albeit a science of the unconscious, is that consciousness, for Jung the tool with which the unconscious must be investigated, is an emergent property of the unconscious itself. Only second-arily does consciousness collect in the center he calls the ego and even then it is not entirely located there. Jung does not make this as explicit in *Psychological Types* as he might have. There he defines consciousness in terms of its relation to the ego:

> By consciousness I understand the relatedness of psychic contents to the ego ... in so far as they are sensed as such by the ego. In so far as relations are not sensed as such by the ego, they are unconscious. Con-sciousness is the function or activity which maintains the relation of psychic contents with the ego. Consciousness is not identical with psyche, since, in my view, psyche represents the totality of all the psychic con-tents, and these are not necessarily all bound up directly with the ego, i.e. related to it in such a way that they take on the quality of consciousness. There exist a great many psychic complexes and these are not all, necessarily, connected with the ego.
>
> (Jung 1921/1971:535–536)

This unfortunate passage, all too self-evidently trying to meet the logical requirements for distinguishing consciousness from the unconscious, has led too many students of Jung's psychology to look for a structure called "ego" and a process of "ego development," neither of which is exactly sup-ported by phenomenological observation of the growth of an individual's consciousness even though some Jungians have made heroic efforts to demonstrate that they are.

Perhaps the most interesting of these attempts is Erich Neumann's landmark book, *The Origins and History of Consciousness*, which offers a model for the development of consciousness out of the unconscious that draws upon quite specific imagery from world mythology (Neumann 1954). Neumann uses myths, particularly myths of the hero in the process of surviving various monsters that can be equated with aspects of the unconscious, to find evidence of the ego's emergence, survival, and progressive strengthening, thus organizing the myths along a continuum of the hero's progress to generate a stage-by-stage model of ego development. The archetypal "stages" of ego-consciousness he educes have generated a clinical mythology among Jungians (e.g. "The patient's ego is contained in the maternal uroborus"). This has been the model of the development of consciousness that many Jungian analysts have drawn upon to gauge where their patients are in the individuation of consciousness. Hillman, Giegerich, and others have criticized this model as unconsciously identified with a nineteenth-century notion of progress.

Jung's own way of speaking about the growth of consciousness tended to be simpler, and, from a contemporary standpoint, more soulful. For instance, Jung was once asked, "Does consciousness help in the process of individuation?" His answer was:

> Living consciously is our form of individuation. A plant that is meant to produce a flower is not individuated if it does not produce it – and the man who does not develop consciousness is not individuated, because consciousness is his flower – it – is his life.
>
> (Jung 1934/1976:296–297)

In allowing the subtitle of the first English translation of *Psychological Types* to be "The Psychology of Individuation," Jung implied that the flowering of consciousness has something to do with the progressive emergence of the psychological types, and it's this idea I prefer to the idea of a monadic "ego" developing over time. Sticking to Jung's metaphor of flowering, I find it best to say that if a person individuates, that is, goes on to flower, then the various functions of consciousness that Jung describes in *Psychological Types* will be the petals of his or her flower. This notion does not assume that consciousness originates in the ego, even though when consciousness emerges it is associated with an ongoing narrative of self, that is, as part of what a person can refer to as "mine." If anything, consciousness would seem to arise out of what Jung described in a talk with students as "the peculiar intelligence of the background" (Jung 1958/1970:178).

The idea that consciousness already resides in some form in the unconscious gives another meaning to the idea of "knowing together with an other." The idea of a teamwork between ego-consciousness and a consciousness that already resides in the unconscious is particularly appropriate to the understanding of the psychological functions Jung has called "thinking," "feeling," "sensation," and "intuition." In *Psychological Types*, he conceives these as two pairs of opposites: thinking and feeling (evaluative functions) defining one axis of consciousness, sensation and intuition (perceptive functions) the other. Asked for definitions of these four functions of consciousness, Jung told an interviewer:

> there is quite a simple explanation of those terms, and it shows at the same time how I arrived at such a typology. Sensation tells you that there *is* something. Thinking, roughly speaking, tells you *what* it is. Feeling tells you whether it is agreeable or not, to be accepted or rejected. And intuition – now there is a difficulty. You don't know, ordinarily, how intuition works. When a man has a hunch, you can't tell how he got that hunch, or where that hunch comes from. There is something funny about intuition. [Jung gives an example.] So my definition of that intuition is a perception via the unconscious.
>
> (Jung 1957/1977:306)

So far, this seems like a reasonable enough orientation to reality from the standpoint of an ego trying to cope with it. But in discussing intuition, the "difficult" function to explain, Jung tells us:

> It is a very important function, because when you live under primitive conditions a lot of unpredictable things are likely to happen. Then you need your intuition because you cannot possibly tell by your sense perceptions what is going to happen. For instance, you are traveling in a primeval forest. You can only see a few steps ahead. You go by the compass, perhaps, but you don't know what there is ahead. It is uncharted country. If you use your intuition you have hunches. There are places that are favorable; there are places that are not favorable. You can't tell for your life what it is, but you'd better follow those hunches because anything can happen, quite unforeseen things … You can also have intuitions – and this constantly happens – in our jungle called a city. You can have a hunch that something is going wrong, particularly when you are driving an automobile. For instance it is the day when nurses appear in the street … And then you get a peculiar feeling, and really, at the next corner there is a second nurse that runs in front of the automobile.
>
> (Jung 1957/1977:307–308)

I like to read that amplification of the intuitive function as a gloss on the purpose that *all* the functions of consciousness – thinking, feeling, and sensation too – serve. All of them are required because life itself presents problems that are already differentiated in such a way that only a particular function of consciousness can solve them. In that case, we would be justified to speak of a problem presented by a patient as a thinking problem, a feeling problem, an intuitive problem, or a sensation problem. Similarly, a dream, which reveals to us "the actual situation in the unconscious" (Jung 1948/1960:505) of a client, lays out the situation for us in such a way that we can "type" it, if we wish, as a thinking situation, a feeling situation, an intuitive situation, or a sensation situation. The problem is then coming up with the function of consciousness appropriate to the situation, or in other words, meeting the situation's own peculiar consciousness as to what it is with a consciousness that matches it. From this perspective, the development of consciousness involves the ability to summon the various functions at appropriate times in appropriate ways.

Unfortunately, we are not always so adaptable. In the book *Lectures on Jung's Typology*, Marie-Louise von Franz and James Hillman (1971) each address the problem of bringing an appropriate function of consciousness to a situation that calls for it. Von Franz's theme is the unevenness in type development that leads one of Jung's four functions to remain "low" in its degree of differentiation. This Jung had called the "inferior function," and I have found the designation accurate, phenomenologically, because each of us usually has an inferiority complex around that particular area of our conscious functioning. Von Franz points out that the inferior function tends to behave like the dummling or idiot youngest son in a fairy-tale and yet, like that son, serves as the bridge to the unconscious that the more differentiated functions (symbolized by the arrogant elder brothers in the typical tale) cannot provide, bringing some kind of renewal to the kingdom, i.e. the sphere of consciousness. This function is the area of our consciousness that is least under the control of our good intentions, slowest to take training despite our best efforts, and most contaminated with the unconscious. Hillman's description of the inferior feeling function well conveys the problem that arises on the basis of this association with what is ordinarily repressed:

> Inferior feeling, to sum it up, may be characterized by contamination with the repressed which tends to manifest, as the Scholastic would have said, in *ira* and *cupiditas* [anger and desire]. Inferior feeling is loaded with anger and rage and ambition and aggression as well as with greed and desire. Here we find ourselves with huge claims for love, with massive needs for recognition, and discover our feeling connection to life to be one vast expectation composed of thousands of tiny resentments. This expectation has been called an omnipotence fantasy, the expression of the abandoned child with his leftover feelings that nobody wants to take care of – but is this enough? Omnipotence is more than a content; rather it expresses, as does the child, an impoverished functioning that insists upon more sway and exercise. Without this exercise, feeling turns upon itself,

morbidly; we are envious, jealous, depressed, feeding our needs and their immediate gratification, then rushing out intermittently to meet someone to help or for help. The cat neglected becomes the unconscious tiger.

(Hillman in von Franz and Hillman 1971:111–112)

It should be pointed out that this description of the emotional attitude of a function of consciousness in the inferior position is strikingly similar to Adler's description of the inferiority complex (Ellenberger 1970:612–613).

Hillman's description of the complex that feeling can display when it is an inferior function helps us to recognize that the behavior of a function of consciousness is affected by its position within the total hierarchy of functions.

Jung had defined this hierarchy according to a fourfold model, specifying a superior function, an auxiliary function, a tertiary function, and an inferior function, which he often diagrammed as follows:

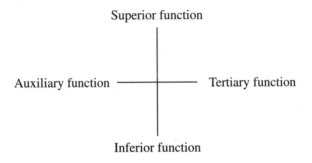

Superior function

Auxiliary function — Tertiary function

Inferior function

This diagram can be read as a stick-figure representation of a right-handed person, who might be imagined standing erect with feet together and back placed flush against a blackboard with his or her arms spread-eagled, for the purpose of revealing the relations of his or her functions of consciousness. Each of the qualifying adjectives for the four functions shown in the diagram – superior, auxiliary, tertiary, and inferior – describes the "position" of one of the person's four functions of consciousness in relation to the others. What is suggested is a hierarchy of the functions that, though it begins according to their degree of differentiation, ends up being as qualitative as it is quantitative. That is to say, the way the function is experienced, both by the person who possesses it and by the others he or she deals with, is as much a result of its position in the total hierarchy of functions as of its actual degree of differentiation. The positions themselves convey certain qualities to the functions that occupy them, as von Franz and Hillman have demonstrated for the "inferior" function and the present author has proceeded to do for the other three positions (Beebe 1984).

Further, these named positions, as the diagram above shows, define a pair of axes, a vertical axis (between the superior function and inferior function), which I think of as the "spine" of consciousness defining the person's conscious standpoint, and a horizontal axis (between the auxiliary and tertiary functions), which can be thought of as the "arms" of consciousness, as it is the task of these functions to articulate the relation to the world once the individual standpoint of the person is established.

Type as a method of analysis

As I have given much attention to the behavior of the functions in each of these positions in the course of my own development of consciousness, I will now offer a series of vignettes from my own analytic process. What follows may be considered an autobiographical case report of a typological analysis.

My discovery of my superior function, intuition, came in the first year of my analysis. I had come into therapy at the age of 26, a few months after graduating from medical school, complaining of "depression," by which I think I meant a general malaise and feeling of blocked libido, the manifest symptom being the inability to finish any professional book I started to read. In the third or fourth session, while I was in the midst of reiterating these complaints, my analyst asked, "Do you ever dream when you're depressed?" It was as if a light had been turned on in a dark room. Of course I dreamed; I had always dreamt, and in fact that's where my mind was when people complained I wasn't paying attention. I was dreaming! No wonder I couldn't keep track of practical things. In a flash I knew that what I was superior at – dreaming – was the cause of what I was inferior at – paying attention, something that in turn my mother, my father, my teachers, and my peers had all tried, with little success, to shame me into being more responsible about. A few months later, I had the Jungian words for those processes that had defined my gift and its accompanying limitation: I was an intuitive type, with inferior sensation. But immediately upon realizing that what I was best at and what I was worst at were two aspects or "ends" of the same thing, I had a dream that I was an obstetrician delivering a baby from myself. In experiencing my superior function and my inferior function as belonging to the same reality, I had discovered the reality of my own vertical axis, and it became a channel for experiencing a new identity.

Realizing that I was an intuitive type gave me a lot of energy. The dreams I was now recording daily and bringing to my analyst twice a week gave me plenty to read, and I found I could also read Jungian books that taught me more about the inner life I was discovering. In my relief at finding something I really liked to study, I discovered my true auxiliary function, introverted thinking. My own father, a military man who had commanded a battalion in Korea, was an extraverted thinking type, and he had bought heavily into the

American cultural belief that knowledge is power. When I would interrupt the nightly radio news broadcast to offer opinions of my own about what the developments might signify, my father would say, "Shut up, son. You don't learn from people who know nothing." My analyst, also a man, never interrupted, or almost never. He let me think out loud about my dreams and my reading to my heart's content. Even though this meant that I was rethinking much of Jungian psychology and making it my own so that I could take it in (and this meant that I was not simply accepting Jung's way of formulating the big ideas, in which my analyst had been trained), he let my thinking go its own introverted, subjective, way. I would only accept something if it was true to my experience, which of course was very Jungian in one way, but would not allow me, in another, to accept the dogma that Jungian psychology had already started to become. I will always be grateful to my first analyst for (1) allowing me to think in his presence without complaining, as many another therapist might have, that I was intellectualizing and avoiding the feelings that were the "real" stuff of depth work and (2) tolerating, without retaliation, a rethinking of the very psychology in which he was so heavily invested. In this way, he let my auxiliary function express itself, which it had never been able to do before, inhibited as it was by the extraverted thinking of my father and other authorities, including the psychiatry professors whose books I could no longer read. As a psychoanalyst might have said at the time, I was fortunate in having a transference situation that would enable me to solve my Oedipal problem in this way.

From a cultural angle, I realize that I was also availing myself of a form of empowerment that was much more open to men than to women in 1966 and 1967, when these events were occurring. I was a doctor, and so was my analyst. There was in medicine a long tradition of learning how to think and function medically, codified in the aphorism we all often heard about learning new medical procedures, "See one, do one, teach one." This was a totemic, patriarchal tradition, for the most part: in some parts of the United States, women were still not even admitted to medical school. I am aware that having my superior function mirrored and my auxiliary function given space would have been far less likely to occur with the very same analyst had I been a woman. Though differently problematic from that of my father, this analyst's anima[4] would, I believe, have been far more likely to insist upon feeling expressions from a woman of my psychological type, in accord with the then prevalent Jungian notion that feeling was more feminine than thinking.

No such impediment to empowering my thinking came up in my analyst's initial overt countertransference, and so I experienced the ideal conditions for a therapy described by Carl Rogers and his colleagues: genuineness, unconditional positive regard, and accurate empathic understanding. (See Rogers and Truax 1967.) For this reason, I became precociously clear about the nature of my own typology as part of my self-experience. I believe that only some such direct experience of the types as one's own, and the permission to consider them in one's own way, can enable a patient to avail himself or herself of the individuation potential of the type theory. Otherwise, type becomes another way to learn from others what one is, and a new set of tasks to be learned in the effort to adapt more effectively to the environment. There can be value in type still in discovering new energy for adaptation, but this is not the same as individuation.

As my dream of delivering a baby from myself perhaps conveys, I came into possession quite early in my analysis of a sense of personal selfhood as my typology unfolded in a way that felt authentic to me in the facilitating environment of the therapy. As I have indicated in other writings (Beebe 1988, 1992), I believe that it is only through experiencing one's personal, little "s," self in a way that has "integrity in depth" that the big "S" Self of Jungian psychology, the instinctive knowledge of how to live, can be authentically accessed.

The opening up of my typology led to a great deal of energy pouring into my psyche from the Self. My new problem, replacing the depression I had come to therapy with, was a tendency to get too excited. I sometimes imagined my superior intuition was like the head of a rocket ship, ready to take off. I needed desperately to hold myself to the earth, to stay with the tasks associated with medical training. At that early stage, my inferior function, sensation, simply did not have the necessary weight, the specific gravity, to anchor me. But I noticed that my auxiliary and tertiary functions could be enlisted to keep me connected to the demands of the world. Thinking, after intuition my strongest function, and therefore my auxiliary, helped me to define my situation and identify the issues I needed to work on. And my feeling, less confident and more vulnerable, kept me guessing what my impact was on other people and working to discover what my actual relationships with them were. The combined effect of using these two processes, thinking and feeling, was to slow me down and keep me out of the most irrational flights of my intuition. I first became aware in an inner way that my thinking and feeling form an axis, just as my superior intuition and inferior sensation do, when I had the following dream.

> A father (a man who was maybe in his fifties) was chasing his son (a young man in his twenties) around a dining room table, waving a butcher knife.

Working on this dream in my analysis, I was able to associate to the image of the young man. Although the echoes of my feeling reactions to a critical father were clear, the young man in my dream, in his fearfulness, was not anything like my waking personality. At that time, if anything, I had not learned to fear. The son in the dream reminded me of a young man I knew at the time, who was strongly feeling and who thought very slowly. The butcher knife, with its capacity to cleave and dissect, seemed to me the image of a thinking function, used to make separating distinctions between things. That an older man wielded it in a bullying way toward a younger suggested to me that a more developed function was somehow bullying a less developed one. The dream may, of course, have been a commentary on the way I used thinking around my feeling type friend, but at the time I was more focused on how I was relating to myself. I decided that the father symbolized my auxiliary thinking and the son my tertiary feeling. That they were father and son suggested that they were on the same axis, but that they were engaged in a sadomasochistic interaction – the chase around the dining room table – suggested that this axis was in dysfunction. It was not enough to reduce the dream to the humiliations I had received from my father when I had tried to express my feelings at the dinner table while his "news briefing" was on the radio. In the manner of an internal object relation, this bullying was something I was now doing to myself with my own thinking. Chastened by the dream, I gradually became less aggressive about applying my thinking formulations to the understanding of my feeling when it was upset. In time, my confident thinking took a more protective attitude toward my shakier, immature feeling.

Up to this time, my use of the type theory to make sense of myself had pretty much concentrated on which functions were strong, and which at risk. I was not particularly focused on whether the functions that I was discovering and analyzing were introverted or extraverted, and indeed I could not make up my mind whether I myself should be described as an introvert or an extravert. My first analyst had said it was a "continuum" and while half of my friends saw me as more extraverted, others who knew me just as well said I was the only true introvert they knew! As I had now entered analytic training, it was an embarrassment to me that I did not know. Around this time, I learned from a member of the training committee at my Institute, Wayne Detloff, to whom I confided my confusion, that there was a point of view not often expressed in the circles frequented by Jungian analysts and candidates, that if the superior function is extraverted, the auxiliary function is introverted and vice versa. Although I had actually taken the Myers-Briggs Type Indicator, as part of a research study in which all the first year residents in my psychiatric residency were asked to participate in 1968, and its finding that I was an ENTP seemed to confirm the "intuitive thinking" diagnosis I had given myself on the basis of my analytic discoveries of my typology, Dr Detloff's explanation was my first introduction to the theoretical ideas of Isabel Briggs Myers about type development, which at that time went largely untaught in my Institute.[5]

The received version of type there was that of Jo Wheelwright (1982), who with his wife Jane and Horace Gray had created their own diagnostic instrument, the Gray-Wheelwrights Type Test. On it, as on the Myers-Briggs, I came out extraverted and an intuitive thinking type. And in my Institute that meant that *both* my leading functions were extraverted. What introversion I had was supposed to come from my inferior function, sensation. But in truth, although *Lectures on Jung's Typology* had now been published and I could follow this argument, as far as it went, I still saw my inferior function in a less differentiated way, as just "inferior sensation," and, as I have indicated, I was really not all that sure about the extraverted diagnosis for my superior function.

Dr Detloff, however, was quite clear that introverted sensation and extraverted sensation were so different that he wondered why they were even both called "sensation." Later I came to see that introverted sensation concerns itself primarily with finding order, organizing experience, and monitoring the comfort of the body on the inside, whereas extraverted sensation involves compelling, often shared, experiences of the textures, smells, sights, sounds, and tastes of the world – a direct relationship with reality. Similarly, I decided that introverted feeling is mainly concerned with the values that matter most to oneself, while extraverted feeling seeks to connect with the feelings of others. Extraverted intuition seemed to be involved in picking up what was going on in other people's minds, and seeing possibilities that others might not have imagined; whereas introverted intuition looked at the big picture in the unconscious, where the gestalts that moved nations, religions, and epochs lay, even in the midst of apparently "individual" experience. And the two kinds of thinking, though both concerned with defining things, also did so in very different ways: extraverted thinking was interested in definitions that would hold true for everyone, according to ideas everyone might agree with, whereas introverted thinking had to reflect on whether a particular construction really accorded with the conviction of inner truth, regardless of what the received opinion might be.

These distinctions were a helpful orientation to other people's psychology, but they were not of the greatest personal interest at this stage of my development, for I had more urgent issues in my analysis to deal with, or so I believed. My core depression was still untouched, and still further years into the analysis I was often beset with migraine headaches and accompanying states of severe exhaustion. In my dreams, I saw stretches of scant and barren vegetation. My analyst (by this time I had switched to a woman) interpreted this as a picture of my vegetative nervous system, as it looked during these periods of burnout.

Then I dreamed of a woman sitting alone in a room. She was Chinese and had a glum look on her face. The room she was in was bare, without other furniture than the chair she was sitting in. This was so because her husband spent all his money doping and gambling and so had nothing to bring home. My analyst was very insistent about the importance of this dream. "She doesn't have anything," she pointed out.

I associated to the woman. I knew her in life: she was the laundress at the Chinese launderette to which I entrusted my washables at that time. A practical, unadorned woman, she worked very efficiently. She was clearly no extravert, but she was quite concerned with sensation matters in her introverted way. I decided she was an introverted sensation type. I had recently read von Franz's essay on the inferior function and also Gareth Hill's essay on "Men, the anima and the feminine," which at that time was unpublished, but described eight types of anima, using both the four function types (feeling, thinking, intuition, and sensation) and the two attitude types (introverted and extraverted) to arrive at his eight possibilities for the type of the anima, just as von Franz had done in establishing eight types of inferior function in her essay.

The husband in the dream who was given to gambling seemed to me to represent a less flattering side of my superior function, extraverted intuition. That seemed to fit the image of the husband as a gambler, someone who pursues possibilities and takes his energy into the world, leaving his introverted wife at home alone, not giving her much. But what did this have to do with me? I did not drink and gamble, but I was drawn to chase after possibilities to extend my life, even after it was time to go home and rest. The newest movie, the latest book, even the next dream one of my patients would bring to me, were causing me to transgress the limits of my personal comfort. For the first time, the importance of the extravert/introvert distinction really was brought home to me. If the husband represented my unbalanced extraversion, the clear message of the dream was that I was neglecting the introverted side of myself, represented by the forlorn and unfurnished anima figure, the Chinese laundress. The dream was saying, very specifically, that my introverted sensation was not getting anything from me. When I conveyed this conclusion to my analyst, she said, "I couldn't agree more."

I thought long and hard about how to rectify that state of affairs. Introverted sensation, I knew by this time, lives on the inside of the body, and seeks to keep it from getting overstimulated, overheated, too tired, too hungry, or too filled with the wrong foods, etc. I looked at what was happening with my patients in my developing psychotherapy practice. I was very excited to hear everything they were telling me, so much so that I was listening with bated breath, neglecting even to breathe properly. No wonder I came home to migraine headaches: I was retaining carbon dioxide. I made up my mind that I would have to attend to my breathing while listening to patients. This opened a series of spaces that allowed me to be aware of my body as I practiced therapy. I then noticed that in my body, as I attended to it, were clues to what was going on in my patient beyond anything dream interpretation could have revealed. If my stomach or chest felt tense, that was a signal that my patient was feeling "uptight." I found if I attended to these sensations, and eventually took up with the patient the feelings I was introjectively identifying, relevant material would emerge which would move the therapy forward. When I succeeded in getting the patient to express the feelings that my body had picked up, I wouldn't leave the session with a headache, and I would end the day of doing psychotherapy energized, not depleted. Apparently this method was a tonic for my inner life. A subsequent dream about the Chinese laundress found her happier: her husband had been taking her out for ice cream!

There is a tradition in Jungian analysis that the type problem becomes especially important when the inferior function starts to "come up" as a topic in analysis, and that then one needs to pay very close attention to the type. Certainly that turned out to be true in my case. Once I knew that my anima was an introverted sensation type, and that I tended not just to be woefully inefficient in this area (as I had recognized as soon as I realized I was an intuitive) but also destructively neglectful (which I had not realized until I dreamed of the Chinese laundress whose husband was not providing for her), I became much more interested in the exact situation of all my functions, and gave a lot of thought to what in me was extraverted and what introverted.

It made sense that my intuition was extraverted and my thinking introverted. I was pretty sure, also, that my feeling, to the degree that it was differentiated at all, was extraverted. Since my sensation had turned out to be introverted, on the evidence of the Chinese laundress anima, I decided that the types alternated through the hierarchy of functions in their extraversion or introversion like a system of checks and balances. In my case, the typology looked like this:

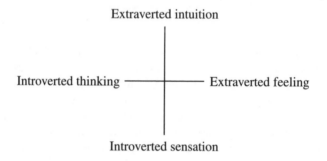

Here at last, in a convincing way, were the four functions that Jung had indicated represented an oriented ego, the fourness suggesting an aspect of selfhood, which I eventually came to call, refusing the heavy Kantian implications of Jung's and Neumann's emphasis on "ego," the little "s" self. This was the typology of my everyday self-experience, the basis of my ongoing consciousness as a person having his own standpoint with its inevitable strengths and weaknesses.

There is something seductive about the sense of wholeness that comes with the number four, which Jung considers the archetypal number designating the big "S" Self. I was at least seven years into my analysis before the four functions that make up my typology were clear to me, and it was hard not to believe that I had somehow "arrived," from the standpoint of individuation, even though I was only 34 years old. Thirty years later, this seems a bit like the naïveté of a relatively young person, but the inflation of self-discovery can threaten at any age. To assume that type development ends with the discovery of the inferior function, at which point the Self is constellated and from then on one is engaged in relating to the unconscious in its deeper aspect, can actually interfere with the development of consciousness. In reality, type remains an issue throughout the individuation process, although analysts do not always recognize this.

Type development

Not long after I had recognized the differentiation of my first four functions, including their alternation of extraversion and introversion, I came across Isabel Briggs Myers's book, *Gifts Differing* (1980), which contained five chapters on the dynamics of type development. I was particularly struck by the chapter "Good type development," which confirmed many of my own discoveries about my type development in therapy, which had indeed felt "good" to me. Elizabeth Murphy also takes up this theme in her book *The Developing Child* (1992:12–13), in which she points out that the superior and auxiliary functions may develop naturally in childhood, but that the superior, the tertiary and inferior functions normally do not appear until adulthood. I believe that my first analysis unblocked this normal developmental process in me. One of Myers's most important ideas, which she and her mother had culled from Jung, was that:

> For all the types appearing in practice, the principle holds good that besides the conscious main function there is also a relatively unconscious, auxiliary function which is in every respect different from the nature of the main function.
>
> (Jung 1921/1971:515, quoted in Myers 1980:19)

As Myers insisted:

> The operative words are "in every respect." If the auxiliary process differs from the dominant process in every respect, it *cannot* be introverted where the dominant process is introverted. It has to be extraverted if the dominant process is introverted, and introverted if the dominant process is extraverted.
>
> (Myers 1980:19)

Myers quotes two other passages from Jung that she feels support this interpretation. The first concerns the attitude type of the inferior, auxiliary, and tertiary functions in someone whose superior function is introverted thinking.

> The relatively unconscious functions of feeling, intuition, and sensation, which counterbalance introverted thinking, are inferior in quality and have a primitive, extraverted character.
>
> (Jung 1921/1971:489, quoted in Myers 1980:20)

The second concerns the attitude of the other functions in someone whose superior function is extraverted.

> When the mechanism of extraversion predominates . . . the most highly differentiated function has a constantly extraverted application, while the inferior functions are found in the service of introversion.
>
> (Jung 1921/1971:486, quoted in Myers 1980:20)

What I find most striking in these passages is Jung's assumption that only one function, the superior, is likely to be particularly differentiated. Therefore, the other functions all take on the unconscious character of the inferior function, and operate in a crudely compensatory way. That actually describes the undifferentiated way my unconscious compensated me before I went into analysis, but it was not particularly helpful to understanding the ways my function types sorted themselves out, as to attitude, once they started to become differentiated in analysis.

One way I was experiencing this differentiation was that I was becoming more particular, and not less, when I practiced psychotherapy, so that I often suffered if a person in my practice had introverted feeling that I could not take care of with my extraverted feeling. I devoted a lot of attention to this problem, and was particularly helped by a passage in von Franz's essay on the inferior function in *Lectures on Jung's Typology* (von Franz and Hillman 1971). She had been asked the question, "Does an introverted feeling type experience introverted thinking, or is it always extraverted thinking?" She replied:

> If you are an introverted feeling type, you *can* also think introvertedly. You can naturally have all the functions all ways, but it won't be such a great problem, and there will not be much intensity of life in it. Jung has said that the hardest thing to understand is not your *opposite* type – if you have introverted feeling it *is* very difficult to understand an extraverted thinking type – but it is even worse to understand [extraverted feeling,] the same functional type with the other attitude! There one feels that one doesn't know how the wheels go round in that person's head, one cannot feel one's way into it. Such people remain to a great extent a puzzle and are very difficult to understand spontaneously. Here the theory

of types is tremendously important practically, for it is the only thing which can prevent one from completely misunderstanding certain people.

(von Franz and Hillman 1971:52)

I addressed the subject of type incompatibility in my first full-length essay on the role types play in transference, countertransference, and the therapeutic interaction (Beebe 1984). There I recommended that analysts try to determine for each of a client's four functions whether that function is being used in an introverted or an extraverted way. I also suggested that the analyst should make an effort to figure out if he or she is deploying that function with the same, or with an opposite, attitude with respect to introversion and extraversion. It is on this basis, rather than whether one person in the therapeutic dyad has feeling as the superior function and the other thinking, or has an extraverted superior function when the other has an introverted superior function, that I established type compatibility, meaning whether there would be easy empathic understanding between the partners or whether there would be frequent clashes.

In that same essay, I looked at the other potential basis of incompatibility Jung discusses, and that Isabel Briggs Myers explores at great length in her book. That, for Jung, is whether the person's superior function is rational (his term for the evaluative functions, thinking and feeling) or irrational (his term for the perceptive functions, sensation and intuition). Because she was working out a test of personality that focused on easily identifiable behaviors in the outer world, Myers felt that she had to get at the difference between rational and irrational modes of consciousness by looking at the individual's leading *extraverted* function, whether superior or auxiliary. On the Myers-Briggs Type Indicator (MBTI), this extraverted function is therefore given a letter code, J or P, to indicate whether it is a judging function (her way of referring to Jung's rational functions) or a perceiving function (her way of identifying Jung's irrational functions).

For me, Jung's approach is the more psychological. When assessing type compatibility between people, I prefer to look at each individual's vertical axis, or spine of consciousness, which connects the superior and inferior function, rather than privileging extraversion. Thus, I noted early on my incompatibility with an introverted feeling type companion (we were both "P"s according to the MBTI system, since his leading extraverted function was his auxiliary extraverted sensation). I found that our spines tended to cross: he often heard my perceptions for judgments, just as I mistook his judgments for perceptions, a source of many misunderstandings.

As the types became more real to me, I became ever more aware of the roles they were playing within my psyche. Following Jung (1925/1989:56–57; 1963:179ff. and 173ff.), I associated the strong, effective superior function with the archetype of the hero. From my dream about the father and son I added the innovation that the auxiliary behaves like a parent, whether helpful or critical, the tertiary like a child, either divine or wounded, and thus in the language of Jungian psychology a *puer aeternus* or *puella aeterna.*

Puer aeternus means "eternal boy," or as one of my patients called it, "endless boy." The term was taken by Jung from Ovid's knowing salutation to the child god Iacchus, who with his "unconsumed youth," figured in the Eleusinian mysteries of renewal: *tibi enim inconsumpta iuventa est, tu puer aeternus, tu formosissimus alto conspiceris caelo; tibi, cum sine cornibus adstas* (Metamorphoses, Book IV, lines 18–29 as found at http://www.sacred-texts.com/cla/ovid/meta/metal03.htm), the last part of which has been rendered by Rolfe Humphries (Ovid 1955) as "Behold *puer aeternus* with his angel seeming face, But oh, those invisible horns!" This archetypal description of a personality style has been applied to a problem in adult development, that of the charming, promising, but ultimately unreliable character of certain eternally youthful and often very seductive men and women. Von Franz (1970) and Henderson (1967), focusing on its role in masculine development, relate the excessive reliance on this archetype in daily interactions with others to the narcissistic mother complex of the immature man. But Hillman (1989) believes that the concept most generally "refers to that archetypal dominant which personifies or is in special relation with the transcendent spiritual powers of the collective unconscious" and is thus an aspect of the creativity in all of us (1989:227). I am using this term, in tandem with *puella aeterna,* Latin for "eternal girl," to refer to the eternal youth in all of us, the brilliant but volatile side of ourselves that is by turns the seemingly immortal Prince or Princess and the helplessly vulnerable, wounded boy or girl.

There was also an analytical tradition, passed onto me by Bill Alex, who had been in the first training class at the C.G. Jung Institute in Zurich, that the anima or animus "carries the inferior function." In her writings, von Franz has associated the inferior function with the anima/animus, but somewhat less specifically than I would assert. She states, "The inferior function is the door through which all the figures of the unconscious come into consciousness. Our conscious realm is like a room with four doors, and it is the fourth door by which the Shadow, the Animus or the Anima, and the personification of the Self come in." She later adds that "when one becomes somewhat conscious of the shadow, the inferior function will give the animus or the anima figure a special quality" so that, if personified by a human being, the anima or animus will "very often appear as a person of the opposite function" (von Franz and Hillman 1971:55–56).

In my own work on myself and with patients, I most often found the inferior function, with its uncanny emotionality, to have the character of the anima or animus,[6] the "other" within us, which becomes profoundly upset when its ideals are not met and nearly ecstatic when they are. It had been symbolized that way by my dreams of the Chinese laundress. I could then diagram my four functions again, showing the archetypes associated with them as I had encountered them.

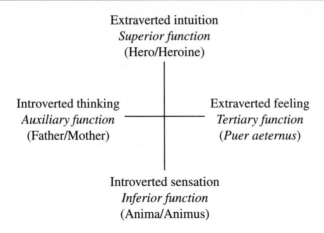

Extraverted intuition
Superior function
(Hero/Heroine)

Introverted thinking   Extraverted feeling
Auxiliary function   *Tertiary function*
(Father/Mother)   (*Puer aeternus*)

Introverted sensation
Inferior function
(Anima/Animus)

My shift into Latin in naming the archetypes associated with the tertiary and inferior functions is deliberate. These functions, though still part of one's complement of ego-syntonic consciousnesses, are more archaic than the superior and auxiliary and present themselves in more classically "arche-typal" ways, having a god-like entitled quality to them, whereas the superior and auxiliary functions are more adapted to this time and place and more considerate of the perspectives of one's contemporaries.

This archetypal analysis of the first four functions provided the basis for the model of type I was able to present at the Chiron Conference for Jungian psychotherapists held at Ghost Ranch in Abiquiu, New Mexico in 1983, and to write up in my 1984 essay. It has proved very helpful both to me and to others in clarifying how a well-differentiated consciousness might arrange itself in the course of individuation. We might note several features of this model.

1   The model asserts, with Jung and subsequent Jungians, that if the superior function is irrational the auxiliary will be rational, and vice versa.
2   It agrees with Myers and the MBTI counselors that if the superior func-tion is introverted the auxiliary will be extraverted and vice versa.
3   The model specifies the tertiary function as opposite in attitude to the auxiliary just as the inferior is opposite in attitude to the superior.
4   Following the Jungian tradition, the model maintains that if the superior function is rational, the inferior will likewise be rational; if the superior function is irrational, the inferior function will also be irrational.
5   The tertiary function is represented as matching the auxiliary with respect to rationality or irrationality.
6   The model therefore defines two axes of consciousness, one between the superior and inferior functions (spine), the other between the auxiliary and tertiary functions (arms). If the spine is rational, the arms will be irrational and vice versa.

(See Figure 4.1.)

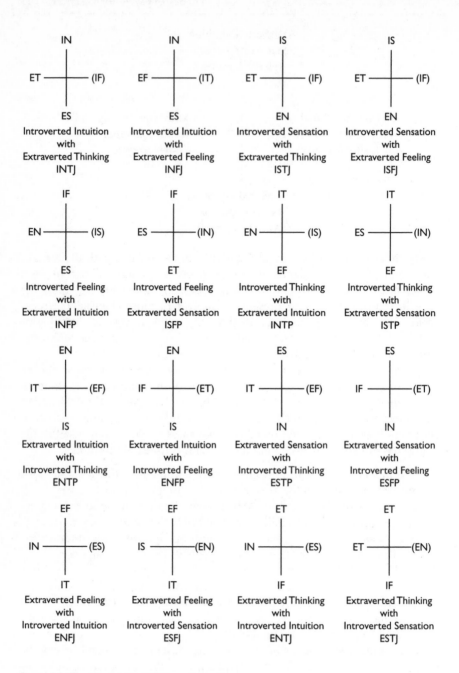

Figure 4.1 The 16 possible MBTI configurations.

I believe that this model makes sense of the way the types differentiate in someone who is showing what Myers calls "good type development" and Jung would call individuating according to the law of his or her own being. It does not account for the many falsifications of type (Benziger 1995) that involve substituting other functions out of a need to satisfy or defend against the type demands of an environment that is not facilitative of individuation.

Types of the shadow

At the 1983 conference were two analysts-in-training – Paul Watsky and Laura McGrew – whose comments proved very helpful to the growth of my understanding of type over the next decade. Watsky pointed out that Jung lists eight functions of consciousness in *Psychological Types*. If someone succeeds in differentiating four of those functions to achieve the good type development of which Isabel Briggs Myers had spoken, Watsky said, it's as if the north 40 of their psychological field has been hoed; the person still needs to cultivate the other four functions: the south 40. These four were presumably in shadow. Laura McGrew came back to Ghost Ranch the next year with a sketch of a diagram indicating what the archetypes associated with the four functions in shadow might be. For the shadow of the mother, she had put "witch."

"Witch" is a deeply problematic term, which, as early as L. Frank Baum's *The Wonderful Wizard of Oz* (1900), was deconstructed for the better as referring to a woman in command of magic that was as potentially good as it was bad, and for a long time I preferred to use the term "negative mother" to convey the quality of the shaming, blaming, limit-setting female parent. But I have decided that *witch* with its freight of negative connotations gets at the specific characteristic of this position of shadow in women (and some men). Like all the shadow archetypes, the witch "fights dirty" to defend the personality. She uses her capacity to cast spells that immobilize in an underhanded way, but this is a survival consciousness that resides in the shadow that can be used to stop others in their tracks when they are threatening the personality or its values. In terms of gender politics, the witch uses her feminine authority in a way that can be extremely paralyzing to the anima of a man. In a man's psyche, the shadow side of the good father would be the *senex*, which exerts the same sinister limit-setting control when he "pulls rank," and which can similarly paralyze a woman's animus.

As I recall, Laura McGrew and I agreed that the shadow of the *puer aeternus* carrying the tertiary function had to be the trickster. Neither she nor I was satisfied with designations for the shadow side of the hero and the shadow side of the anima/animus. It was clear that the shadow archetype carries the same function of consciousness as its ego-syntonic counterpart, but with the opposite attitude with respect to extraversion and introversion. Here, then, was my shadow, in terms of the types of consciousness involved:

Introverted intuition
Shadow of my superior function

Extraverted thinking
Shadow of my auxiliary

Introverted feeling
Shadow of my tertiary

Extraverted sensation
Shadow of my inferior function

I set it as my task to learn how this shadow was actually expressed in my dreams and my outer behavior. In this way, I was able to do some of the work Paul Watsky suggested still needed to be done by someone who laid a claim to "good type development," and I was able to answer Laura McGrew's question empirically, by noting the characteristics of dream figures who seemed to display the negative of my preferred typology. This work occupied me for another seven years, so that it was not until 1990 that I had finally come up with the following model to describe my shadow in terms of a complement of consciousnesses that were more negative and destructive in their archetypal functioning than the consciousnesses I had identified as mine thus far in the course of my analysis:

Introverted intuition
Shadow of superior function
(Opposing personality)

Extraverted thinking
Shadow of auxiliary function
(Senex/Witch)

Introverted feeling
Shadow of tertiary function
(Trickster)

Extraverted sensation
Shadow of inferior function
(Demonic personality)

There is much in the Jungian literature already about senex[7] and witch and trickster, just as there is much about father and mother and *puer aeternus*. I introduced the archetypal roles I describe here as "opposing personality" and "demonic personality," and this introduction can be found in the second revised edition of Murray Stein's *Jungian Analysis* (1995), in the chapter

I wrote with Donald Sandner, "Psychopathology and analysis," in a section entitled "The role of psychological type in possession."

The most unexpected discovery was the archetype I call the opposing personality, which is characterized by behaviors that may be described in the language of character pathology: oppositional, paranoid, passive-aggressive, and avoidant. This is a shadow that is very hard to see in oneself (it seems to fall in the blind spot of the superior function) and very easy to project onto another person, especially a person of the opposite sex. The archetype of the opposing personality often appears in dreams as a contrasexual figure, but, unlike the anima, the opposing personality is antagonistic to the ego rather than helpful in connecting it to the needs of the Self. Classical Jungians have sometimes identified this figure that opposes, criticizes, and seduces the ego as the "negative" animus or anima, but this intuitive shorthand ignores the real type difference between the opposing personality and the anima or animus. In adopting the rather clinical sounding term, "opposing personality," rather than a name such as "the Adversary" or "the Antagonist" that has a more dignified and archetypal connotation, I have tried to convey the unconscious and undeclared quality with which this archetype usually operates. It is often more like a symptom than like a dashing enemy on a black horse.

In associating to a dream figure, it is important to try to establish the figure's psychological type, which is often surprisingly easy to determine. At the Ghost Ranch conference, I called attention to Jung's foreword to the Argentine edition of *Psychological Types* (1936/1971:xiv) in which he had emphasized that the theory of psychological types should be used not as a way of classifying people but for "sorting out the empirical material" that comes up in the course of a therapeutic analysis. The method of analysis that results has the advantage of enabling a patient to see where a particular complex lives in the psyche.

The opposing personality lived in me as a tendency to become detached and avoidant in a schizoid way in relation to certain kinds of situations that I didn't immediately know how to handle. This came up in my practice as a tendency to "tune out" in the face of affects I didn't know how to deal with. It was as if my introverted intuition was working in this shadowy way to find some kind of image that would make sense of the emotion for me, but mostly my patients experienced me at such moments as leaving them. As I meditated on that behavior, I realized it was a defense of the self I had often used in my life – to the extent that some of my friends in college had complained, after a summer of putting up with my withdrawn inattentiveness, that I had become more "John-ish" than ever. Until I decided, however, to look hard at the shadow side of my superior function, an extraverted intuition that many had experienced as extraordinarily "present" to them, I never took such complaints seriously. Instead, as is so often the case with a shadow function, I tended to project the difficulty within me onto other people whose avoidant traits were particularly pronounced. In my practice, I seemed to keep encountering a certain kind of introverted intuitive woman who I felt would not "come clean" with her intuitions, so that I would experience her as being stubbornly resistant to the therapy. Only gradually did I come to recognize that the oppositional woman was even more characteristic of a side of myself, and that to some extent I had been projectively identifying her onto introverted intuitive clients who might have certain "hooks" to catch the projection.

The trickster was the one aspect of my shadow that I had worked on fairly early on in my analysis. However, I had not thought of my trickster as having a type. It had, however, often been projected onto difficult male or female analysands whose intense subjectivity seemed constantly to undercut my efforts to help them with psychological understanding. These were analysands who might have fit the diagnostic criteria for borderline personality disorder, which I have elsewhere discussed as a "primary ambivalence toward the Self" (Beebe 1988), but the issue that kept coming up for me was the degree to which my feeling was no match for the patient's. In the service of being a good doctor, I was trying to use extraverted feeling in a sincere, compassionate way that begged the hostility the patients were directing toward me. As one man put it to me, "Western medicine, Eastern too if you consider Buddhism, is based on compassion. When people are compassionate toward me, I become this bitch."

It was in this feeling context that I came more personally to understand the difference between extraversion and introversion. I had concentrated on developing my extraverted feeling, since I recognized that as a relatively weak function in myself, and since this consciousness was carried in me by the archetype of the *puer aeternus*, I could leap to unusual heights of empathic compassion, privileging the other person's feeling above my own. I would, however, plunge to the depths of despair when the person I was dealing with abandoned my feeling for their own and did not show any gratitude for the compassion I was dispensing. Gradually, I learned that this was a normal difference between extraversion and introversion. In meeting a situation that involves another person, extraversion moves to create a shared experience, by reaching out to "merge" in some way with the other person (Shapiro and Alexander 1975), whereas introversion steps back from the experience to see if it "matches" an archetype within that carries an *a priori* understanding of what an experience like this is supposed to consist of. As I learned to honor my introverted feeling, which in the manner of a trickster did not feel bound by medical and Christian cultural expectations, I learned to make statements like "I'm not sure I can work with you if it's going to be this negative." I had realized that the bullying I had been receiving from my "borderline" patients did not accord with my introverted feeling sense of what a mutually respectful medical treatment ought to be like, and once I had grasped the validity of this perspective, I was able to assert it in a way which, though it was a manipulation of the transference, enabled my difficult patients and me to work together in an atmosphere of more regard, if not for each other, which would be extraverted feeling, at least for the value of what we were trying to accomplish. I found my patients could accept this, even though they still had much ambivalence, envy, and negativity to work through in their actual experience of me as a person.

The senex extraverted thinking was particularly hard to see as a part of myself. I had thoroughly projected this onto my father, who did affect a stentorian, nineteenth-century personality that was aloof and, to my ear, somewhat pompous. I always imagined myself to be more laid-back. But there was a side of me, too, that could be quite arrogant and dogmatic in the way it delivered its opinions and interpretations. This was my senex extraverted thinking.

In coming to terms with my demonic extraverted sensation, I felt that I was encountering the problem of evil in myself. My colleague Herbert Wiesenfeld, an introverted feeling type whose anima grappled with ideas, finally decided that "evil" in Jungian psychology refers to the quality of being undermined. The demonic personality, then, is that part of ourselves that operates in the shadow to undermine others and ourselves. Certainly in my own case that is extraverted sensation. My body language is often the opposite of what I mean to convey. My relation to physical geography is such that, when trying to find my way along an unfamiliar route, the opposite of where I think I should be going is almost always the correct way. But most importantly, I sometimes misjudge in therapy the relative distance from consciousness of an unconscious complex and assume, with my optimistic extraverted intuition, that the client is ready to benefit from openly discussing something that the client is, in fact, not ready to look at yet. This miscalculation can lead to interventions that shock the client and, for a time, undermine the therapy. Occasionally, such interventions can also enliven a therapy that has become too polite, reminding us that, just as Lucifer is the light-bringer, the demon is sometimes a daimon.

As I surveyed my shadow, I could see that it too carried "consciousness," but consciousness used in antagonistic, paradoxical, depreciating, and destructive ways. The archetypal complexes of the shadow could sometimes move a stuck situation, but they could also be quite hurtful to others and myself. Specifying these defensive consciousnesses was, however, helpful in getting a handle on them and developing a measure of choice in how I deployed them.

By this point, I was convinced I had been able to locate all eight functions of consciousness in myself and to see how the archetypes that were carrying them operated to structure my dealings with others. What I then realized would be necessary was a validation of this eight-function/eight-archetype model as generally applicable. Although I experimented with it often in clinical situations, seeing the figures in my patient's dreams as so many personifications of typological part-personalities, which could not only be typed but matched to an archetype within the scheme I had developed, I realized I would need a more generally available arena where the types and archetypes could be readily visualized by others. This came through movies, at least those that could be recognized as personal expressions of an auteur director putting out his or her own complexes for an audience to see. I found that my model worked particularly well as a way to analyze films (by then already a topic of intense cultural scrutiny) and I have recorded the results of this kind of analysis in numerous lectures and in two essays that analyze *The Wizard of Oz* and Woody Allen's *Husbands and Wives* (Beebe 2000, 2002).

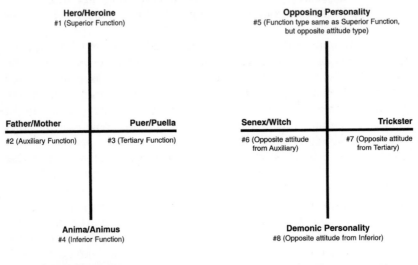

Figure 4.2 Archetypal complexes carrying the eight functions.

The eight-function model I have developed (see Figure 4.2), as an "addition and extension" to Jung's analytical psychology (Henderson 1991), asks that we re-examine some of the earlier findings that our field made about type using a four-function model. For instance, Hillman's description of "inferior feeling," cited earlier in this chapter, might better be understood as a description of demonic introverted feeling in an introverted thinking type. My dream about the "father" brandishing a butcher knife chasing his "son" around the dining room table, though it opened me up to the idea of the "father" and "*puer*" as referring to the more and less developed types on the axis of my auxiliary and tertiary functions, is actually such a shadowy situation, with an obvious reference to Saturn's sickle, that it is more likely a depiction of senex vs trickster. (At the time of the dream, I had not developed my introverted feeling enough to notice that the young man my unconscious selected to serve as the "son" was actually a very provocative person, who used his introverted feeling in a manipulative way, thus occasioning the senex response in the unconscious.) I now see my early, somewhat faulty, interpretation of the dream as a "creative misreading" – one of those helpful misunderstandings which not infrequently serve to advance our thinking (Bloom 1985).

Let us close with a look back at the inferior function and, implicitly, its demonic shadow, in the following passage from von Franz:

> The little open door of each individual's inferior function is what con-
> tributes to the sum of collective evil in the world. You could observe
> that very easily in Germany when the devil slowly took over the situ-
> ation in the Nazi movement. Every German I knew at that time who fell
> for Nazism did so on account of his inferior function. The feeling type
> got caught by the stupid arguments of the party doctrine; the intuitive
> type got caught by his dependence on money – he could not give up his
> job and did not see how he could deal with the money problem, so he
> had to stay in it despite the fact that he did not agree, and so on. The
> inferior function was in each personal realm the door where some of
> this collective evil could accumulate. Or you could say that each one
> who had not worked on his inferior function contributed to this general
> disaster – in a small way – but the sum of millions of inferior functions
> constitutes an enormous devil! Propaganda against the Jews was very
> cleverly made up in that respect. For example, the Jews were insulted as
> being destructive intellectuals, which completely convinced all the feel-
> ing types – a projection of inferior thinking. Or they were accused of
> being reckless moneymakers; that completely convinced the intuitive, for
> they were his inferior sensation, and now one knew where the devil was.
> The propaganda used the ordinary suspicions that people had against
> others on account of their inferior function. So you can say that behind
> each individual the fourth function is not just a little kind of deficiency:
> the sum of these is really responsible for a tremendous amount of
> trouble.
>
> (von Franz in von Franz and Hillman 1971:66–67)

What she is describing here is a relation between the inferior function and a demonic function that tests the integrity of the inferior function. To the degree that the inferior function has not been taken up as a problem by the individual in the course of the development of his consciousness, it is no match for the demonic aspect of the unconscious, rather like the Chinese laundress in my dream who has no power to stop her husband from spending all his money drinking and gambling. At the time I had that dream, I felt the husband represented my own superior function of extraverted intuition; now I would say he represents a much more shadowy aspect of me, my extraverted sensation (which, like the husband in the dream, is usually not even seen). At the time I had the dream, I felt it was necessary for him to take better care of her, i.e. that I should take better care of my anima. But a healthier anima would also have the integrity to stand up to him, bringing her integrity to bear upon his problem of character (Beebe 1998).

As the notion of good type development moves, both in MBTI counseling and in Jungian analysis, toward a "whole type" eight-function model,[8] in which each of Jung's eight types of consciousness is represented within a picture of the person's consciousness that includes both ego-syntonic functions and functions in shadow, the ethical aspects of this development will become ever more evident. Gradually, perhaps, consciousness will realize its potential to become conscience.

Notes

1   This passage from *The Correspondence of Sigmund Freud and Ernest Jones 1908–1939* (ed. Paskauskas) is cited by Jung's faultfinding biographer Frank McLynn (1996:267), who devotes much of his chapter on *Psychological Types* to the objections that have been raised to Jung's contribution within depth psychology.
2   For a comparison of Gardner's multiple intelligences and Jung's functions of consciousness, see Keith Thompson's (1985) review of Howard Gardner's *Frames of Mind: The Theory of Multiple Intelligences* (1983). Thompson found strong analogies between Gardner's seven "intelligences" and seven of Jung's eight "function types of consciousness" (the Jungian function for which he could not find an analogue in Gardner's system was introverted intuition). This article is cited in Gardner (1999).
3   For a discussion of Damasio's work in relation to analytical psychology, see Tresan (1996).
4   Anima is the Latin word for soul, which is defined by Jung in *Psychological Types* as referring to "a definitely demarcated function complex that is best characterized as a 'personality' " (1921/1971:588). For Jung, anima as a feminine noun refers to the contrasexual character of the inner, subjective attitude in a man, which is often symbolized in dreams by a feminine figure and in the man's outer behavior by the kind of soulful opinionatedness about woman's obligations to men that we now recognize as sexist.
5   I have addressed the development of thinking about type in both the Jungian and the MBTI movements in my chapter in the *Handbook of Jungian Psychology* (Beebe 2004).
6   Animus, which is Latin for mind or spirit, is often used differently in Jungian psychology from its standard English dictionary meaning as "hostile opinion," to represent the spirit of a woman that helps her to focus her self-experience and express it in the world. Despite excellent discussions of the animus and its development by Emma Jung (1957/1985) and Ann Ulanov (1971), there is still a tendency even among analytical psychologists to depreciate the woman's sometimes-severe spirit as a form of competitiveness and spite, confounding it with the "opposing personality" that I will discuss later in this chapter.
7   "*Senex* is the Latin word for 'old man.' We find it still contained within our words *senescence, senile,* and *senator* … As natural, cultural and psychic processes mature, gain order, consolidate and wither, we witness the specific formative effects of the senex … Longings for superior knowledge, imperturbability, magnanimity

express senex feelings as does intolerance for that which crosses one's systems and habits . . . The temperament of the senex is cold, which can also be expressed as distance" (Hillman 1989:208).

8   For the development of an eight-function model within the wider type community represented by the Association for Psychological Type, an organization with more than 4000 members that consists for the most part of type counselors using the MBTI in educational and work settings, see Thompson (1996), Geldart (1998) Myers and Kirby (2000), Clark (2000), Haas *et al.* (2001), and Beebe (2004).

References

Baum, L.F. (1900) *The Wonderful Wizard of Oz*, Chicago: George M. Hill Co.

Beebe, J. (1984) "Psychological types in transference, countertransference, and the therapeutic interaction", in M. Stein and N.S. Salant (eds), *Transference/ Countertransference*, Wilmette, IL: Chiron Publications.

—— (1988) "Primary ambivalence toward the Self", in M. Stein and N.S. Salant (eds), *The Borderline Personality in Analysis*, Wilmette, IL: Chiron Publications.

—— (1992) *Integrity in Depth*, College Station, TX: Texas A&M University Press.

—— (1998) "Toward a Jungian analysis of character", in A. Casement (ed.), *The Post-Jungians Today: Key Papers in Contemporary Analytical Psychology*, London and New York: Routledge, pp. 53–66.

—— (2000) "*The Wizard of Oz*: a vision of development in the American political psyche", in T. Singer, *The Vision Thing*, London: Routledge, pp. 62–83.

—— (2002) "An archetypal model of the self in dialogue", *Theory and Psychology*, **12**(2), pp. 267–280.

—— (2004) "Psychological types", in R.K. Papadopoulos (ed.), *The Handbook of Jungian Psychology: Theory, Practice and Applications*, Hove: Brunner-Routledge.

Benziger, K. (1995) *Falsification of Type*, Dillon, CO: KBA.

Binet, A. (1903) *L'Etude expérimental de l'intelligence*, Paris: Schleicher.

Bloom, H. (1985) *A Map of Misreading*, New York: Oxford University Press (paper).

Brachfeld, O. (1954) "Gelenkte tagträume als hilfsmittel der psychotherapie", *Zeitschrift für Psychotherapie*, **IV**, 79–93.

Clark, P. (2000) "Work and the eight function model", *Bulletin of Psychological Type*, **23**(7).

Corsini, R.J. (2002) *The Dictionary of Psychology*, Hove: Brunner-Routledge.

Damasio, A. (1995) *Descartes' Error: Emotion, Reason and the Human Brain*, New York: Pan Macmillan.

Dennett, D.C. (1991) *Consciousness Explained*, New York: Little Brown & Company.

Edinger, E.F. (1984) *The Creation of Consciousness*, Toronto: Inner City.

Ellenberger, H. (1970) *The Discovery of the Unconscious*, New York: Basic Books.

Gardner, H. (1983) *Frames of Mind: The Theory of Multiple Intelligences*, New York: Basic Books.

—— (1999) *Intelligence Reframed: Multiple Intelligences for the 21st Century*, New York: Basic Books.

Geldart, W. (1998) "Katharine Downing Myers and whole MBTI type – an inter-view", *The Enneagram and the MBTI: An Electronic Journal*, http://tap3x.net/ EMBTI/journal.html (February 1998).

Haas, L., McAlpine, R., and Hartzler, M. (2001) *Journey of Understanding: MBTI©*

Interpretation Using the Eight Jungian Functions, Palo Alto, CA: Consulting Psychologists Press.

Henderson, J. (1967) *Thresholds of Initiation*, Middletown, CT: Wesleyan University Press.

—— (1991) "C.G. Jung's psychology: additions and extensions", *Journal of Analytical Psychology*, **36**(4), 429–442.

Hill, G. (1998) "Men, the anima, and the feminine", *San Francisco Jung Institute Library Journal*, **17**(3), 49–61.

Hillman, J. (1989) *A Blue Fire* (T. Moore, ed.), New York: Harper Perennial.

Humphrey, N. (1992) *A History of the Mind: Evolution and the Birth of Consciousness*, New York: Simon and Schuster.

James, W. (1904) "Does 'consciousness' exist?", *Journal of Philosophy, Psychology, and Scientific Methods*, **1**, 477–491.

Jung, C.G. (1921/1971) *Psychological Types* (trans. H.G. Baynes), New York: Harcourt & Brace.

—— (1925/1989) *Analytical Psychology: Notes of the Seminar Given in 1925*, W. McGuire (ed.), Princeton, NJ: Princeton University Press.

—— (1934/1976) *The Visions Seminars*, Vol. 2, New York: Spring Publications.

—— (1936/1971) Foreword to the Argentine edition of *Psychological Types*, CW 6, pp. xiv–xv.

—— (1948/1960) "General aspects of dream psychology", CW 8, Princeton, NJ: Princeton University Press.

—— (1957/1977) "The Houston films", In W. McGuire and R.F.C. Hull (eds), *C.G. Jung Speaking*, Princeton, NJ: Princeton University Press, pp. 276–352.

—— (1958/1970) "Fragments from a talk with students" (recorded by Marian Bayes), *Spring*, 177–181.

—— (1963) *Memories, Dreams, Reflections*, New York: Pantheon.

—— (1972) "On psychological understanding", CW 3.

Jung, E. (1957/1985) *Animus and Anima*, H. Nagel and C.F. Baynes (trans.), Thompson, CT: Spring Publications.

Kohut, H. (1959/1978) "Introspection, empathy, and psychoanalysis: an examination of the relationship between mode of observation and theory", in P.H. Ornstein (ed.), *The Search for the Self*, Vol. 1, New York: International Universities Press, pp. 205–232.

McLynn, F. (1996) *Carl Gustav Jung: A Biography*, New York: St Martins.

Murphy, E. (1992) *The Developing Child*, Palo Alto, CA: Davies Black Publishing Co.

Myers, I.B. (with Myers, P.B.) (1980) *Gifts Differing: Understanding Personality Type*, Palo Alto, CA: Consulting Psychologists Press.

Myers, K. and Kirby, L. (2000) *Introduction to Type Dynamics and Development*, Palo Alto, CA: Consulting Psychologists Press.

Neumann, E. (1954) *The Origins and History of Consciousness*, Princeton, NJ: Princeton University Press.

Ovid (1955) *Metamorphoses*, R. Humphries (trans.), Bloomington, IN: Indiana University Press.

Paskauskas, A. (1993) *The Correspondence of Sigmund Freud and Ernest Jones 1908–1939*, Cambridge, MA: Harvard University Press.

Rogers, C. and Truax, C.B. (1967) "The therapeutic condition's antecedent to change:

a theoretical view", in C. Rogers (ed.), *The Therapeutic Relationship and Its Impact*, Madison, WI: University of Wisconsin Press, pp. 97–108.

Sandner, D. and Beebe, J. (1995) "Psychopathology and analysis", in M. Stein (ed.) *Jungian Analysis*, LaSalle, IL: Open Court.

Shapiro, K.J. and Alexander, I.E. (1975) *The Experience of Introversion: An Integration of Phenomenological, Empirical, and Jungian approaches*, Durham, NC: Duke University Press.

Thompson, H.L. (1996) *Jung's Function-Attitudes Explained*, Watkinsville, GA: Wormhole Publishing.

Thompson, K. (1985) "Cognitive and analytical psychology", *The San Francisco Jung Institute Library Journal*, **5**(4), 40–64.

Tresan, D. (1996) "Jungian metapsychology and neurobiological theory", *Journal of Analytical Psychology*, **41**(3), 399–436.

Ulanov, A.B. (1971) *The Feminine in Jungian Psychology and in Christian Theology*, Evanston, IL: Northwestern University Press.

Von Franz, M.L. (1970) *Puer Aeternus*, New York: Spring Publications.

Von Franz, M.L. and Hillman, J. (1971) *Lectures on Jung's Typology*, Zurich: Spring Publications.

Wheelwright, J. (1982) "Psychological types", in *Saint George and the Dandelion*, San Francisco: C.G. Jung Institute of San Francisco.

Chapter 5

Analytic methods revisited

Joseph Cambray and Linda Carter

The methods for handling unconscious material in analysis which we will discuss in this chapter, specifically amplification, active imagination, and work with dream images, form a core of methods that Jung evolved after his separation and differentiation from Freud's psychoanalysis as practiced prior to 1914, i.e. before Freud's papers on technique. While Jung had considerable experience in working with transference and countertransference material, he generally did not focus on them in his writing, though he published a mature monograph devoted to the subject in 1946. Chapter 6 will take up contemporary views on transference and countertransference.

Jung's clinical practice as a psychiatrist began with his arrival at the Burghölzli hospital in December 1900. He was introduced to the patient-centered approach of his chief Eugen Bleuler in what can be seen as a fore-runner to the milieu model of inpatient treatment (see Graf-Nold 2001; Bair 2003). Psychological research also was performed by the medical staff often assisted by patients; Jung first became proficient and then highly creative in his use of the word-association experiment in this context (Jung 1981). This research served as the first experimental verification of Freud's hypothesis of a dynamic unconscious and was a link to his method of free-association which Jung used ambivalently if at all before abandoning it (Hoffer 2001). Jung preferred an image focused, directed approach, staying close to the phenomenology of psychological experience.

In the process of breaking with Freud, Jung struck out on his own in both his theoretical formulations and his clinical practices. His methods originating in this period are profoundly experiential and privilege the personality of the therapist. While refined by Jung as his investigations of the psyche matured, these methods remained grounded in the immediacy of the psychological material together with the clinician's use of the self. The first generation of Jung's followers tended to elaborate descriptively on his approach. However, as the larger analytic world came increasingly to understand and utilize countertransference as a source of information and communication, Jungian methods underwent some adaptive alterations by those followers who were interested in these approaches, especially members of the Society of

Analytical Psychology (SAP) in London and the Deutsche Gesellschaft für Analytische Psychologie (DGAP) in Germany.

In this chapter we will extend reconsideration of Jung's methods in the light of contemporary scientific findings. This is consonant with a broader reassessment of goals and methods occurring across most schools of psychodynamic therapy. While several seemingly disparate lines of research will be drawn upon, they all partake of a paradigm shift towards an emergentist model of the psyche and the world, a holistic approach requiring a multidisciplinary effort to capture a fuller description of reality. However, before seeking the horizon, we begin with the ground of Jung's approach.

An individuation model

In reflecting on methods, it is useful to start with the purpose for which they will be applied. From a teleological perspective, to which all the methods discussed in this chapter can be referenced, a uniquely defining, ultimate "goal" of Jungian analysis has been, from the publication of *Psychological Types* in 1921 on, to foster or facilitate the process of *individuation*. A richly nuanced, multifaceted concept, individuation cannot be captured in a single definition; however, some hints can be gained from basic statements by Jung and post-Jungians on the matter.

In the second of the *Two Essays on Analytical Psychology*, Jung devotes four chapters specifically to "individuation". He begins by stating that it:

> means becoming an "in-dividual," and, in so far as "individuality" embraces our innermost, last, and incomparable uniqueness, it also implies becoming one's own self. We could therefore translate individuation as "coming to selfhood" or "self-realization."
>
> (Jung 1928:para. 266)

A similar description of this concept, from Jung's essay "Conscious, unconscious, and individuation" (1939:para. 490), has already been noted in Chapter 3, and in a footnote (n. 2) to that statement Jung observed: "Modern physicists (Louis de Broglie, for instance) use instead of this [separate, indivisible unity or 'whole'], the concept of something 'discontinuous.' " Thus, the sense of wholeness and self-realization which is entering analytic thought here is not being directed towards an amorphous or fusional enmeshment in unconsciousness, nor the oceanic bliss about which Freud wrote ambivalently; rather it is one which values and celebrates the unique qualities that at the deepest levels define our individual beings. Jung was also careful here to identify inflationary dangers (narcissistic misuse), differentiating this process from individualism, and of the potential for psychological trauma if methods used to activate unconscious processes were applied prematurely.

The individuating self, in Jung's model of the psyche, is conceived as much more than a function of consciousness; it is "not only the centre, but also the whole circumference which embraces both conscious and unconscious; it is the centre of this totality, just as the ego is the centre of consciousness" (1944:para. 44). Samuels *et al.* have offered a concise way to understand this with regard to individuation: "ego is to integration (socially seen as adaptation) what the self is for individuation (self-experience and -realization) . . . the process of individuation is a circumambulation of the self as the centre of the personality which thereby becomes unified" (1986:76).

For Jung, analytic work approaching the undivided self is a multi-tiered process, requiring a modicum of successful adaptations to collective values before the individuation urge, which at times he even refers to as a drive (1980:para. 1198), can become fully operative. His notion long predates Margaret Mahler's formulation of the same name and is considerably broader in scope. While they both see the origins of individuation in the separation and differentiation from the mother (see e.g. Jung 1967a:para. 624, n. 15), Jung explores this process through the lifelong development of the personality. The actual articulation and application of the Jungian view of individuation throughout the lives of children and youths had to await the work of Michael Fordham and members of the SAP in the UK from the late 1940s on.

While an overt focus on the individuation process and with it an ongoing dialectic between conscious and unconscious comes to the fore "almost regularly during the later stages of analytical treatment" (Jung 1939:para. 489), it nevertheless forms the backdrop to any analytic approach characterized as Jungian. Analytic attention to the relationship between the individual and the collective socio-cultural world in which he or she is embedded creates a dialectic process starting with the value of adaptation in the formative stages of the mind and proceeds towards greater differentiation from collective norms with increasing psychological maturation. The value and dangers inherent in this approach have been discussed by various authors, notably Lambert in *Analysis, Repair and Individuation* (1981). Mario Jacoby in *Individuation & Narcissism* (1990) discusses the use of Jung's own life as a model for this process and wisely cautions against mimesis. For an exploration of contemporary long-term analyses that proceed into psychological terrains outside the vicissitudes of psychopathology, bringing attention to the *non-linear* evolution of consciousness and the spirit at personal and collective levels, see Tresan (2004).

The combination of a commitment to psychological holism (most actively engaged in well-differentiated individuals), together with the archetypal hypothesis that includes an understanding of the self as a supraordinate organizing principle of the personality, lends itself to a restatement of individuation in terms of the multidisciplinary field of complexity. At whatever level we choose to view psychological processes (intrapsychic, interpersonal, sociological, global), transformative engagements seeking to foster greater awareness can be usefully examined employing models that borrow from the findings derived from complexity theory, especially those from complex adaptive systems (CAS).[1] A key feature of such systems is their propensity for self-organization arising in response to environmental, competitive pressures, i.e. they exhibit emergent properties. The quality of complexity in CAS is driven by these external forces; it is not inherent in individual units. In the words of science writer Steven Johnson: "In these systems (CAS), agents residing on one scale start producing behavior that lies one scale above them ... the movement from low-level rules to higher-level sophistication is what we call emergence" (2001:18). This aspect of complexity can be discerned throughout the whole of nature, from the subatomic to the cosmological, and is postulated to be an essential organizing principle at every level including the emergence of the mind out of the neural interactions of the brain as well as human social behaviors such as traffic jams, stock market trends and the evolution of city neighborhoods (see Morowitz 2002).

To maximally retain Jung's system requires the self also to be reconsidered as an emergent property of the interactions of the components/complexes constituting the psyche. The viability of Jung's formulation of the self is an area of contention among analytical psychologists, especially in its innatist form; however, for the purposes of the present discussion, the concept will be retained. If the self is deleted, the argument for emergence can still hold for a model of the psyche composed of emergent archetypal processes, though it then is necessarily polycentric without an overarching unity. For a discussion of alternative theoretical viewpoints on archetypes more generally, see Chapter 2 and references therein.

If, as is being proposed in various chapters of this book, archetypal patterns are emergent properties of the psyche, then the interactive network of these patterns serves in effect to identify them as nodes or hubs (nodes with large numbers of connections) in what are termed scale-free or small world networks (Barabasi 2003; Strogatz 2003). Such networks are identifiable by their self-organizing properties and independence of scale.[2] Strogatz cites research demonstrating the tendency for clustering of word association in English sentences, which follow power laws, a hallmark of scale-free topology (Strogatz 2003:256–257; see Chapter 9, note 3 for an explanation of power laws). Jung's own word association experiments demonstrated clustering driven by feeling-tone complexes (1934); these studies were the linguistic precursor of his associative method of amplification (see below). The contemporary research on networks may bear out the wisdom operating in Jung's use of amplification to flesh out archetypal patterns – in effect using cultural associations to identify nodes of psychic structure in and through the context of their interconnectedness. Jung, in fact, remarks, "It is a well-nigh hopeless undertaking to tear a single archetype out of the living tissue of the psyche; but despite their interwovenness they do form units of meaning that can be apprehended intuitively" (1940:para. 302). At the largest scale of such organization within the human psychological system we expect to find the urge towards individuation as the driving dynamic force. Therefore, we can now turn toward the methodology for facilitating such a process as first articulated by Jung and see how the means of approach can be modified in light of our increased scientific knowledge of complex systems.

Emergent methods

Jung's well-known discomfort with analytic technique caused him to eschew systematic presentation of the details of his way of working clinically. Even his most important paper on the methodology of analytical psychology, "The transcendent function", written in 1916 was not published until 1957 and then only because of the activities of the students at the C.G. Jung Institute in Zurich. The seeming deprivation in how to work with analysands that Jung's reluctance produced may be partially forgiven when we realize that in this paper he was attempting what may be seen as a highly novel, even precarious form of practice (which he acknowledges in the paper). Not only are there risks in any attempt to codify engagement with unconscious processes, but also, as Jung was acutely aware, there is the danger of opening oneself to attack by making self-revelatory explorations. Read in tandem with his biography, especially Chapter 4, "Confrontation with the unconscious" (1963), it is apparent that Jung's methods are based on his first-hand experiences, which, like Freud's with his dream book, are derived from self-healing in what Ellenberger termed a "creative illness." Jung's willingness to only gradually make these investigations more widely known also reflects a profoundly intuitive sensitivity that could not be fully delineated, in part due to evolving limitations of scientific knowledge through the course of his long life.

Educated at the end of the nineteenth century in the German-speaking world, Jung, as a young man, was among the group of scientists who were intent on re-imagining the disciplines of science of their times from the mechanistic positivism then in ascendancy, to a "holistic," more "soulful" viewpoint that could be grounded in Kant's writing (see Harrington 1996). In their attempts to bridge divisions between the physical, biological and human sciences, the models available at that time were insufficient; the ideas remained intuitions. It was not until the development of dynamic systems theory and the advent of high-speed computers with the ability to arrive at testable solutions to previously insoluble non-linear problems through simulations, together with the groundbreaking work of scientists, such as Nobel laureate Ilya Prigogine on the non-equilibrium thermodynamics of dissipative structures, that real headway in the search for a holistic paradigm could be subjected to verification. This was not realizable until nearly two decades after Jung's death. Nevertheless, his attempts at a psychotherapeutic approach which would attend to the personality as a whole, at the heart of his methodology, prove to be congruent in the main with the findings from modern complexity theory.

Jung began his essay on the transcendent function by noting his derivation of the concept from the analogy with the mathematical function of the same name (what we now tend to refer to as "complex numbers"[3]). He continues, "[t]he psychological 'transcendent function' arises from the union of conscious and unconscious contents" (1916/1957:para. 131). The radical nature of this formulation in 1916 resides in its sweeping synthetic approach. It is not reducible to making the unconscious conscious but is a search for the means of engaging with unconscious processes that allow ongoing mutual influence (conscious and unconscious upon one another). Jung recognizes that the transformative potential in such an encounter can only emerge out of the interaction through the creation of "a living, third thing . . . a living birth that leads to *a new level of being*, a new situation" (Jung 1916/1957:para. 189, emphasis added). This new level of being arising out of the interaction of components operating at a lower (less complete) level is precisely an emergent quality of the psyche (conscious + unconscious). Thus the holistic methodology Jung is seeking can now be more fully appreciated from a CAS perspective. The methods derived from this approach would be intended to facilitate emergence of new psychological realities capable of reconfiguring the underlying personality. Therefore, these methods need to be congruent with such transformations, partaking of the emergent third as "something more than" the approaches of classical psychoanalysis, to which Jung was exposed, could yield.

As a constructive form of treatment, the dialectic between conscious and unconscious processes can be mediated by the analyst through encounters with what Jung identified as "symbols." Symbols are "taken to mean the best possible expression for a complex fact not yet clearly apprehended by consciousness" (Jung 1916/1957:para. 148). They arise as the synthetic products from encounters with affectively charged states of mind, saturated with activated unconscious material. In a CAS formulation, they are the psychological instantiation of the emergent "third" of the interactive field (whether intrapsychic or interpersonal) in those moments when the field is poised at the edge of chaos and order, the locus for the origins of life itself (see Chapter 9). The ephemeral quality of these forms, which Jung also termed "living symbols," is vulnerable to either chaotic dissolutions in excess activations of unconscious processes or rigidification in over-intellectualized understandings. The approach used to enter and engage symbolic reality must therefore seek to stay near the creative edge. For Jung this translated into a needed tension between aesthetics and meaning:

> we could say that aesthetic formulation needs understanding of meaning, and understanding needs aesthetic formulation. The two supplement each other to form the transcendent function.
>
> (Jung 1916/1957:para. 177)

This dialectic forms the key to the actual methods suggested by Jung; they must be artful and intelligent, linking the sensual with the mental, embracing feeling and cognition, or psyche and soma including affective states.

The recommended methods involve allowing an unconscious process to gain expression in consciousness, usually through an initial non-judgmental receptivity to a mood, fantasy, parapraxis, dream or similar phenomenon. Consciousness is deliberately relaxed into the preconscious dimensions of the sensory modalities operative (Jung gives examples of visual imagery, internal dialogue, kinesthetic movement including dance, sculpture, painting and automatic writing). Only after the expression has taken form and been developed into an embodied psychological reality is a reflective or hermeneutical understanding employed. While the forms of these activities most obviously derived from the arts were identified as forms of "active imagination" by Jung and were primarily aimed at engaging and metabolizing fantasy productions, the methods can be used with various manifestations of dynamic unconscious material. The application to dreams will be discussed below; the relevance of this approach for transference–countertransference dynamics will be touched on briefly in this chapter and noted in the following one. In passing it should be noted that Jung first pointed out the archetypal dimensions of transference–countertransference fantasies in his 1946 "Psychology of the transference."

The overt, deliberate and direct means Jung used to dialogue with unconscious material may no longer be required in all cases, though in some instances the incorporation of more derivative means of engagement may amount to an erosion of discernment in quality of imagination (Schaverien, submitted). Analytic techniques allowing recognition of more quotidian unconscious processes have entered and evolved within the Jungian community, notably through the researches of Fordham and others in the SAP, and in Germany through the work of Dieckmann (1991), as well as incorporations based on borrowings of techniques from various psychoanalytic schools. Thus with Plaut (1966) we learned that the ability to imagine requires the capacity to form a trusting relationship and that when this is not intact it must first be cultivated through working with early mental states in the transference. As the play of unconscious fantasy was increasingly acknowledged as shaping the interactive field in analysis, Davidson (1966) extended the parallels between these fantasies and those employed in active imagination. This opened the way to investigate countertransferential fantasies not only for potential pathology in the analyst, or to help metabolize projective identifications from the patient, but also as a means of engaging in the here-and-now with what is emerging in the field itself.

Similarly, in the psychoanalytic community the uses of countertransferential reactions have gradually developed. With this, a renewed appreciation of the value of the therapist's preconscious has emerged, especially in exploring the vicissitudes of the co-constructed field or analytic third. Although this version of the third is more contracted than the Jungian view – it lacks an archetypal, objective base – the technical innovations stemming from these explorations as developed by psychoanalytic theorists can be beneficially transcribed into a Jungian mode without excessive distortion (e.g. Cambray 2001). The study of the therapist's reveries (see Ogden 1997), the play of enactments (Ellman and Moskowitz 1998) and the role of implicit memory (see below) operating in the interactive field are some of the more useful avenues for augmenting the methods for engaging emergent phenomena. We now turn to contemporary applications of selected methods in analytical psychology (due to limitations of space we will limit discussion to work with dreams, amplification and active imagination).

Amplification

Even prior to his first formulations, in a 1914 contribution, of what was to become the method of amplification (Jung 1914/1915:para. 412–414; also see the editor's n. 12), Jung had already begun to explore the practice in his breakaway book, now known as *Symbols of Transformation* (1967b). The method as formulated consisted of applying contextually appropriate cultural and archetypal analogies to expand and deepen understanding of the meaning of unconscious contents once personal associations prove inadequate for a full analysis of this material (for a cogent summary of the three-tiered system of association/amplification see Hall 1983:35–36). In these publications Jung was seeking a way to analyze that was not only reductive, back to infantile causes, but constructive, expansively moving toward the underlying goal or purpose of a psychic content (like acorn to oak tree). By proceeding in this way Jung opened to the therapeutic community the possibility of truly interdisciplinary discourse, offering both subjective (personal) and objective (cultural and archetypal) modes to our understanding of the notion of the unconscious. As detailed elsewhere, in clinical work the subjectivity inherent in the choices of objective analogies to be applied must also be taken into consideration and examined for coutertransferential components (Cambray 2001).

As Samuels has pointed out, Jung continued throughout his life to refine and elaborate his thoughts on amplification (in Casement 1998:23–24). Over time, with his and his colleagues' growing ability to use external, objective analogies from multiple sources (history, folklore, myth, alchemy, religious practice, scientific theories, etc.; in short the world of cultural productions) to enrich analytic comprehension of symbolic material and to decipher archetypal patterns, Jung also reflected on the process of the method. At his Tavistock lectures in 1935, after reframing amplification in terms of discovering the "mental tissue" in which a psychological content is embedded, he continues, "I am looking for what the *unconscious is doing* with the complex, because that interests me very much more than the fact that people have complexes" (Jung 1980:para. 175, emphasis in original). The implicit relations between complexes being envisioned here can be seen as forming intrapsychic as well interpersonal fields, so that Jung is articulating a psychological network with complexes as nodes gathering clusters of associations (see also Jung 1944:para. 48).

While the associational network view of amplification was operationalized in the classical school of Jungian analysis (for examples see von Franz 1970; Jacobi 1973: 84–88; Edinger 1985), the focus was on articulating the layers of context informing a content (see below). This had the positive effect of linking a given word or image into a web of personal and collective associations. Therapeutic benefit can be derived by helping an analysand to discover a deeper human background to their suffering and can bring the individuation narrative into greater relief. This also often can activate and/or intensify the motivational dynamics of individuation slumbering in a person. The skillful use of this method not only can have prospective value for a client but also can assist a therapist in dealing with a difficult or trying period in a treatment, as shown recently by John Beebe (in Young-Eisendrath and Dawson 1997:192).

The integration into Jungian analysis of viewpoints and techniques from other schools of psychotherapy has increasingly clarified the limitations and dangers in this method. Thus Whitmont and Perera in their book on dreams end the amplification chapter with a cautionary section on thoroughly exploring countertransference before introducing any amplificatory contribution (1989:54–55) and sensitively discuss a number of potential dangers and benefits when assessing the use of an amplification (ibid.: 109–110); Peters offers similar advice and even amplifies the dangers themselves by citing the "bed of Procrustes" (in Alister and Hauke 1998:139). Samuels offers another way of seeing into this method, by looking at "thinking behind the idea" (in Casement 1998:24). In doing so he observed that "the ordinary, everyday procedure of interpreting the patient's material, especially the transference contents, in infantile terms may also be seen as a kind of amplification" making the thin and vague more accessible (Casement 1998:24). He goes on to note that "relating the (psychological) material to general models of unconscious functioning and personality development has a very similar effect to that of amplification in its classical, Jungian sense: to expand the horizons and to deepen the patient's experience in the here-and-now, turning the events of analysis into experiences in analysis" (Casement 1998: 24). The impact of this line of reflection has been to facilitate greater cross fertilization between Jungian and other schools of psychotherapy, demonstrating the usefulness of interactive discussions between groups.

A further step towards mutual engagement, at various levels within the Jungian world and increasingly with other schools and disciplines, has been the revaluing of Jung's later writings, especially as they articulate an interactive field model. With regard to amplification this has been discussed by Cambray (2001), along with references to some of the relevant Jungian literature on fields. A collection of differing psychoanalytic views can be found in the January 2002 issue of the *Journal of Analytical Psychology* where a questionnaire explores how psychoanalysts from various schools view selected Jungian ideas; see especially responses to question 3. In Cambray's 2001 paper he focuses on how the therapist subjectively processes the qualities of the interactive field that become enacted whenever an amplification is offered, or even just held in mind silently, along with the traditionally under-stood countertransferential components in such enactments. By examining an analytic day (a series of sessions on a particular day) instead of the usual case vignette format, he was attending to affective-image patterns emerging in a set of fields having the analyst as a node. Though not formulated in such terms, a supraordinate, self-organizing system was observed to be shaping the field and an amplification of the enactment paradigm itself was offered using the mythologem of Pandora.

Over the past several years a fresh perspective on the nature of archetypal processes has been gaining currency in the Jungian community, especially applications of dynamic systems theory as mentioned earlier in this chapter. Two aspects of this deserve specific mention here; the first is the emergent quality of Jung's methods. Amplification is an intentionally *non-linear* cir-cumambulation of an image or psychic content; it operates by allowing con-textually meaningful associations to be gathered up and enter consciousness. As the limit of personal associations is reached, if further analysis is required, the net is widened to include cultural and archetypal elements. For this expansion to remain clinically relevant it must offer an experiential dimen-sion as well as being an intellectual event; affective involvement is crucial, as will be discussed with dream work.

A precondition for entering a state of (analytic) consciousness that can facilitate a mutative employment of transpersonal material was noted by Jung and more fully discussed by Bion, the suspension of ordinary knowing – this link between Jung and Bion was delineated by Fordham along with a number of other areas of overlap between them (in Hobdell 1995: 223–224). Through the work of Bion, Thomas Ogden has recently adopted a similar perspective, finding value and importance in an emergentist perspective. He observes: "the philosophical concept of emergence closely corresponds to Bion's (1970) notion of the 'emergence' of ('evolution' of) O in the realm of apprehensible, 'sensible' experience (K) ... in psychoanalysis, the analyst and analysand make 'things' (analytic objects such as interpretations) in ver-bal and non-verbal form which emerge from, and gesture toward, what is true to the present emotional experience" (Odgen 2004). The openness to unconscious processes, with the dangers and novelty that the setting aside of memory and desire can induce, also orients the mind towards the edge of order and chaos, the locus of deeper psychological creativity. This is what Jung sought with amplification, where the collective associations were intended to be spontaneously discovered in a manner that permitted a glimpse of the constellating archetypal forms, but only after the material presented had already been thoroughly engaged. This formulation reached its full expression in Jung's later ideas on "active imagination" (see below), which he saw as a "natural amplification process" that had a profound affective core essential for transformation (see Cambray 2001:300, n. 1).

The second aspect of amplification that takes on new features in the light of contemporary science is the web or network aspect of association clustering around specific images or ideas. In one of her books Jacobi gives three graphic examples, diagrams 2, 3, and 4 (1973:85–88); Edinger (1985) begins each of his chapters on alchemical operations (as metaphors for psychological transformations) with a map of associational links among symbols, and these maps themselves are found to interlink when studied, forming a multidimensional, interconnected system. To help the reader better grasp these webs, Figure 5.1 reproduces Jacobi's diagram 3 and Figure 5.2 reproduces Edinger's association net for *Calcinatio*. The associational clusters bear a striking resemblance, indeed are a form of what contemporary scientists from various disciplines are identifying as "scale-free networks" (see above). Such networks are characterized by having interconnected nodes, with the

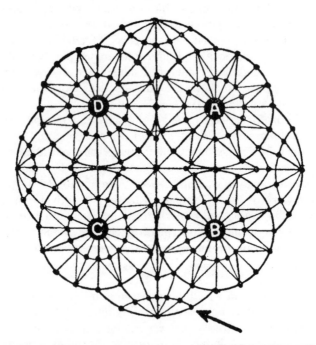

Figure 5.1 Nodal network of amplifications. A, B, C, D: the dream elements. The nodal points of the net of connections indicated by the arrow represent the individual parallels or amplifications. Reprinted from Jacobi, J. (1973) *The Psychology of C.G. Jung*, © Yale University Press.

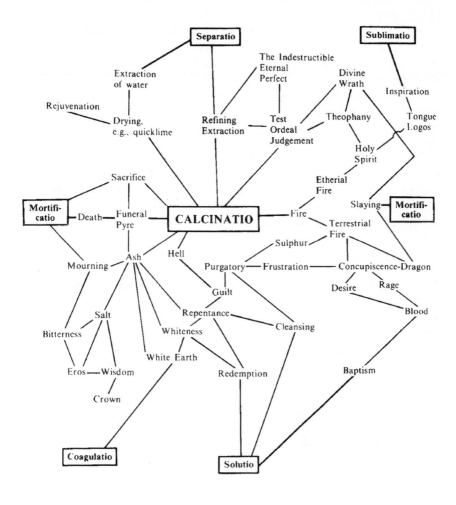

Figure 5.2 **Network around the** *Calcinatio.* Reprinted by permission of Open Court Publishing Company, a division of Carus Publishing Company, Peru, IL, from *Anatomy of the Psyche* by E. Edinger, copyright © 1985 by Open Court Publishing Company.

more highly linked nodes designated "hubs." The patterning in these systems creates a previously unappreciated architectural dimension to networks, which Barabasi and Bonabeau say are "ruled by fundamental laws – laws that appear to apply equally to cells, computers, languages and society" (2003:60–69; see also Barabasi 2003). The most important of these, as previously mentioned, is the power law distribution of node linkages.

As discussed in Chapter 9, emergent behavior of CAS is characterized by power law distributions; scale-free networks have likewise been shown to have self-organizing properties. Thus, without detailing the scientific finding here, we can favorably compare the amplificatory model to a contemporary scientific reframing of Jung's vision of the psyche and find profound correspondence. The emergent properties of complexes and archetypes have already been detailed. Here we would add that *the network of complexes* in an individual and/or between individuals (or in communities, or between groups, etc. – a series of increasingly complex systems) have differentially, affectively charged, numinous archetypal cores, or nodes of symbolic attraction, activated to greater or lesser degrees based on biological, environmental, and learned/cultural conditions, manifesting what some Jungians refer to as the degree of constellation.

As Barabasi and Bonabeau (2003) discuss, the implications for understanding scale-free networks are widespread, for example allowing new strategies in considering how to handle various kinds of systemic dilemmas: from differential responses to accidental failures versus systematic attacks on computer networks, to vaccination campaign strategies (focusing on treating hub individuals), to designing drugs that target hub molecules in certain diseases, to protecting economies from cascading financial failures. Applied to Jung's model, we recognize that select complexes tend to infiltrate the psychic structure more heavily, for example patterns of interaction formed early in life with parents, i.e. introjects identified by object relations theory. While psychotherapy generally works with these hubs, seeking to repair the damage from traumatic events, inner and outer, the later stages of Jungian analysis privilege nodes less frequently explored in other systems. These involve various archetypal nodes activated in the individuation process; the methods of amplification and active imagination are the means Jung devised to access and interact with these organizers of experience that lie at the far margins of ordinary consciousness.

Active imagination

Active imagination is a way of engaging with unconscious contents that Jung developed into a method following his break with Freud. Drawing on his experience with altered states of consciousness, from séances with trance states, hypnotism, and therapeutic work with individuals suffering with more extreme forms of psychopathology, Jung deliberately experimented with suspending focused rational consciousness, entering what would today be understood as a light meditative or trance state to gain access to the unseen workings of the mind. This can be seen to be a means of approaching the emergent edge of the personality, as previously noted in the similarity between Jung and Bion in their attitudes towards entering the analytic space.

Through his explorations, Jung came to feel that an *active* encounter with the depths of the imagination, responded to as psychologically real, would have a beneficial impact on the conscious personality, making it less defensive and more creative in dealing with the problems of life. This in turn was felt to have a potential healing impact on neurotic symptoms. Jung was cautious in applying the method, concerned that whoever would attempt it have adequate ego strength; his uncertainties about how he and it would be received caused him to write sparingly about the actual practice of the method. Hence, as noted, his first paper on the subject written in 1916 was not published until 1957. He presented his own experiences with the method in his various seminars and these served as the primary source of methodological information for many years. The method has plasticity allowing many modalities of expression, usually beginning with a dream image or a mood then cultivating an open, curious attitude that seeks engagement with the contents that arise. These contents if imaged as personified figures can be dialogued with, or emerging images can be drawn, painted, sculpted, danced, etc. Jung was in fact a major pioneer in the application of the arts to psychotherapy. Chodorow in her recent, playful and insightful compilation of Jung's writing on the subject notes that "many fundamental concepts of Jung's analytical psychology come from his experiences with active imagination" (1997:3).

Several of Jung's early followers published monographs on the subject (von Franz 1979; Hannah 1981) as well as the Australian Rix Weaver (1973) and the method was discussed and debated from different perspectives in the Jungian world for its values, dangers and clinical efficacy – for a review of selected aspects of this debate see Cwik, who also closely links the practice with Jung's complex theory (in Stein 1995). The privileging of psychic imagery and the imagination by advocates of this approach became a central tenet of the archetypal school of analysis (see Adams in Young-Eisendrath and Dawson 1997). However, one of the more interesting clinical observations about this method was that of Davidson, who wrote a paper entitled "Transference as a form of active imagination" (1966), thereby challenging those who would split the "clinical" aspects of Jungian practice from a "symbolic" approach. This paper can also be seen as a precursor for contemporary thinking about the applications of reverie in investigations of transference/countertransference fields.

Hopefully it is now clear that amplification and active imagination can be treated as emergent processes that can foster and facilitate an individuation process. In conjunction with explorations of dream imagery they provide a potent set of tools for engaging with the full range of our humanness. In the next section we turn to dream work, but with a shift in focus regarding the systems approach employed. We move from discussion of networks to recent relevant findings in the neurosciences and attachment research. These allow a closer look at physiological processes that are activated in Jungian work and help to contextualize the Jungian approach in terms of the mind/brain/therapeutic-dyad relationships.

Dreams

Dream work has been and remains a centerpiece of the Jungian approach to personality development (see Jung 1974; Hall 1983; Whitmont and Perera 1989; Vedfelt 1999). Juxtaposing traditional Jungian methods valuing mytho-poetic consciousness with contemporary neuroscientific thinking, we hope to demonstrate that there is now solid support for traditional practices which embrace story, narrative, and metaphor. Beginning with the act of a client telling a dream in analysis, taken as a kind of ritual of engagement between therapeutic partners, disparate activities of the brain/mind/interpersonal systems can be noted operating simultaneously at various levels mutually impacting one another. For example, opportunities for hemispheric integration occur in concert with the presentation of core conflicts within the context of an evolving, supportive co-constructed therapeutic dyad (see below). Formulating interactions derived from general systems theory among such nested sets has been employed similarly by infant researchers, psychoanalysts and neuroscientists to explicate an emergentist paradigm, which as various chapters here suggest, resonates with contemporary Jungian theorizing about unconscious processes including dreams.

Turning first to the mythological, sleep personified as *Hypnos* and dream as *Oneiros* are inseparable brothers and children of *Nyx* (night) who rule over gods and mortals alike (Meier 1987: 38–39). Archetypal psychologist James Hillman says, "each dream is a child of Night, affiliated closely with sleep or death and with forgetting (Lethe) all that the daily world remembers" (1979:53). With the embrace of sleep, the dream emerges from the collaborative contributions from a number of brain areas (usually during REM periods) to form images that dazzle, amaze, and terrify us. Analysands often seek Jungian work because they are curious about a dream or series of dreams that they have pondered for years, sensing that there is something more to these visitations than wish-fulfilling day residues. Not unlike visitors to the Greek temple of Aesclepius, they long for a healing dream (*enhypnion enarges* = effective dream) to function as guide through life's trials (see Meier 1987:42). Some analysands look to the analyst for oracular pronouncements and need help in appreciating that dream analysis is a co-constructed process evolving within the context of an ongoing, containing relationship.

Although it is useful to consider dreams both reductively and prospectively, traditional Jungian thinking has favored the latter, privileging personality expansion through creative integration of unconscious contents and self-regulation through compensatory balancing of the tensions between conscious and unconscious forces. Communication and discussion of dreams is generally facilitated by attention to the symbols and metaphors which provide imagistic descriptions of these ephemeral experiences that are frequently nonverbal. While dreams can be experienced with immediacy, comprehension generally requires processing through multiple channels. As is often the case, the *feeling* associated with a dream stays with us throughout the day; thus Shakespeare remarks (quoted in Meier 1987:63):

> The dream's here still. Even when I wake it is
> Without me, as within me; not imagin'd, felt.
> Shakespeare, Cymbeline, Act IV, Scene II

This portrays a kind of holistic awareness rather than an articulated thought. Even so, analysands write down their dreams translating them to verbal form, leaving us to wonder what is lost in this kind of conversion process. At times an artistic expression of a dream experience may best render the dream essence. Critical for therapeutic value is that the dreamer discovers/recovers in the analytic process the affective experience residing in the dream (see Reed 1976 on the art of remembering dreams). A parallel from the mood congruity hypothesis can be found in LeDoux (2003:222): "memories are more easily retrieved when the emotional state at the time of memory formation matches the state at the time of retrieval." Recapturing an embodied presence may be facilitated through a thoughtful, slow spirit of inquiry (Fosshage 2004) where the analyst encourages elaboration of dream images. Detailed descriptions make more ample the ephemeral quality of the dream which can contribute to its felt presence in the analytic encounter (e.g. Bosnak 1986, 1996) and often give first shape to feelings that have been unbearable.

Premature interpretation threatens to collapse the imaginal field (see Cambray 2001 for the negative impact of a premature amplification), resulting in an intellectual understanding devoid of the richness brought forward by re-experiencing the implicit realm in the present moment. With the image more established, associations can be solicited. The Jungian tradition has returned consistently to the dream as a kind of touchstone to avoid drifting away from the direct experience as Jung feared with the free associative method of Freud. Jung's phenomenological approach respects the truth and integrity of the dream as a communication of a psychic state at a particular moment. This contrasts with Freudian notions of hidden and disguised meanings with manifest and latent content. Patricia Berry of the archetypal school cautions against such reduction, stating that "for Jung, images opened out, i.e., had telos or purpose beyond themselves" (Berry 1982:82). Staying close to the image, attending to the feelings engendered, is likely to provoke concordant affect during the exploration of a dream (parallel to LeDoux's mood congruity hypothesis); this kind of reproduction allows both analyst and analysand the opportunity to value, get to know, and be led by the image itself.

Infant research, neuroscience and adult analysis

Modern Jungian theorizing has benefited from an infusion of innovative ideas and practices from other fields, as detailed throughout this book. Like-wise, Beebe and Lachmann (2002), Sander (1982, 2002), and Stern *et al.* (1998), all psychoanalysts looking at the applications of infant research to adult analysis, subscribe to variants of an emergentist paradigm grounded in non-linear dynamic systems. Sander's ideas about paradox and polarity are resonant with Jung's core perception of the dissociability of the psyche that leads to his theory of complexes with the consequent aim in analysis to foster synthesis and integration via the transcendent function (see Feldman 2003 for a recent Jungian review of Sander's contribution). Thus in discussing the infant-caregiving systems Sander (1982:317) notes three principles:

1   polarities exist in dynamic opposition
2   paradoxically opposite processes proceed together
3   integrative mechanisms harmonize these polarities and paradoxical tendencies.

He goes on to say:

> The organism gains coherence as ever new coordinations between organism and environment are created in new combinations of action and function that serve to bridge the disparities generated within and between systems.
>
> (Sander 1982:317)

Every living system must cope with uncertainty that places it in a state some-where between continuity and change, core polarities for Sander (1982:318). In the therapeutic setting, fluctuations in relational certitude and doubt provide an emergent edge through which the co-constructed third of the relationship becomes the locus of the transcendent function. A kernel of this found in Jung is: "In terms of energy, polarity means a potential, and wherever a potential exists there is the possibility of a current, a flow of events, for the tension of opposites strives for balance" (1945/1948:para. 426). Such vacillation can be mutative for both partners, as evidenced in the bidirectionality of influence that has been nicely documented in the microprocessing (via video tape) of mother–infant interaction and convincingly applied to the analytic dyad by Beebe and Lachmann (2002). Jung presaged this fundamental idea as follows: "When two chemical substances combine, both are altered. This is precisely what happens in the transference" (1946:para. 358). But, one wonders, how does this transformation actually unfold?

A seminal paper by the Process of Change Group led by Daniel Stern called "Non-interpretive mechanisms in psychoanalytic therapy: the 'something more' than interpretation" attempts to answer this question by describing two complementary systems of therapeutic action: one is explicit through verbal, content-oriented interpretation of transference, the other is implicit through nonverbal, process-oriented knowing in the context of the shared current relationship:

> Such *knowings* integrate affect, cognition and behavioral/interactive dimensions. They can remain out of awareness as Bollas's "unthought known" (1987) or as Sandler's "past unconscious" (Sandler and Fonagy, 1998) but can also form a basis for much of what may later become symbolically represented.
>
> (Stern *et al.* 1998:906)

Jungians may think of this as intuition. Continuing on Stern *et al.* (1998), note that interpretation rearranges the explicit relationship and "moments of meeting" reconfigure implicit relational knowing. They say that "The change [through a *moment of meeting*] will be sensed and the newly altered environment then acts as the new effective context in which subsequent mental actions occur and are shaped and past events are reorganized" (ibid.). According to Beebe and Lachmann:

> In a moment of meeting, two states of consciousness are matched such that the way that one is known by oneself is matched by the way one is known by the other (Beebe 1998). This match in the moment of meeting facilitates the development of agency and identity. In the moment of meeting, a mutual recognition occurs that changes the patient's ability to act as an agent, in his own self-regulation.
>
> (Beebe and Lachmann 2002:32)

This system radically expands our understanding of transference and points to the creative possibilities inherent in a "new" experience. Which complexes are constellated in the analyst, in the patient and between them at such moments should likely be considered. For example, a traumatized patient with an abuse history including an intrusive, critical and abandoning mother may experience through the positive pole of the archetypal mother, a figure of nurturance in a moment of meeting with the analyst who conveys through voice, intonation, and facial expression the granting of space, acceptance, and connectedness. A new way of *being together* can begin to emerge.

Ideas about implicit and explicit memory from neuroscience are being integrated as above in contemporary theory and practice (see LeDoux 1996, 2002; Pally 1998; Damasio 1999; Fonagy 1999; Kandel 1999; Siegel 1999;

Stern *et al.* 1998; Knox 2001). Explicit memory, also known as declarative memory, tends to be verbal and requires conscious awareness and focal attention for encoding (Siegel 1999:33). It includes both semantic (factual) memory and episodic autobiographical memory which begins to operate at about age two. Implicit or non-declarative, procedural memory (Siegel 1999:33) is present at birth and is devoid of a sense of recall. This includes behavioral, emotional, perceptual, and perhaps somatosensory memory. These memories have never, for the most part, been "conscious" and there-fore cannot be forgotten. (An exception occurs, for example, when learning a new skill such as playing the piano; one needs focused conscious attention on acquiring the skill but having accomplished this ability, it falls into pro-cedural memory.) Coordination and integration of these two domains are influenced through early attachment experiences (Stern *et al.* 1998; Beebe and Lachmann 2002) and profoundly affect self and interactive regulations. How one relates to others and to one's internal world emanates not simply from internalization of the object but from internalization of the "process of mutual regulation" (Stern *et al.* 1998:907). Memory then is a dance between factual content and more subtle emotional and bodily processes. One can cue the other. For example, a dream can sometimes be recalled by getting hold of a feeling about it; by the same token a remembered face in a dream may bring forward an emotional sequence. (More will follow but it is important to note here that traces of explicit and implicit knowing and memory may arise in the interactions between and among dream figures; mythology can also in part encode implicit processes at the cultural and archetypal levels.)

Another aspect of this dance has to do with brain laterality. Siegel says that "memory processes are also specialized in each hemisphere" (1999:197) and quotes Daniel Schacter as follows:

> Neurologists and neurophysiologists have known for over a century that language and verbal abilities are heavily dependent on the left hemi-sphere, whereas nonverbal and spatial functions are more dependent on the right hemisphere. Memory is similarly lateralized. Patients with dam-age to the left hippocampus and medial temporal lobe tend to have dif-ficulties explicitly remembering verbal information but have no problems remembering visual designs and spatial locations. Patients with damage to the right hippocampus and medial temporal lobe tend to show the opposite pattern.
>
> (Siegel 1999:197)

The right and left brain offer two different ways of knowing, simplified as the left being responsible for logical, linear detail and focused thoughts, while the right is based on sensations and images (Siegel 1999). Schore expands on this in his recent book, saying that the right hemisphere:

is dominant for the cognitive processing of facial, prosodic, and bodily information embedded in emotional communications, for attention, for empathy, and for the human stress response. These essential processes – central to both regulation of homeostasis and the capacity to flexibly alter the internal environment to optimally cope with external perturbations – take place extremely rapidly, at levels beneath conscious awareness. Converging neuropsychologic and neurobiological data strongly suggest the right hemisphere is critically involved in the maintenance of a coherent, continuous and unified implicit sense of self.

(Schore 2003:xv)

This right brain description fits well with Stern *et al.*'s (1998) notion of implicit relational knowledge as a fundamental aspect of therapeutic action, which is complemented by interpretation, associated with left brain function. Collaboration of the two hemispheres is highly dependent on early attachment experiences which have been regulating and secure, or maladaptively have been dysregulating and disorganized. Along these lines, Schore states:

The psychobiologically attuned therapist then has an opportunity to act as an interactive affect regulator of the patient's dysregulated state . . . We can directly engage and therefore regulate the patient's inefficient right-brain processes with our own right brains. On the part of the therapist, the most effective interpretations are based on the clinician's "awareness of his own physical, emotional, and ideational responses to the patient's veiled messages" (Boyer 1990:304). On the part of the patient, the most "correct understandings" can be used by the patient "only if the analyst is attuned to the patient's state at the time the interpretation is offered" (Friedman and Moskowitz 1992:xxi).

(Schore 2003:53–54)

Interpersonal interaction, then, influences brain functioning which in turn influences interactional capacities. Affective engagement of the analyst through the emergent qualities of the new relationship as well as through metabolized countertransference is necessary for any real transformation to occur; without the therapist's capacity to be influenced, the patient does not change. Such interactive regulation leads to self-regulation, integration, coherence, and a sense of self.

Emotional engagement via enactment cannot be overemphasized. Although "what" we say may be important, "how" we communicate via the implicit realm gives shape and contour through voice tone, prosody, and body posture. Coordinated interactions developed by the fluctuation of matching and disengaging create "schemas of ways of being with another" (Stern *et al.*, 1998: 905) ever present in the nonverbal subtext. *The Oxford English Dictionary* tells us that the word *implicit* actually means "entangled, entwined, folded or twisted together; involved." We feel this entanglement in the midst of enactment. Schore says:

> in the heightened affective moment of an enactment, the key to sustaining a co-created right-brain-to-right-brain holding environment is the clinician's capacity of "avoiding closure" and tolerating ambiguity, uncertainty, and, lack of differentiation in order to "wonder."
>
> (Schore 2003:94)

We view the implicit realm as partaking of the complicated, murky, nonlinear world of constellated complexes. Within this domain, the analyst really comes to know empathically the patient's experience felt as pressures, discomforts and anxieties. When inhabiting a liminal state, the analyst may become distracted by thoughts, images, and emotions that if attended to may be reveries opening to emergent processes pertinent to the here and now engagement (see e.g., Ogden 1997, 1999). How these feelings, hunches, or clinical intuitions come about is an interesting open question. One supposition is that in charged moments at times prematurely (mis)construed as synchronicities in clinical work, we are witnessing implicit knowing conveyed in voice, movement, and/ or facial expression, residing at the edges of awareness, exerting influence over perceptions and judgments and organizing interaction.

Clinical vignette I

We come to know the feeling of significant others in our analysands' lives through their implicit conveyance of them. The presence of these "others" may be helpful as guiding spirits or intrusive as ghosts in the analytic field. The memory of an inspiring teacher, for example, may manifest in the analysand's incorporation of mannerisms, gestures or voice tone. On the other hand, the incarnation of a psychotic mother may cause the analysand to experience inexplicable hyperaroused panic via the sympathetic system manifesting as anxiety or hypoaroused dissociation via the parasympathetic system causing shutdown and silence in the session. Through this implicit communication in the analytic hour and in dreams we, too, become well acquainted and respond, often preconsciously, to these embodied "others."

An example of the presence of such an "other" occurred when a patient attended analysis on her brother's birthday. This brother had died 10 years before at 24 and we had been talking a good deal about him in relation to my patient's current romantic interests as they emerged in dreams. During the previous session, she had reported a dream in which a man for whom she had unrequited feelings had fallen out of a tree and died. The centrality of the relationship with her brother and the consequent loss that his death entailed powerfully affected relational, emotional, and career choices. Now this new man had become the center of longing and we discovered multiple resonances between his personality and that of her brother; however, also like her brother, he was unavailable. Subsequently, we discussed the tree as a world axis and the pivotal position that this man had symbolized in her psychic life.

As my analysand reminisced fondly about her brother, his endearing qualities and quirks, I (LC) found myself enjoying his presence through her implicit knowledge of him. I knew much more than factual information, I had a "feel" for what this man really had been like. I got hold of a sense of his charm and flirtatiousness and found myself attracted to him. He was magnetic in personality and my patient had found it hard to ever say no, even though she was aware of his inclination toward narcissistic manipulation. This pattern had replicated itself in my patient with boyfriends who were charming but emotionally unavailable. To truly develop an intimate relationship, the patient would have to face and grieve the unavailability of her brother and the man in her life who was now the focus of her attention. This process had begun as she was now letting in feelings of sadness and grief. Along with the patient, I felt the excitement of her brother's presence and subsequent gaping loss over not having access to him due first to incest barriers and then to his untimely death. I commented on the aliveness of his presence as she conveyed it and how overwhelming the loss of that presence must be. This brought a watershed of tears that gripped me as well. Implicitly her voice, facial expression, giggles over his humor and tears over his death had fully positioned him between us in the room, giving me the sense that I actually knew and recognized this complex young man. She and I experienced intense togetherness typical of a moment of meeting. We had managed to coordinate implicit knowing of her brother and of each other with explicit factual information and direct interpretation of dream symbols. Letting go of her brother as a core complex eventually opened the patient up to other creative aspects of herself and to other kinds of relational choices. In this sense, the dream imagery predicted a much needed but painful change.

Memory, archetype and narrative

The interplay of explicit and implicit memory often manifests in the expressive arts and literature. Personified mytho-poetically as Mnemosyne, the Greek goddess of Memory incarnates as The Muses, her daughters. Says Eliade (1996:21): "The past thus revealed is much more than the antecedent of the present; it is its source . . . the poet inspired by the Muses has access to the original realities." Although organization and planning are necessary for a creative piece, what inspires us is a feeling, a spirit, an awareness that is implicit, as in Virginia Woolf's view of rhythm given in a letter of 16 March 1926:

> Now this is profound, what rhythm is, and goes far deeper than words. A signal, an emotion, creates this wave in the mind, long before it makes words to fit it; and in writing (such is my present belief) one has to

recapture this, and set this working (which has nothing apparently to do with words) and then, as it breaks and tumbles in the mind, it makes words to fit it.

(Desalvo and Leaska 1984:93–94)

This kind of knowing seems to come from implicit memory not available as recollection or conscious thought but through a sense of patterning at the archetypal level. A presence is felt incarnating in words, artwork, or dramatic production. Image and metaphor may capture an integrated aliveness of conscious and unconscious systems interacting, moving, living. Says Hillman:

Archetypes are the skeletal structures of the psyche, yet the bones are changeable constellations or light-sparks, waves, motions. They are principles of uncertainty. Since they cannot be confronted directly, they become defined, as Jung always insisted, as "unknowable in themselves."

(Hillman 1979:157)

Archetypal processes are not directly available to consciousness but only known indirectly with an "as if" quality in myth, story, and narrative. Telling and listening to these stories can serve an organizing function and, according to Siegel, may foster integration. He says:

In the co-construction of stories, parent and child enter into a dyadic form of bilateral resonance. Each person enters a state of interhemispheric integration, which is facilitated by interpersonal communication. This highly complex form of collaborative communication allows the dyad to move into highly resonant states, and also enables the child's mind to develop its own capacity for integration. Such a capacity may be at the heart of self regulation.

(Siegel 1999:334)

Jungians have been reassessing the value of story, narrative and practice such as in the papers by Covington (1995), Dieckmann (1997) and Ekstrom (2002). There are parallels between Siegel's work and Covington's as she emphasizes that psychic healing comes with the patient's incorporation of the narrative process. She says:

It is by creating a narrative that we realize and express our need to internalize the other and to experience ourselves as internalized by another in a meaningful way. The construction of narrative, derived from our desire to know and to form connections with one another, and to explore what we can love in one another, has a mutative effect, that is, it produces psychic change.

(Covington 1995:43)

Again, Siegel speaking of narratives, says:

> Narratives reveal how representations from one system can clearly inter-
> twine with another. Thus the mental models of implicit memory help
> organize the themes of how the details of explicit autobiographical
> memory are expressed within a life story. Though we can never see men-
> tal models directly, their manifestation in narratives allows us to get a
> view of at least the shadow they cast on the output of other systems of
> the mind.
>
> (Siegel 1999:63)

Metaphors in analysis are woven into narratives, which offer a creative domain
for playful interaction and allow multiple strands of a life to be interwoven.
Psychoanalyst Arnold Modell (1997) argues that linguists, neurobiologists,
and psychoanalysts can share a common paradigm through metaphor. He
holds the forces of poetic consciousness in relation to contemporary theories
about memory within an emergentist view. He says:

> Metaphor, as is true of memory, rests on the border between psychology
> and physiology. It can be said that metaphor represents an emergent
> property of mind. Perhaps the clearest evidence that metaphor is the
> currency of mind is the fact that dreaming, a neurophysiological process,
> automatically generates visual metaphors . . . Metaphor is a fundamental
> and indispensable structure of human understanding, a basic and irredu-
> cible unit of mental functioning . . . I believe that affects, metaphor and
> memory form a synergistic unified system.
>
> (Modell 1997:106)

Pally notes that both Levin (1997) and Modell (1997) believe that the use of
metaphor also serves bilateral integrative coherence. She continues, "[b]y containing within them sensory, imagistic, emotional, and verbal elements,
metaphors are believed to activate multiple brain centers simultaneously;
they are ways of perceiving, feeling and existing" (Pally 1998:576). This sim-
ultaneity may be the neurophysiological correlate facilitating the transcendent function relating conscious to unconscious and affect to insight and
cognition (Siegelman 1990). Underlying the multimodal importance of
metaphors, Hillman says, "Metaphors are more than ways of speaking; they
are ways of perceiving, feeling and existing" (1979:156). From our point of
view they are the vehicles for explicit and implicit knowing and allow for
a complex and full means for expression and communication.

Within the Jungian paradigm this use of metaphor can be extended into
explorations of the collective unconscious. To access the archetypal layer
of the psyche after exhaustive exploration of personal associations to
unconscious material, Jungians rely on methods such as amplification by

analogical expansion (see above) to move beyond the limits of genetic, causal interpretation. Describing dreams through component images is story-telling no matter how illogical the narrative, and an apt amplificatory response can foreground an archetypal pattern capable of providing a sense of containment through discovered coherency.

In following the purpose of a dream, it often becomes important to track its images as they recur over time in a sequence of dreams. Dream series often portray core problems in multiple, evolving ways thus detailing, completing or complementing what is already known. Jung demonstrated this in great detail in his study of an extended series of dreams chronicling the emergence of symbols depicting a new center in the personality of the renowned physicist Wolfgang Pauli (1944:para. 44–331).

Dreams, active imagination, sandplay or artistic productions, also offer windows into the implicit domain that falls outside conscious cortical control. Specifically, interactions between figures within a dream may reveal internalized representations of significant regulatory functioning that lead to coherence and integration or alternatively to disintegration and fragmentation. When attended to, these interactive patterns can provide insight into the vicissitudes of emergent processes.

Clinical vignette II

"E", a man in his thirties, dreamed during a three-times-a-week analysis that he backed his car into the analyst's office, which had two large archways at either end, in an effort, along with his wife, to take home a baby animal that would grow to the size of a horse. The analyst (LC) was on a ladder with her back to the analysand arranging books and pamphlets on a shelf. After some discussion of the dream, E decided to work with the sandtray[4] and have a three-dimensional experience in the analyst's presence. What gripped E emotionally from the tray was his felt experience of the analyst being up on a ladder with her back turned, paying no attention to the drama in the room. Recovering feelings of hurt, disappointment, and abandonment, he then associated to his mother who was usually distracted by his three brothers and household duties. Wounded by this recurrent lack of sensitivity and attunement to his needs, E left home at an early age "turning his back" on his mother. Seeing the analyst turned away from him surprised both of us as he consciously experienced me as engaged and present, in contrast to his history with his mother, presenting us with an apparent paradox, since covert pressures towards intellectualization were not yet evident. The dream revealed a transferential constellation in polar opposition to our conscious interaction. What emerged in subsequent sandtrays based on the same dream imagery was his rage at the "analyst" (mother) for not looking, seeing him and this amazing creature in the room. Through countertransference feelings of being devalued and left alone, a glimpse of the narcissistic injuries suffered by

E came into focus, which on reflection allowed transformation of initial frustration into compassion. Simultaneously, between sessions, E did an active imagination in which he powerfully expressed his anger and frustration and insisted that the analyst turn around. This was followed by ongoing sandtray work involving an analyst figure in the tray watching as E played with and took care of the baby animal. No interpretation was offered, as the need to play and experience had the privileged position as a form of elaboration. E often expressed gratitude for the "room" and "space" he felt in the regulating environment of the analysis.

Play and metaphor

Neuroscientist Panksepp states that "play may be the functional counterpart of dreaming" (1998:295). He goes on to say that:

> REM sleep may exercise the potentials for organizing affective information in emotional circuits in the relative emotional safety of a positive affective state. In other words dreaming and play may have synergistic functions – providing special opportunities for exercising the psychobehavioral potentials of emotional operating systems within socially supportive environments.
>
> (Panksepp 1998:295)

According to Siegelman, who draws upon Plaut's (1966) classic paper, the capacity for play in analysis depends on the capacity to trust which has often been damaged at the preverbal level, therefore requiring repair not through interpretation but through what we have been calling here "the implicit domain" (1990:173–174). She says:

> What we strive to supply, then, is an atmosphere or environment, a space or place in which the patient can count on our steadiness, dependability, benign lack of judgment, our relative predictability and our "thereness" – that very going-on-being, as Winnicott calls it, that may have been so disrupted in the patient's infancy.
>
> (Siegelman 1990:174)

This attitude of the analyst would, then, support and enhance the synergistic effect of sandplay, art work, and active imagination as well as dream work as they manifest in the analytic dyad.

The serious play with dreams in analysis, activating the reflective function and stimulating the creative imagination, can initiate the construction of a richer, more nuanced life narrative. Writing about the importance of memory, narrative, and dreaming, Siegel makes the following statement:

Dreaming is a multimodal narrative process containing various elements of our daily experience, past events, mental models, and present perceptual experience. The unit of a day, marked by the consolidation process [of memory] of REM sleep, may thus be seen as a form of chapter in a life story. Each day is literally the opportunity to create a new episode of learning, in which recent experience will become integrated with the past and woven into the anticipated future.

(Siegel 1999:61)

During REM sleep cortical consolidation of memory takes place, leading to narrativization of episodic memory (Siegel 1999:62). The process of reporting dreams, together with image-focused methodology, links implicit and explicit memory resulting in emotional modulation, self-organization, and coherence of past, present, and future (Siegal 1999:62–63). E's animal dream and subsequent sandplay reveal an implicit interactive pattern of dysregulation from the past entering the transference, which when metabolized led to a lysis of the internalized tension due to maternal abandonment. The freed libido was then available for an enhanced connection to self in the context of an evolving relationship with the analyst. Dreaming the dream on allowed for explicit articulation of disappointment and anger and a renegotiation of this within the analytic frame facilitating an experience of the transcendent function, or what infant researcher Tronick calls "dyadic expansion of consciousness":

In this process, each partner's state of consciousness expands to incorporate elements of consciousness of the other in a new and more coherent form. Since both partners are affected by this process, there is a dyadic expansion of consciousness into a more coherently organized and complex state of dyadic consciousness (p. 13). Tronick (1996) suggests that this process describes a view of therapeutic action: both analyst and patient create and transform unique dyadic states of consciousness through mutual and self regulation.

(Beebe and Lachmann 2002:42)

The project of story-telling, story-listening, and image exploration generates attachment that, although asymmetric, impacts both participants, expanding mind and soul. The narrative, story, or image description unfolds within a co-constructed relational field in flux where two separate systems engage to hold the tensions of polarity and paradox generating the possibility of a dyadic expansion of consciousness. Such dynamic fluctuation of constellated polarities implies movement in a situated field between constituents and leads to the notion that archetypal patterns may best be conceived as emergent processes of multidimensional fields.

Jung believed that dream figures could be taken subjectively, reflecting different aspects of the individual or objectively reflecting relations with external others (Whitmont and Perera 1989:59). Interactions between dream figures at the subjective level are influenced by attachment history and by ego flexibility or rigidity which may be mirrored in the quality of interpersonal connectedness. The capacity to accept more problematic aspects of oneself as evident in subjective shadow representations tends to be dependent on how accepting significant others have been in daily life as well as intrapsychic distress including the management of shame. At the extreme, for example, are trauma survivors who tend to dissociate under mild stress and whose dreams often reflect this fragmentation with associated affects that are frightening; it has been shown that this may be the result of insecure and disorganizing attachments (Schore 2003:66–69). What have been represented internally are dysregulating interactions that have become persecutory in nature and now impede relatedness with oneself and others. Mediation of this can come through right brain to right brain contact, provided by the empathically attuned therapist within the implicit realm as demonstrated by Wilkinson (2003) within a Jungian framework. Trauma survivors do not need abreaction but expansion of their capacity to be *present* which can be modeled by the tolerance and attention of the regulating therapist (Van der Kolk 2003). Of course, the dissociative experiences of trauma survivors represent a magnified version of what we all experience as a multiplicity of selves, so well articulated in Jung's complex theory and now adopted by relational psychoanalysts who credit Janet but rarely Jung. (For links between Jung's theories and those of Janet, see Haule 1999.)

Jung's dissociative model with a belief that there are unconscious contents not due to repression is clearly supported by contemporary ideas of the implicit domain. The implicit is not the same as the psychoanalytic territory of repressed early history. Further explication of this idea can be found with Lyons-Ruth, who says:

> although implicit knowings are often not symbolically represented, they are also not necessarily dynamically unconscious in the sense of being defensively excluded from awareness. Implicit relational knowing, then, is operating largely outside the realm of verbal consciousness *and* the dynamic unconscious [but can often be preconscious].
>
> (Lyons-Ruth 1998:285)

Again, this is the territory of unconscious complexes, or "splinter psyches" as Jung called them, which become known through multiple dream figures that are representations of different aspects of the self.

We have attempted here to suggest the utility of bivalent Hermetic consciousness attuned to metaphor as applied to dreams by valuing the mythopoetic nature of traditional Jungian ideas in conjunction with contemporary findings from psychoanalysis, infant research, and neuroscience. Through the tension of polarity and paradox, we hoped to convey a sense of regulation

which may result in the emergence of the transcendent function. The therapeutic focus is on facilitating a coordinated integration of explicit and
implicit relational memory and knowing as manifest in images, dreams,
stories, and narrative, as well as the analytic relationship.

Notes

1 For a growing body of applications of related approaches to Jungian psychology in addition to various chapters in this book, see Tresan (1996), Hogenson
(2001), Saunders and Skar (2001), McDowell (2001), Cambray (2002), Knox
(2003); the forthcoming papers from the most recent *Journal of Analytical
Psychology* conference, "Science in the Symbolic World" held in Charleston, SC,
May 2003; and the upcoming International Congress of the IAAP, "Edges of
Experience: Memory and Emergence" to be held in Barcelona in late August
2004.
2 These networks are characterized by what seems paradoxical from the mathematics of random or hierarchical networks, i.e. they are small and highly clustered at
the same time (Strogatz 2003:242). As with other emergent phenomena, such
networks are found throughout the natural and human world. They describe the
form of the internet's backbone, and of neural structures including the brain, they
are also found in the structure of language.
3 Those having a real and an imaginary (containing a multiple of the square root
of minus one) component, i.e. $z = x + \iota y$, where the complex number, or transcendent function, z is composed of a real number x plus an imaginary number
with ι = square root of -1 and y being any real number.
4 Sandplay is a Jungian three-dimensional method made well known by Dora Kalff
in which an analysand is invited to use small figures in a $30 \times 20 \times 30$ inch tray of
sand that has a blue bottom beneath. For details see C.G. Jung Institute (1981),
Kalff (2003) and Weinrib (1983).

References

Alister, I. and Hauke, C. (eds) (1998) *Contemporary Jungian Analysis*, London:
Routledge.
Bair, D. (2003) *Jung: A Biography*, Boston: Little, Brown and Company.
Barabasi, A.-L. (2003) *Linked*, New York: Plume.
Barabasi, A.-L. and Bonabeau, E. (2003) "Scale-free networks", *Scientific American*,
288(5), 60–69.
Beebe, B. (1998) "A procedural theory of therapeutic action: commentary on the
symposium on 'Interventions that effect change in psychotherapy' ", *Infant Mental
Health Journal*, **19**, 333–340.
Beebe, B. and Lachmann, F.M. (2002) *Infant Research and Adult Treatment*, Hillsdale,
NJ: The Analytic Press.
Berry, P. (1982) *Echo's Subtle Body*, Thalwill, Switzerland: Spring Publications.
Bion, W.R. (1970) "Attention and interpretation", in *Seven Servants*, New York:
Jason Aronson, 1977.
Bollas, C. (1987) *The Shadow of the Object: Psychoanalysis of the Unthought Known*,
New York: Columbia University Press.
Bosnak, R. (1986) *A Little Course in Dreams*, Boston: Shambahala Publications.

—— (1996) *Tracks in the Wilderness of Dreaming: Exploring Interior Landscape Through Practical Dreamwork*, New York: Delacorte Press.

Boyer, L.B. (1990) "Countertransference and technique", in L.B. Boyer and P.L. Giovacchini (eds), *Master Clinicians on Treating the Regressed Patient*, Northvale, NJ: Jason Aronson, pp. xiii–xxvi.

Cambray, J. (2001) "Enactments and amplification", *Journal of Analytical Psychology*, **46**(2), 275–303.

—— (2002) "Synchronicity and emergence", *American Image*, **59**(4), 409–434.

Casement, A. (ed.) (1998) *Post-Jungians Today*, London: Routledge.

C.G. Jung Institute (1981) *Sandplay Studies*, San Francisco.

Chodorow, J. (ed.) (1997) *Encountering Jung: On Active Imagination*, Princeton, NJ: Princeton University Press.

Covington, C. (1995), "No story, no analysis", *Journal of Analytical Psychology*, **40**(3), 405–416.

Damasio, A. (1999) *The Feeling of What Happens*, New York: Harcourt Brace.

Davidson, D. (1966) "Transference as a form of active imagination", *Journal of Analytical Psychology*, **11**(2), 135–146.

Desalvo, L. and Leaska, M. (eds) (1984) *The Letters of Vita Sackville-West to Virginia Woolf*, San Francisco: Cleis Press.

Dieckmann, H. (1991) *Methods in Analytical Psychology: An Introduction*, Wilmette, IL: Chiron.

—— (1997) "Fairy-tales in psychotherapy", *Journal of Analytical Psychology*, **42**(2), 253–268.

Douling, D.M. (ed.) (1996) "Arcs", *Parabola*, **XI**(4), 46–49.

Edinger, E. (1985) *Anatomy of the Psyche*, La Salle, IL: Open Court.

Ekstrom, S. (2002) "A cacophony of theories: contributions towards a story-based, understanding of analytic treatment", *Journal of Analytical Psychology*, **47**(3), 339–358.

Eliade, M. (1996) "Mythologies of memory and forgetting", *Parabola*, **XI**(4), 68–76.

Ellman, S. and Moskowitz, M. (eds) (1998) *Enactment: Toward a New Approach to the Therapeutic Relationship*, Northvale, NJ: Jason Aronson.

Feldman, B. (2003) Journal review of "Thinking differently: principles of process in living systems and the specificity of being known", *Journal of Analytical Psychology*, **48**(4), 534–535.

Fonagy, P. (1999) "Memory and therapeutic action", *The International Journal of Psychoanalysis*, **80**, 215–223.

Fosshage, J.L. (2004) "The explicit and implicit dance in psychoanalytic change", *Journal of Analytical Psychology*, **49**(1), 49–65.

Friedman, N. and Moskowitz, M. (1992) "Introduction", in M. Moskowitz, C. Monk, C. Kaye and S. Ellman (eds), *The Neurobiological and Developmental Basis for Psychotherapeutic Intervention*, Northvale, NJ: Jason Aronson, pp. xiii–xxvi.

Graf-Nold, A. (2001) "The Zurich School of Psychiatry in theory and practice. Sabina Spielrein's treatment at the Burghölzli Clinic in Zurich", *Journal of Analytical Psychology*, **46**(1), 73–104.

Hall, J.A. (1983), *Jungian Dream Interpretation*, Toronto: Inner City Books.

Hannah, B. (1981) *Encounters with the Soul: Active Imagination*, Boston: Sigo Press.

Harrington, A. (1996) *Reenchanted Science*, Princeton, NJ: Princeton University Press.

Haule, J.R. (1999) "From somnambulism to the archetypes: the French roots of Jung's split with Freud", in P. Bishop (ed.), *Jung in Contexts: A Reader*, London: Routledge.

Hillman, J. (1979) *The Dream and the Underworld*, New York: Harper & Row.

Hobdell, R. (ed.) (1995) *Freud, Jung, Klein – The Fenceless Field*, London: Routledge.

Hoffer, A. (2001) Jung's analysis of Sabina Spielrein and his use of Freud's free association method, *Journal of Analytical Psychology*, **46**(1), 117–128.

Hogenson, G. (2001) "The Baldwin effect: a neglected influence on C.G. Jung's evolutionary thinking", *The Journal of Analytical Psychology*, **46**(4), 591–611.

Jacobi, J. (1953) *C.G. Jung: Psychological Reflections*, New York: Bollingen Foundation.

—— (1973) *The Psychology of C.G. Jung*, New Haven, CT: Yale University Press.

Jacoby, M. (1990) *Individuation & Narcissism*, London: Routledge.

Johnson, S. (2001) *Emergence: The Connected Lives of Ants, Brains, Cities, and Software*, New York: Scribner.

Jung, C.G. (1914/1915) "On psychological understanding", CW 3, Princeton, NJ: Princeton University Press.

—— (1916/1957) "The transcendent function", CW 8.

—— (1928) "The relations between the ego and the unconscious", CW 7.

—— (1934) "A review of complex theory", CW 8.

—— (1939) "Conscious, unconscious and individuation", CW 9i.

—— (1940) "The psychology of the child archetype", CW 9i.

—— (1944) *Psychology and Alchemy*, CW 12.

—— (1945/1948) "The phenomenology of the spirit in fairytales", CW 9i.

—— (1946) "The psychology of the transference", CW 16.

—— (1963) *Memories, Dreams, Reflections*, New York: Vintage Books.

—— (1967a) "The battle for deliverance from the mother", CW 5.

—— (1967b) *Symbols of Transformation*, CW 5.

—— (1973) *Letters*. Vol. 1: 1906–1950, eds. Gerhard Adler & Aniela Jaffe. London: Routledge & Kegan Paul.

—— (1974) *Dreams*, Princeton, NJ: Bollingen Series, Princeton University Press.

—— (1980) *The Symbolic Life*, CW 18.

—— (1981) *Experimental Researches*, CW 2.

Kalff, D. (2003) *Sandplay: A Psychotherapeutic Approach to the Psyche*, 2nd edn., B. Turner (ed.), Cloverdale, CA: Temenos Press.

Kandel, E.R. (1999) "Biology and the future of psychoanalysis: a new intellectual framework for psychiatry revisited", *American Journal of Psychiatry*, **1561**(4), 505–524.

Knox, J. (2001) "Memories, fantasies, archetypes: an exploration of some connections between cognitive science and analytical psychology", *Journal of Analytical Psychology*, **46**(4), 613–635.

—— (2003) *Archetype, Attachment, Analysis, Jungian Psychology and the Emergent Mind*, Hove: Brunner-Routledge.

Lambert, K. (1981) *Analysis, Repair and Individuation*, London: Karnac.

LeDoux, J. (1996) *The Emotional Brain*, New York: Simon and Schuster.

—— (2002) *Synaptic Self: How Our Brains Become Who We Are*, New York: Penguin.

—— (2003) "The emotional brain revisited", conference paper, *Psychological Trauma: Maturational Processes and Therapeutic Interventions*, Boston.

Levin, F. (1997) "Integrating some mind and brain views of transference: the phenomena", *Journal of American Psychoanalysis*, **45**, 1121–1152.

Lyons-Ruth, K. (1998) "Implicit relational knowing: its role in development and psychoanalytic treatment", *Infant Mental Health Journal*, **19**(3), 282–289.

Maduro, R.J. (1987) "The initial dream and analyzability in beginning analysis", *Journal of Analytical Psychology*, **32**(3), 199–226.

McDowell, M. (2001) "Principle of organization: a dynamic-systems view of the archetype-as-such", *Journal of Analytical Psychology*, **46**(4), 637–654.

Meier, C.A. (1987) *The Meaning and Significance of Dreams*, Boston: Sigo Press.

Modell, A.H. (1997) "The synergy of memory, affects and metaphor", *Journal of Analytical Psychology*, **42**(1), 105–117.

Morowitz, H. (2002) *The Emergence of Everything: How the World Became Complex*, Oxford: Oxford University Press.

Ogden, T. (1997) *Reverie and Interpretation*, Northvale, NJ: Jason Aronson.

—— (1999) " 'The music of what happens' in poetry and psychoanalysis", *International Journal of Psychoanalysis*, **801**, 979–994.

—— (2004) "An introduction to the reading of Bion", *International Journal of Psychoanalysis*, **85**(2), 285–300.

Pally, R. (1998) "Emotional processing; the mind-body connection", *International Journal of Psychoanalysis*, **79**(2), 349–362.

Panksepp, J. (1998) *Affective Neuroscience: The Foundations of Human and Animal Emotions*, Oxford: Oxford University Press.

Plaut, A. (1966) "Reflections about not being able to imagine", *Journal of Analytical Psychology*, **11**(2), 113–134.

Reed, H. (1976) "The art of remembering dreams", *Quadrant*, **9**(1), 48–60.

Samuels, A., Shorter, B. and Plaut, F. (1986) *A Critical Dictionary of Jungian Analysis*, London: Routledge.

Sander, L.W. (1982) "Polarities, paradox, and the organizing process", in J. Call *et al.* (eds), *Proceedings of the 1st World Congress on Infant Psychiatry*, New York: Basic Books.

—— (2002) "Thinking differently: principles of process in living systems and the specificity of being known", *Psychoanalytic Dialogues*, **12**(1), 11–42.

Sandler, J. and Fonagy, P. (eds) (1998) *Recovered Memories of Abuse: True or False?* Madison, CT: International Universities Press.

Saunders, P. and Skar, P. (2001) "Archetypes, complexes and self-organization", *Journal of Analytical Psychology*, **46**(2), 305–323.

Schaverien, J. (submitted) "Art, dreams and active imagination: a post-Jungian approach to the image", *Journal of Analytical Psychology*.

Schore, A.N. (2003) *Affect Regulation*, New York: W.W. Norton & Co.

Siegel, D.J. (1999) *The Developing Mind*, New York: Guilford Press.

Siegelman, E.Y. (1990) *Metaphor and Meaning in Psychotherapy*, New York: Guilford Press.

Stein, M. (ed.) (1995) *Jungian Analysis*, 2nd edn, Chicago: Open Court.

Stern, D.N., Sander, L.W., Nahum, J.P., Harrison, A.M., Lyons-Ruth, K., Morgan, A.C., Bruschweilerstern, N. and Tronick, E.Z. (1998) "Non-interpretive mechanisms in psychoanalytic therapy: the 'something more' than interpretation", *International Journal of Psychoanalysis*, **79**, 903–921.

Strogatz, S. (2003) *Sync: The Emerging Science of Spontaneous Order*, New York: Hyperion.

Tresan, D. (1996) "Jungian metapsychology and neurobiolgical theory", *Journal of Analytical Psychology*, **41**(3), 399–436.

—— (2004) "This new science of ours", *Journal of Analytical Psychology*, **49**(3), 369–396.

Tronick, E. (1996) "Dyadically expanded states of consciousness and the process of normal and abnormal development", presented to Colloque International de Psychiatrie Perinatal, Monaco, January.

Van der Kolk, B. (2003) "The psychobiology of post-traumatic stress disorder", Conference paper, *Psychological Trauma: Maturational Processes and Therapeutic Interventions*, Boston.

Vedfelt, O. (1999) *The Dimensions of Dreams*, New York: Fromm International.

Von Franz, M.-L. (1970) *An Introduction to the Interpretation of Fairy Tales*, Dallas, TX: Spring Publications.

—— (1979) *Alchemical Active Imagination*, Irving, TX: Spring Publications.

Weaver, R. (1973) *The Old Wise Woman: A Study of Active Imagination*, New York: G.P. Putnam's Sons.

Weinrib, E.L. (1983) *Images of the Self: The Sandplay Therapy Process*, Boston: Sigo Press.

Whitmont, E.C. and Perera, S.B. (1989) *Dreams, a Portal to the Source*, New York: Routledge.

Wilkinson, M. (2003) "Undoing trauma: contemporary neuroscience. A Jungian clinical perspective", *Journal of Analytical Psychology*, **48**(2), 235–253.

Young-Eisendrath, P. and Dawson, T. (eds) (1997) *The Cambridge Companion to Jung*, Cambridge: Cambridge University Press.

Chapter 6

Transference and countertransference: contemporary perspectives

Jan Wiener

There have probably been more words written on the subject of transference and countertransference from a wide variety of different perspectives than on any other subject within the domain of depth psychology. This is as true among psychoanalysts as it is for analytical psychologists. Today it remains as "hot" a topic for debate and dispute as it was between Jung and Freud almost a century ago. Our definitions of the concepts and the focus of these debates have evolved and changed over time. We now have a wealth of clinical experience and theoretical evidence built up during these years. We know a good deal more about how to define transference and countertransference, the dynamics of transference projections from the patient and their effect on the analyst, and how technically to approach and work with transferences in the analytic relationship.

Jung is often quoted as uninterested in working with the transference, but although, unlike Freud, he did not leave us extended clinical case studies illustrating how he worked with transference material, his writings and clinical vignettes show evidence of a profound intellectual and emotional interest in the phenomenon from both its personal and archetypal perspectives, developed, often at some cost, out of his own clinical practice.

The movement over time from seeing a phenomenon as a pathological process – an impediment to analysis – to seeing it as a normal part of all conscious and unconscious interactions is nowhere more evident than in discussions of transference and countertransference. I imagine that it would be difficult to find a Jungian analyst around the world who would dispute the inevitability of transference projections making themselves felt within the analytic relationship and their significant role in the service of individuation. However, thinking about and writing about these complex concepts today raises the crucial question of whether we are actually thinking, talking and writing about the same thing. In order to creatively explore our views and differences about an issue, we need to be clear about what we mean and while we may use concepts comfortably, it is often more difficult to describe what we are doing in the consulting room. Problems of definition, of differences in emphasis, context and culture, can all influence the way in which interest in modern concepts evolves, affecting analytic discourse and leading sometimes awkwardly to a confusion of dialects, rather than the provision of a creative space for genuine difference to be acknowledged and disagreements aired.

Notions of transference and what we mean by it are predicated on our views about the nature of the psyche and the development of mental functioning, the analytic relationship and our aims of analysis. This raises the question of the relative significance of transference within the network of concepts that influence analysts' practice, recognizing of course, that some of these may not be fully conscious and again may be difficult to verbalize. Hamilton uses Freud's *the analyst's preconscious* to explore variations in psychoanalysts' preconscious beliefs and practice:

> It is in the area between avowed theoretical orientation – "I am a Freudian", "I am a Jungian" – on the one hand, and therapeutic actions in the "here-and-now" exchanges of the clinical situation on the other, that analysts reveal the muddled overlaps and uncomfortable coexistence of parts of belief systems.
>
> (Hamilton 1996:2–3)

Her interest in the mind of the analyst highlights the value of investigating and trying to clarify the organizing principles of different depth psychologies so that we can learn more about the significance and emphasis that different analysts invest in concepts: in this case, transference and countertransference.

It is my impression that analysts have diverse views about their aims, about what is therapeutic, affected by their affiliations to analytic institutes and key individuals within them, social factors, clinical experience and their own personalities. One of the central beliefs that bring us together as analytical psychologists is in the self as an organizing and unifying centre of the psyche – an archetypal impulse to bring together and mediate the tensions between opposites. Analysis seeks access to the unconscious and the self in all its aspects, but may privilege different "sites of therapeutic action" (Colman 2003:352), leading to different methods of making sense with patients of their psychological experience. Some analytical psychologists, especially those influenced by psychoanalysis, would assert that working in the transference, this specific way of being with another individual and coming to understand them, provides the most meaningful access to the unknown parts of the self and the development of identity. These analysts privilege the *process* of the analytic relationship over its content, preferring patients to use the couch to facilitate the process. Samuels (1985:194) refers to this method as the *interactional dialectic*. Other Jungians privilege the objective psyche, relying more extensively on dreams, associations, active imagination and amplification to locate the unconscious contents of the psyche, collaborating more consciously with patients to allow different aspects of the psyche to come into better alignment with each other. Samuels (1985:194) refers to such a method as the *classical–symbolic–synthetic*. Here, the *contents* of the psyche as they emerge within the analytic relationship take precedence over the process and the transference is less significant.

Our beliefs extend outside the consulting room, affecting how we think, write and teach. Institutionally, they will determine the aims of each training curriculum and the syllabus for trainees, whether the course is more academic or clinical in emphasis. Jung claimed to want no disciples, yet the emergence of different clusters of beliefs, advocated by key individuals, has continued to lead to differences and some tense projections between different societies across the world; what Eisold (2001:343) has called "a continuum from Jungian orthodoxy to psychoanalytic collaboration".

My aims in writing this chapter are firstly to trace the theoretical and clinical development of the concepts of transference and countertransference in analytical psychology from Jung to the present day, turning to psychoanalysis as appropriate. Drawing on some recent evidence from infant research and cognitive neuroscience, I then locate what I believe are some of the present central theoretical and clinical controversies for analytical psychologists, exploring how this new evidence affects our conceptualizations of transference and its implications for clinically fruitful work in the service of our patients.

Theory, pluralism and transference

A chapter that considers contemporary theory needs some preliminary thoughts about the nature of theory in analytical psychology and more particularly theory about transference and countertransference. The cumulative wisdom of our profession is embodied in our theory, and analytical psychology has probably outgrown its initial classification as "a pure" natural science in favour of an approach more familiar to the social sciences, taking account of both the observed and the observer.

Frosh (1997:233) highlights how the central interest of analytical psychology and psychoanalysis – the unconscious – means that theory can never be completely objective: "if there is always unconscious activity, then one can never stand outside the system in order to observe its operations in a perfectly 'objective' way". Forrester (1997:235–236) thinks that rather than debating whether or not psychoanalysis is a science, we should ask what kind of discipline it is. In his view, it is a stable discipline which produces knowledge, "an observational, naturalistic science of human beings; coping with complexity and variety". Parsons (2000:67) highlights the subjective nature of our theory: "psychoanalysis uniquely combines the scientific and the personal . . . its scientific nature is embedded in its personal nature: it is scientific only in so far as it is personal as well".

Theory-making is a natural activity and can be a means of advancing the knowledge of our profession. Pluralism does not uphold a one-worldview,

valuing equally a range of alternatives that can encompass conflict and compromise. Implicitly it acknowledges a role for subjectivity. But pluralism itself
is complex. Samuels defines it as an "attitude to conflict that tries to reconcile
differences without imposing a false resolution on them or losing sight of the
unique value of each position" (Samuels 1989:1).

This is the public face of theory. However, projections onto the concept of
"transference" and its use in analysis, the "transference onto transference", if
you like, reveal a darker personal face and can all too easily become the
heated trigger for criticism and emotional conflict among colleagues. Com-
peting theories of transference find those who work extensively in the transference considered by others to have lost the essence of their Jungian identity
to the psychoanalysts. On the other hand, those who downplay the transference, seeing it as a distortion of the task that is analysis, are often seen as
over-intellectual, clinging blindly to Jung's ideas in the face of new evidence
or overlooking significant aspects of the transference that demand attention.

The pluralist ideal may be all very well in theory, but much more difficult in
practice, since theory-making carries so much investment of feeling and,
however well-analysed we are, it is often difficult to separate the theories we
believe in from our allegiances to their original proponents, be they valued or
disdained internal objects.

For some authors pluralism has real dangers. Knox thinks:

> There is the danger of a scientific and deterministic imperialism which
> attempts to reduce the complexity of the human psyche to explanation in
> terms of one unified theory ... however if the scientific paradigm is
> discarded altogether, pluralism can slide too easily into a postmodern
> multiplicity of theoretical narratives which have no connection with the
> growing body of empirical research in other disciplines about the way the
> mind takes in and organizes information.
>
> (Knox 2003:202–203)

She thinks we must draw on theory from elsewhere, especially about cognitive
and developmental capacities that have been empirically verified in other
disciplines.

Stevens too is rather sceptical about pluralism:

> My position is that there exists a place for pluralism and contextualiza-
> tion but that Jungian psychology will destroy itself if it does not recog-
> nise certain basic principles, which are not "beliefs" or "fictions", but
> hypotheses which have passed certain empirical tests.
>
> (Stevens 2002:349)

Hamilton (1996:24) thinks pluralism is an ideal we rarely live up to; "psychoanalysis has developed into a conglomerate of monistic systems that compete

with one another, each advancing itself as the most comprehensive explanation of human pathology and development". People seem to aspire to pluralism but it can seem grey in comparison to more black and white theories.
Her point seems resonant with some of the present-day debates between
Freudian and Kleinian psychoanalysts.

In this chapter, I hope to consider different approaches to transference and
countertransference, showing some of the nodal points of difference. However, my training at the Society of Analytical Psychology and the cultural
atmosphere in which I practise have inevitably biased my thinking in favour
of a central role for transference in my clinical practice. I recalled Jung's
statement about his own writing:

> Not everything I bring forth is written out of my head, but much of it
> comes from the heart also, a fact I would beg the gracious reader not to
> overlook if, following up the intellectual line of thought, he comes upon
> certain lacunae that have not been properly filled in.
>
> (Jung 1917:para. 200)

A history of theory about transference

Different authors have defined transference in similar but actually subtly
different ways. All seem to agree that transference is a form of projection
from the patient onto the analyst and a universal phenomenon. In the
Tavistock Lectures, Jung referred to transference as follows:

> The term "transference" is the translation of the German word *Übertra-
> gung*. Literally, *Übertragung* means: to carry something over from one
> place to another . . . the psychological process of transference is a specific
> form of the more general process of projection . . . that carries over
> subjective contents of any kind into the object.
>
> (Jung 1935:para. 311–312)

His emphasis is a broad one, on "subjective contents of any kind". Freud
(1912:104) acknowledged the key role for transference resistance: "these circumstances tend towards a situation in which finally every conflict has to be
fought out in the sphere of transference". He saw transference as an ally in
the analytic process, and that it could take different forms with different
patients. He introduced the concept of "transference neurosis" (Freud 1914),
the pressure to repeat in the present repressed material from the past, instead
of remembering it.

Blum (Blum and Fonagy 2003:499), a Freudian psychoanalyst, considers
the complex relationship between transference projections and their relationship with past experiences. He points out that transference is not literally a
replay of the patient's early object relationships but more of a compromise

formation, an unconscious fantasy that includes different components including real experience but also self- and object-representations, defences and superego factors. From this, we can conclude that it tends to be the representations and fantasies about internal objects that are projected onto the analyst which are analysed.

Fordham's (1963:7) definition of transference is more specific, "an unspecified number of *(unconscious)* perceptions of the analyst by the patient, caused by the projection of *split-off, or unintegrated parts of the patient onto or into the analyst*" (my italics). He uses two words here, "onto" and "into", and although he does not differentiate between them, they seem to imply that the nature and power of the projective processes can be different. "Onto" conveys something less powerfully projected and introjected by the analyst, who seems in the traditional way to act more neutrally, available to "deal with" patients' projections. "Into" is more suggestive of a forceful projective identification that invades the analyst who will be affected, whether he likes it or not. Fordham also talks of "split-off or unintegrated" parts of the patient, showing his attempts to link Jungian and Kleinian ideas in developing his pioneering theory of the self and its development in infancy and childhood. These two terms ("split-off" and "unintegrated") actually have rather different meanings (Astor 1995:63; Mizen 2003:292). "Splitting" was a term used by Klein and her followers to describe the primitive defence mechanism employed to preserve good experience and evacuate the bad and intolerable so that they cannot contaminate each other. This was the earliest process by which internal objects were formed. She has been criticised for developing a model of "normal" functioning using clinical data from her work with ill and damaged children. Fordham reserves the term "splitting" for disintegrative experiences that are pathological, threatening to overwhelm the infant or adult, preferring the more Jungian idea of deintegration and reintegration to describe the dynamic process where the primary self reaches out towards objects and internalises experience. His phrase "unintegrated parts of the patient" suggests that he is referring to the not-yet-known rather than the pathological or defensive. Splitting is only necessary when this process is significantly interfered with.

One has only to survey Jung's writings on transference to discover a variety of different points of view. Jung left a confusing legacy about his thoughts and feelings about transference to his followers, which may contribute added heat to the intensity of debate and difference today. This ambiguity permits authors wishing to find evidence from Jung for their personal beliefs about transference every opportunity for extensive "narrative smoothing" (Spence 1987:133)!

Steinberg (1988) and Fordham (1974a) have written chronological accounts of Jung's developing ideas about transference which spanned more than 35 years. Over these years, he was often contradictory in his views, sometimes even within the same paper. Authors develop and change their ideas, hopefully with humility, and such changes of view may be understood in the context of the time they were written, the debates of the day and to whom they were presented (Fordham 1974a). However, the question must indeed be asked as to why Jung's writings on transference are so ambiguous.

Steinberg (1988) thinks that it is the only area in his writings where such major contradictions may be observed because Jung was hurt and angry with Freud for not sufficiently valuing his ideas. Steinberg is also of the opinion that Jung had emotional difficulties with his patients' transferences, particularly the erotic, and their effect on him: "This may have led him to play down the significance of the personal component of the transference and try to find other means of treating his patients" (Steinberg 1988:36).

Jung's writings do indeed support Steinberg's view:

> I am personally always glad when there is only a mild transference or when it is practically unnoticeable. Far less claim is then made upon one as a person, and one can be satisfied with other therapeutically effective factors.
>
> (Jung 1946:para. 359)

Jung's treatment of Sabina Spielrein provides compelling evidence of his struggles with the transference. In a recently discovered letter of Jung's first approach to Freud after Sabina Spielrein's discharge from the Burghölzli, he writes:

> During treatment the patient had the misfortune to fall in love with me . . . In view of this situation her mother therefore wishes, if the worst comes to the worst, to place her elsewhere for treatment, *with which I am naturally in agreement.*
>
> (Minder 2001:69; emphasis added)

Similarly, in Jung's personal letters to Spielrein:

> I have eliminated from my heart all the bitterness against you which it still harboured. To be sure this bitterness did not come from your work . . . but from earlier, from all the inner anguish I experienced because of you – and which you experienced because of me.
>
> (Jung 1911:para. 180)

Fordham (1974a:122) is more generous about Jung's inconsistencies in terms of his attitude to the transference, finding a greater consistency of evidence as to why at crucial points Jung held the views he did if the reader shows perseverance. He points out helpfully, using the Tavistock Lectures as an example, how Jung may have taken a negative view of transference out of annoyance that his audience distracted him away from his devoted study of archetypal dream material to ask about his views on transference.

Despite the inconsistencies, Jung has made significant theoretical contributions to the study of transference, emphasising as he did both its purposive and therapeutic aspects and the significance of the "real" personality of the analyst.

In Lecture 5 (Jung 1935:para. 367–380), Jung outlines what he considers to be four necessary stages of working with transference. I have summarized these in my own words:

1   to help patients come to acknowledge and value their subjective images, personal figures, inner objects, etc. that are projected onto the analyst
2   when these are worked through, to help patients distinguish between the personal projections and those that are impersonal or archetypal
3   to help patients differentiate the personal relationship to the analyst from impersonal factors, helping them to realize consciously that they are not just personal but carry an impersonal, archetypal value that can take them forward
4   what Jung called the "objectivation of impersonal images", an essential part of the process of individuation, helping the patient to realize that "the treasure" lies within him, not outside, "no longer in an object on which he depends".

These stages contain very complex ideas about the nature and role of the transference and, as stand-alone statements, they will not help the budding analytical psychologist grasp "how" to work with transference material. Questions arise as to how to distinguish between personal and archetypal transference projections; whether the process evolves in neat stages like this, and how to work with defences against the processes Jung outlines. Jung did not tell us how to do it and was of the view that "technique" devalued the individual nature of analysis. It is also to be remembered that Jung did not extend his theory to include the role of infancy and the development of the self from birth. He took what might be seen as a more adult and sophisticated approach to transference.

Whatever the clinical limitations of his four stages, implicit within them are some of Jung's core beliefs about transference:

(a)   Jung is in agreement with Freud in supporting analysis of the infantile transference:

> His [the analyst's] highest ambition must consist only in educating his patients to become independent personalities, and in freeing them from their unconscious bondage to infantile limitations. *He must therefore analyse the transference*, a task left untouched by the priest.
>
> (Jung 1912:para. 435; emphasis added)

(b) In contrast to Freud, who was interested in causality, Jung stresses the purposive value of the transference. In an early letter to Dr Löy, Jung writes:

> As long as we look at life only retrospectively, as is the case in the psychoanalytic writings of the Viennese school, we shall never do justice to these persons (neurotic) and never bring them the longed-for deliverance . . . But the impulse which drives the others out of their conservative father-relationship is by no means an infantile wish for subordination; *it is a powerful urge to develop their own personality*, and the struggle for this is for them an imperative duty.
>
> (Jung 1913:para. 658; emphasis added)

Jung made a helpful distinction between two kinds of causality, which he called *causa efficiens* and *causa finalis* (Jung 1945:para. 281). *Causa efficiens* seeks to find reasons for happenings – "why did they happen?", whereas *causa finalis* asks the question "to what purpose is it happening?" Helping patients connect past experiences with the present is not simply to find causes, but to help them move forward. Understanding the roots of patients' emotional difficulties and the inevitable regression involved actually facilitates movement towards contact with the archetypal experience.

(c) Jung is more comfortable with a synthetic method. He criticised Freud's heavy emphasis on infancy and the reductive method as failing to value sufficiently the present meaning to the individual of unconscious spontaneous productions such as dream images and symptoms. His preference (though not exclusively) for working towards a synthetic method embodied his view of the purposive character of the unconscious and its symbol-making capacity:

> we know that it is possible to interpret the fantasy-contents of the instincts either as signs, as self-portraits of the instincts, i.e. reductively; or as symbols, as is the spiritual meaning of the natural instinct.
>
> (Jung 1946:para. 362)

(d) Jung made a distinction between personal and archetypal transference. Jung's stages of the progress of analysis distinguish between images that emerge in the transference from patients' personal experience and those images emanating from impersonal structures of the psyche. The way Jung writes can easily give the impression that he wanted the personal out of the way, moving with more interest to archetypal transferences, but his acknowledgment of the significance of both is observable in his writing:

> The personal projections must be dissolved; and they can be dissolved through conscious realization. But the impersonal projections cannot

be destroyed because they belong to the structural elements of the psyche. They are not relics of a past which has to be outgrown; they are on the contrary purposive and compensatory functions of the utmost importance.

(Jung 1935:para. 368)

(e) Jung placed extremely high value on the analytic relationship and its potential to change not only the patient, but also the analyst:

this bond is often of such intensity that we could almost speak of a "combination". When two chemical substances combine, both are altered. This is precisely what happens in the transference . . . this bond is of the greatest therapeutic importance in that it gives rise to a *mixtum compositum* of the doctor's mental health and the patient's maladjustment.

(Jung 1946:para. 358)

(f) Jung understood intuitively and intellectually the archetypal nature of the transference process itself. This is expressed clearly in "The psychology of the transference" and holds up well to this day:

Once the transference has appeared, the doctor must accept it as part of the treatment and try to understand it, otherwise it will be just another piece of neurotic stupidity. The transference itself is a perfectly natural phenomenon which does not by any means happen only in the consulting room – it can be seen everywhere and may lead to all sorts of nonsense, like all unrecognised projections. Medical treatment of the transference gives the patient a priceless opportunity to withdraw his projections, to make good his losses, and to integrate his personality.

(Jung 1946:para. 420)

In the absence of a personal analyst, Jung turned to studies of history, anthropology and mythology to amplify his intuitions about the unconscious psyche and the relationship between patient and analyst. Some view his detailed unfolding of the analytic relationship through the alchemical text of the *Rosarium Philosophorum* as his main work. Not to everyone's taste, it is difficult to understand, and can leave students keen to advance their clinical practice floundering in its abstract metaphors, but Jung's parallels between the individual's striving for inner unity and the alchemists' search for the lapis, the philosopher's stone, are truly original. I refer the reader to Perry's (1997:146–155) skilled exposition of the woodcut series and their relevance to day-to-day work in the consulting room.

Post-Jungian contributions on transference

One of the most methodologically significant post-Jungian contributions to the theory and clinical use of transference is Williams's (1963) paper on the relationship between the personal and the collective unconscious. She thinks that Jung did not separate these concepts in an arbitrary manner when treating patients, although his writings can give this impression. She points out how the personal and collective unconscious in image-making and pattern-making activities are always interdependent:

> nothing in the personal experience needs to be repressed unless the ego feels threatened by its archetypal power. The archetypal activity which forms the individual's myth is dependent on material supplied by the personal unconscious ... the conceptual split, though necessary for purposes of exposition, is considered to be undesirable in practice.
>
> (Williams 1963:45)

Much contemporary Jungian writing on transference has more clinical emphasis, developing Jung's ideas and making them more relevant and accessible for practitioners. Fordham (1957, 1967, 1974b) was one of the first analysts to explore and question some of Jung's key beliefs about transference, giving frequent case illustrations in his extensive writings. He mistrusted Jung's reliance on the personality of the analyst, thinking that it could lead easily to idealizations from patients and acting out from analysts. In his view, it is how analysts manage the transference that is crucial. Analytical psychologists who turn away from the word "technique" risk using the unique nature of each analysis to deter them from more careful scrutiny of the interactive process. His researches into Jung's synthetic method revealed doubt that an educative approach could deal helpfully with patients with a delusional transference.

Following Jung's distinction between the personal and archetypal transference, and taking account of his early personal difficulties managing some transference projections, Plaut (1956, 1970) thinks that analysts cannot avoid being affected by archetypal transferences and they inevitably "incarnate" the internal figure projected. The danger for the analyst lies in identifying with this figure and either not recognizing it, or sensing it and resisting.

Other authors have made bridges between Jung's central ideas and modern day practice. Davidson (1966) illustrates how a good analysis can be thought of as a lived-through active imagination, emphasising the need for the analyst to receive transference projections from patients with an attitude favourable to an internal process of active imagination. More recently, Cambray (2001:283) draws on the literature on subjectivity and intersubjectivity to reformulate Jung's method of amplification as an internal process that occurs as part of analysts' countertransference responses to their patients. His paper helps to bridge the division between analysts who uphold and those who dismiss the value of amplification in their work, stressing that "to most fully employ amplifications, recognition of our felt engagements with the images and stories that come to mind is essential".

A history of the concept of countertransference

Freud introduced the term "countertransference" in "The future prospects of psycho-analytic therapy", presented at the second International Nuremberg Congress in 1910 (Freud 1910:144–145). In this paper, Freud described countertransference as the analyst's emotional response to stimuli coming from the patient, affecting the doctor's unconscious. In his view, it was an obstacle to progress in analysis, leading him to advocate self-analysis as a way of helping the analyst overcome his blind spots. Despite his significant acknowledgement of analysts' limitations in understanding their patients, he never returned to the theme.

Jung was specific in his early recognition of the need for the analyst to be analysed:

> I even hold it to be an indispensable prerequisite that the psychoanalyst should first submit himself to the analytical process, as his personality is one of the main factors in the cure.
>
> (Jung 1913:para. 586)

Unlike Freud, the supreme value Jung placed on countertransference is implicit in much of his writing. He seemed to recognize intuitively the value of countertransference affects as part of the interactive, unconscious relating in analysis. Although he used the term only rarely, his commitment is evident:

> all projections provoke counter-projections . . . The countertransference is then just as useful and meaningful, or as much of a hindrance, as the transference of the patient, according to whether or not it seeks to establish that better rapport which is essential for the realization of certain unconscious contents.
>
> (Jung 1916:para. 519)

It is nowhere more evident than in his now famous quotation highlighting the significance of the analyst's personality in treatment:

> By no device can the treatment be anything but the product of mutual influence, in which the whole being of the doctor as well as that of his patient plays its part. In the treatment there is an encounter between two irrational factors, that is to say between two persons who are not fixed and determinable quantities but who bring with them, besides their more

or less defined fields of consciousness, an indefinitely extended sphere of non-consciousness. Hence the personalities of doctor and patient are often infinitely more important for the outcome of the treatment than what the doctor says and thinks.

(Jung 1929:para. 163)

Definitions of countertransference can be confusing since the term is sometimes used in a general sense to describe all the analyst's feelings and thoughts towards his patient. I prefer a meaning restricted to the feelings and thoughts arising in the analyst directly from the patient's transferences. Etchegoyen's (1999:269) musical analogy puts it nicely: "there is first canto, to which the contracanto responds". Fordham's (1960:41) definition is consistent with this:

> transference and countertransference are essentially part and parcel of each other because both processes originate in the unconscious. The term will therefore be used here to cover the unconsciously motivated reactions in the analyst that the patient's transference evokes.

Sandler *et al.* (1992:84) have pointed out that the prefix "counter" has two different meanings. It conveys something that is "opposed", a reaction to the patient's transference, but also something that is "parallel", implying a counterpart. These distinctions have contributed to the way in which contemporary writers have mapped out different kinds of countertransference reaction the analyst may experience.

Post-Jungian contributions on countertransference

Studies of the nature and dynamic process of countertransference blossomed from the 1950s when authors realised that analysts' affective responses, their subjectivity, and the capacity to reflect on communications from patients was an indispensable therapeutic tool and one pathway to the unconscious. Although it is woven into the fabric of Jung's fundamental conceptions about the nature of the analytic process, it was later authors such as Winnicott (1949), Heimann (1950) and Little (1951) that paved the way for the wealth of ideas about countertransference in the context of intersubjectivity and its related processes – projection, introjection, projective identification, containment and enactment. Jacobs (2002:15–16) thinks that analysts were severely affected by the traumas of their patients just after the Second World War and that this may have contributed to the accelerating interest in the subject.

Racker (1968) published the first systematic study of countertransference, considering the analytic relationship as involving two individuals, each with a healthy and a more neurotic aspect to their psyches, a personal past and present and their own phantasies and relationship with reality. His work focused on the inner experience of the analyst and how it affected work in the transference. He distinguished first of all between countertransference affects that were neurotic, developing if the analyst became too identified with his own infantile feelings in relation to his patient, and secondly, "true" countertransference affects. Racker's true countertransference could be of two types. First, more comfortable *concordant* responses, when the analyst finds himself feeling empathic with the patient, identifying his ego with the patient's ego. The capacity for concordant countertransference affects is in turn related to the analyst's own experiences of "good enough handling by another when in a state of dependence" (Lambert 1981:148). Then there are the often more disturbing *complementary* reactions, when the analyst receives and identifies with the patient's internal objects. Grinberg (1970) extended the idea of complementary countertransference, putting forward the concept of *projective counteridentification* when, in response to patients' projective identifications, analysts can react with projective identifications of their own. In other words, when there are intense affects in the room, these are not necessarily just the projected inner world of the patient.

Among analytical psychologists, Fordham (1960) developed his ideas about countertransference from Jung's use of empathy and also *participation mystique*, a concept similar to projective identification. He made a distinction between illusory and syntonic countertransference. Like Racker, he considered that analysts project their own material into their patients in a way that obscures understanding of the patient. This unconscious process he termed *illusory*. Fordham used the concept of *syntonic* countertransference to express the analysts' identifications with patients' inner objects. He encompassed Racker's concordant and complementary distinctions. Later, Fordham (1979, in Shamdasani 1996:172) proposed restricting the use of countertransference to the illusory: "it is when the interactive systems become obstructed that a special label is needed and, to my mind, it is then that the term countertransference is appropriate". This idea has not been taken up by subsequent writers.

Jungian authors have contributed significantly to elaborating the shadow aspects of countertransference. Jacoby (1984:94–113) describes a range of potentially dangerous countertransference enactments by the analyst, focusing on money, power, erotic feelings and the neurotic need for therapeutic success. Lambert (1981) warns of enactments in the countertransference when the analyst becomes caught up in the talion law, unconsciously treating attack with counter-attack when identified with the patient's hostile inner objects. Guggenbuhl-Craig (1971) and Groesbeck (1975) elaborate how analysts can become identified with the "healer" archetype, leaving their patients as the only "wounded" ones.

Countertransference is actually a most complex phenomenon. It is a joint creation between patient and analyst, implying as it does the significance of both the analyst's subjective responses and projected aspects of the patient's inner world. It both influences the process and also holds within it rich opportunities for its understanding. Countertransference now embraces the notion that both the analyst's professional and personal identity are inevitably involved in the analytic process. What continues to be debated today is how this translates into individual methods of practice and whether the analyst's reflections on countertransference affects are, with all their attendant dangers, the central mutative activity in analysis.

New contexts for thinking about transference and countertransference

It is beyond the remit and scope of this chapter to consider all the research findings from different disciplines that could provide evidence for different authors' positions on the theory of transference and countertransference. For comprehensive overviews, the reader is referred to Chapters 3 and 5. There is now sufficient consistency of view in the fields of mind–brain research and infant research to demonstrate how the development of the brain and the development of mind are significantly related and further, that the development of a mind and the capacity to make meaning emerges through relationship. Non-verbal and unconscious interactive processes go on continuously in infancy and adulthood and therefore, by implication, within the transference–countertransference relationship. Implicit processing that is beyond awareness can be as important as that which is explicit, conscious or verbal. There has been some excellent experimental and clinical research showing the implications of damage to these implicit interactive processes (Kaplan-Solms and Solms 2000; Davies 2002; Wilkinson 2003).

Schore (1994, 2001) describes how the brain always organizes itself in the context of another person with another brain. He stresses that affect regulation underlies and maintains the functioning of the individual. It in turn is affected nonverbally and unconsciously through relating. His findings have implications for both psychoanalysis and analytical psychology, which have tended until relatively recently to focus more heavily on the symbolic meaning of verbal communication. Schore's research supports the idea that non-verbal communication regulates mind and body between people and by implication between patient and analyst:

> Non-verbal transference–countertransference interactions that take place at preconscious–unconscious levels represent right hemisphere to right hemisphere communications of fast-acting, automatic, regulated and dysregulated emotional states between patient and therapist . . . In a growth-facilitating therapeutic context, meaning is not singularly discovered, but dyadically created.
>
> (Schore 2001:315–319)

Pally (2000:99) is in agreement with Schore:

> How the analyst feels, both "in the body" and "in the mind", may be as important an indicator of what is going on in the patient as whatever the analyst is thinking. How the analyst communicates may be as important as what the analyst says.

The implications for analysts to find the capacity to access both their subjective responses and their rational thoughts are clear. Working from the central premise that the nature of interactive processes is now seen as central both to infant development and to the success of the analytic endeavour, Beebe and Lachman (2002) use a dyadic systems model to study the origins of relatedness and patterns of non-verbal communication in infancy and adulthood:

> a person is affected by his own behaviour (self-regulation) as well as by that of his partner (interactive regulation). Interactive regulation flows in both directions, on a moment-to-moment basis.
>
> (Beebe and Lachmann 2002:141)

Stern *et al.* (1998) capture the essence of these ideas with their phrase "implicit relational knowing", the intersubjective unconscious experiences in analysis that are "moments of meeting", just as important in precipitating change in analysis as interpretation. The process of making implicit knowing conscious is not the same as accessing repressed material. What is significant is that these "moments of meeting" are new; something is created intersubjectively which alters the analytic atmosphere. Lyons-Ruth (1998:288) stresses that "these moments of meeting open the way to the elaboration of a more complex and coherent way of being together, with associated change in how relational possibilities are represented in each participant's implicit relational knowing".

These and other findings lend credible support to the value for analysts of attending carefully to the processes of transference and countertransference, as they promise to be central in the recognition and facilitation of change. Jungian theory stands up pretty well to the research tests of time in the context of the finding that subjectivity is an emergent and interactive process. Jung's emphasis on the mutuality of change in analysis, and on an indefinitely extended sphere of non-consciousness, is supported by the findings of neuroscience and infant development research. Jung's concept of the transcendent function, the capacity in the individual that enables the rational and the irrational, the conscious and the unconscious to be compared and ultimately to come together, sits well with Stern's implicit relational knowing and the need for the analyst to bring together what he senses with what he thinks – to develop a capacity for self-regulation and interactive sensitivity. The research findings give food for thought as to how we can train potential analysts to fine-tune their subjective experiences with their patients and internalize the capacity to self-regulate and contain primitive experience. Tracking patients' affective states in relation to those of the analyst would seem to be an essential component of the analytic attitude. How these may be converted into a meaningful language with which to talk to our patients remains controversial. The specific controversies among depth psychologists about transference and countertransference have been reframed but not resolved. What we know now from the fields of infant research and cognitive neuroscience promises to help us understand the precise mechanisms by which transference and countertransference processes operate.

Controversy in contemporary attitudes to transference

Fordham's address to members of the Society of Analytical Psychology at the Society's Annual General Meeting in July 1954 highlighted the central role of transference in debates among its members:

> a new sign of activity within the Society has been the continued interest in the transference, round which is circulating some of the conflicts with the society. *If my reading of these conflicts is correct, they turn on the questions, not of the existence of transference phenomena, but upon the desirability, or otherwise of interpreting some of them in personal terms, and on the ways of handling and reacting to transpersonal contents.*
>
> (Shamdasani 1996:6; emphasis added)

These minutes reflected the work of a small group of SAP members meeting 16 times to engage creatively with the subject of transference and countertransference. While the central tenet of Fordham's address holds true today, the areas of difference and dispute have shifted in focus. Two central controversies (not the only ones by any means) are much in debate today.

I. Transference: the total or partial situation?

The term "transference: the total situation" is the provocative title of Betty Joseph's (1985) paper stressing her idea that transference is the central framework for all analyses. She follows Klein's (1952:48–57) ideas emphasizing transference as "total situations transferred from the past into the present as well as emotion, defences and object relations". In other words, it is not just transference onto the analyst that is significant and may be interpreted, but rather everything patients bring give clues about their unconscious anxieties aroused in the transference relationship. Joseph (1985:452) states:

my stress has been on the transference as a relationship in which something is all the time going on, but we know that this something is essentially based on the patient's past and the relationship with his internal objects or his belief about them and what they were like.

Later she summarizes her position:

everything in the patient's psychic organization based on his early and habitual ways of functioning, his fantasies, impulses, defences and conflicts, will be lived out in some way in the transference. In addition, everything that the analyst is or says is likely to be responded to according to the patient's own psychic make-up, rather than the analyst's intentions and the meaning he gives to his interpretations.

(Joseph 1985:453)

Joseph believes that the main site of therapeutic action lies within the transference relationship. It seems to me that the Kleinian attitude to transference is predicated on the supreme significance of the infant–mother dyad as the location of disturbance. Troubles start at this earliest point and it is only if these "hot spots' can become lived experience within the analysis, and interpreted through the here-and-now of the transference, that internal change becomes possible. For this to happen, there has to be a regression. Appropriate attempts to interpret past experience as significantly influencing the present are not excluded, but are downplayed as defensive on the part of patient or analyst and of lesser therapeutic value than here-and-now interventions.

This view has led to much difference of opinion among psychoanalysts. There is an ongoing debate between Blum and Fonagy (2003:497–515) as to whether the here-and-now transference experience of self and other is the most important site of therapeutic action. Given Fonagy's (1999) distinctions between explicit and implicit memory, he questions the usefulness to the analytic endeavour of the process of recovering memories from childhood and agrees with Joseph when he states that "therapeutic work needs to focus on helping the individual identify regular patterns of behaviour based on childhood fantasy and experience, for which autobiographical memory can provide no explanation" (Fonagy 1999:220). In his view the only way we can really know what goes on in a patient's mind is in the transference.

Blum (Blum and Fonagy 2003:498) challenges Fonagy's position: "we do not know our patients' character through transference alone and the analyst is not the only transference object ... extratransference interpretations involve extra-analytic transferences". Blum values transference as one useful element for understanding our patients, but thinks it is no more reliable than others, such as dreams, symptoms and other behaviour. In a more emotional tone, he criticises analysts whose sole focus is on the transference:

How does the patient feel when only transference is interpreted and other issues are ignored? All associations, interventions and reactions are forced into the Procrustean bed of transference. A strictly analytic transference focus is consistent with a narcissistic position of the analyst; he/she is not only a very important person, but is considered the most important person in the patient's life. The patient identifies with the idealized analyst and the narcissism of the analytic dyad is then gratified and promoted. This is especially problematic in a long analysis if real-life relationships have been devalued, and cannot compare to the exceptional status and satisfactions.

(Blum and Fonagy 2003:498–499)

Blum overstates his case a bit, but his voice resonates among some analytical psychologists. Peters (1991) considers that transference develops naturally and should not be forced through premature or dogmatic transference inter-pretations by the analyst. He considers that patients bring transferences onto figures other than the analyst, which if worked with do not preclude effective analysis. He joins with Blum in warning analysts of the dangers of incarnat-ing excessively the archetype of the infant–mother relationship, leading them, in his view, to draw with hunger their patients' transferences towards them.

Astor (2001), using detailed clinical case material, considers his inner rela-tionship between his psychoanalytic supervisor and his Jungian supervisor as they interact and are played out in the analysis of a female patient. He maps out from within himself the controversy of the relative importance of the transference. His Jungian supervisor trusts in the organizing capacity of the self, values the manifest content of his patient's material, finds a valid role for empathy and non-transference interpretations. Transference material is not necessarily always buried. His psychoanalytic supervisor sees the task of analysis as bringing unconscious fantasy into the open. The communications of his patient always have unconscious meaning in the here-and-now of a session. Astor uses his empathy and intuition about his patient's feelings and state of mind to find an approach most helpful for her at that time.

Kast (2003) and Proner (2003) enter into debate about the relative significance for them of the transference. Kast is clear about her view:

Facilitating the development of symbols is more important than the pro-cess of transference–countertransference itself. Symbols are not only vehicles for the individuation process, but also refer to life history and future development . . . They shape the emotions that are connected with complexes, archetypes and the real relationship.

(Kast 2003:107)

Proner (2003:96) disagrees, conceptualizing the analytic relationship as "analogous to an early mother–infant couple", emphasizing the need for access to feelings and images associated with infantile parts of the psyche reworked with the analyst. He agrees with Joseph, placing transference as the central site of therapeutic action. He sees Kast's approach as "*analysing the transference*" whereas he works "*in the transference*", highlighting a methodologically significant difference in emphasis between them: "all material brought to the analytic session, whether verbal or non-verbal, whether dreams or free associations, communicates something about the ongoing inner relationship between the patient and the analyst" (Proner 2003:100–101).

These controversies highlight three central differences of opinion. First, is transference theoretically the "fulcrum of analysis" (Gordon 1993)? Second, is it the case that everything the patient brings emanates only from the infantile parts of the psyche? Third, what is the effect on the patient of the analyst taking up all communications in the transference?

I agree with Fonagy (Blum and Fonagy 2003:506) that "the crucial component is the provision of a perspective or a frame for interpreting subjectivity that is beyond that which the patient has ready conscious access to apart from the analytic encounter". In my view this perspective crucially involves the transference. But, like Etchegoyen (1999:83), I feel that "not everything is transference, but transference exists in everything, which is not the same thing".

Although I work *in* the transference, I cannot agree that transference is "the total situation". Transference is always there, and when it emerges from the earliest experiences of patients, it is obvious within the analytic relationship and must be "received" by the analyst. Frequent sessions and the use of the couch are likely to foster pre-verbal and intense transference projections, but the transference is not always infantile. If we view (and interpret) transference as emanating only from infancy, then we risk losing both the complexity and the temporality of the meaning of our patients' communications and how the mind functions at different developmental stages. If *all* interpretations are transference interpretations with the aim of uncovering patients' complexes in relation to the analyst, this can become a particular kind of reductionism and risks patients learning "a method" from the analyst that limits their possibilities for creative play where symbols can find meaning and dreams herald new possibilities. The analyst can become a new object and is not necessarily always the incarnation of a former object.

2. The personality of the analyst

Jung stressed frequently the important role of the personality of the analyst and the mutuality of the analytic process, but it is not always obvious what this means in practice. Obviously, the personality of the analyst is significant since we all bring to the analytic situation the essential and unique characteristics of the people we have become. I think Jung is referring here to the way in which analysts use themselves when working with patients. Jung's considerable emphasis on personality was in part his reaction to the much-caricatured Freudian emphasis on neutrality, abstinence and anonymity – vestiges of the old medical model. Although the findings of neuroscience and infant research show that non-verbal unconscious processes are going on all the time, influencing both patient and analyst, the personal analysis, training and clinical experience of analysts put them in a better position to bring these interactions into consciousness. The relationship between patient and analyst is not symmetrical.

Analysts need the capacity both to hold back and to move forward in the analytic relationship. Anonymity, abstinence and neutrality can be seen as intrinsic constituents of a professional analytic and ethical attitude (see Solomon, Chapter 10). We do not reveal too much of our personal lives to our patients, leaving "space" for transference projections (anonymity). We try to limit enactments and acting out (abstinence) and to maintain a non-judgemental attitude (neutrality). These contribute to the creation of a *vas bene clausum* or containing space in which relating can evolve safely. We also need the capacity to move forward in the sense of making ourselves emotionally fully available to our patients. Receptiveness to projections and projective identifications is a vital component of the analytic attitude. I think this is what Jung was talking about when he advocated a new theory for each patient, and what Fordham (1993) was encouraging by "not knowing before-hand", creating the potential for the emergence of new theories in each session. It is Bion's (1970:34) eschewing of memory and desire so that the analyst increases his ability to exercise "acts of faith". This involves what I prefer to describe as the "self of the analyst". Schafer (1983:291) says something similar, discussing the analyst's need to subordinate his personality in analytic work and referring to "a second self". He thinks it is artificial to separate this second self from the analyst's personality, but it is "a form that integrates one's own personality into the constraints required to develop an analytic situation". I think he is talking about his way of using himself in the service of his patients.

A consideration of the role of personality includes debates about whether analysis is a "real" relationship and how much of themselves analysts should reveal to their patients. Although Greenson (1973) recommends that the analyst constrain himself from expressing genuine feelings to his patients, he cites frequent examples of situations when he considers such revelations to be therapeutically helpful. Renik (1995) too challenges contemporary ideas about countertransference, believing that since the analyst's subjectivity is inevitably transmitted to the patient, the analyst might as well bring his views out into the open. In my experience this can often be counterproductive. It is the analyst's self-knowledge that patients really need.

The range of different views about how much analysts should give of themselves is aired in a debate between Caper (2003) and Colman (2003). Caper, a psychoanalyst, thinks we always unconsciously wish to influence our patients rather than analyse them. He considers this an aspect of the analyst's neurotic countertransference and that it happens because the analyst cannot hold back from offering himself freely in the presence of obvious suffering. We must necessarily exclude "too many of the elements vital to any ordinary, natural human relationship" (Caper 2003:345). Being too real leads to collusions with the patient and even if it appears superficially therapeutic, it is not, in his view, analytic.

He considers that the main role of the analyst is to make interpretations:

> The real job of the real analyst is to identify and understand the meaning of both the transference and countertransference fantasies in terms of split-off parts of the patient's personality, and to communicate this understanding to the patient. In this view, providing the patient with anything else, such as love, advice, guidance, or support for his self-esteem is the analyst's acting in his countertransference, and represents his resistance to analysis.
>
> (Caper 2003:346)

Caper's view of analysts' technical stance and their attitude to the transference could be considered to be one where there is more holding back by the analyst than moving forward. The analytic attitude privileges neutrality because without it, patients will not discover their destructive impulses.

Colman thinks that Caper's attitude risks inhibiting the development of a natural unconscious process between patient and analyst. For him, "the therapeutic action of psychoanalysis occurs directly through the relationship between analyst and patient, rather than through the interpretation of its transference elements . . . analysis is left after the interpretations have been forgotten" (Colman 2003:352). I think he is saying that patients' experiences of their analysts as empathic and "real" can facilitate growth and do not constitute a longed-for but defensive collusion. It is what comes from the "self" of the analyst that is important and will be felt unconsciously by the patient. Colman is not advocating countertransference enactments by telling patients what he feels in sessions, but rather supports Jung's view that "an uncontaminated transference" is impossible and interpretations make themselves out of this intensely personal relationship. Colman's stance gains support from recent research studies (Pally 2000; Beebe and Lachmann 2002), showing how what is felt in relationship can be more important than what is thought and how interpretations are conveyed may be more significant than their content. The person of the analyst, however much is revealed, cannot be avoided in the analytic relationship and it is this emotional contact that potentially facilitates change.

Conclusions

The controversies discussed in this chapter show the extent to which our attachment to specific theories becomes intensely personal. Since as analysts we all need to become experts in the management of uncertainty, it is perhaps understandable that we long for a coherent theory, a universal truth and method of enquiry. It is also understandable that pulls between pluralism and unity, between learning from experience and the hard sciences are nowhere more potent than in our theories of transference and countertransference, since these lie at the heart of the subjective, personal and unique meeting of two selves, trying to come together in an authentic way to make meaning together.

In this chapter I have emphasized that analysts' skilled use of countertransference experiences and their ability to process projective identifications can be a major therapeutic factor in the analysis. If these affects remain unscrutinized, they can lead to dangerous enactments and impasse; if they are used dogmatically, patients may not feel heard or understood or will feel forced by technique to become compliant to its method. The emerging topical concepts of affect regulation, implicit memory function and co-constructed intersubjectivity, which integrate clinical thinking with data from cognitive neuroscience and infant research, can help us reconsider divergent views of transference and countertransference as well as the physiological and emotional processes through which they operate.

I would like to return to Anthony Stevens' (2002:349) plea that Jungian psychology continue in its quest to "recognise certain basic principles, which are not 'beliefs' or fictions, but hypotheses which have passed certain empirical tests". Recent research findings about the value of the analysts' subjectivity as an emergent process uphold Jung's heartfelt views about the interactive nature of the analytic relationship, where the selves of patient and analyst consciously and unconsciously influence each other, and also his concept of the transcendent function. They support a central role for projective identification or, in Jung's language, *participation mystique*, at the core of intersubjective relating. We ignore transference and countertransference phenomena at our peril.

Careful research has helped and will continue to help us to examine our long-held theories, refine them and cast some reluctantly to the history books. Hamilton (1996:311) thinks that research into analysts' descriptions about how they work with transference and countertransference affects has "moved analysis onto a more horizontal, transparent plane. Gone is the search for the mysterious, for the inner, the latent and for historical fact". With reference to the mysterious, I hope she is wrong. However much contemporary research encourages us to re-evaluate present theory and its clinical usefulness, the search for the mysterious, the not-yet-known, remains paramount. The knowledge we acquire from imaginative theory-making in the consulting room is as important as objective data from other disciplines. We should not lose touch with this lived experience, where the subjective, interactive processes provide complementary natural theory-making opportunities. We cannot separate our theory from ourselves. It evolves from unconsciousness hopefully to find a place where eventually it can be articulated. Meaning and understanding come as we acquire the capacity to integrate knowledge that comes from outside – from colleagues, from books, and from other disciplines – with the knowledge that comes from within. It is this process of finding, forming and reforming that goes on continuously with our patients that gives meaning to our professional work and allows us to continue to assess the usefulness of our concepts and to modify them when necessary.

References

Astor, J. (1995) "Ego development in infancy and childhood", in J. Astor, (ed.), *Michael Fordham: Innovations in Analytical Psychology*, London: Routledge.
—— (2001) "Is transference the total situation?", *Journal of Analytical Psychology*, **46**(3), 415–431.
Beebe, B. and Lachmann, F.M. (2002) *Infant Research and Adult Treatment*, Hillsdale, NJ and London: The Analytic Press.
Bion, W. (1970) *Attention and Interpretation*, London: Tavistock Publications.
Blum, H.P and Fonagy, P. (2003) "Psychoanalytic controversies", *International Journal of Psycho-Analysis*, **84**(3), 497–515.
Cambray, J. (2001) "Enactments and amplification", *Journal of Analytical Psychology*, **46**(2), 275–305.
Caper, R. (2003) "Does psychoanalysis heal? A contribution to the theory of psychoanalytic technique", in R. Withers, (ed.), *Controversies in Analytical Psychology*, Hove and New York: Brunner-Routledge. Also in *International Journal of Psycho-Analysis* (1992), **73**(2), 283–293.
Colman, W. (2003) "Interpretation and relationship: ends or means?", in R. Withers (ed.), *Controversies in Analytical Psychology*, Hove and New York: Brunner-Routledge.
Davidson, D. (1966) "Transference as a form of active imagination", *Journal of Analytical Psychology*, **11**(2), 135–147.
Davies, M. (2002) "A few thoughts about the mind, the brain, and a child with early deprivation", *Journal of Analytical Psychology*, **47**(3), 421–436.
Eisold, K. (2001) "Institutional conflicts in Jungian analysis", *Journal of Analytical Psychology*, **46**(2), 335–355.
Etchegoyen, R.H. (1999) *The Fundamentals of Psychoanalytic Technique*, London: Karnac Books.
Fonagy, P. (1999) "Memory and therapeutic action", *International Journal of Psycho-Analysis*, **80**(2), 215–225.
Fordham, M. (1957) "Notes on the transference", reprinted in *New Developments in Analytical Psychology*, London: Heinemann, 1974. Also published in S. Shamdasani (ed.), *Fordham, M. Analyst–Patient Interaction: Collected Papers on Technique*, London: Routledge, 1996.
—— (1960) "Countertransference", in S. Shamdasani (ed.), *Fordham, M.*

Analyst–Patient Interaction: Collected Papers on Technique, London: Routledge, 1996.

—— (1963) "Notes on the transference and its management in a schizoid child", *Journal of Child Psychotherapy*, **1**(1), 7–15.

—— (1967) "Active imagination – deintegration or disintegration", *Journal of Analytical Psychology*, **12**(1), 51–67.

—— (1974a) "Jung's conception of transference", *Journal of Analytical Psychology*, **19**(1), 1–22. Also in S. Shamdasani (ed.), *Fordham, M. Analyst–Patient Interaction: Collected Papers on Technique*, London and New York: Routledge, 1996.

—— (1974b) "Technique and countertransference", *Journal of Analytical Psychology*, **14**(2), 95–119. Also in M. Fordham, R. Gordon, J. Hubback and K. Lambert, (eds), *Technique in Jungian Analysis*, Library of Analytical Psychology, vol. 2, London: Heinemann, 1974. Also in S. Shamdasani (ed.), *Fordham, M. Analyst–Patient Interaction: Collected Papers on Technique*, London and New York: Routledge, 1996.

—— (1993) "On not knowing beforehand", *Journal of Analytical Psychology*, **38**(2), 127–137.

Forrester, J. (1997) *Dispatches from the Freud Wars*, London and Cambridge, MA: Harvard University Press.

Freud, S. (1910) "The future prospects of psycho-analytic therapy", Standard Edition 11, London: The Hogarth Press.

—— (1912) "Dynamics of the transference", Standard Edition 12, p.104, London: The Hogarth Press.

—— (1914) "Remembering, repeating and working through (Further recommendations on the technique of psycho-analysis)", Standard Edition, 12, London: The Hogarth Press.

Frosh, S. (1997) *For and Against Psychoanalysis*, London: Routledge.

Gordon, R. (1993) "Transference as fulcrum of analysis", *Bridges: Metaphor for Psychic Processes*, London: Karnac Books.

Greenson, R. (1973) *The Technique and Practice of Psycho-Analysis*, London: The Hogarth Press.

Grinberg, L (1970) "The problems of supervision in psychoanalytic education", *International Journal of Psycho-Analysis*, **51**, 371–374.

Groesbeck, C.G. (1975) "The archetypal image of the wounded healer", *Journal of Analytical Psychology*, **20**(2), 122–146.

Guggenbuhl-Craig, A. (1971) *Power in the Helping Professions*, Zurich: Spring Publications.

Hamilton, V. (1996) *The Analyst's Preconscious*, Hillsdale, NJ and London: The Analytic Press.

Heimann, P. (1950) "On countertransference", *International Journal of Psycho-Analysis*, **31**, 81–84.

Jacobs, T. (2002) "Countertransference past and present: a review of the concept", in M. Michels, L. Abensauer, C.L. Eizirik and R. Rusbridger (eds) *Key Papers on Countertransference*, London: Karnac Books.

Jacoby, M. (1984) *The Analytic Encounter*, Toronto: Inner City Books.

Joseph, B. (1985) "Transference: the total situation", *International Journal of Psycho-Analysis*, **66**(4), 447–455.

Jung, C.G. (1911) "The Letters of C.G. Jung to Sabina Spielrein", *Journal of Analytical Psychology* (2001), **46**(1), 173–201.
—— (1912) "The theory of psychoanalysis", CW 4, Princeton, NJ: Princeton University Press.
—— (1913) "Crucial points in psychoanalysis (Jung and Löy)", CW 4.
—— (1916) "General aspects of dream psychology", CW 8.
—— (1917) "General remarks on the therapeutic approach to the unconscious", CW 7.
—— (1929) "Problems of modern psychotherapy", CW 16.
—— (1935) "The Tavistock Lectures", CW 18. Also in *Analytical Psychology: Its Theory and Practice*, London: Routledge and Kegan Paul.
—— (1945) "On the nature of dreams", CW 8.
—— (1946) "The psychology of the transference", CW 16.
Kaplan-Solms, K. and Solms M. (2000) *Clinical Studies in Neuro-Psychoanalysis*, London: Karnac Books.
Kast, V. (2003) "Transcending the transference", in R. Withers (ed.), *Controversies in Analytical Psychology*, Hove and New York: Brunner-Routledge.
Klein, M. (1952) "The origins of transference", *Envy and Gratitude and Other Works, 1946–1960*, London: Hogarth Press.
Knox, J. (2003) *Archetype, Attachment Analysis*, Hove and New York: Brunner-Routledge.
Lambert, K. (1981) *Analysis, Repair and Individuation*, Library of Analytical Psychology, London: Academic Press.
Little, M. (1951) "Countertransference and the patient's response to it", *International Journal of Psycho-Analysis*, **32**, 320–340.
Lyons-Ruth, K. (1998) "Implicit relational knowing: its role in development and psychoanalytic treatment", *Infant Mental Health Journal*, **19**(3), 282–291.
Minder, B. (2001) "A document. Jung to Freud 1905: a report on Sabina Spielrein", *Journal of Analytical Psychology*, **46**(1), 67–73.
Mizen, R. (2003) "A contribution towards an analytic theory of violence", *Journal of Analytical Psychology*, **48**(3), 285–307.
Pally, R. (2000) *The Mind–Brain Relationship*, London: Karnac Books.
Parsons, M. (2000) *The Dove that Returns, the Dove That Vanishes: Paradox and Creativity in Psychoanalysis*, London and Philadelphia: Routledge.
Perry, C. (1997) "Transference and countertransference", in P. Young-Eisendrath and T. Dawson (eds), *The Cambridge Companion to Jung*, Cambridge: Cambridge University Press.
Peters, R. (1991) "The therapist's expectations of the transference", *Journal of Analytical Psychology*, **36**(1), 77–93.
Plaut, A.B (1956) "The transference in analytical psychology", *British Journal of Medical Psychology*, **29**(1), 15–20. Also in M. Fordham, R. Gordon, J. Hubback and K. Lambert (eds), *Technique in Jungian Analysis*, vol. 2, London: Heinemann, 1974.
—— (1970) "Comment: on not incarnating the archetype", *Journal of Analytical Psychology*, **29**(1), 88–94. Also in M. Fordham, R. Gordon, J. Hubback and K. Lambert (eds), *Technique in Jungian Analysis*, vol. 2, London: Heinemann, 1974.
Proner, B. (2003) "Working in the transference", in R. Withers (ed.), *Controversies in Analytical Psychology*, Hove and New York: Brunner-Routledge.
Racker, H. (1968) *Transference and Countertransference*, London: Maresfield Library.

Renik, O. (1995) "The ideal of the anonymous analyst and the problem of self-disclosure", *Psychoanalytic Quarterly*, **64**, 466–495.

Samuels, A. (1985) *Jung and the Post-Jungians*, London: Routledge and Kegan Paul.

—— (1989) *The Plural Psyche*, London: Routledge.

Sandler, J., Dare, C. and Holder, A. (1992) *The Patient and the Analyst*, London and New York: Karnac Books.

Schafer, R. (1983) *The Analytic Attitude*, New York: Basic Books.

Schore, A.N. (1994) *Affect Regulation and the Origin of the Self: The Neurology of Emotional Development*, Hillsdale, NJ and Hove: Lawrence Erlbaum Associates.

—— (2001) "Minds in the making: attachment, the self-organizing brain, and developmentally-oriented psychoanalytic psychotherapy", *British Journal of Psychotherapy*, **17**(3), 297–299.

Shamdasani, S. (ed.) (1996) *Analyst–Patient Interaction: Collected Papers on Technique by M. Fordham*, London: Routledge.

Spence, D. (1987) *The Freudian Metaphor: Toward Paradigm Change in Psychoanalysis*, New York and London: W.W. Norton and Co.

Steinberg, W. (1988) "The evolution of Jung's ideas on the transference", *Journal of Analytical Psychology*, **33**(1), 21–39.

Stern, D.N., Sander, L.W., Nahum, J.P., Harrison, A.M., Lyons-Ruth, K., Morgan, A.C., Bruchweilerstern, N. and Tronick, E.Z. (1998) "Non-interpretive mechanisms in psychoanalytic therapy", *International Journal of Psycho-Analysis*, **79**(5), 903–923.

Stevens, A. (2002) *Archetype Revisited: An Updated Natural History of the Self*, Hove and New York: Brunner-Routledge.

Wilkinson, M. (2003) "Undoing trauma: contemporary neuroscience. A Jungian clinical perspective", *Journal of Analytical Psychology*, **28**, 235–255.

Williams, M. (1963) "The indivisibility of the personal and collective unconscious", *Journal of Analytical Psychology*, **8**(1), 45–51. Also in M. Fordham, R. Gordon, J. Hubback, K. Lambert and M. Williams (eds), *Analytical Psychology: A Modern Science*, vol. 1, London: Academic Press, 1980.

Winnicott, D. (1949) "Hate in the countertransference", *International Journal of Psycho-Analysis*, **30**, 69–75.

Chapter 7

The emerging theory of cultural complexes

Thomas Singer and Samuel L. Kimbles

The purpose of this chapter is to build for the reader a step-by-step foundation for a theory of cultural complexes. Through a hundred years of clinical
experience, Jungians have come to know well and accept that complexes are
powerful forces in the lives of individuals. Most simply, we define a complex
as an emotionally charged group of ideas and images that cluster around an
archetypal core. The basic premise of this chapter is that another level of
complexes exists within the psyche of the group (and within the individual at
the group level of their psyche). We call these group complexes "cultural
complexes" and they, too, can be defined as an emotionally charged aggregate
of ideas and images that cluster around an archetypal core.

Jungian theory at its best is open and evolving, with a long and meaningful
history of modification and adaptation. Jung himself was never static in the
development of his ideas and as a result, there are several different "theories"
that exist side by side: complex theory, a theory of psychological types, a
theory of archetypes and the collective unconscious and ultimately, his theory of the Self. These theories taken together form a whole, but were never
intended to be a tight, carefully constructed architectural gem. One might
think of them as a bit ramshackle – which is how many of us like it. Our
theory of cultural complexes is a new addition, conceived in the style of
a New England farmhouse addition.

The structure of this chapter will reflect the construction of this new addition. The name "cultural complex" is itself a theory-building title – putting
two traditional building blocks of Jungian psychology together in a new way.
First is Jung's theory of complexes. Second is Joseph Henderson's elaboration on Jung's earlier design of the structure of the unconscious itself, in
which Henderson introduced the concept of the "cultural unconscious."
Third, we are now putting these two theories together with the idea of "cultural complexes." Indeed, we chose "cultural complex" rather than "group
complex" as the name for this psychological phenomenon to stay consistent
with the nomenclature of our predecessors. It is clearest to think of cultural
complexes emerging from the cultural level of the unconscious. The first
three sections of this chapter will develop these three themes: Jung's theory

of complexes; Henderson's theory of the cultural unconscious; and our theory of cultural complexes. The final two sections of this chapter will give examples of how the theory of cultural complexes can be applied in specific situations. Thomas Singer will discuss an example of a cultural complex in the psyche of the group. And finally, Samuel L. Kimbles will give a clinical case example of a cultural complex in the psyche of an individual.

Therefore this chapter introduces a theme that is both very old and, at the same time, quite new – or at least conceived with a new "spin" – in analytical psychology. Jung's theory of complexes was his first major contribution to psychology and remains one of the fundamental building blocks of the Jungian tradition. This is the "old" part of the story and should be familiar to most readers of this volume. The "new" part of the story which this chapter wants to tell is that Jung's complex theory can and should be applied in ways that – up until now – the tradition for the most part has overlooked or neglected. We think that Jung's complex theory can and should be applied to the life of groups (and nations) and that these cultural complexes exist within the psyche of the collective as a whole and the individual members of the group. This raises several questions right away: why do you call them "cultural complexes?" Didn't Jung explore this theme in his discussion of "national character," a discussion with an ugly history that has led mostly to acrimony and rarely to fruitful application? These and many other questions should come to the reader's mind in working through this essay and, hopefully, the answers will become clearer along the way. Before getting into these issues, however, we would like to back up and suggest why Jung's complex theory didn't get extended into the life of groups and also why, at this time, the subject of "cultural complexes" offers such a fruitful avenue for creative exploration and even a potential way for our tradition to make a meaningful psychological contribution to the understanding of forces that are tearing the world apart.

Part of Jung's genius was his sensitivity to the perils of the individual's falling into the grip of collective life. Like all who lived through the twentieth century, Jung witnessed the terrible side of collectivity. Beginning with the deadening effect of collective religious life on his father's spirit, Jung went on to *dream* and then see the map of Europe and much of the rest of the world bathed in blood, violence, and terror through two world wars (McGuire 1989:41–42). In the later part of his life, he shared in the nightmare horror of imagining nuclear holocaust. It is easy to see why Jung had such a dread of the psyche's falling into possession by collective and archetypal forces. For these very good reasons, collective life as a whole, more often than not, has slipped into the Jungian shadow – so much so that it is easy to feel within the Jungian tradition as if the life of the group and the individuals' participation in it exist in a no man's land, suspended in the ether somewhere between the much more important and meaningful individual and/or archetypal realms. We would argue that this tendency for collective life to fall into the

Jungian shadow has done a great disservice to our tradition and its potential to contribute to a better understanding of group forces in the psyche.

Jung's natural introversion (and his appeal to other introverts) and his fundamental focus on individuation had an unacknowledged tendency to set the individual up against or in opposition to the life of the group. Quite naturally, group life was left to the shadow and is most easily seen by Jungians as monstrous and magically destructive, thereby setting up the individual as the hero whose task it is to slay the group's devouring hold on him or her. Individuation and whole-hearted participation in the life of the group do not seem to readily work together. We would argue, however, that part of seeing the shadow of the group more objectively (rather than seeing the group as the shadow) is to understand its complexes as differentiated from the individual's complexes.

And, God knows – whether he/she be Zeus, Yahweh, Allah or some other divinity – that group life is teeming with complexes. Everywhere one turns today, there is a group that is feeling the effects of or is in the grip of a complex in its relationships and behavior to other groups. Group complexes are ubiquitous and one feels swamped by their affects and claims – if one still has the energy to pay attention to them. Often, to suggest that a group is under the spell of a complex in its behavior, affect or mood – particularly if there is merit to the claim that the group has been discriminated against by a colonial power or a white power or a male power or a female power or a black power – is to risk being attacked with the full fury of the collective psyche's group defenses. Mostly these group complexes have to do with trauma, discrimination, feelings of oppression and inferiority at the hands of another offending group – although the "offending groups" can just as frequently feel discriminated against and unfairly treated. Group complexes litter the collective psychic landscape and are as easily detonated as the literal landmines that scatter the globe and threaten life – especially young life – worldwide.

Jungian psychology – with its theory of complexes – was well positioned in its earliest theoretical conceptions to understand these cultural, collective and group phenomena. But, with its own anti-group bias and preference for understanding such material in terms of archetypal possession, analytical psychology has not lived up to its promise and potential. Our tendency to archetypal reductionism, our fear and distaste for the collective, and our primary and legitimate focus on individuation are all factors that have not lent themselves to a careful, objective consideration of group phenomena within the individual and collective psyche.

Concept of complexes in analytical psychology (by Thomas Singer)

Jung's first papers on the "word association test" were published in 1905, almost one hundred years ago. Out of those early experiments based on timed responses to lists of words was born Jung's idea of complexes. Interestingly, when the early group which had formed around Jung was considering a name separate from the founder's, Jung himself thought it should be called "complex psychology." For many analytical psychologists, Jung's theory of complexes remains the cornerstone of the day-to-day work of psychotherapy and analysis. Like the Freudian theory of defenses, Jung's notion of complexes provides a handle for understanding the nature of intrapsychic and interpersonal conflict.

Most simply, a complex is an emotionally charged group of ideas and images that cluster around an archetypal core. Jung wrote:

> The complex has a sort of body, a certain amount of it own physiology. It can upset the stomach. It upsets the breathing, it disturbs the heart – in short, it behaves like a partial personality. For instance, when you want to say or do something and unfortunately a complex interferes with this intention, then you say or do something different from what you intended. You are simply interrupted, and your best intention gets upset by the complex, exactly as if you had been interfered with by a human being or by circumstances from outside.
>
> (Jung 1964:para. 72)

Complexes express themselves in powerful moods and repetitive behaviors. They resist our most heroic efforts at consciousness, and they tend to collect experience that confirms their preexisting view of the world. An activated complex can have its own body language and tone of voice. It operates beneath the level of consciousness, almost like the psychological analog of automatic, vegetative systems that control blood pressure and digestion. We do not have to think about complexes for them to carry out their autonomous processes of structuring and filtering our experience of ourselves and others.

A further characteristic of complexes, elegantly elaborated by John Perry in his paper titled "Emotions and object relations" (Perry 1970), is that they tend to be bipolar or consist of two parts. Most often, when a complex is activated, one part of the bipolar complex attaches itself to the ego and the other part is projected onto a suitable other. For instance, in a typical negative father complex, the angry and defiant rebel projects itself onto the ego of the young man and inevitably the other half of the unconscious complex seeks out the authoritarian father in every teacher, coach or boss who provides a fine hook on which to be caught. This bipolarity of the complex leads to an endless round of repetitive skirmishes with the illusory other – who may or may not fit the bill perfectly. Complexes can be recognized by the simplistic certainty of a worldview and one's place in it that they offer, in the face of the conflicting and not easily reconcilable opposites. A colleague likes to tell a story about herself that well illustrates this psychological fact. After a day of "holding the opposites" in the office with her analysands, she enjoys watching John Wayne movies in which it is clear who the bad guys and the good guys are. She points out that it is far easier to settle for the certainty of a complex than wrestle with the emotional ambiguity of inner and outer reality that is constantly challenging the ego. Finally, it is important to remember that although complexes can present enormous problems to oneself and those one has to live with, they are naturally occurring psychological realities and everyone has them. Jung suggested that our complexes – whether we become more conscious of them or simply live them out – determine the course of our lives:

> Archetypes are complexes of experience that come upon us like fate, and their effects are felt in our most personal life. The anima no longer crosses our path as a goddess, but, it may be, as an intimately personal misadventure, or perhaps as our best venture. When, for instance, a highly esteemed professor in his seventies abandons his family and runs off with a young red-headed actress, we know that the gods have claimed another victim.
>
> (Jung 1935:para. 62)

This synopsis of the nature and structure of complexes as worked out by analytical psychologists over the past century has, for the most part, been thought of and applied to the psyche of individuals. Indeed, the goal of Jungian analysis in its individuation process has been to make one's personal complexes more conscious and free up the energy contained within them to be more available for the purposes of more creative psychological development. Elizabeth Osterman, a well known Jungian analyst of another generation, liked to say of herself that she had learned that complexes never completely disappear, but a lifetime of struggling with them sometimes could result in their debilitating effects, including foul moods, lasting only five minutes at a time rather than decades at a time. Some of the cultural complexes that we are exploring have caused uninterrupted foul moods in cultures for centuries, if not millennia. After Sam Kimbles discusses the notion of the "cultural unconscious" we will put together the building blocks of complexes and the cultural unconscious to construct the theory of cultural complexes. In that discussion, we will carry the characteristics about complexes noted above into the realm of cultural complexes.

The cultural unconscious (by Samuel L. Kimbles)

Analytical psychology and culture

The concept of the cultural unconscious had a recent birth and a relatively unelaborated history. Analytical psychology's relationship to culture has been an ambivalent one at best. In Jung's own approach to cultural issues we can see at least three strands interwoven. First, he was sensitive to how Eurocentric, rationalistic attitudes alienated many Westerners from their primal, instinctual roots. Secondly, in his conceptualization of the collective unconscious he made a series of assumptions that had implicit within them a privileging of Western attitudes and values but also a derogation of traditional cultures. Finally, the concept of the collective unconscious was defined in a way that did not allow room for the cultural matrix to have its own field of action coexistent with personal and archetypal layers.

Taking the above three strands in order, first about the impact of the development of rationalistic, Eurocentric attitudes on Westerners, we find Jung stating in a rather mournful tone:

> Man feels himself isolated in the cosmos. He is no longer involved in nature and has lost his emotional participation in natural events, which hitherto had a symbolic meaning for him. Thunder is no longer the voice of a god, nor is lightning his avenging missile. No river contains a spirit, no tree means a man's life, no snake is the embodiment of wisdom, and no mountain still harbors a great demon. Neither do things speak to him nor can he speak to things, like stones, springs, plants, and animals. He no longer has a bush-soul identifying him with a wild animal. His immediate communication with nature is gone for ever, and the emotional energy it generated has sunk into the unconscious.
>
> (Jung 1964:para. 585)

Here Jung laments the loss of connection with our instincts, the unconscious, and the Self which have accompanied Western development. Analytically, this collective loss of connection to the Self means that the numinous symbols that grip us and allow us to experience a relationship to the transpersonal world (which we typically feel as religious) have disappeared into the unconscious. Jung suggests that our personal and collective psyches are profoundly disturbed by this loss of soul connection. Nowadays connection to the numinous is likely to be experienced in our heightened suggestibility, fearfulness, prejudices, and irrationality that survive within the rationalistic psyche and get expressed in "isms," cults, holy wars, terrorism, political movements and a host of other mass processes. These forces represent the return of the transpersonal in horrific, cultural garb. The language of our day has shifted since the attacks on the World Trade Center in New York and the Pentagon in Virginia on 11 September 2001 (hereafter referred to as 9/11) to include a plethora of numinous words and phrases: evil doers, axis of evil, jihad (holy war), crusade, sacrifice, weapons of mass destruction, shock and awe.

In a recent paper titled "Cultural property and the dilemma of the collective unconscious," Waldron (2003) addresses an issue which touches on the second strand in analytical psychology mentioned above. Waldron argues that Jung made a series of assumptions about the collective unconscious that had implicit within them a privileging of Western attitudes and values and a derogation of traditional cultures. A synopsis of her argument is that through his theoretical framework of the collective unconscious, Jung:

1   "links the psyche of primitive cultures and children to the unconscious" and "to the evolutionary process of humanity, which he found comparable to the evolutionary development of consciousness"
2   holds the "view that 'primitive' is incapable of personal reflection which can stand over and against the collective"
3   maintains the notion of a collective unconscious that "negates to some extent a belief that culture can be owned exclusively by any group of people" (Waldron 2003:38–40).

With a certain unconsciousness regarding the role of his own cultural assumptions, Jung at times placed himself above traditions and cultures by adopting an archetypal perspective and seemed to lose the awareness that his own attitude and theory were the product of his particular cultural time and place. In general, Jung searched for human universality; the archetypal took precedence over issues of human diversity. He seemed to assume that there was an unconscious symbiosis between the individual and the collective. But we observe much more variety and see more diversity than the homogeneity implied in the concept of the collective unconscious. In a seminar on 6 July 1925, Jung introduced a "geological" diagram showing the individual coming out of a common level that connects animal ancestors, primate ancestors, large groups, nations, clans, and families. Individuals are the small tip on the top of this mountain. But there is a great diversity suggested in that vast region of larger groups, nations, clans and families (McGuire 1989:133).

Though he was clearly aware of culture as a different level or field of functioning, Jung nevertheless did not identify and/or define a distinct level of the unconscious called the cultural unconscious. This was left to Henderson.

Joseph Henderson and "the cultural unconscious"

In his paper on "The cultural unconscious", Dr Henderson (1990) defined the *cultural unconscious* as:

> an area of historical memory that lies between the collective unconscious and the manifest pattern of the culture. It may include both these modalities, conscious and unconscious, but it has some kind of identity arising from the archetypes of the collective unconscious, which assists in the formation of myth and ritual and also promotes the process of development in individuals.

> (Henderson 1990:102)

We want to call attention to two aspects in Dr Henderson's definition: first, the location of the cultural unconscious and secondly, his emphasis on "an area of historical memory." The location defines this level of the unconscious as a group level unconscious that is neither personal nor archetypal, but grounded in the collective unconscious of a culture.

Exemplifying the first point, Carolyn Forche in her book *Against Forgetting*, speaking of poetry as witness, states:

> we are accustomed to distinguish between "personal" and "political" poems – the former calling to mind lyrics of love and emotional losses, the latter indicating a public partisanship . . . The distinction between the personal and the political gives the political realm too much and too little scope; at the same time, it renders the personal too important and not important enough. If we give up the dimension of the personal, we risk relinquishing one of the most powerful sites of resistance. The celebration of the personal, however, can indicate myopia, an inability to see how the larger structure of the economy and the state circumscribe, if not determine, the fragile realm of individuality . . . We need a *third* term, one that can describe the space between the state and the supposedly safe havens of the personal. Let us call this space "the social".
>
> (Forche 1993:31)

We, along with Henderson, would now see that space between the personal and the political as a manifestation of the cultural unconscious within an energetic field.

Dr Henderson's reference to an area of historical memory points to a kind of living continuity between past and present at the level of the group unconscious. In his paper on "The cultural unconscious," Henderson says, "it has repeatedly rescued me and my patients from the arrogant assumption that history lives only in books and in pronouncements concerning the future" (1990:106). He goes on to quote Henry Corbin who makes a distinction between history as external, versus the esoteric history that "is in man." According to Corbin, "Therefore essentially man always brings with him something prior to history, something he will never cease to carry in himself that will save him from external history. Then it becomes a matter of internal history, happenings in the 'Heaven' or 'Hell' that man carries within himself" (Corbin 1980:8).

Even though Jung did not specifically name an area of the psyche the "cultural unconscious," he implied the existence of such an intermediate realm, as Murray Stein says in his paper "Looking backward: archetypes in reconstruction":

> Jung's inclusion of archetypes within the historical nexus leads to the realization that the influence of history upon the individual is ubiquitous,

rooted in culture and the unconscious, pervasive through all segments of emotional and mental functioning, and fundamental to identity. For this reason he warns of the danger of departing too far from one's personal and cultural roots.

(Stein 1987:61)

More recently, in his book *The Multicultural Imagination*, Michael Vannoy Adams makes some significant distinctions as he speaks about the cultural unconscious as it relates to race. In reviewing the Freudian method, Adams states that it privileges latent contents as basic and regards manifest contents as derivative. For instance, a dream in which there is a racial conflict is reduced to a struggle over aggression. This has the effect of denying the significance of race. Referring to Freudian analysis, Adams says: "Historically, it has tended to reduce cultural factors to instinctual factors, especially sexual factors" (Adams 1996:39). On the other hand, Jungians, in spite of emphasizing constructive approaches to the psyche, reduce psyche, to "typical components" (ibid.). As an example, Adams notes, "Jungian analysis tends to regard blacks in dreams (especially in the dreams of whites) as images of the 'shadow' and to reduce them to personifications of 'dark,' negative, or inferior aspects of the dreamer, a self who unconsciously projects them onto another" (ibid.:40). In brief, Adams states, "If Freudian analysis has tended to be sexually reductive, then Jungian analysis has tended to be archetypally reductive" (ibid.:39).

Henderson notes that "much of what Jung called personal was actually culturally conditioned" (1990:104) and Adams says that "much of what Jung called collective was cultural" (1996:40). The concept of the cultural unconscious allows us to begin to become conscious of the connective tissue in which group life is lived out, embodied and structured both within and outside the individual. We can become better participant observers. The cultural unconscious becomes a way of understanding a symbolic dimension of human experience created by human interactions, narratives, and images that are preserved and transmitted through a kind of centripetal dynamic (see below). Indeed at the group level, we begin to notice a kind of "group skin," a containing function for collective condensations, vulnerable to disseminations, ruptures, deaths and renewals. Cultural memory, as we understand it from the point of view of the cultural unconscious, is not a warehouse or a retrieval process but a living, dynamic field. From a process perspective, this field is at the core of our capacity for reflection that ultimately allows for a relationship to living history.

By making past events meaningful, the historian exercises an important psychic capacity, that of reflection: This does not confer retrospective truth on the past – indeed, almost the contrary – but creates a new meaning that did not exist before, one that could not exist were it not based on past events and did it not transform them into a tapestry holding them in a new place.

(Bollas 1995:143)

We believe this place or energetic field of transformation is organized by cultural complexes.

Cultural complexes: a working definition

(a) Thomas Singer

It is time to put together the building blocks of Jung's theory of "complexes" with Henderson's theory of the "cultural unconscious" and make the "cultural complex" addition to the ramshackle theoretical framework of analytical psychology. As personal complexes emerge out of the level of the personal unconscious in its interaction with deeper levels of the psyche, cultural complexes can be thought of as arising out of the cultural unconscious in its interaction with both the archetypal and personal realms of the psyche. As such, cultural complexes can be thought of as forming the essential components of an inner sociology. But this inner sociology does not pretend to be objective or scientific in its description of different groups and classes of people. Rather, it is a description of groups and classes of people as filtered through the psyches of generations of ancestors. It contains an abundance of information and misinformation about the structures of societies – a truly inner sociology – and its essential building blocks are cultural complexes.

To get at what we think cultural complexes actually are, we may begin with what they are *not*, following Thomas Aquinas's *via negativa*. Cultural complexes are not the same as cultural identity, although sometimes they can seem impossibly intertwined. Groups emerging out of long periods of oppression struggle to define new psychological and political identities by incorporating sometimes long submerged traditions, which can easily become confused with potent cultural complexes that have accrued over centuries of trauma. In the fierce and legitimate protest to forge a new group identity that is freed up from the shackles of oppression, it is very easy for both sides in such a conflict – oppressor and oppressed groups alike – to get caught up in cultural complexes. And for some people, their complexes – cultural and personal – are their identity. But, for many others, there is a healthy cultural identity that can clearly be seen as separate from the more negative and contaminating aspects of cultural complexes. Jung was probably also getting at this idea in his discussion of national character, but that notion took an ugly and controversial turn when the discussion of national character became entangled with the controversy around Jung and anti-Semitism.[1]

One might say that Jung's discussion of national character itself became contaminated by the swirling emotionalism activated by the very cultural complexes that lead to fascism, racism and all of the other horrors committed in the name of perceived differences between groups of peoples. So the notion of cultural complexes is not the same as either cultural identity or national character, but can easily be confused with them.

Another way to make this most important distinction is to turn again to the idea which John Perry (1970) introduced in his seminal paper on complexes. Perry spoke of the everyday ego as separate from the ego which has been taken over by a complex. When a complex is activated, its potent affect and frequently one-sided perceptions of the world take hold of the everyday ego and create what Perry called "the affect-ego." The other part of the bipolar pair is projected onto the person with whom one is caught in the complex and they, in turn, become what Perry labeled an "affect-object." Hence, you get the ragged and highly charged interactions between an "affect-ego" and an "affect-object." Neither party in this unholy pair usually fares very well. This same notion of "affect-ego" and "affect-object" can be carried over into our discussion of cultural complexes to help make the distinction between cultural identity and cultural complex. A cultural identity not in the grip of a complex is much freer to interact in the world of other peoples without being subject to such highly charged emotional contents that can quickly alter the perception and behavior of groups in relation to one another. Once the cultural complex is activated, however, the everyday cultural identity can be overtaken by the affect of the cultural complex, often built up over centuries of repetitive traumatic experience. Then you are in the territory of what Perry called "affect-ego" and "affect-object" – but at the level of the cultural complex as it manifests itself in the psyche of the individual and the group as a whole. So it is important to make a distinction between cultural identity, cultural complex and national character – how they differ from one another and how they can very easily get caught up in one another.

Having said what cultural complexes are not, it is time to be more specific about what they are. Cultural complexes structure emotional experience and operate in the personal and collective psyche in much the same way as individual complexes, although their content might be quite different. Like individual complexes, cultural complexes tend to be repetitive, autonomous, resist consciousness, and collect experience that confirms their historical point of view. And, as mentioned above, cultural complexes tend to be bipolar, so that when they are activated the group ego or the individual ego of a group member becomes identified with one part of the unconscious cultural complex, while the other part is projected out onto the suitable hook of another group or one of its members. Individuals and groups possessed by a particular cultural complex automatically take on a shared body language and postures or express their distress in similar somatic complaints. Finally, like personal complexes, cultural complexes can provide those caught in their potent web of stories and emotions with a simplistic certainty about the group's place in the world in the face of otherwise conflicting and ambiguous uncertainties.

Because of its primary focus on the individuation process, the Jungian tradition has tended to emphasize the development of the individual out of his or her particular collective experience, but has not been particularly clear or helpful in differentiating individual from cultural complexes. Certainly, Jung and his followers have had a keen sense of different cultural types which is evident, for example, in Jung's discussion of national personality characteristics (Jung 1989:246–247). But this perception of different cultural types has never been adequately linked to Jung's theory of complexes or to how these differences get incorporated into the psyche of the individual and the group. Both in the clinical work of individual analysis and in the broader Jungian tradition of archetypal and cultural commentary, it is of enormous potential benefit to begin to make clearer distinctions between an individual complex and a cultural complex. It offers both the individual and groups the opportunity of not having to telescope or condense everything into the personal or archetypal realm – but to recognize the legitimate (and illegitimate) cultural and group contributions to their struggles, suffering and meaning.

One can easily imagine how the individual's ego can identify with a cultural complex as a defense against a more painful and isolating personal complex. It is far easier to split off one's individual suffering (or to see it all as a result of group trauma) and get caught up in a mass movement than it is to carry the burden of one's individual pain. Within analytical psychology itself, there is a growing tradition of archetypal commentary on cultural experience which tends to neglect how the individual relates to the culture through more personal experiences and complexes. Archetypal commentary on the culture's underlying myths and failings can easily camouflage the need to work hard at grappling with individual complexes. But it is also equally true that the most personally difficult complexes can have their grounding in longstanding cultural complexes. Differentiating the personal, cultural and archetypal levels of complexes requires careful attention to each of these realms, without collapsing one into the other, as if one were more real or true than the other.

To summarize, cultural complexes are based on repetitive, historical group experiences which have taken root in the cultural unconscious of the group. At any opportune time, these slumbering cultural complexes can be activated in the cultural unconscious and take hold of the collective psyche of the group, and through this channel the individual psyches of the members may become impacted. The inner sociology of the cultural complexes can seize the imagination, the behavior and the emotions of the collective psyche and unleash tremendously irrational forces in the name of their "logic."

(b) Samuel L. Kimbles

The five key elements to consider in a working definition of cultural complexes are that they: (1) function at the group level of the individual psyche and within the group; (2) function autonomously; (3) organize group life; (4) facilitate the individual's relationship to the group and functioning within the individual; and (5) can provide for a sense of belonging, identity and historical continuity.

1   A "cultural complex" is a way of describing how deeply held beliefs and emotions operate in group life and within the individual psyche by mediating an individual's relationship to a specific group, nation or culture. These complexes are dynamic systems of relations that serve the basic individual need for belonging and identity through linking personal experiences and group expectations as these are mediated by ethnicity, race, religion, gender and/or their social identity processes. Jung's metaphor of the spectrum can be applied along a personal–collective axis: "psychic processes ... behave like a scale along which consciousness slides" (Jung 1947:para. 408). Hence, consciousness may manifest itself or be pulled in the direction of identification with the most collective cultural expressions of behavior, i.e. black Muslim, Hasidic Jew, to the most individual expressions, i.e. Buddhist black man, pagan Jew (Kimbles 2000:160). Drawing on the bipolarity inherent in the archetypal perspective:

> the individual and group poles of identity are different manifestations of one underlying process. At the level of this underlying process of collective and individual, a psychological attitude allows us to ask what the psyche is doing with the fact of differences and similarities, both individually and culturally.
>
> (Kimbles 2000:162)

Thus the group level of the psyche and the individual level simultaneously make their contribution to the sense of the group and to individual subjective experience.

2   Cultural complexes operate autonomously beneath our awareness. They are expressions of a field phenomenon where a group complex operates within the field of the cultural unconscious. Their functioning implies levels of meaning that bind individuals to each other and provide a sense of coherence, producing continuity for the group. The cultural complexes are nucleating centers that allow for a continuous movement of affect and images, leading to narrative and rituals passed from generation to generation. At the collective level they constitute the "unthought known" of group life (Bollas 1995). They are centripetal in direction, imposing constraints on the perception of differences or accentuating them; emphasizing identification with or differentiation from the group-defining enemies; and allowing for feelings of belonging to or being alienated from the group.

3   Energetic fields created by cultural complexes constitute impersonal dynamics. Cultural complexes function through psychic induction. They create a resonance among people which produces a sense of familiarity.

Negatively, they function through collective emotional sign language, bypassing thinking and reflection, readying individuals and groups for action. By putting together complex theory and the concept of the cultural unconscious we are pointing to psychological structures that organize groups and individuals around the group's expectations, its definition of itself, its destiny, its uniqueness and its projective/introjective processes, i.e. what is taken in and what is rejected at the boundary of the group's skin.

4   Though we feel that cultural complexes are positively involved in the individual's sense of belonging to and identification with his or her reference group and provide a nucleating center for group life; negatively on the basis of this belonging, we generate stereotypes, prejudices and a whole psychology of otherness threat. Every group has a volume of images about those who are different. Those different ones are generally pathologized or demonized but rarely idealized.

5   That the issues around economics, politics, and discrimination are socially constructed does not diminish their archetypal significance for kinship (or belonging) and for individuation (or identity formation).

We now move on to group and individual examples of how these cultural complexes actually take shape in specific situations.

A type of cultural complex in the psyche of the group: archetypal defenses of the group spirit and *Constantine's Sword* (by Thomas Singer)

This section of the chapter presents an example of how the concept of "cultural complexes" can be used to think about the psyche of the group. The first part of this section will describe an archetypal pattern that fuels a particularly explosive and virulent type of cultural complex that one can identify in any number of conflicts occurring around the world today. I call this pattern "archetypal defenses of the group spirit." The second part of this section will give a specific example of how this particular type of cultural complex has expressed itself in the collective psyche of two groups and the individual psyche of one extraordinary writer, James Carroll, whose *Constantine's Sword: The Church and the Jews: A History* (2001) will be examined as "case study" of a cultural complex.

Archetypal defenses of the group spirit

To lay the groundwork for the discussion of *Constantine's Sword* and its history of anti-Semitism in the Catholic Church as an example of a cultural complex, I want to introduce another piece of the ramshackle theoretical renovation we are suggesting – the notion of archetypal defenses of the group spirit. Donald Kalsched's work offers a compelling model of how the individual psyche responds to trauma in its defense of the self. Can his model be extended to include specific categories of group behavior and allow us to see more clearly the structure and content of certain types of group or cultural complexes? Basically, I am suggesting a reformulation of the title of Kalsched's book, shifting the focus from *The Inner World of Trauma: Archetypal Defences of the Personal Spirit* to "The Group World of Trauma: Archetypal Defenses of the Group Spirit." I will briefly summarize the central elements of Kalsched's formulations about the activation of "archetypal defenses" in traumatized individuals in order to establish the foundation for considering them in relation to group processes (Kalsched 1996).

1   Trauma alone does not shatter the psyche. The psyche shatters itself through its own self-defense system. In a sense, the psyche's defense system is as traumatogenic as an original extreme trauma because its focus is on survival and it interprets any attempt to grow and individuate as dangerous and needing to be punished. Kalsched labels this the *Daimone*-Protector defense system which prevents the severely traumatized individual from reaching out beyond a closed system of certainty which would expose the personal spirit to further traumatization.

2   This occurs because the *daimonic* defense system is unleashed against the psyche for the purpose of converting annihilation anxiety into a more manageable fear. This self-protective mechanism preserves a fearful ego in the face of shattering trauma rather than permitting the ego to be annihilated altogether. This self-protective mechanism which results in self-attack can be likened to the autoimmune system having gone haywire when it turns its substantial arsenal of defenses back on one's own tissues. Fragmentation of the psyche is the result.

3   The *Daimone*-Protector defenses are internalized representations of the original perpetrators of the trauma. Even more than that, they are archaic, typical and archetypal.

4   Following the psyche's fragmenting, a false self takes up residence in the outer world which can function well enough in ordinary situations, although it is most likely to break down in intimate relationships. This false self can take on a caretaker function as well as becoming a compliant, good adult.

5   On the other side of the fragmentation, the true self goes into inner hibernation behind the ferociously protective barrier of the *Daimones* – which can be alternately protective and torturing.

6   The individual has very little access to effective aggression in the world.

7   The shadow of being a traumatized victim is the tendency towards an imperious sense of entitlement and its accompanying demands for reparation. A false, imperial self can take root that demands love, respect, sexual pleasure, freedom and happiness.

8   At the heart of this fragmented psychic "balance" resides a vulnerable,

wounded child surrounded by an archaic defense system that can alternate between sheltering protection and ruthless torturing of the self and others.

What if this highly schematized outline of the psyche's response to trauma applies as much to a severely traumatized group psyche as it does to the individual? I hypothesize that the same dynamics so elegantly described by Kalsched may come alive in the traumatized group psyche as well as in the private horror of a traumatized individual. The traumatized group may develop a cohort of Protector/Persecutor leaders who function like the *Daimones* in the individual psyche where archetypal defenses are employed to protect the wounded spirit – whether it be of the group or the individual or both. In other words, the traumatized group spirit may well be subject to the same nurturing protection and/or violent torture at the hands of its *Daimones* leaders. All of the group's defenses are mobilized in the name of a self-care system which is designed to protect the injured divine child of the group identity, as well as to protect the group "ego" from a terrifying sense of imminent annihilation.

The group may develop a defensive system akin to the individual's, but in this case its goal is to protect the group or collective spirit rather than the individual spirit. Such a traumatized group presents only a "false self" to the outer world, which is unable to "see" the group in its more authentic and vulnerable identity. Such a cultural complex can easily give birth to a book such as Ralph Ellison's *Invisible Man*, where the black man is literally invisible to the white man (Ellison 2002). Or, the rest of the world which is not part of the traumatized group may not see the invisible or compliant "false self" of the group persona, but rather be confronted with the more hardened "*daimonic*" front men or women who are identified with the archetypal defenses of the group spirit. It is easy to respond to the carriers of the group's defenses as if their aggression and impenetrability is characteristic of the psyche of the whole group, so that, for instance, all Muslims are seen as if they are part of Bin Laden's al-Qaeda.

Traumatized groups with their defenses of the collective spirit may find themselves living with a history that spans several generations, several centuries, or even millennia with repetitive, wounding experiences that fix these patterns of behavior and emotion into what analytical psychologists have come to know as "complexes." These group complexes create bipolar fields in the same way that personal complexes activate or constellate in external reality the very splits that have splintered the inner world. The traumatized life of the group gets incorporated into the inner life of the individual through a group complex – which may be mistaken for or get confused with a personal complex.

I am not suggesting that all cultural complexes behave in the particular model of a traumatized, vulnerable child and the Protective/Torturer *Daimones*, as described by Kalsched. But many of them do. There are two separate but related points that I want to emphasize here:

1   There is a continuum in the content and structure of complexes that
      ranges from the personal to the cultural to the archetypal. At the same
      time, some complexes have become such a part of a group's identity over
      time through repetitive experience that the group level of the complex
      becomes dominant or paramount, even in the psyche of an individual.
      Individuals are frequently swallowed whole by the group complex that
      has come to define their ethnic, religious, racial, gender, or other primary
      sense of identity.
2   Sometimes groups as a whole behave as if they are in the grip of a specific
      type of cultural complex. This type of cultural complex mobilizes in the
      group's behavior, and emotional life functioning as a defensive self-care
      system akin to that described in individuals by Kalsched. In the group
      version of the complex, however, the goal of the self-care defensive sys-
      tem is the protection of the group spirit, not the personal spirit. The
      Daimones are mobilized to protect the traumatized divine child or other
      symbolic carrier of the collective spirit of the group and can do so with
      a mixture of sheltering kindness and persecutory attack which, directed
      inwardly, results in self-loathing and, directed outwardly, results in
      impenetrability and hostility to other groups.

One has only to glance at the daily newspaper to see the proliferation in
popular culture of these group complexes at work. Indeed, it has almost
become a national sport for traumatized groups to send out *Daimones* (attor-
neys and others) to attack the general public for neglecting the entitled interests of their particular victimized group. A large part of the public has grown
weary of this institutionalization of group defenses of the collective spirit.
Frequently members of the victimized group are so identified with themselves
as wounded divine children that it is hard for them to understand how their
Daimones-Protectors, embodied in public spokespersons/attackers, are perceived as an aggressive, destructive, hostile turnoff by those who are not
identified with their plight. In the psychic arena of our global network of
group life, it is as if many groups display signs of group trauma, with their
group divine child, and their group *Daimones* (Protectors/Persecutors) ready
to swing into action. Perhaps this is the inescapable cost of living in a global
marketplace where ease of transportation, communication, and the rapid
import/export of goods, ideas, values, money, and people also facilitates the
wholesale and almost instantaneous exchange of cultural complexes that are
on high alert, ready to explode just about anywhere and anytime.

An example of a cultural complex: James Carroll's Constantine's Sword

No flare-up of collective emotion in Western history is older or more repetitive than anti-Semitism. As a cultural complex, it is the lightning rod

for almost unending strife between various groups. Most visible today, of course, is the Muslim–Jewish form of the cultural complex, but the history of anti-Semitism in the Catholic Church has nearly a 2,000-year history, which in James Carroll's *Constantine's Sword* finds a remarkable historian whose narration reveals the personal, cultural and archetypal dimensions of the complex. Carroll's history can be read as a stunning example of the dynamic interplay between cultural complex and archetypal defenses of the group spirit. It also offers a rare glimpse of the continuum of a cultural complex as it interpenetrates and moves from individual to cultural to archetypal levels. In searching for a familiar example of a cultural complex, it would be easiest to focus on groups such as gays, blacks, women, the disabled and other obviously disenfranchised and historically traumatized peoples to see how the dynamics of cultural complexes and defenses of the group spirit play out. But James Carroll's *Constantine's Sword: The Church and the Jews: A History* suggested to me that the same dynamics can be seen in the Catholics, a group that few would now characterize as a disenfranchised and traumatized minority (Carroll 2001).

Constantine's Sword is a history of Christian – more specifically Catholic – anti-Semitism. Starting with the old Christian belief that Jews were the "Christ-killers," Carroll systematically examines layer upon layer of historical event, political context, emotional climate, theological justification and psychological consequence. He begins his narrative by describing contemporary Catholic and Jewish reactions to a memorial cross placed at Auschwitz as the latest episode in a stormy and violent two-millennia relationship. His reflections on the Auschwitz cross are placed in the context of his memories of growing up in Germany right after the Second World War and his own early childhood belief that Jews were in fact the "Christ-killers." After carefully probing the details of his Catholic up-bringing, Carroll opens up to an in-depth exploration of the entire historical sweep of Catholic–Jewish relations. Obviously, Carroll does not claim to tell the whole story of the development of Catholicism or Judaism or of the relations between the two religions.

Let us briefly follow the thread of Carroll's work. On the personal side, the early development of his faith took place in the epicenter of one of the most traumatic events of modern Western history – the Holocaust. Carroll's father was commander of the American air force in Germany immediately following the Second World War. The family lived at headquarters in Wiesbaden, Germany. Accompanying his devoutly Catholic mother, an adolescent Jim Carroll traveled to many of the important Catholic shrines of Western Europe. Through his deep love of his mother and his intimate knowledge of her suffering because of the crippling illness (polio) of his brother, Carroll developed a faith rooted in the cross, the mother and the suffering son. Growing up in post-Nazi Germany, Carroll had an extensive view of the great Catholic tradition and the devastation of the Second

World War, but learned little of the Holocaust and the suffering of the Jews at that time.

This is where Carroll's personal complex and the Jewish–Catholic cultural complex became entangled – not just in his childhood story but in the 2,000-year history that he sets out to explore in this book. The Christian religion that nurtured a youth aspiring to the priesthood placed suffering and traumatic death at the center of the Western collective experience, indeed at the center of all human history. And right at the very heart of that story, as he heard it, was the belief that the Jews were responsible for the suffering and traumatic death of the young god who truly incarnated the group spirit, Jesus Christ. The belief that the Jews were the "Christ-killers" – reinforced through a long history of theological amplification together with political, social and religious persecutions – has fueled virulent collective emotions of loathing and rage that have burned without interruption for centuries. Two millennia of collective emotion demanding vengeance on the "Christ-killers" has fueled a long line of *Daimones* from the Crusaders to the Nazis.

One of the many surprising revelations of Carroll's historical journey is that the suffering and traumatic death of the young god for which the Jews have been held responsible has not always been at the center of Christian faith. In fact, the cult of the cross does not seem to come to center stage until the time of Constantine in the early part of the fourth century CE. Even today, the Eastern Orthodox Church places more emphasis on the mystery of the resurrection or rebirth than the traumatic death symbolized by the crucifixion. Imagine for a moment what the history of the Western world might have been like if suffering and trauma had not been at the core of the Western story since the time of Christ. Of course, we now know that the traumatic death of the crucifixion has been the focal point of Western orthodoxy since the time of Constantine.

When Constantine was crossing the Milvian Bridge to attack Rome in 312 CE, he had a vision and a conversion experience in which his sword and the cross became one. Carroll writes:

> The place of the cross in the Christian imagination changed with Constantine. "He said that about noon, when the day was already beginning to decline" – this is Eusebius's account of Constantine's own report of what he saw in the sky on the eve of the battle above the Milvian Bridge – "he saw with his own eyes the trophy of a cross of light in the heavens, above the sun, and bearing the inscription CONQUER BY THIS." The story goes on to say that Constantine then assembled his army – "He sat in the midst of them, and described to them the figure of the sign he had seen" – and gave them the new standard to carry into battle. "Now it was made in the following manner. A long spear, overlaid with gold, formed the figure of the cross by means of a transverse bar laid over it." As we saw, the army behind this standard did conquer, and

Constantine, so Eusebius heard him say, was thus convinced of the truth of Christianity. "The emperor constantly made use of this sign of salvation as a safeguard against every adverse and hostile power, and commanded that others similar to it should be carried at the head of all his armies."

(Carroll 2001:175)

Constantine became a Christian, and in him the Christian faith found a Protector/Persecutor/*Daimone* of the first order. At the moment of Constantine's vision, the symbol of traumatic injury – the cross – and its avenging protector in the form of Constantine's sword were conjoined. I would argue that this symbolic marriage of cross and sword is an example of the historical emergence of an "archetypal defense of the group spirit." The inevitable, archetypal coupling of the endangered divine child and the protective, warrior *Daimones* who surround him are at the heart of this story. Christ falls into that lineage of human/divine beings who eventually attracted potent *Daimones*/Protectors willing to commit unimaginable atrocities in his name.

Groups go on the attack in defense of their collective spirit when they fear being annihilated, especially if there is a history of trauma at their beginnings. The Christian story originates in trauma. Some three hundred years after the crucifixion of Christ, the suffering divine being finds his archetypal and historical *Daimone*/Protector/Persecutor in Constantine, from whose sword Carroll traces a direct line to the Crusades, the Inquisition and finally the Holocaust. One can argue, in summary, that at the heart of the central cultural complex and narrative event of the western Christian psyche is the emergence of an archetypal defense of the group spirit whose primary features are: (1) traumatic injury to a vulnerable divine being representing the group spirit; (2) fear of annihilation of the group spirit; and (3) emergence of avenging protector/persecutor defenses of the group spirit.

In the Christian coupling of cross and sword, the archetypal defenses of the group spirit turned all of its more shadowy aggressive energy outward and one sees self-righteousness rather than self-hatred. (Note: obviously this is not the whole story of Christianity or of Judaism since Constantine. Rather, it is following one thread only that has contributed to a particularly potent/virulent cultural complex.) The Jews bore the brunt of attacks from this 2,000-year Catholic archetypal defensive system and to some degree mirrored its aggressiveness in self-hatred, until Zionism and the Holocaust gave birth to a generation of Jews that could say with equal aggressive self-affirmation "Never Again." "Never Again" grew out of unimaginable human suffering and the resolve to protect the Jewish group spirit at any cost, giving birth to a whole new generation of Jewish *Daimones* which the Palestinians and Israelis know quite well.

If we apply John Perry's idea of the bipolarity of complexes to group life and cultural complexes, we can see in these awful histories of Jews and

Catholics or Jews and Palestinians that when the unconscious bipolar cultural complex is activated, one half of the complex seizes the everyday ego of the group identity and it become an affect-ego. The other half of the complex seeks its suitable hook on which to project itself and that becomes the affect-object. Both the affect-ego and the affect-object are identifiable by the intensity of emotion generated in their interaction. The greater the intensity of emotion in such flare-ups between two groups, the more one is likely to be in the territory of cultural complexes. Irrational collective emotion is the hallmark of a cultural complex at the core of which is an archetypal pattern.

Carroll's book, from one perspective then, can be viewed as the extraordinary effort of an individual to sort out his personal complexes from a cultural complex; until consciously examined, these are in fact so interwoven and continuous that it would be impossible to know where the personal part of the complex ends and the cultural complex begins. Carroll would not describe his effort in the language of Jung's complex theory, but it is clear that all of his considerable emotional and intellectual passions have been devoted to teasing out the different levels of personal, cultural and archetypal conflict that are at the heart of his history of the Catholics and the Jews. Carroll's personal journey to free himself from the myth of the Jews as "Christ-killers" and all of the collective emotion that has been ignited in the name of that belief is deeply entangled with the long history of animosity, misunderstanding, persecution and trauma which characterize Jewish–Christian relations. One of the most important aspects of his book from a Jungian perspective is that he gives us an X-ray of the layering of the personal, cultural and archetypal dimensions of the complex he is probing. This approach opens him up to criticism from the more "objective" historians, some of whom have dismissed his work as too "personal."

Indeed, Carroll's search for historical objectivity begins with an examination of his own subjectivity. In my opinion, the objectivity he gains from the hard introspective work of looking at his own individual and family history is more authentic than the carefully cultivated dispassionate objectivity of a conventional historian who is trained to refrain from injecting his own experience and biases into the story. Carroll's method is truer to our own experience of how the personal and cultural become intertwined in the unconscious of our family lives and in the cultural and religious history of mankind. Paradoxically, by publicly wrestling with the personal dimensions of his development as a devout Catholic, he leads us to a profound consideration of the unfolding of the historical relations between Catholics and Jews. This is because Carroll's self-revelations naturally evoke and invite us to consider our own personal and cultural complexes in relation to this history. His story opens us to our story and we are plunged into a very old history to which we are intimately related. From one point of view, then, this book is a record of a personal complex set in the context of a two-millennia-old cultural complex, as well as this cultural complex set in the context of a personal complex. As such, it is an extraordinary example of a cultural complex in which archetypal defenses of the group spirit are mobilized in the most destructive way for generation upon generation. And, it is a monumental example of the effort it takes for a single individual to make more conscious in himself the corrosive effects of a cultural complex that has been predominant in Western civilization for so long.

A cultural complex in the psyche of an individual: a clinical case example (by Samuel L. Kimbles)

In the clinical area some of the challenging questions that the exploration of cultural complexes raise are: What is the relationship of individual complexes to cultural complexes? A related question is how do cultural complexes enter the clinical/analytical situation? What are the relationships of cultural complexes to transference and countertransference dynamics? Do cultural complexes initiate unconscious dynamics which become expressed in individual experiences that are manifested through transference/countertransference dynamics? If so, what is their purpose? In the following case example the events surrounding 9/11 seemed to activate and intensify a personal complex while expressing a cultural complex. We can see the bare emergence of a cultural complex as it becomes part of the clinical process in this case.

Introduction to the case

The events of 9/11 constituted a narcissistic blow to the American psyche and exposed many of us to a new level of collective and personal vulnerability. Something of the numinous "other" seems to have broken through the sense of invulnerability so characteristic of America's collective consciousness. Our collective level of vulnerability and the sense of threat can be read partially by the words and language that emerged to express the group's feelings about these events: axis of evil, evil doers, the enemy, innocence, holy war, sacrifice, victim, vengeance, etc. These words constitute a collective language of signs that induced us to act in accord with our cultural complexes, especially those elucidated earlier in this chapter by Tom Singer in his notion of the archetypal defenses of the group spirit. During the period of 9/11 and immediately thereafter, the interplay between what was going on inside us and what was going on in the outer world seemed to reach a resonating pitch that called out for community – a group response. In my description of the case to follow, I will first share a dream which I had two months following the cataclysm that was 9/11, then describe a brief aspect of my work with a patient, Julie, that took place in two analytic sessions following my dream. The patient's as well as my resonance to the collective event of 9/11 affected the transference/countertransference through the activation of both personal and cultural complexes. But first my dream:

I was in a war-torn city. Soldiers were everywhere. At one point I ran and hid inside a doorway to a locked building. An American soldier with a rifle on his shoulder saw me and motioned to me to come out of hiding. I did and offered him a handful of toy soldiers like the ones I use in my sandplay work. He rejected them and the next thing I knew I had a gun and was in an army uniform.

The dream reminded me of a line from the *I Ching* (Hexagram 7, "The Army"). The line is: "When danger threatens, every peasant becomes a soldier; when the war ends, he goes back to his plow." I took my dream to point to the inevitable transformation occurring in my psyche and that of most Americans as this country approached war. Collectively moving in that direction, there was no standing on the sidelines and there was little room for a symbolic attitude, i.e. toy soldiers and sandplay. My psyche, in an attempt to wrestle with the collective process that I and many others were experiencing, produced this dream. I thought of my dream as the expression of an emerging cultural complex in which the dilemmas being created by possible war were symbolized by my efforts to create a symbolic attitude during the time that a collective situation was moving with its own force and direction. In other words, the dream grew partially out of my reactions to the group. My response is an expression of my anxiety in conjunction with the group's anxiety. The emergence of the cultural complex in my psyche at the time was changing my relationship to myself, manifesting in a heightened sense of vulnerability and fear. I felt less articulate and that the analytic space had been invaded by the events of daily life, activating in me a kind of archaic confusion that became part of the analysis, thus creating a new psychological situation with which I had to work.

The patient

Julie is a 57-year-old married woman. Though she helped raise a stepson and a stepdaughter, she has no biological children of her own. The stepdaughter was killed in a car accident about 10 years before the start of analysis. Julie works as an attorney in a small law firm where she specializes in estate law. She began analysis complaining of isolation and depression after having suffered a series of setbacks both at work and at home. At work she was not selected to an important committee because she was seen by her co-workers as "too unassertive." In her marriage she felt little libido but felt rejected and unwanted by her husband, who paradoxically expressed demanding, obsessive sexual interest in her. She was raised in a conservative Midwestern community where she described her father as domineering, critical and angry. On the other hand she felt close to her mother but angry at her passivity that prevented her from intervening with the father. I have worked with Julie for about three years.

In the analysis, Julie typically spoke in a disjointed and guarded way about events in her life as if describing a play that she was observing. Rarely would I have a clear sense of where she was emotionally. Interpreting her distance from me in terms of defensive anxiety (about connection) seemed to leave her with a vacant look on her face – as if she did not know what I was talking about. Often she seemed to have difficulty accessing feelings, much less expressing them. The sessions that are the present focus took place two weeks following my dream which I reported at the beginning of this section.

First session

J: I identify with the Afghanistan people! We brought the Twin Towers bombing on ourselves.

S: What happened has affected all of us.

J: Maybe I am autistic, since I don't seem to get it.

S: What is the it?

J: This touchy-feely therapy. What about the politics of what's going on? Bush? Iraq? America's arrogance? What's happening in the world? You and I are having a problem. You are trying to get me to give up my political feelings! (Julie had told me earlier in our work that she was a sixties radical. This had been said in an unemotional and flat manner and seemed to be said in passing.) You do not understand me! You reduce everything to an internal touchy-feely world.

S: You are making a difference between the two of us by putting the feeling world into me and the political world into yourself. (My interpretation made her angry.)

J: Ah! (Julie responded with a disgusted look.)

S: (I then had the image of a great wave coming down on my office.) Though I value your passion we are both in danger of being drowned out by the strength of your feelings and I want to understand better what is important to you here.

J: Sam, you don't get it!

S: (At that moment I remembered my dream of the soldiers and the sand-play toys. I felt that we were both being moved by an emerging cultural complex related to our anger, fear and powerlessness in relationship to each other and the world situation.)

Second meeting

J: (Julie came in looking discouraged and dispirited.) I've given up! You have no hope that my political attitude will have any effect on the world.

S: Maybe your statement, "you don't get it, Sam" is your experience of me as not supporting you . . . that I'm trying to take something important from you.

J: There's not enough love in the world, for me.

S: I'm interested in your attitude toward the world but equally in the "for me" part of your attitude. The part of you that wants my support, love and wants the world to be a more loving place.

J: I didn't mean to turn the session into a discussion of politics, but I want my thoughts about politics respected.

S: You have brought more of yourself into the room by talking about something that is really important to you, politics (wanting a more loving world) and wanting love and support from me . . . and that feels like positive movement.

Discussion

Though the content (you don't get it!) expressed by Julie during her outburst with me made sense from both a political and psychological point of view (i.e. her feeling not seen or supported in her family, work, marriage and therapy), she did not appear to me to be interested in understanding the relationship between her emotional intensity and the political attitude she was expressing. She was caught in a personal complex that reflected her sense of not feeling safe in a situation in which she would not get supported. Furthermore, she did not feel she could speak about the situation she was in. Through her politics, Julie reflected a world focused on power dynamics only and this reinforced her belief that she would not find understanding of the helplessness and vulnerability she was experiencing in relationship to the 9/11 event and to me. Her confrontation with me was an attempt both to express her wish for support and to cover it over through a return to an encapsulated position. In short, an external event, 9/11, had activated a cultural complex (in the analytic field) expressed through a political attitude and a related personal complex around Julie's distrust of others. Her need for reassurance was hidden by her outburst.

Julie's emerging anger at me in the transference expressed also her feelings that she was not safe in the analytic container. Neither the analytic container nor the analysis had protected her from her felt vulnerability in the world. Instead, her feelings about the events of 9/11 had activated her personal conflict around trust. Both her basic expectations of being held in the larger American environment and in the analytic setting were ruptured. The narcissistic blow at the level of the group psyche resonated with the pain from her family's (of origin) failure to hold her, disappointments in her marriage, and frustrations at work, which were expressed as a disappointment in the analysis to hold or keep her safe. By presenting political feelings she was utilizing a social attitude to cover over her conflict around her need to trust and find support. Henderson refers to the relationship between social attitude and personal defense in his book *Cultural Attitudes in Psychological Perspective* when he states:

I have often found this [social] attitude provides a particular resistance to analysis, since the patient may assume that if the social problems of our time were solved, all conflict would vanish and psychotherapy would be unnecessary.

(Henderson 1984:17–18)

In the countertransference, my image of the wave had gathered intensity from my own inability to adequately symbolize and hold my feelings about the world situation. Instead, my dream suggested that unconsciously I, too, had become a reluctant soldier, i.e. merged with the collective effort to fight the enemy, which is both internal and external aggression. There was little room for me to be separate or differentiate from Julie without that being experienced as an insult to her. When I became aware that her anger at me for my "touchy-feely" world was an expression of her wish for relatedness to me and her desire to feel empowered in relationship to the world, I could trust the reparative activity in both the personal and cultural complex, that is, her wish to feel love and a sense of belonging. It would seem that in this case the activated cultural complex was partially in the service of Eros.

Conclusion

Cultural complexes mediate the two-way relationship between cultural and social influences on the individual psyche as well as the individual's reciprocal impact on the culture. The concept of cultural complexes builds upon the earlier work by Jung on complexes and Joseph Henderson on the cultural unconscious. These complexes exist within the psyche of the collective as a whole and within the individual members of a group. On an individual level, cultural complexes are expressions of the need to belong and have a valued identity within the context of a specific reference group, even though this may lead to splitting, rigidities and the whole range of phenomena that we recognize as psychological disturbances. At the level of the group, cultural complexes seem to offer cohesion which provides a sense of kinship and group spirit. At the pathological extreme this kinship is expressed in archetypal defenses of the group spirit.

We are barely in a place where we can identify the ubiquity of cultural complexes. We need to develop a language to include a new cultural sensitivity in combination with individual intrapsychic dynamics in order to deal with the manifestation of both kinds of complexes in the clinical situation as well as in everyday life. Just as in our work with individual complexes, the goal is awareness obtained through persevering with the suffering produced by the cultural complex until a consciousness is developed that can contain and tolerate the energy. Similarly, cultivating an attitude toward cultural complexes, whenever they manifest, has the potential to develop a personality capable of consciously utilizing the connectedness of group and individual identity. In this sense the activation of a cultural complex becomes a kinship-furthering process that contributes to developing psychological consciousness.

Notes

1   In *The Shadow of Anti-Semitism*, Jung writes:

> The question I broached regarding the peculiarities of Jewish psychology does not presuppose any intention on my part to depreciate Jews, but is merely an attempt to single out and formulate the mental idiosyncrasies that distinguish Jews from other people. No sensible person will deny that such differences exist, any more than he will deny that there are essential differences in the mental attitude of Germans and Frenchmen ... Again, nobody with any experience of the world will deny that the psychology of an American differs in a characteristic and unmistakable way from that of an Englishman. To point out this difference cannot possibly, in my humble opinion, be in itself an insult to the Jews so long as one refrains from value judgments. If anyone seeking to pin down my peculiarities should remark that this or that is specifically Swiss, or peasant-like, or Christian, I just wouldn't know what I should get peeved about, and I would be able to admit such differences without turning a hair. I have never understood why, for instance, a Chinese should be insulted when a European asserts that the Chinese mentality differs from the European mentality.
>
> (Jung 1992:147–148)

References

Adams, M.V. (1996) *The Multicultural Imagination*, London: Routledge.

Bollas, C. (1995) *Cracking Up*, New York: Hill and Wang.

Carroll, J. (2001) *Constantine's Sword: The Church and the Jews: A History*. Boston and New York: Houghton Mifflin.

Corbin, H. (1980) *The Question of Comparative Philosophy*, Dallas, TX: Spring Publications.

Ellison, R. (2002) *The Invisible Man*, New York: Random House.

Forche, C. (1993) *Against Forgetting*, New York: W.W. Norton & Co.

Henderson, J. (1984) *Cultural Attitudes in Psychological Perspective*, Toronto: Inner City Books.

Henderson, J. (1990) "The cultural unconscious", *Shadow and Self*, Wilmette, IL: Chiron Publications.

Jung, C.G. (1935) *Archetypes and the Collective Unconscious*, CW 9i, Princeton, NJ: Princeton University Press.

—— (1947) "On the nature of the psyche", CW 10.

—— (1964) "Symbols and the interpretation of dreams", CW 18.

—— (1989) *Memories, Dreams, Reflections*, A. Jaffe (ed.), rev. edn, New York: Vintage Books.

—— (1992) *C.G. Jung Letters, vol.1, 1906–1950* (eds G. Adler, A. Jaffe and R.F.C. Hull), Bollingen Series XCV, Princeton, NJ: Princeton University Press.

Kalsched, D. (1996) *The Inner World of Trauma: Archetypal Defences of the Personal Spirit*, London: Routledge.

Kimbles, S. (2000) "The cultural complex and the myth of invisibility", in T. Singer (ed.), *The Vision Thing*, London: Routledge.

Maidenbaum, A. (ed.) (2002) *Jung and the Shadow of Anti-Semitism: Collected Essays*, Berwick, ME: Nicolas-Hays.

McGuire, W. (ed.) (1989) *Jung's Analytical Psychology: Notes on the Seminar Given in 1925*, Princeton, NJ: Princeton University Press.

Perry, J.W. (1970) "Emotions and object relations", *Journal of Analytical Psychology*, **15**(1), 1–12.

Singer, T. (ed.) (2000) *The Vision Thing: Myth, Politics and Psyche in the World*, London: Routledge.

Singer, T. (2003) "The cultural complex and archetypal defenses of the collective spirit: baby Zeus, Elian Gonzales, Constantine's sword, and other holy wars", *The San Francisco Jung Institute Library Journal*, **20**(4), 4–28.

Stein, M. (1987) "Looking backward: archetypes in reconstruction", *Archetypal Processes in Psychotherapy*, Wilmette, IL: Chiron Publications.

Waldron, S. (2003) "Cultural property and the dilemma of the collective unconscious", *Quadrant*, **XXXIII**, 35–49.

Chapter 8

Spiritual and religious aspects of modern analysis

Murray Stein

The religious function

Jung proposed that a native religious function exists within the human psyche (see, among many references, Jung 1966:para. 150). *Homo religiōsus* is by no means an exceptional creature. In fact, everyone is to some extent religiously inclined, at least implicitly. The religious function is a mythopoetic instinct of sorts, and it bespeaks humankind's inherent tendency to create myth. This function manifests wherever people make culture and try to find meaning. It arises spontaneously in individuals, and it can be studied in the historical records of religions and in the ritual practices of all human beings in all time periods.

In modern times, too, the religious function continues to display its effects. Since these may be dressed in our contemporary fashions of thought and imagination, they are often not recognized as religious phenomena. In a late paper entitled "Flying saucers: a modern myth of things seen in the skies," Jung (1958) discussed the frequent "observations" of circular extraterrestrial spaceships as evidence that a new myth was being elaborated in the collective psyche of Western people. Whenever humans confront the unknown – in this case "outer space" and the prospect of exploring it or being confronted by its inhabitants – archetypal images and psychological patterns are projected and experienced. The manifestation of these primordial images, woven together in typical narrative structures common to mythologies since time immemorial, represents the activation of the religious function as humans attempt to map the territory beyond the frontiers of the known. Death is another such frontier, and archetypal images of an afterlife are generated at this borderland in order to gain some sort of conscious mastery over the mystery of death.

When a person enters analysis, too, a space for projections opens up and becomes available for the religious function to be stimulated into action. At first, this is unknown territory. The reality of the analyst is and remains largely an enigma, as is the general notion of "the unconscious" from which so many interpretations derive. The aspects of the inner world that lie beyond the reach of simple reflection and introspection present a challenging puzzle.

Much needs to be made conscious and sorted out. As one enters this terrain, it becomes evident that more than personal memories and associations are hidden here. Peculiar dynamic factors come into play in the transference and through synchronistic events that cannot be easily explained or understood. In analysis a person is entering a *terra incognita*, and therefore archetypal projections are called forward.

As Jung observed, the religious function is present and actively at work in the analytic relationship, typically elaborating itself in the transference. It is instructive to note that when Jung introduces the notion of archetypes in his seminal work, *Two Essays in Analytical Psychology* (1966), he does so by discussing transference. The analyst becomes mythologized in the analysand's psyche because the analyst's reality remains more or less concealed and shrouded in obscurity throughout the analytic treatment. Archetypal images (e.g. hero or demon, savior or guru) and themes (e.g. going on an adventure, crossing the open seas) are woven into the concrete experience of this intimate human encounter.

The analysand's psyche responds to the analyst and to the analytic space, characteristically, by projecting mythic features into them. The physical and mental frame of the human being conducting analytic sessions is tarnished or embellished with content from the analysand's personal and collective unconscious. Something uncanny, hidden, and at times even numinous is perceived and felt to be at work in the analysis. As an "analytic field" develops, the physical space in which analysis takes place also becomes highly symbolic in the perception and feeling of the analysand. Objects such as lamps and wall hangings can become invested with numinous symbolic value. Sometimes this aspect of analysis is vividly shown in dreams, which can portray the analyst as a mythical figure, larger than life, with demonic or godlike features. (This is no different in kind from the collective projections that fall upon celebrities and political leaders. Those too reveal the religious function at work, for good or ill.)

Jung put the religious function on a par with "instinct," as compelling and omnipresent as sexuality, aggression, or hunger. The religious function, as Jung understood and wrote about it, generates archetypal projections and experiences of numinosity using the rather ordinary objects and things in the surrounding world. Following Rudolf Otto's understanding of religious experience in *The Idea of the Holy*, Jung understood it as the experience of the *numinosum*, and he defined the "religious attitude" as one that calls a person to pay careful and scrupulous attention to "a dynamic agency or effect not caused by an arbitrary act of will" (Jung 1937:para. 6) but by the "powers" that lie beyond the visible and known world and create numinous effects within it. The religious attitude and the religious function go hand in hand as the individual develops sensitivity to manifestations of the archetypal dimension of the unconscious. As Jung conceived of the religious attitude, it is not primarily defensive in that its aim and purpose are not fundamentally to ward off anxiety about insecurity or death. Rather it is observant and respectful of archetypal aspects of experience, which traditional religious people ordinarily attribute to the agency of an objective God. (It is of course well known that religion can be used for defensive purposes, but its real purpose is to conserve and respect the Powers and with its rituals to reproduce the experience of numinosity that generally lies at its point of origin.)

Jung used both of the two possible derivations of the word "religion." On the one hand, it can be seen as originating in the Latin *relegere*, meaning, "gather together, peruse"; alternatively and perhaps more accurately it is considered to derive from *religāre*, meaning "bind fast" (Onions 1966:754). (In Catholic parlance, a "religious" is someone "bound" by vows.) Jung employed both options: the "religious attitude" (from *relegere*) entails paying "careful and scrupulous attention" to numinous experience; the "religious function" (from *religāre*) links or binds together ego consciousness and the archetypal levels of the unconscious.

Jung considered the vital link between the ego and the archetypal level of the psyche, later termed the "ego-Self axis" by Erich Neumann and Edward Edinger, essential for mental health. This forms the very foundation and necessary precondition for human wholeness. Neurosis occurs when this link is disturbed, that is, when the conscious ego drifts away from its moorings too far into a state of inner alienation from the Self, the psychic source and ground of its existence. Jung called this pathological condition "one-sidedness." The religious function calls a person back to the source, and thus the innate striving of the psyche for its own health and wholeness is intimately related to the religious function.

Since the goal of analysis, as Jung practiced and taught it, is to foster psychological wholeness, its purpose coincides with the goal of the religious function. In this sense, analysis stands in the service of the religious function. Both seek to foster and promote psychological wholeness by creating and maintaining a strong and vital connection between the conscious ego and the inner ground of its existence, the primordial archetypal images of the collective unconscious at the center of which is the Self.

As a side comment here, it should be noted that Jung (and most analysts after him) all too frequently found that analysands had appropriated and used the teachings and structures of established religion actually to thwart the work of the religious function. The practice of organized religion gets in the way of the religious function when it is used defensively or is taken too concretely and applied by the ego's defensive operations. Instead of assisting people to make and maintain a vital contact to the primordial images of the psyche, religious beliefs and practices may be misused by people primarily to defend themselves against abandonment anxiety or annihilation fears. If religious belief offers the comforting and soothing doctrine of eternal life for its adherents, for example, they may fall into the trap of infantile dependency on the priests and religious authorities who control the means of grace. In such an event, analysis aims to undo the effects of religious habits that foster neurotic traits and behavior patterns such as obsessive-compulsive disorders ("scrupulosity"), exaggerated guilt reactions for perceived sins, fear of punishment by parental figures, infantile dependency on others, and so forth. Religions are no panacea for mental illness. On the contrary, they may exacerbate it, if not actually encourage or even create it. Religious leaders are famous for traumatizing people into belief and discipleship.

Analysis and modernity

Analysis arose within the cultural and historical context of modernity (for an excellent discussion of this, see Homans (1995). Here it found its special role as a method for the "cure of souls." Analysis as a profession distinct from medical psychiatry would never have taken hold in a traditionally religious culture, which covers the contingencies of meaning in its own manner and offers other methods for dealing with mental conflict and emotional anguish. To this day, analysis thrives only where modernity has put down deep roots and has shaped cultural expectations and concomitant anxieties. Traditional societies, and the more traditional parts of modern societies, are generally inhospitable to the analytic profession. In fact, many religious traditionalists and fundamentalists consider analysis subversive and dangerous.

Jung was keenly aware of his cultural context and comments on it in many places in his writings. Generally the people who came to him and to his followers and students for analysis were "modern people." That is, they were not religious in the familiar sense of the word, although many of them had grown up in traditionally religious families and surroundings, as had Jung himself. In his own analysis of the cultural situation in which he found himself working as a physician and analyst, Jung followed the well-known distinction between traditional and modern cultures. Traditional ones are rooted in and based upon religious myth, while modern culture grew out of a rational ("enlightened") critique of religion with its mythical images and metaphysical assumptions. As Karen Armstrong has written so persuasively in *The Battle for God*, using Johannes Sloek's (1996) useful distinction between *mythos* and *logos* forms of thinking, traditional cultures are grounded in *mythos* and modern culture is based on the principle of *logos* (Armstrong 2001). Analysis originated and continues to have its home primarily in the *logos* culture of post-enlightenment Europe, i.e. in modernity. Jung considered himself a Kantian in the sense that he accepted Kant's critique of pure reason and metaphysical knowledge. Jung did not believe that one can prove God's existence or that theology has access to special knowledge ("revelation") about the nature of the cosmos. Like most people around him, he subscribed to the scientific approach to knowledge. He was "modern."

The religious and spiritual problems that Jung addressed in his practical work with patients and in his writings are those of modern people who have departed from the beliefs of religious tradition. They are no longer contained religiously in a defined belief system and must make their way spiritually within a scientifically oriented culture that offers little guidance on questions of a spiritual nature. Modernity rejects (if it does not actually ridicule) all myth-based patterns of thought and behavior. The great advantage of modern scientific culture is that it works. It has produced steady improvement in the technical effectiveness of tools and instruments that can powerfully shape and change nature. It fails, however, to deliver what *mythos* cultures can, namely a sense of personal destiny and meaning within the framework of history and a cosmological symbol system.

Jung struggled with the bias of modernity against the mythic and symbolic. The basic problem of "modern man in search of a soul" (the title of one of Jung's better known works in English) is the absence of "soul." There is no transcendence in modernity. So the problem is that without the possibility for imagining personal meaning in a vast and impersonal, wholly material universe, the religious function fails and psychological wholeness becomes diminished as a viable option. In modernity, the human is generally seen to be merely a temporary phenomenon in a time-bound material universe. Religious experience, i.e. the experience of the *numinosum*, becomes interpreted as nothing more than a subjective emotional surge based on the arbitrary flow of brain chemistry and hormones. It carries no intrinsic value, and it points to nothing beyond itself. There are no true symbols in such a universe, only signs and delusions. This is the modernist bias.

Moreover, the modern person, once inculcated with the scientific and enlightened (*logos*) worldview, finds it impossible to return to traditional religion as a source of meaning. An existential purchase on myth becomes essentially impossible. Religious belief is indefensible from a scientific perspective. Unlike *mythos*-based culture, *logos*-culture operates strictly on the basis of scientific rationality, where every "truth" is continuously questioned and there are no permanent certainties. There are no unassailable spiritual facts, only theories, and every theory is open to doubt and revision. Thus modern people, it seems, are condemned to live a life of psychological poverty and partialness in the midst of material plenty, without the option of wholeness because the religious function has been disabled. They cannot create an effective link to the numinous archetypes of the collective unconscious. They must live a barren egoic existence, godless, without transcendent meaning, and sealed off from access to deeper layers of the psyche. They have no myth to live by and are cursed to make do without.

This is the dilemma that Jung sought to address in analysis. Is wholeness possible for modern people? Is there a way to allow the religious function to do its natural psychological work within the culture of modernity?

The religious function in analysis

How can people be spiritual while maintaining their cultural connections to modernity and their commitment to a scientific approach to knowledge? From this question blossomed many of Jung's written statements concerning the relation of analysis and the religious function. In such works as "Psychology and religion," "The symbolic life," "Psychotherapists or the clergy?" "Psychoanalysis and the cure of souls," and "A study in the process of individuation," Jung laid out the case for tending to the spiritual needs of modern men and women within the frame of analytic practice. (In recent times, the term "spiritual" has replaced "religious," to differentiate it from traditional religious forms and practices.) For many of the people who came to see him for psychological treatment, Jung stated more than once, the major problem was not medical but spiritual. It came down to the problem of absence of meaning and lack of contact with the archetypal. They were suffering from lack of wholeness because the religious function was not operating effectively. They were alienated from their own psychological roots, without inner mooring, adrift on the open seas of modernity without a compass. Jung also came to recognize that neurotic symptoms could be an expression of unsatisfied spiritual needs, and were therefore often the distorted expression of a poorly operating religious function. He would occasionally state that people should be grateful for their neuroses because these keep them from going even further into rationalistic one-sidedness. The neurosis paradoxically brings them back to themselves and to the careful and scrupulous observation of the powers at work in the psyche that cannot be controlled by the ego. Neurosis is, ironically, a modern type of religious attitude. Woody Allen would be emblematic of this state of affairs.

No matter what may be going on at the surface of conscious life, Jung theorized, the religious function may still be active in the unconscious. He therefore enlisted dreams to study the religious function at work within the unconscious of modern scientific people, on the theory that dreams offer a sort of X-ray of what is going on under the surface in the unconscious. In one such study, presented as an interpretation of a dream series in *Psychology and Alchemy*, Jung sought to demonstrate the teleological movement of the psyche toward symbols of wholeness. The dreamer was a "modern man" with high scientific credentials (we now know it was Wolfgang Pauli, the physicist) who was under the psychological treatment of a student of Jung's. In this work, Jung argued that the religious function could be detected in the production of dream symbols. In his commentary he says nothing about the personal aspects of "the case." He sticks to the images of the dreams and links them into a chain of pieces that leads to several highly numinous, symbolic symbols of the Self.

In his own analytic practice, too, Jung would often spot the signs of thwarted spirituality in the dreams of patients as well as in the archetypal transference. His method of active imagination, moreover, as used in conjunction with analysis of complexes, dreams, and the transference, became a modern type of spiritual discipline, akin to the Spiritual Exercises of Ignatius Loyola or the meditation practices of some Eastern religious traditions. In the analytic experience, a person could discover and recover the religious function.

What Jung did in analysis with patients became a means for opening the modern person to the religious function active within the unconscious. If the "facts" from the unconscious, as they become available through dreams and transference, are carefully followed and observed in the course of a detailed analysis, the analysand comes into contact with the *spiritus rector* (i.e. the spiritual function) that resides inherently within the psyche. This contact brings about a breakup of the modern defenses against the spiritual (the cultural bias of modernity) and opens the way for a new type of spiritual and religious awareness outside of any defined religious traditions. Analysis became for Jung a road around the spiritual impasse created by modernity.

Jung's followers: the Jungians and the post-Jungians

This road became heavily trafficked by Jung's followers, who expanded upon his original insights and carried his model of analysis into many other areas of the world. Even a modest and cursory review of Jungian literature on the subject of spirituality and the religious function in analysis yields a plethora of titles and authors. Among the most notable in the first generation of Jungians was C.A. Meier (1977), whose small book, *Jung's Analytical Psychology and Religion*, summarizes beautifully Jung's views and the minimal additions of the early Jungians. Many other well-known Jungians of that generation contributed to this topic as well: Gerhard Adler, Barbara Hannah, Esther Harding, Jolande Jacobi, Aniela Jaffe, James Kirsch, M.L. von Franz, to name only some of the more outstanding. The Guild for Pastoral Psychology in London – for which Jung himself gave a talk in 1939 entitled "The symbolic life," James Kirsch offered the first printed pamphlet lecture on "The religious aspect of the unconscious," and Michael Fordham (who was not known for an emphasis on the religious function) gave the forty-sixth pamphlet lecture on "Analytical psychology and religious experience" – has been sponsoring annual lectures on the subject of analytical psychology and spirituality since 1939. The number of pamphlets published by now numbers nearly 300. This is an indication of the amount of attention given to the religious function by Jungians during the course of the past seven decades. Not all of these have to do, of course, with spirituality in analysis, but nearly all the works by Jungians assume analysis as the primary location in which the spiritual takes form within the cultural context of modernity.

With the era of the "post-Jungians," who are commonly identified as those who followed the first generation of "Jungians," a change in tone and emphasis took place, and a new group of authors with a different kind of sensibility entered the scene. James Hillman's early books *Suicide and the Soul* (1964) and *Insearch* (1967) struck the new tone. Hillman gave the term "soul" psychological definition and wide credibility in the English-speaking world. This culminated in his bestseller, *The Soul's Code* (1997). Among the post-Jungians who followed Hillman's lead, spirituality became subsumed under the term "archetypal," which was subtly redefined to mean "essential" or "important" without reference to "the unconscious" or "the archetypes of the collective unconscious." Hillman's "archetypal psychology" also powerfully challenged the notion of psychological "monotheism" as represented by the centrality of the Self in the writings of Jung and his first generation of followers. Instead he proposed opening psychology to "polytheism," which presented a type of spirituality with a multiplicity of images and centers. Using the myths of the Greeks as the template for this version of the action of the religious function in the psyche, the appearance of the spiritual within analysis became more broadly available and generalized. Now it would also include the appearance of archetypal images in consciousness whether from "the unconscious" as in dreams, from "projections" as in transference, or from the phenomenal world of everyday experience. Contemporary life in the city and in the cinema, in relationships such as marriage and friendship and in family life, as well as in analysis, was scanned for archetypal images at play. Wherever these were found would be the occasion for a momentary epiphany, an insight into the psyche as an underlying *unus mundus* or *anima mundi* inhabiting the entire phenomenal world. The doors of analysis were sprung open and depth psychology was taken out of the clinical setting into the world at large. This offered a kind of psychological re-sacrilization of the modern world, as myth-making could be taken up by individuals with an eye for archetypal image and structure. Spirituality became a way of seeing, through an archetypal perspective. In turn, this sensitivity to archetypal image in conscious experience was taken back into analysis, where a multiplicity of archetypal fields were found to be constellated in the dynamic interplay of psyches within the analytic setting.

From Hillman's work flowed the popular books of Thomas Moore (e.g. *Care of the Soul: A Guide for Cultivating Depth and Sacredness in Everyday Life*), the more devotional works of Robert Sardello (e.g. *Love and the World: A Guide to Conscious Soul Practice*), the psychological and theological books and lectures of David Miller (e.g. *The New Polytheism: Rebirth of the Gods and Goddesses*), and the philosophically inclined works of Robert Romanyshyn (e.g. *Mirror and Metaphor: Images and Stories of Psychological Life*).

At the same time, however, other contemporary post-Jungians drew more straightforwardly upon the works of Jung and the early Jungians and extended this into the clinical area with important contributions. Among these perhaps the most notable have been Ann Ulanov, professor of psychology and psychiatry at Union Theological Seminary in New York City (see, for example, her paper "Spiritual aspects of clinical work"), and Edward Edinger, one of the deans of American analysts (see his classic work *Ego and Archetype*). In addition, Lionel Corbett has made a significant statement in his work, *The Religious Function of the Psyche*.

A critical approach to religious and spiritual aspects in analysis

What makes modern Jungian analysis different from traditional analysis is a critical attitude with respect to technique and interpretation, as well as the incorporation of perspectives from modern psychoanalytic figures such as Winnicott and Bion. As Jungian analysis evolved during the years since the founding of formal training institutes after the Second World War, a strong and ongoing debate took place (and still continues to a degree) between what are sometimes referred to as the clinical and symbolic, or the developmental and classical, approaches to analysis. This argument, sometimes quite acrimonious, has sharpened the thinking on both sides of the divide, and in recent times a sort of rapprochement has come about in that both sides now seem to hear and understand as well as respect one another. Moreover, there are today many "blends" of the two polar opposites that attempt to incorporate the strengths of each and minimize the deficits.

The way the fault lines appeared was as follows. An emphasis on the symbolic (i.e. archetypal and spiritual) aspects of analysis was seen to be characteristic of the Zurich school and those most heavily influenced directly by Jung himself. The critique mounted against this, deriving primarily at first from the London school led by Michael Fordham and his students, was that the symbolic approach missed important features of analytic work by overlooking the personal features of transference and early development. The London school analysts, deeply influenced by object relations theory as it was being elaborated in England in the 1940s and 1950s, sought to bring Jungian analysis closer in line with emerging psychoanalytic (i.e. Kleinian and Middle School) technique and understanding. Their strong emphasis on greater frequency of sessions (four or five times weekly vs the twice per week Zurich standard), the use of the couch rather than sitting *vis-à-vis*, the positive valuation placed on regression in analysis to childhood and infantile levels of transference, and the detailed working through of early developmental phases within the structured space of analysis seemed to contradict Jung's emphasis on the experience of the numinous, the elaboration of personal meaning in one's life and destiny looking forward, and the symbolic. Whereas Jung emphasized the religious aspect of analysis in the careful and scrupulous attention to the activity of the archetypal factors at work in the analytic process, the critics attacked his reliance on dream interpretation and activation of the archetypal layers of the unconscious through active imagination and his relative neglect of personal transference. They claimed that the

Zurich ("classical") analysts were missing the most important dimensions of analysis, namely the careful reconstruction of early psychological development and the attachment between parent and infant as this was re-experienced in the transference. In short, the symbolic approach, they argued, was not clinically sharp and grounded enough. It did not address the psychological difficulties of patients who sought help for their common neurotic conditions, most of which revolved around problems with their relationships.

To this the symbolically oriented analysts answered that the so-called clinical approach failed to deliver on the most important issue of all, namely establishing the ego–Self connection and generating a sense of personal meaning. It lacked the religious element, just as modernity lacks it, and it therefore failed to connect the modern ego to the transcendent, to the Self. Without this connection, wholeness is impossible. A person could be in analysis for hundreds of hours, could understand all the reasons for his or her suffering based on early childhood traumas, could be made more rational and competent in ordinary human relationships, but would not be "cured" of the disease of the modern, namely the lack of connection to the religious function and to the symbols that bring the ego into a more conscious relationship with the Self.

As the debates raged in Congresses and publications, the two sides gradually began hearing one another and changes took place on both parts. The Zurich people became less archetypal and symbolic, and the London people started to talk about the Self in a way that could justify capitalizing the word. An important crossover figure is Mario Jacoby, a senior training analyst in Zurich but who did part of his own training in London. His book on transference, *The Analytic Encounter*, demonstrates a smooth joining of clinical and archetypal/symbolic perspectives and techniques. Similarly, Rosemary Gordon, one of the doyennes of the London school, has written works that embrace the symbolic attitude and perspective and weave it together with a solid clinical approach in works such as "The symbolic experience as bridge between the personal and the collective" and "Masochism: the shadow side of the archetypal need to venerate and worship."

Today it has become generally accepted in psychotherapy and psychoanalysis that there is legitimate human need for religious experience and that the religious function has a healthy role to play in psychological life. Religious feeling is more than simply a holdover from childhood's dependence on the parental figures. Jung's understanding of symbols as links between the rational and the irrational, which bring the ego and the unconscious into closer contact, has become understood as not quite so "mystical" as it had been earlier. In fact, in many psychological and psychoanalytical circles mysticism has become less demonized and more respected than it was in the first and middle parts of the twentieth century. Mysticism is not necessarily contradictory to rationality and practicality. It can even be extremely useful medically. Prayer has been shown experimentally to "work" in helping people recover from physical illness. And today many therapists accept the notion that human beings are naturally spiritual if they are not blocked from it by collective prejudices. Spirituality is seen as potentially a part of mental health, not as a sign of illness.

As Jungian analysts became more critical, technique and interpretation also changed. It is no longer quite so easy as it once was to make purely reductive or purely synthetic interpretations. There is awareness that both bases need to be covered.

In addition, adding to the critical thinking about spirituality and the religious function as it enters into analytic practice, a new stream of thought has entered into the discussion of the religious and spiritual elements in analysis. This thinking has been centered on the destructive potential of archetypal constellations within the psyche and within the analytic process. In a challenging paper delivered in 1985, Jeffrey Satinover contended that archetypally based psychic structures are compensatory for developmental deficits. They come into play when ordinary ("good enough") care-taking is not available, and they serve the purpose of making up for the deficit by offering imaginal figures and projections that serve the purpose of providing soothing reassurance, protection, comfort, and presence. In this view, the religious function is seen as fundamentally defensive in nature. This view came out of Satinover's work on narcissistic personality disorders, where compensating grandiose fantasies replace actual achievements in the service of bolstering self-esteem. Similar defensive and at times highly destructive and toxic activity on the part of archetypal images and structures were noted by Nathan Schwartz-Salant in his book on narcissism and in his later work on borderline personality disorder. Donald Kalsched provided the capstone for this angle of vision in his book *The Inner World of Trauma*, where he argues that archetypal defenses of the Self arise from early childhood experiences of severe trauma. The "self-care system" that comes into play from the experience of early and severe psychological trauma employs primitive, archaic (i.e. archetypal) defenses to insure the psychic survival of the individual on the one hand, but like autoimmune diseases that attack the body they also have the unfortunate effect of undermining and often destroying the social and psychological viability of the people they are meant to protect. These are the seemingly impenetrable and thorny defensive structures facing the analyst who attempts to work with early trauma victims, who often show severe borderline personality disturbances.

This view that the religious function has a negative potential is not altogether without reference in Jung's own work. Jung recognized the shadow side of the Self clearly in such works as *Answer to Job*, but he and his immediate followers did not employ this insight in their clinical work with patients. It was later, as analysts began working with narcissistic and borderline personality disorders, that this aspect of the religious function began to come into clear view. (The same phenomenon can be found in social and political reactions to warfare and economic trauma. Societies and cultures show the same proclivity to resort to religious defenses as they seek to protect their embattled national and cultural identities. The "group spirit" becomes the focus of defensive actions, which often have the effect of further traumatizing the people who are supposed to be receiving protection.)

On "negative spirituality"

Jungian analysts from all schools today are trained to be open to the manifestation of the religious function in analysis, whether it manifests positively in numinous dream symbols, for example, or negatively in the defenses of the Self. What does this mean in practice? Fundamentally it means that analysts are prepared to pay "careful and scrupulous attention" to the unconscious factors at work in the analytic process, which can appear in the form of reported dream images, transference and countertransference phenomena, defensive reactions, or any other "field phenomena" as these may appear in the "here and now" of analysis. It is important to note, too, that analysts are taught to refrain from "suggestion" and in their training are not encouraged to create "spiritual enactments" within the analytic frame. This combination of openness to the spiritual and religious (i.e. the archetypal) emergences of the psyche, combined with abstinence from suggesting or enacting spiritual scenarios (such as prayer, quotation from Scriptural texts, encouragement of altered states of consciousness within the session) is what I have come to call "negative spirituality." By this term I mean to distinguish it from the "positive spirituality" that is practiced in religious settings such as churches, temples, mosques, etc. where ritual action is aimed precisely at calling forth or invoking the numinous powers of the archetypal dimension.

The adjectives "negative" and "positive" do not denote value but rather the absence or presence of content. This distinction between "negative" and "positive" spirituality borrows from Isaiah Berlin's distinction between two types of liberty. "Negative liberty" is freedom from external compulsion and constraint; "positive liberty" is freedom to carry out a program of action. In analysis, one practices the discipline of emptiness ("abstinence"), which sets up a "free and sheltered space" (in Dora Kalff's fine phrase) for the analysand's psyche to enter and reveal itself as fully as possible.

Analysis rests upon an inherently uneven relationship between analyst and analysand, because the analyst accepts ethical, professional, and legal responsibility for the process and is paid for it on the one hand, and more importantly because it is fundamentally "for the patient" and his or her psychological benefit, healing, and growth toward wholeness. What the analyst brings to this is training (including many years of personal analysis and supervision), a methodology (technique), self-discipline, and respect for the psyche as it unfolds and reveals its deficits and potentials. The analyst must remain more or less free of expectation, programmatic pressures, or self-gratifying enactments. In this respect, there are no Christian analysts, Jewish analysts, Hindu analysts, or Moslem analysts – there are only analysts. Their own positive religious, philosophical, and even theoretical (except for the bare methods employed) positions should be bracketed when working with individual analysands. The "analytic space" therefore is ideally empty (negative) until material enters from the individual analysand who walks into a session. (I recognize that this is an "ideal" to be sought, not a given that is guaranteed or for that matter even fully achievable. All analysts, regardless of their own personal convictions or beliefs, grow up in and are deeply influenced by their cultural settings, an important part of which is the prevailing religious ethos.)

I will offer some clinical examples to illustrate how I understand negative spirituality in analysis. The first is a case in which the spiritual appeared as a dangerous predatory figure lurking in wait, a dark angel. A new patient brought a first dream to analysis. He is having breakfast in a resort hotel room, and the window is wide open. Outside he sees the ocean. A moderately strong sea breeze billows a white curtain into the room. I ask him to describe this detail more carefully.

"It's a mild breeze," he says, "very fresh. Sometimes there is a gust of wind and the curtain, you know, billows," he adds, gesturing widely with his arms. "It's a clear sunny day and the breeze is fairly strong, but not threatening. It's a good day for the beach, or for sailing."

As he tells me this, he enters into a mild state of reverie, and I follow him. For a moment it seems like we have entered the dream together and I can almost feel the breeze and taste the salty air. He goes on associating to the image, and I muse to myself: the window is open, there is access to the unconscious, and the timing looks propitious. I also think: wind = *pneuma* = spirit. Something mildly spiritual is stirring. He also tells me that I, the analyst, appear in the dream. I am watching him eat breakfast, and he wonders if I am going to be critical of him. So I realize that a potentially negative transference is already at work, and I can easily be turned into a judging and rejecting parental figure.

Several weeks later he brought in a second dream, which became the centerpiece of analytical work for months. In this one, he is standing on the bank of a large river. Again the element of water is central. Around him and in the water he sees many women and children playing, bathing, and generally relaxing. It is a peaceful, nearly paradisal, scene. As he enters the water and begins swimming, he notes how clear and clean this river is. He can see the bottom, and he enjoys the refreshing cool feeling of the clean water on his bare skin. He swims out a long distance and is about to round a bend when suddenly he spots the form of a great white shark lying quietly on the bottom of the river some 20 or 30 feet beneath the surface. He is stunned, quickly turns back, and gets out of the water. He cannot understand why the women and children do not seem to care and go on swimming and playing around in the water. Don't they see the shark? Or do they know it is not dangerous? Or has he hallucinated the shark and it's not real? He does not know.

This dream was disquieting but in fact not terribly frightening. He associates the shark to a psychotic break he had during a drug trip many years earlier. This was a major traumatic experience in his life. His life was completely changed by it, and it took him years to recover ego integrity. In the paranoid state he entered during the drug experience, he said, "I was frozen in the eye of God. I could see my sin. God was pointing his finger of accusation right at me. I *knew* [said with strong emphasis] that I was utterly corrupt and rotten. Everything I did was bad. I was the greatest sinner in the world. Only there was nobody else around: I was all God was looking at, and His judgment was absolute and final."

The great white shark – a psychic predator – had once upon a time attacked and devastated his ego. For him this was a spiritual experience of the first order, but also it resulted in a severely pathological reaction. The angry and rejecting side of an awful God of judgment appeared in the drug experience, and his weakened ego became severely traumatized. On the personal level, he could associate this to scenes of childhood scolding and brutality delivered by an alcoholic parent. His parents were not reliable. Surprising and frightening destructive things could happen suddenly and without warning.

"That's why I got out of the river of life," he said, referring to the bad drug trip. "My life stopped at that moment. I longed to go back to being the person I was before the attack, but I couldn't. I was trapped by this knowledge that God had me in his vision and that I was totally bad. And I couldn't figure out why other people weren't equally devastated by this knowledge." The famous preacher and Puritan divine, Jonathan Edwards, would have recognized this spiritual crisis as familiar enough.

In this dream image of the latent shark, produced within the context of analysis many years later, we are given an entry point back to a traumatizing event and a traumatized ego. The dream points to the archetypal factor underlying it, the shadow side of the Self. The presence of this potentially traumatizing force in the unconscious continued to haunt him in the years following. And now it enters the analytic space, looking mild and docile enough at the moment, but potentially explosive and dangerous. Perhaps it can be tamed and metabolized through reflection and be made somewhat more benign through the experience of the transference.

The working through of his pathological guilt and fear of divine retribution, experienced in the psychotic break and imaged by the dream of the shark, showed evidence of some improvement (i.e. normalization) in another (also archetypal) dream that came about a year later. He dreamed:

A strange spider, having three parts to its body (a head, a thorax, and a body proper), sits on a plastic sphere, which is a hollow container full of liquid from which it can feed. [See drawing by patient, Figure 8.1.] This

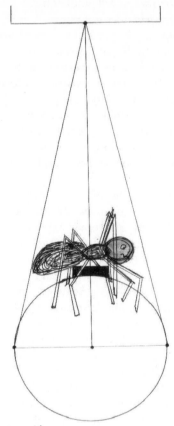

Figure 8.1 Drawing of a dream spider.

sphere hangs on the front verandah of a house, near the entrance. I live in the house with other people, perhaps family members. The spider looks synthetic, but it is alive and real. The legs are hollow, the head is blue and spherical, and some elements look sort of abstract. It is a female spider, a mother with children. The spider is completely happy, enraptured and totally alive, doing what it needs to be doing. Suddenly and without provocation I kill it. I pull off four of its legs. It grimaces in agony as I destroy its complete and whole small world. Then I stare at the sphere and see that the spider is not there any more. I am very upset to see its place is empty. Someone in the house asks: "Where is the spider?" The spider is of course irreplaceable. I feel terrible for killing it, and I realize that something essential has disappeared from the house. I feel very depressed as I awaken.

This dream was understandably deeply troubling to the analysand (and to me), and we spent several sessions reflecting on it. The analysand feared he had done some irreparable damage to himself, to his wholeness and his psychological balance. Had he perhaps even destroyed the Self, he wondered? His gratuitous act of wanton destructiveness was as surprising to him as it was to me. He is a kind and gentle soul, environmentally sensitive and nurturing. Turn this dream as we might, exploring every facet and avenue at length and in great detail, nothing "clicked" for him, and both of us remained unsatisfied with the interpretation. Some six weeks later he had another dream that provided the satisfactory answer. It was a simple dream in which reference was made to the spider dream, and the phrase "RESPECT FOR OTHERNESS" appeared and was registered. The thought was that the spider, living in her own world, represented radical "otherness." The word "respect" turned the key in the lock of meaning. Out of experiences like this is born what Hester Solomon has called "the ethical attitude." It is an attitude grounded in awareness of and respect for "the other." But this dream goes even further, to advocate respect for "otherness" itself. This is precisely what Jung meant by the term "religious," which rests on "careful and scrupulous attention" (i.e. respect) toward otherness, toward the factors at work in the psyche and in the world that are beyond the ego's understanding, with which the ego cannot identify short of delusion and insanity. Following Kierkegaard, we can say that the "religious" reaches even beyond the "ethical" dimensions of psychological experience and maturity to embrace respect for otherness itself as this becomes manifest in the numinous. These dreams became the teacher of the religious attitude.

I offer this as an example not of clinical or interpretive brilliance on my part or his. It is rather an example of what I mean by "negative spirituality," which is akin to the similarly named "negative capability" espoused by John Keats and recommended to poets. One dream proposed a puzzle, and another dream answered the puzzle. The task of the analyst here is simply to keep the space open enough to receive both and to live with the frustration and ambiguity of not knowing the answer until the psyche offers its own solution.

Another clinical example of how negative spirituality plays a role in analysis is the following. A patient I had been seeing for a little more than a year brought in a dream that totally surprised him. It is, in my view, an example of the unconscious spirit's freedom and genius for turning our conscious attitudes upside down. This too is the work of the religious function. The context of the dream was extraordinary. The analysand told me that he had the dream while sitting on a bench at the hospital waiting for his daughter to have her third baby. He and his wife were not at all pleased that their daughter was having this child – she was not married and had no means to support herself and her other children, let alone yet another. The baby's father had disappeared. She had refused to undergo an abortion and had insisted on carrying the child to term. So here he was at 2 a.m., waiting with her until she would be taken into the delivery room. He fell asleep on the bench and dreamed that he found himself in his daughter's hospital room. Some women were hovering around and tending to things. Suddenly he has a vision (in the dream), and in the vision he sees some 20 people standing around his daughter's bed waiting for the birth to take place. They are here to celebrate this *joyful* event. Then he realizes that he recognizes all of these people. Each one is someone he knows from the past. He searches their faces – there is his childhood chum, there is his friend from college, there is his former mentor, on and on. He knows them all. In the dream vision, they are the ages they were when he knew them. He becomes ecstatic and filled with joy because he realizes that while some of these people are actually dead now, still they are here and have returned to be with him at the birth of his new grandchild. He is overcome by gratitude and is weeping for joy to be with his friends again, when his daughter wakes him up and says it is time to go in and give birth.

This dream/vision of a living network of relationships, of links between past (his childhood friends), present (the hospital situation), and future (the new grandchild, a symbol of futurity), is akin to mystical visions of the interconnectedness of all things and beings in the cosmos, seen and unseen. In such moments we are privileged to transcend our limited ego views and preferences. There are larger realities, temporal and atemporal. The ego's position is relativized. The ego puts aside its own limited and immediate concerns as a greater perspective takes hold. The dream helped this man to change his attitude toward his child and grandchild.

The spirituality that arises in analysis is spontaneous, surprising, and almost always contrary to the ego's limited attitudes and expectations. This is possible only if the analyst practices negative spirituality and does not fill the analytic container with positive content and procedures. The patient's psyche does the necessary work.

Another clinical vignette illustrates the appearance of the religious function through a synchronistic event reported in analysis. Synchronicity is the meaningful coincidence of subjective and objective factors. Most often this moment of being shown the surprising interconnectedness of things inner and outer derives from the context of a close human relationship. A patient, who was not at all given to mystical-mindedness and strove to be a rational, skeptical, modern man in all ways, related an unusual happening. He was nonplussed by an incident that took place the day before our session. His daughter had called from another country and told him about a near fatal accident she had been in while driving an old rented car over a narrow mountain road. A tire blew out on her vehicle and nearly caused her to leave the road and tumble to her death in the deep ravine below. She was shaken up but OK. He was recounting this fearful event to another child of his as they were driving into the city to see a show. Just when he was about to tell him about the blowout on her car, one of the tires on his own car blew out with a terrific noise and with such force that the rim of the wheel was instantly grinding on the pavement. He was speechless. The hidden network of object relations, which includes the psychological and physical domains of our lives, shows its presence sometimes in astonishing ways. If we could see the full extent of it, we would see that we are each connected by threads in a great fabric whose extent and intimate design are beyond our comprehension, and we touch each other in strange ways and surprising places. The net result of such a synchronistic experience is a conviction that there are unseen factors at work behind the scenes, which we do not control or understand. If we pay attention to them, we are engaged in what Jung called the religious attitude.

References

Armstrong, K. (2001) *The Battle for God*, New York: Balantine Books.
Berlin, I. (2002) *Liberty*, Oxford and New York: Oxford University Press.
Corbett, L. (1996) *The Religious Function of the Psyche*, New York: Routledge.
Edinger, E. (1972) *Ego and Archetype*, New York: Putnam.
—— (1984) *The Creation of Consciousness*, Toronto: Inner City Books.
Geoghegan, W. (2002) *Jung's Psychology As a Spiritual Practice & Way of Life*, Lanham, NY and Oxford: University Press of America.
Gordon, R. (1977) "The symbolic experience as bridge between the personal and the collective", *Journal of Analytical Psychology*, **22**(4), 331–343.
—— (1987) "Masochism: the shadow side of the archetypal need to venerate and worship", *The Archetype of Shadow in a Split World* (Berlin: Tenth International Congress of Analytical Psychology, 2–9 September 1986), pp. 283–295. Einsiedeln, Switzerland: Daimon Verlag.
Hillman, J. (1964) *Suicide and the Soul*, London: Hodder and Stoughton.
—— (1967) *Insearch: Psychology and Religion*, New York: Charles Scribner's Sons.
—— (1971) "Psychology: monotheistic or polytheistic?", *Spring*, 193–207, New York: Spring Publications.
—— (1997) *The Soul's Code: In Search of Character and Calling*, New York: Warner Books.
Homans, P. (1995) *Jung in Context: Modernity and the Making of a Psychology*, Chicago: University of Chicago Press.
Jacobi, J. (1965) *The Way of Individuation*, New York: New American Library.
Jacoby, M. (1984) *The Analytic Encounter: Transference and Human Relationship*, Toronto: Inner City Books.
Jung, C.G. (1922) "Psychoanalysis and the cure of souls", CW 11, para. 539–552, Princeton, NJ: Princeton University Press.
—— (1932) "Psychotherapists or the clergy", CW 11, para. 488–538.
—— (1937) *Psychology and Religion*, CW 11, para. 1–168.
—— (1952) *Answer to Job*, CW 11, para. 553–758.
—— (1958) "Flying saucers: a modern myth of things seen in the skies", CW 10, para. 389–824.
—— (1966) *Two Essays in Analytical Psychology*, CW 7.
—— (1968) *Psychology and Alchemy*, CW 12.
Kalsched, D. (1996) *The Inner World of Trauma: Archetypal Defenses of the Personal Spirit*, London and New York: Routledge.

—— (2003) "Daimonic elements in early trauma", *Journal of Analytical Psychology*, **48**(2), 145–170.

Meier, C.A. (1977) *Jung's Analytical Psychology and Religion*, Carbondale and Edwardsville, IL Southern Illinois University Press.

Miller, D. (1974) *The New Polytheism: Rebirth of the Gods and Goddesses*, New York: Harper and Row.

Moore, T. (1994) *Care of the Soul: A Guide for Cultivating Depth and Sacredness in Everyday Life*, New York: HarperCollins.

Neumann, E. (1954) *The Origins and History of Consciousness*, New York: Pantheon.

Onions, C.T. (ed.) (1966) *The Oxford Dictionary of English Etymology*, Oxford: Clarendon Press.

Otto, R. (1923) *The Idea of the Holy* (trans. J.W. Harvey), Oxford: Oxford University Press.

Romanyshyn, R. (2001) *Mirror and Metaphor: Images and Stories of Psychological Life*, Pittsburgh, PA: Trivium Publications.

Sardello, R. (2001) *Love and the World: A Guide to Conscious Soul Practice*, Great Barrington, MA: Lindsfarne Books.

Satinover, J. (1985) "At the mercy of another: abandonment and restitution in psychosis and psychotic character", in N. Schwartz-Salant and M. Stein (eds), *Abandonment*, pp. 47–86, Wilmette, IL: Chiron Publications.

Schwartz-Salant, N. (1982) *Narcissism and Character Transformation*, Toronto: Inner City Books.

—— (1989) *The Borderline Personality: Vision and Healing*, Wilmette, IL: Chiron Publications.

Sloek, J. (1996) *Devotional Language*, New York and Berlin: Walter de Gruyter.

Solomon, H. (2001) "Origins of the ethical attitude", *Journal of Analytical Psychology*, **46**(3), 443–454.

Ulanov, A. (1995) "Spiritual aspects of clinical work", in M. Stein (ed.), *Jungian Analysis*, Chicago: Open Court.

Chapter 9

Synchronicity as emergence[1]

Joseph Cambray

> The aim of science is not things themselves, as the dogmatists in their simplicity imagine, but the relations among things; outside these relations there is no reality knowable.
>
> (Henri Poincaré, *Science and Hypothesis*, 1905)

Historical background

Many of the pioneers in depth psychology had an interest in what would today be referred to as anomalous phenomena. For example, Jung's, Freud's and Ferenczi's ambivalent fascination with spiritualist mediums is now well known. Jung wrote his medical dissertation "On the psychology and pathology of so-called occult phenomena" (1902) based upon his analysis of séances he attended, observing his mediumistic cousin, Helly Preisewerk (Goodheart 1984). Ferenczi, whose first, pre-psychoanalytic paper was on mediumship, induced Freud to join him on trips to visit several mediums. Thus, from the various correspondences between these pioneers now published, we know that Freud and Ferenczi went to see the medium Frau Seidler in Berlin in 1909 on the trip home from the USA, as soon as Jung departed for Zurich. Freud, who wrote variously on telepathy, the uncanny, dreams and the occult (see e.g. Rieff 1963; Devereux 1953), also remarked to Karl Abraham that his daughter Anna possessed "telepathic sensitivity" (Falzeder 2002:550).

The background to this persistent interest has various sources, from Mesmer's ability to cure patients through the use of "animal magnetism" – a victory over Gassner with his traditional method of exorcism (Ellenberger 1970:53–57) – to the rise of the popular spiritualist movement from 1848 on (Taves 1999), to the medical use of hypnotic techniques proper, especially in France during the later nineteenth century. Jean-Martin Charcot's use of these techniques allowed the first clinical differentiation of patients with functional illnesses (psychologically based symptoms) from those with "organic" problems (having primary neurobiological impairments) and became part of a psychological treatment regime. If we maintain an attitude of openness to clinical data, regardless of its "fit" with prevailing theory, then one of the most immediate and important sources for depth psychology's fascination with anomalous phenomena can be traced to the Society for Psychical Research (SPR), which in the 1880s initiated a series of "thought transference" experiments. Frederic W.H. Myers, who was a founding member of the SPR, renamed "thought transference" with the neologism "tele-pathy" (emotional touch at a distance) in the context of the "tele-" technologies then emerging (the telegraph and the telephone being the most prominent). Myers in his later works drew parallels between his own notions of a "subliminal consciousness" (derived from Charcot's work) and Freud's unconscious – Myers was also responsible for introducing Freud's thought into England in 1897 and, according to Luckhurst, his writings were the source of both Joan Riviere's and James Strachey's first contact with Freud's ideas (Luckhurst 2002:269 and n. 94; Thurschwell 2001:19 and n. 21); even Ernest Jones, one of the staunchest opponents to Freud's interest in occult-ism, had read Myers at the start of his career (Luckhurst 2002:270 and n. 95). Myers' influence on Jung's thought has been highlighted at a *Journal of Analytical Psychology* (*JAP*) conference by both Eugene Taylor and Sonu Shamdasani (Taylor 1998; Shamdasani 1998); other aspects of Jung's interest in séances, the occult and related matters can be found in Ellenberger (1970), the introductory chapter of Main's (1997) selection of Jung's writings, the numerous publications of Sonu Shamdasani, and F.X. Charet's (1993) book.

According to several scholars of the history of this period, Freud, despite his involvement with the SPR (he published "A note on the unconscious" in the Proceedings of the SPR in 1912 as part of his election to be a "corres-ponding member"; see Jones 1957:397), was especially concerned with the SPR experiments and related theories. He was at pains to assign a physio-logical mechanism to "thought transference" in order to differentiate it from his nascent intrapsychic model of analytic transference, as an affective recapitulation of infantile prototypes displaced onto the analyst. After visit-ing Frau Seidler, Freud in a letter to Ferenczi wrote: "Should one now, as a result of this experience, commit oneself to occultism? Certainly not, it is only a matter of thought transference. If this can be proved, then one has to believe it – then it is not [a psychoanalytic] phenomenon, but rather a purely somatic one, certainly a novelty of the first rank" (Thurschwell 2001:123). Freud's concern persisted, so that 24 years later he wrote in "Dreams and the occult": "as regards thought transference . . . it would seem actually to favor the extension of the scientific (or, as opponents would say, mechanistic) way of thinking onto the elusive world of the mind . . . [B]y inserting the unconscious between the physical and . . . the mental, psychoanalysis has prepared the way for the acceptance of such processes as telepathy" (Devereux 1953:108).

Chertok and Stengers have examined the anxiety behind Freud's thinking on this:

if thoughts could be transferred in a direct way, then how could suggestion and analysis be told apart? . . . As Freud portrays it, the context is
one of potentially dangerous rivalry between the science of psychoanalysis on the one hand and the occult and fascinating character of
telepathy on the other . . . The task of psychoanalysis is, on the one hand,
to avoid being fascinated by telepathy, and, on the other, to elucidate the
materials of thought transference just as it elucidates fantasies, ordinary
dreams, and other subjective productions.

(Chertok and Stenger 1992:71–73)

As Thurschwell and Luckhurst each discuss in their books, behind this differentiation of the mechanisms for types of transference lay concerns about
unboundaried states of mind, with fears ranging from those around plagiar-
ism to contamination by psychotic processes. In addition I believe we are
catching sight here of Freud's political anxieties. He is struggling to save the
purity of the young psychoanalytic movement from identification with
occultism, especially that aspect associated with hypnoidal phenomena
through a dichotomizing, Cartesian sleight of hand, or mind. The disengaging
of psychological from somatic communication in the face of anomalies that
breach the boundaries of intrapsychic formulations falsely compartmental-
izes unconscious processes, which are irreducibly psychosomatic. Jung's concept of the "psychoid" is an alternative approach that does not get trapped in
this split.[2]

Throughout the first generation of analytic thinkers following Freud,
there was a persistent interest in telepathy and clairvoyance, especially as
observed in the clinical encounter – the more general public interest in these
matters during this period is an enormous topic beyond the scope of a single
chapter. Curiously, the book edited by Devereux, *Psychoanalysis and the
Occult* – a compilation of 31 papers on these topics, published from 1899 to
1950 – came out in 1953, shortly after Jung's publications *On Synchronicity*
(1951) and *Synchronicity: An Acausal Connecting Principle* (1952) (I thank
Roderick Main for first bringing this to my attention). There is a striking
absence of any mention of Jung or his work in the Devereux book, though it
should be noted that Jung's conception of synchronicity as a basic principle
of the world is much broader in scope than the clinical focus of the
Devereux anthology. It may be that one of the undeclared tasks of the book
was to counter Jung's innovations, reminiscent of Freud's attempts to
arrange for Ferenczi to attack Jung for his publication of *Wandlungen und
Symbole der Libido* (*Psychology of the Unconscious*) (Falzeder and Haynal
2003). Since 1953, psychoanalytic commentary on matters "occult" has
persisted, going in and out of fashion (the pep-CD-Rom of psychoanalytic
articles lists more than 150 new publications in the 45 years between 1953
and 1998). However, only rarely do these writings touch on Jung's reflections
and contributions to the field. Many, though not all, of these publications

retain a conservative framework, maintaining a reductive model to explain such radically transgressive occurrences in the therapeutic frame. I believe this is a problem of the scientific models of the world and the mind that informs analytic thinking. This chapter will attempt to redress some of these concerns and, in keeping with the series of which this volume is a part, will stay close to the clinical experience rather than the whole of Jung's vision of synchronicity.

Recently, psychoanalyst Elizabeth Lloyd Mayer has put forward several papers and lectures in which she has taken a more expansive view of anomalous phenomena from a contemporary scientific and psychoanalytic perspective. In some of these she details co-leading groups with Carol Gilligan on "Intuition, Unconscious Communication and 'Thought Transference' " at the American Psychoanalytic Association's bi-annual meetings. Although applicants had to write a report on an anomalous experience of either a personal or a clinical nature as a requirement for joining a group, the organizers were overwhelmed with applicants, many of whom were well-known and respected master clinicians (Mayer 2002a). Mayer is also involved with PEAR (the Princeton Engineering Anomalies Research group) and in this has been turning to various contemporary scientific disciplines in a search to find a more up-to-date grounding for these phenomena. In the process she has become something of a psychopomp to her psychoanalytic colleagues, providing a vessel of containment for the divulging of secret, clinical occurrences that generally have been discussed openly only by Jungians. In this vein she has recently published a posthumous paper by Robert Stoller on telepathic dreams that, as she tells in an article in *JAPA* (2001), he sequestered at the urging of a supervisor.

The concern with the relationship between boundaried and unboundaried, or as Mayer sees it, radically connected states of mind, was presented by her in a *JAP* paper (2002b) and at greater length at a *JAP* conference on "Science and the Symbolic World." The fundamental divergence of models of the nature of the psyche, implicit in the scientific worldviews informing each, makes braiding strands of Jungian and Freudian thought difficult at best, requiring a postmodern, multi-perspectival stance to hold the tension necessary for any synthesis to emerge. An interesting attempt in this direction is an eclectic group of essays edited by Nick Totton (2003) with contributions from a multicultural, multidisciplinary selection of scholars and analysts. All of these efforts compel readers to consider experiences outside the traditional confines of ego psychology, requiring we examine the specter of our credulity. This was one of the persistent problems for the SPR in its failed attempt to divest itself of nineteenth-century spiritualism and put its data on the firm "scientific" footing of the day, and this approach when applied to parapsychological research has tended to meet with similar difficulties. Rather than trying to fit these experiences into a scientific paradigm that is itself being deeply reconsidered for its limitations, this chapter will look towards scientific models that deliberately explore complex phenomena that often cannot be completely described by unambiguous mathematical solutions.

Coincidence

Jung's first formal use of the term "synchronicity" was on 4 December 1929 in a seminar on dreams; his first public (and published) mention of the term followed a few months later on 10 May 1930 at his memorial address for his friend, the sinologist Richard Wilhelm (1930:para. 56). But it was only with some trepidation, following his heart attack, that Jung proceeded on the urging of Wolfgang Pauli to publish the details of his ideas on synchronicity in 1951 and 1952 – the letters between Jung and Pauli, edited by C.A. Meier, have recently appeared in English with an instructive introduction by Beverley Zabriskie, under the title *Atom and Archetype* (Meier 2001).

In putting forth a new principle, at least for Western science, of acausal connectedness stemming from years of recorded observations of meaningful coincidences, Jung was at pains in his exposition to explicate the limits of understanding of "chance" and "coincidence" within the causal framework of the science of his day. The justification for introducing a new principle was failure of the prevalent, strictly Cartesian description of events used by the science of the times to account for phenomena outside a straightforward cause and effect paradigm. Jung drew upon the famous Duke University ESP researcher J.B. Rhine's results, especially those with precognitive, future-predictive indicators, to buttress his critique of the classical views of space, time and causality. At the core of his argument Jung employs an energy hypothesis:

> it is impossible, with our present resources, to explain ESP, or the fact of meaningful coincidence, as a phenomenon of energy. This makes an end of the causal explanation as well, for "effect" cannot be understood as anything except a phenomenon of energy. Therefore it cannot be a question of cause and effect, but of a falling together in time, a kind of simultaneity. Because of this quality of simultaneity, I have picked on the term "synchronicity" to designate a hypothetical fact equal in rank to causality as a principle of explanation . . . I consider synchronicity as a psychically conditioned relativity of space and time.
>
> (Jung 1952:para. 840)

Although Rhine's work and Jung's use of it have been subjected to criticisms over the years, the energy hypothesis at the core of Jung's argument for an acausal principle operative in meaningful coincidence has not been adequately explored to date. Jung's understanding of energy was based on the laws of thermodynamics articulated in the nineteenth century, which apply only to closed systems at or near equilibrium. Scientific description of energic processes in open systems far from equilibrium was not available in Jung's day. As modern scientists note: "The common statements of the first and second law are that energy is conserved and entropy increases respectively. Unfortunately entropy is strictly defined only for equilibrium situations. Thus these statements are not sufficient for discussing non-equilibrium situations, the realm of all self-organizing systems including life" (Schneider and Kay 1994:631).

Before exploring this, however, let us first look at modern views of "chance" events that are not considered psychologically meaningful. Generally the occurrence of these events has been modeled using statistical techniques and probability theory. One of the most important applications of such modeling has been in the study of biological evolution through natural selection based on the theory of genetic mutations. Random, chance occurrences, such as radiation or chemically induced changes in components of DNA, have been taken as leading in rare cases to adaptive advantage. This gives creatures with traits stemming from such changes a competitive edge for survival. Therefore the offspring of individuals with such traits, if inherited, will tend to persist in a stable environment over others lacking these traits. Minor variations are seen to accumulate gradually, creating the complicated order and organs we see in the diverse organisms of our world. This view of biological evolution is again Cartesian, in that the psyche has had no role. In effect, *coincidence drives evolution*, but is explained solely through probability theory and treated as wholly accidental.

Attempting to extend this perspective by applying statistical analysis to the study of coincidences in the human realm, mathematicians Persi Diaconis and Frederick Mosteller sought to evaluate Jung's model of synchronicity. In a published paper they conclude that:

> Once we set aside coincidences having apparent causes, four principles account for large numbers of remaining coincidences: hidden cause; psychology, including memory and perception; multiplicity of endpoints, including the counting of "close" or nearly alike events as if they were identical; and the law of truly large numbers, which says that when enormous numbers of events and people and their interactions cumulate over time, almost any outrageous event is bound to occur. These sources account for much of the force of synchronicity.
>
> (Diaconis and Mosteller 1989:853)

They do leave a door ajar, however, at the very end of their article: "Where we have solid control and knowledge, the rates of occurrences seem about as expected ... but our inexperience with and lack of empirical information about the kinds of problems coincidences present do make for many surprises" (ibid.: 860). In the statistical model used to date, meaning is treated as wholly subjective, not inherent in the world. This again embraces a Cartesian separation of inner and outer worlds rather than exploring their interpenetration.

Pauli in his interactions with Jung takes a radically different stance, as when he comments: "whenever an application of statistical methods, without consideration of the psychic state of the people involved in the experiment does *not* show such a 'pernicious influence' [of the statistical method itself on the determination of synchronicity], then there is something very different from synchronicity going on" (Meier 2001:54). Pauli was referring here to Jung's observation that an initial synchronistic set of responses to a survey he had done for his monograph on the topic had faded and been lost with subsequent data collection *along with* the decreased affective interest in the project, a factor not accounted for in the statistical approach.

Similarly the use of quantum mechanics as a source of metaphors for psychological experience is potentially problematic, especially as quantum phenomena primarily operate at the micro-level and do not generally translate into phenomena at the macro, or human scale. Some philosophers such as Kirk Ludwig have argued that quantum mechanics does not offer greater insight into the mind/body dilemma than classical mechanics (1995). Instead, contemporary mind–body theorists have increasingly turned to the concept of "supervenience" to try to capture the nature of the relationship between physical and mental events (e.g. Kim 1998; Tresan 1996), a project that has its roots in the seventeenth century after Descartes with the work of the philosopher-polymath Leibniz, curiously one of Jung's stated major precursors for his idea of synchronicity (this is developed elsewhere; see Cambray 2003). Moving outside the realm of microphysics (where Jung was in part deriving his concerns about energy, in addition to classical thermodynamic formulations), are there now other ways of looking scientifically at seeming coincidences occurring at the scale of normal perceptions besides the statistical, probabilistic approach?

Emergence

Overlapping the same period as the SPR research there were a group of parallel cultural and intellectual movements, especially in English- and German-speaking countries that challenged the mechanistic models of life and the universe that were derived from nineteenth-century positivistic scientific disciplines. Various formulations of holistic perspectives, including Gestalt psychology, had their birth in these movements. The British group included such figures as John Stuart Mills, George Henry Lewes, Samuel Alexander, Conway Lloyd Morgan and C.D. Broad, who were known collectively as "emergentists." Lloyd Morgan, who gave the 1922 Gifford lectures on the topic "Emergent Evolution," was a source for Jung's entomological example when constructing his theory of archetypes; for example, Jung uses the example of the leaf-cutting ant from Morgan's *Habit and Instinct* in "On the nature of the psyche" (see CW 8, para. 398, n. 112). Lloyd Morgan was also a friend of James Mark Baldwin, an American developmentalist, whose views on the relationship of cultural learning to evolution have had a renaissance in the era of computer simulations and who may also have impacted Jung's thinking (Tresan 1996; Hogenson 2001). Harrington traces the Germanic fascination with wholeness back to Kant in his positing of a teleological causality when considering how living systems, which have component parts, were organized into a whole (Harrington 1996:xvii). From Kant it is a short step to Goethe and then the whole German Romantic tradition with its *Naturphilosophie*. This lineage is, of course, the one Jung identified himself with throughout his life, though Paul Bishop offers careful, critical reexamination of Jung's relationship to his sources in his various publications (for a critique of Jung's use of Kant in formulating synchronicity, see Bishop 2000).

With the rise of molecular biology these movements foundered, as much of the behavior of living systems seemed ultimately to be derived from and explained by genetics. Matters rested there, for the most part, until the 1970s when a new mode of scientific thinking began to open up scientific investigations in areas previously designated as too complex to solve. The work of Nobel laureate Ilya Prigogine on the non-equilibrium thermodynamics of dissipative structures was one of the keys to this breakthrough. Prigogine developed a view of energetics that supersedes the simplistic cause/effect models of the positivistic science. Together with Stengers, he went on to point out that his conclusions approximate many phenomena in our ordinary daily lives, which are lived far from the stasis of equilibrium (Prigogine and Stengers 1984). The field of study which has grown out this approach is called "complexity theory" and explores the ways in which order can emerge through self-organization at the edge of chaos. Unlike quantum mechanics, the findings from this approach are applicable to both micro and macro worlds. The underlying organizational processes operate across all levels of the physical and human worlds and thus do not conform to specialist categories. In terms of theory this paradigm transgresses and transcends classic disciplinary divisions such as physics, biology or economics. Complexity, as a feature of dynamic systems, occurs when interactions between component parts give rise to novel, unpredictable behaviors such as can be found in certain chemical reactions, the weather, ecosystems, socio-political events, economic trends, and so on. Emergence is postulated to be an essential organizing principle operating at every level (e.g. Morowitz 2002); this includes the way mental events supervene on the neural interactions of the brain.

To explore the ramifications involved in adopting complexity, a "think tank", the Santa Fe Institute, was set up. This institute is made up of an eclectic group of brilliant scientists from many disciplines. A particularly interesting subset of the studies coming out of the work of this group is on "complex adaptive systems" (CAS). These are systems that have what is termed "emergent" properties, self-organizing features arising in response to environmental, competitive pressures – in effect, this effort is providing scientific formulation for the previous intuitions of the emergentists; however, at times reaching different conclusions. While external forces drive the quality of complexity in CAS, this complexity is not inherent in individual components. CAS form patterns or Gestalts in which the whole is truly greater than the sum of the parts. As noted in Chapter 5, CAS have agents operating on one scale producing behaviors that lie one scale above them and the transition from lower to higher levels of organization is "emergence." Complex systems tend to exhibit "scale-free" features, showing similar patterns in a homologous series, or nested emergent phenomena. The evolving network of neighborhoods forming cities over time is one of Steven Johnson's (2001) examples derived from the work of Jane Jacobs. In general, systems are not considered emergent until "local interactions result in some kind of discernible macrobehavior" (Johnson 2001:19). Among Johnson's examples of biological emergence is one in which individual slime mold cells aggregate into a swarm entity during times when the forest floor is replete with decaying organic matter, i.e. when there is excess food, then spontaneously revert to single cell life during times of less bounty, all of which is done without a "leader" but rather is collective organization from below upwards.

Another striking example from the world of insects was noted in *Scientific American* by Diane Martindale:

> Hundreds of the parasitic tiny blister beetle larvae clump together to mimic the shape and color of a female bee. When an amorous male bee attempts to mate, the beetle larvae grab his chest hair and are carried off. Then, when the duped male mates with a real female bee, the larvae transfer to her back and ride off to the nest, where they help themselves to pollen. The cooperative behavior of the beetle larvae had been virtually unknown in the insect world except among social species such as bees and ants. The report also notes that beetle larvae clumps must also smell like female bees, because painted models do not fool the male bee.
>
> (Martindale 2000)

The collective bee-ing here appears as an adaptive emergent form.

The self-organization manifesting in CAS appears transcendent from what is known about the behavior of the individual agents (and transcendent from the perspective of consciousness if the ˉsystem is biological, including human). This of course brings us to a reconsideration of Jung's formulation of archetypes as discussed throughout this book, but especially in Chapter 2. When an emergent model is extended to human psychology, Jung's concept of archetypal patterns recast in terms of CAS seems far less "occult" and more truly visionary than has been generally appreciated. There does appear to be a growing reassessment of Jung's theory in terms of emergence as discussed in various places. Thus, Saunders and Skar, using physical examples that are described with the aid of contemporary mathematics and physics, argued that "the archetype is an emergent property of the activity of the brain/mind" (2001:305). George Hogenson has shown how Jung's sources of biological understanding were predominately neo-Darwinian, a perspective which ultimately brings Hogenson to the conclusion that "the archetypes are the emergent properties of the dynamic developmental system of brain, environment, and narrative" (2001:607). Jean Knox in a recent book (2003) has synthesized a great deal of neurobiological, cognitive science and attachment research into a Jungian view of the emergent mind. A measure of the general importance of the emergentist reformulation of Jungian theory can be discerned from the title of the XVI international congress of Jungian analysts (2004): "Edges of Experience: Memory and Emergence." Jung's vision of archetypes, as nodal patterns in the collective unconscious (discussed in Chapter 5) engendering order and shaping our psychologies, seems a remarkable, intuitive articulation of the CAS model now being scientifically constructed.

As open systems capable of dissipating energy from the environment, CAS are not constrained by the thermodynamic considerations Jung held in his original framing of synchronicity and so allow reconsideration of the definition of causality to be used when evaluating them. In this view, emergent phenomena do look like meaningful, if inexplicable, coincidences to ordinary consciousness. Aspects of the assembled higher order or supraordinate structures can appear in the mind as images, such as those Jung identified as symbols of the Self, which when related to affectively often coincide with a sense of deeper purpose or function that often can barely be intuited, if perceived at all. This leads me to suggest that synchronicities may be explored as a form of emergence and can have a central role in individuation, or psychological maturation (taken as a homologue of biological evolution), strengthening this line of Jung's thinking.

Stuart Kaufman, a founding member of the Santa Fe Institute, has in a number of books spearheaded a reexamination of the role of self-organizing systems in the origins and evolution of life. Hailed by eminent biologists such as Steven Jay Gould, Kaufman's works have presented in detail how CAS are a factor of equal significance to natural selection in evolution. Highlighting the interconnected quality of these systems, Kaufman states: "Networks in the regime near the edge of chaos – this compromise between order and surprise – appear best able to coordinate complex activities and best able to evolve as well. It is a very attractive hypothesis that natural selection achieves genetic regulatory networks that lie near the edge of chaos" (1995:26). If this hypothesis provides a more complete understanding of somatic evolution, we can anticipate that it will likewise have correlates in the evolution of the psyche, for as Jung noted in "On the nature of the psyche": "In view of the structure of the body, it would be astonishing if the psyche were the only *biological* phenomenon not to show clear traces of its evolutionary history, and it is altogether probable that these marks are closely connected with the instinctual base" (1947/1954:para. 398; emphasis added). Even beyond this, in a letter to Erich Neumann (10 March 1959) speaking about the events involved in mammalian evolution, Jung goes on to comment:

> [i]n this chaos of chance, synchronistic phenomena were probably at work, operating both with and against the known laws of nature to produce, in archetypal moments, syntheses which appear to us miracu- lous ... This presupposes not only an all-pervading, latent meaning which can be recognized by consciousness, but during that preconscious time, a psychoid process with which a physical event meaningfully coincides. Here the meaning cannot be recognized because there is as yet no consciousness.
>
> (Jung 1975:494–495)

From Jung's remarkably prescient intuitions, I extrapolate that just as som- atic evolution occurs at the edge of physical chaos, so too does psychological "evolution" originate at an interface of mental order and chaos. The network aspect of the model also lends support to Jung's methodological approach. For example, as mentioned in Chapter 5, Jung's use of amplification in effect generates scale-free networks of symbols. The value and purpose of these networks rests in their ability to engender awareness of interactive fields and emergent states of mind, those poised at the edge of order and chaos as will be discussed in the next section. It also follows, then, that what had been seen as random events – meaningless chance grouping – in a strictly Darwinian view driving evolution, has been replaced by a non-reductive, deterministic reading of the same events employing complexity theory. By analogy, mean- ingful coincidences in the synchronistic sense can be recognized as psycho- logical factors that spur the evolution of the psyche (personal and collective). They can serve, when understood this way, as motivational spurs that poten- tially organize images and experiences into previously unimagined forms. How then might this perspective be considered in clinical work?

Clinical views

The core of analytic work can be viewed as an opening to and experiencing of the emergent properties of the psyche, i.e. coming into contact with levels of psychological organization that transcend ego psychology such as detected through meaningful coincidences – in effect all discovery of unconscious mental life stems from observing and ascribing meaning to "coincidence" between patterns in conscious life and unconscious dynamics. The manifestations of emergence which are potentially transformative can be anticipated to involve constellated archetypal fields, especially those involv- ing encounters with the Self, Jung's postulated supraordinate organizing principle composed of the network of all archetypal nodes. The optimal mental state for analytic work from a CAS model would be for the personalities involved to be poised near the interface of order and chaos – the creative edge (NB: Jung did refer to synchronicity as an "act of creation"). One way of conceiving good analytic technique is to see it as orienting to and when possible attempting to shift the analytic dyad in an intersubjective field towards this region. A recent book by Palombo, *The Emergent Ego* (1999), provides a valuable analytic model based on this perspective but is, for me, incomplete as it lacks any discussion of an emergent or supraordinate dimension to the self.

To date, most reports of synchronistic occurrences associated with the clinical encounter have tended to fall into two broad areas of discussion in the Jungian literature. In one group, the emphasis is on these occurrences as evidence of archetypal processes at work showing how the conscious personality of the patient stands in relation to the archetypal contents. Jung's well known scarab beetle case is paradigmatic here. Jung gave several renditions of this relevant vignette in his 1952 monograph; in the longer version he reports:

> a young woman patient who, in spite of efforts made on both sides, proved to be psychologically inaccessible. The difficulty lay in the fact that she always knew better about everything. Her excellent education had provided her with a weapon ideally suited to this purpose, namely a highly polished Cartesian rationalism with an impeccably "geometrical" idea of reality. After several fruitless attempts to sweeten her rationalism with a somewhat more human understanding, I had to confine myself to the hope that something unexpected and irrational would turn up, something that would burst the intellectual retort into which she had sealed herself. Well, I was sitting opposite her one day, with my back to the window, listening to her flow of rhetoric. She had had an impressive dream the night before, in which someone had given her a golden scarab – a costly piece of jewellery. While she was still telling me this dream, I heard something behind me gently tapping on the window. I turned round and saw that it was a fairly large flying insect that was knocking against the window-pane from outside in the obvious effort to get into the dark room. This seemed to me very strange. I opened the window immediately and caught the insect in the air as it flew in. It was a scarabaeid beetle, or common rose-chafer (*Cetonia aurata*), whose gold-green colour most nearly resembles that of a golden scarab. I handed the beetle to my patient with the words, "Here is your scarab." This experience punctured the desired hole in her rationalism and broke the ice of her intellectual resistance. The treatment could now be continued with satisfactory results.

> (Jung 1952:para. 982)

In this case Jung's knowledge of the symbolism of the scarab (amplification) led him to postulate that the archetype of rebirth was being resisted through the patient's fear of the irrational until the synchronistic event "punctured the desired hole in her rationalism . . . [and] treatment could now be continued with satisfactory results."

In the second group, attention has been directed towards the interactive aspects of the treatment, with synchronistic occurrences being read as commentary on the state of the transference/countertransference relationship. This approach stems from Michael Fordham's 1957 remarks on the topic, especially; "synchronicity depends upon a relatively unconscious state of mind, i.e., an *abaissement du niveau mental*" (a lowering of the mental level first discussed by Pierre Janet). That is, synchronicities tend to occur in times of stress when both partners lose important dimensions of awareness. Several clear clinical examples of this kind of reading can be found in Rosemary Gordon's *Bridges* (1993), especially in Chapter 24.

Examples from the first group are often presented as support for the archetypal hypothesis. One danger with this stance is that archetypal contents can easily be overvalued or reified and taken as the only legitimate source of motivation for transformation; the relational dimension of the exchange is thrust into the background. Clinically such an approach runs the risk of stasis, especially if symbolic experiences become prescribed and are taken as the goal of treatment. Described in terms of energetics, this would be a return to a closed system equilibrium state. The net effect of such an attitude actually will be a decrease in emergent experience as analysis shifts back towards the safety of ordinary rationality foregoing the sustained uncertainty of remaining near the edge of engagement with unconscious processes. When this stance is in ascendancy, synchronistic events can be reduced to being the means for dismantling irritating stuckness, breaking through resistances so that the "real" business of analysis can proceed. Such an approach lacks dynamic reflections on the meaningfulness of the experience in the specific context in which the event is embedded. Thus Fordham criticized Jung's handling of the scarab incident for his ignoring the transference. I would add with emphasis the countertransference implications of the event: as described in *Memories, Dreams, Reflections*, Jung's mother had for him a strong sense of the uncanny associated with one aspect of her personality, which served as a partial model for his views about himself (his personalities one and two). In Jung's stories about his mother, she unconsciously endorses her son's aggressive narcissistic behaviors (1963:48–50). These elements can be seen infiltrating Jung's treatment of his patient: his irritation with her rationalism, waiting for the ingress of the irrational to assist him and the barely concealed pleasure he took in offering up the synchronicistic beetle with a flourish, practically a magical gesture, a conjuration that produced "satisfactory results." At a deeper level he seems to have broken the silence that constrained him with his mother; for example, after his mother had made a slip of the tongue unconsciously confirming her agreement with his "growing religious skepticism" focused on complaints about "the dullness of the tunes of certain hymns," Jung remarks: "As in the past I pretended that I had not heard and was careful not to cry out in glee, in spite of my feeling of triumph" (1963:50).

Paul Bishop (2000:17 and n. 24) has also pointed out that Jung reported an active imagination in 1913 at the time of his painful break from Freud that included a "gigantic black scarab and . . . a red, newborn sun rising up out of the depths of the water" which Jung amplified as a rebirth image. However, the active imagination also contained images of the corpse of a youth with a head wound and jets of blood which nauseated Jung; he realized the abnormal quality of the image and at the time "abandoned all further attempt to understand" (Jung 1963:179). Thus when he encountered a parallel image in his patient's dream, we can speculate that there would have been some activation of his own preconscious and unconscious processes as the image evoked a time of great suffering, both personal and collective, that could not be relieved by rational understanding. This of course was at least part of Jung's contribution to the analytic field in this case and offers some insight into his relief at being able finally to metaphorically catch, penetrate and pin down the "beetle."

On the other hand, the attitude of the second group, oriented to the interactive aspect of such events, attempts to avoid the grandiosity frequently associated with these experiences but then leans towards a pathologizing of such events. Synchronistic occurrences are viewed in terms of unresolved complexes of the patient and, at times, of the analyst. The implicit goal in this group is to analyze the material until such occurrences cease, which then is read as an at least partial resolution of the complex. While this has clinical merit, I believe it is a subtle distortion of the synchronicity theory.

Robert Aziz points out that in synchronistic phenomena the events partake "of mutual complementary rather than that of mutual identity" (1990:188). He notes that synchronicity as described by Jung is to be understood symbolically, not concretely, and is therefore not a matter of *participation mystique* because subject and object are ultimately differentiated. Aziz argues instead that it is an abnormal reaction for the individuals involved not to sort out and distinguish what "belongs" to each in the compensatory sense. He proceeds to identify three types of pathological reactions to synchronistic events: first,

> participation mystique with the object . . . [i.e.] for the subject not to differentiate the specific compensatory import that the object has for him from what the object is in itself; second, the failure to interpret correctly the compensatory meaning of the synchronistic event [for example read as an idea of reference] . . . and third, wrongly seeing the

synchronistic event as a manifestation of one's or another individual's personal power.

(Aziz 1990:191)

Thus he notes that typical misreadings of these events are based on psychopathological employment of defenses such as archaic identification of the subject with object as well as being in the service of the subject's grandiosity.

The approach outlined by Aziz is, I believe, in keeping with Jung's view that synchronistic experiences are "normal," but that difficulties arise from how they are interpreted. In fact, Jung did argue for the non-pathological quality of these experiences when he responded to L. Kling, MD, an analytical psychologist, regarding his question about ideas of reference and synchronicities occurring in the treatment of schizophrenics: "the synchronistic effect should be understood not as a psychotic but as a normal phenomenon" (1975:409). In the present model this would mean that the ability to detect and intuit accurately the psyche's emergent processes through our handling of meaningful coincidences can be compromised by whatever pathological structures and dynamics are operative in and around such events. This is, of course, in keeping with the acknowledged requirement for the analyst to employ self-analytic reflections in the analytic field as needed, i.e. the analyst's personality is crucial as the instrument of analysis. What may be new here is the opportunity to consider more systematically the use of meaningful coincidences as a guide to such reflection. To this end, I've proposed a brief outline of the way synchronicities may be distorted in selected sectors of the psyche associated with different forms of pathology.

As has been noted frequently in the wider analytic literature, the more dramatic forms of what can be labeled synchronicity often occur in the treatment of individuals with psychotic and borderline features. This is thought to follow from expectations of strongly constellated archetypal fields that are not well mediated, due to the chronic emotional distress such patients tend to suffer and their inadequate ego resources. I would note that synchronicities often come into play in highly traumatized states, which matches Jung's view that such events often occur when serious risk or danger is perceived. A parallel in the CAS framework would be the recognition that the psychological states of highly disturbed patients are located far from the optimal edge of order and chaos; they are trapped in dysfunctional states, either immersed in chaos, such as in hysterical psychoses or manic states, or frozen far from it, as in catatonic stupors, psychotic depressions, and dissociative phenomena generally. Synchronicities, although frequent at times in such states, can be radically disruptive to them while such patients' understanding of these events is vulnerable to massive distortions. Homoeostatic forces are often mobilized in an attempt to sustain these patients in their previously equilibrated states, however dysphoric. Thus, such patients' framing of their experience, whether or not they are conscious of the occurrence of a synchronicity, will provide valuable information on their relationship to emergent phenomena.

By accenting the affective *intensity* associated with synchronistic experiences of severely disturbed patients, the possibility is raised of viewing intensity as a variable functioning along a spectrum. If this is descriptively accurate, it could lead to a novel way of approaching these experiences, i.e. through the study of self-organizing criticality. This would entail applying the model pioneered by Per Bak, in which "complex behavior in nature reflects the tendency of large systems with many components to evolve into a poised, 'critical' state way out of balance, where minor disturbances may lead to events called avalanches, of all sizes" (1996:1), to synchronicities, assuming they can manifest across a large range of intensities. To verify this would require a research project which would systematically examine the distribution and intensity of meaningful coincidence in analysis – as a first step, I have offered a qualitative scaling of such experiences with intensity being matched to unconscious activation (Cambray 2002). If these occurrences were shown to follow a power law, have fractal geometry and/or exhibit 1/f noise,[3] then there would indeed be strong experimental support for the hypothesis that these coincidences are evidence of a self-organizing complex system poised at or near a critical state. This would not explain the mechanism by which they occur but would demonstrate that a broad range of such coincidences have a common, underlying dynamic, even if that dynamic is not itself elucidated, just as Bak has shown to be true for various geophysical phenomena such as earthquakes, all of which therefore must share a common dynamic. These considerations also hold for many human activities, especially creative acts. Thus investigations have shown that the striking and distinctive features of Jackson Pollock's "drip painting" are due in part to their fractal nature and identifying this can even be used to detect frauds (Taylor 2002). Sole and Goodwin note that "it has been shown that Mozart's music is fractal [in time]" (2000:50).

In a previous publication I gave the rudiments of a nosology for synchronistic events occurring within the clinical setting (Cambray 2002). Here I will include several clinical vignettes to give the reader a feeling for the way I think about applying this model in actual practice. In the first example, a severely traumatized patient in multiple times/week analysis during the first year of treatment required prophylactic hospitalization around breaks in treatment of a week or more. After considerable analytic work, the patient asked to remain out of the hospital during a 10 day hiatus with the use of her psychopharmacologist as back-up and with one scheduled phone call from me. The call was arranged before I left town and we spoke at the designated hour. At first during the call, the patient was quite agitated, quickly recounting her dream from the night before that: I (the analyst) was in the Black Forest and lost to her. She was terrified and asked if I were in Germany. Because I was aware that her inability to retain the analytic experience in memory was leaving her exposed to severe abandonment trauma, I responded concretely, perhaps naively, reassuring her that I was not in Germany (I did not disclose my location, in the Caribbean) but could see that she felt in danger of losing contact with me. We discussed her concerns; she acknowledged the fragmentation occurring and I focused on helping her reestablish her links with me and through that to reality as she seemed in danger of becoming lost herself in a childish but terrifying Grimm Brothers-like world of archetypal figures, witches and monsters. The contact was sufficiently containing that my patient's regained stability was sustained and she remained at home, out of the hospital, until I returned. The day after the phone call, I went for a second lesson in scuba-diving. After a morning of work in the pool, the diving instructor decided on the spot that I should come along on the afternoon's dive, my first in open water. It was therefore with some trepidation that I joined the other seasoned divers as we headed out to sea. It was only as we neared the site that the divemaster told us about the dive. I was thoroughly shocked to discover that the site chosen was called "the Black Forest." After the momentary disruption caused by recognition of the pre-cognitive aspect of my patient's dream, I found myself aware of the asymmetry in our respective attitudes about the "Black Forest." The realm I was about to enter, though unknown and containing some real risks, was in fact a potential source of enjoyment. Indeed, the name of the site refers to the black corals that grow on the reef at that spot and the trip underwater to visit them was exquisite to say the least, not marred by external incident. There is also a related, larger transference concern expressed in the dream: if the "black forest" is taken as a metaphor for the numerous anomalous experiences that surrounded this patient, then there was the danger that I, as analyst, would become absorbed (or fascinated) and lost in these elliptical, synchronistic communications and miss her human suffering.

The terribly traumatic history of this patient left her immersed in a hysterical psychosis whenever loss of containment threatened, here linked to my going on vacation. She was absorbed in a world of psychic chaos. However, in the act of providing my patient a measure of containment, offering a sense of ordered understanding, I was left more vulnerable to the dissolving effects of the chaotic elements in the field. My more rational orientation towards the dream contents was undermined by a shift toward the chaotic pole. Although I chose not to disclose to the patient what had occurred to me while on vacation, my attitude and attention to the communicative power of her unconscious processes were certainly heightened. The synchronicity of the dream/dive-site appears to have had an opposite effect on each of us resulting in both of us, and the analysis itself, moving more towards the edge of chaos and order. Alternatively, this could be described as increasing engagement with a series of analytic thirds that converge towards the emergent processes as revealed through that series.

Psychosomatic symptoms form another cluster of clinical observations that have been debated in the Jungian literature as to the involvement of synchronicity. C.T. Frey-Wehrlin (1976) and M.L. von Franz (1992:249–251) have argued for a causal view of the psyche–soma relationship, whereas C.A. Meier has defended the thesis of an acausal connection between them. He says:

> It is proposed to approach the entire problem of psychosomatic phenomena as an acausal relationship, in accordance with the views held by the physicians of ancient Greece, expressed in the word *symptoma* [Greek synonym of Latin *coincidentia*], the acausal but meaningful coincidence of at least two distinct magnitudes. This concept is identical with that expressed in the modern term *synchronicity*; it presupposes a *tertium*, higher than soma or psyche, and is responsible for symptom formation in both – approximating to the theory of the *subtle body* . . . It appears that healing can take place only through the constellation of a *tertium* of a higher order – a symbol or the archetype of totality – but as a synchronistic event and not as a cause–effect chain.
>
> (1986:188)

However, if the *tertium* or third is understood as an emergent phenomenon, then we now have a way of appreciating these symptoms that allows for an exploration of the "coincidental" nature of their occurrences in terms of a self-organizing system without having to resort to strictly reductive causality.

This leads to the second clinical example: a rather obsessional young man had been in weekly treatment with me for about a year when we had the following two sessions. In the first, we met at the last hour of a rather long day, not his usual time; he had requested to reschedule several weeks prior. The session was laborious for me. While I was familiar with the constricted states that often accompanied his difficulties in expressing himself, especially if feelings were involved, I felt unusually exhausted as the session wore on. In the last minutes of the hour, the patient surprisingly produced a dream that contained the image of a child in a closet. There was no time for associations or exploration of the imagery. After he left, I felt so depleted that I needed to lie down and rest before driving home; I felt on the verge of flu; however, I felt fine the next day. The following week we met at our usual daytime hour. And while the affect field was not much different than the week before, we were able to return to the dream; the patient had not seemed to have noticed my state of fatigue in the previous session (no references or derivatives were detectable in the material he discussed). In exploring the images of the dream, however, we did uncover a bit of his history previously unknown to me. By asking the age of the child in the closet, and then getting associations to that time in his life, I found that he had had a specific food allergy, the symptoms of which were remarkably similar to what I had experienced after the session the previous week. During the next phase of the analysis this dream figure came to be understood by us as representing a time in his life when much of his natural spontaneity had receded. Beginning to get the frightened, frozen playfulness "out of the closet" was the starting point for some long, at times torturous work on obsessional defenses that operated at a somatic level.

This case was symmetrically inverted from the previous one. Here the patient was stranded, locked into a rigid order that constricted body and psyche. In a wounded-healer-like model, I, as analyst, somewhat unwittingly absorbed a portion of the unconscious defenses; I was made ill but able to metabolize enough of the complex in the field through the aid of the dream to regain a measure of order in my own mind, recognizing the meaningful coincidence between my symptoms and his history so that a slow dissolution of the defenses could begin.

Given the postulate of an archetypal core, however deeply buried, within all psychological phenomena synchronicity may be a ubiquitous feature of clinical work. Under "normal" conditions, those of the world of mundane consciousness, synchronistic occurrences are of low intensity and undramatic in appearance, perhaps near to vanishing, depending upon the degree of constellation of the archetypal field and the quantity of affective tension residing in any event. How then might we consider the more mundane coincidences in analytic work? In the past several decades there have been developments in psychoanalytic thinking that I believe offer new pathways for examining such coincidences on which Jungian formulations might shed alternative light. In particular I am referring to the study of enactments and the use of reverie in the analytic process – see Cambray 2001 for a discussion of countertransference enactments within a Jungian model. Similarly, the study of what is loosely termed "parallel process" in supervision is based on observing meaningful coincidences between dynamic features of a therapy and the supervision of that therapy (Cambray, submitted). The specific moment in which such processes manifest may partake of a synchronistic field. In addition to whatever subtle causal (unconscious) communication may be involved in these experiences, I suggest from a CAS model that they may also be indicators of emergent processes that from the perspective of ordinary consciousness have a synchronistic quality to them.

While infantile or regressive features are obvious factors in these analytic explorations, we should not restrict ourselves to such formulations. For example, Ogden recently reexamined Winnicott's concern that the good enough mother "tries to insulate her baby from coincidences" (Winnicott 1949/1958:245). In puzzling out his own understanding of this enigmatic remark, Ogden suggests that "the coincidences or complications from which a baby needs to be insulated involve chance simultaneities of events that take place in the infant's internal and external realities at a time when the two are only beginning to be differentiated from one another" (2001:230). From this I draw the conclusion that wherever differentiation is weak, great care must be used in the clinical handling of synchronistic phenomena, but in more mature states when the compensatory meaning of a synchronistic event can be reflected upon, then an opportunity to glimpse psyche in emergence can be transformative. This brings us to the issue of "analytic attitude", how and by what we are guided in the clinical encounter.

In 1997 George Bright published a key paper, "Synchronicity as a basis of analytic attitude." In this he cogently argues that Jung's theory of synchronicity offers an orientation towards psychological experience where connections are made on the basis of meaning rather than through attributions of cause and effect (something that Winnicott was also keenly aware of), and which in the guise of transference/countertransference formulations applies "relentless pressure on both analyst and analysand to attempt to impute meaning and order" (Bright 1997:613) rather than allowing them to be both found and created, objective and subjective. Within this model "any conscious attribution of meaning, such as an analytic interpretation, must be seen as subjective and provisional" (ibid.:618). If taken seriously, I think this allows for enhanced tolerance of uncertainty and increases capacity to grant a greater degree of autonomy to unconscious processes as they occur in the clinical setting.

In the treatment of analysands who have reasonably well-developed sectors of their personalities with pockets of unresolved traumatic complexes, an intersubjective approach often can be employed with benefit. A combination of forming a working alliance with the more mature aspects of the personality while together analyzing infantile roots of disturbances in the transference/countertransference field can be a viable method of treatment in such cases. Under these conditions, working with dreams as productions emanating from the analytic third can be mutative. Jung effectively suggested this on at least several occasions, for example in 1934 commenting to James Kirsch on a series of explicit transference dreams that one of Kirsch's patients was having:

> With regard to your patient, it is quite correct that her dreams are occasioned by *you* . . . In the deepest sense we all dream not *out of ourselves* but out of what lies *between us and the other*.
>
> (Jung 1973:172)

When discussing "telepathic dreams" with Charles Baudouin that same year, Jung summed up his thoughts on the matter, according to Baudouin, by:

> act[ing] them out as follows: with brief, firm gestures he touched first my forehead, then his own, and thirdly drew a great circle with his hand in the space between us; the three motions underscored the three clauses of this statement; "In short, one doesn't dream here, and one doesn't dream here, one dreams there." And *there* the hand kept turning, like the above-mentioned sling and the idea, like the messenger, was launched.
>
> (McGuire and Hull 1977:80)

This can operate with the analyst's dream material as well as the analysand's. Indeed, this was borne out in the case of a man who despite numerous early abandonments had become rather successful in business but was prone to subtle dissociative disconnections when the following dream "coincidence" occurred. In the midst of a session where we had touched upon some painful affect with which the patient was allowing himself gradually to come into limited contact, requiring me to remain silent but receptive, I found myself suddenly recalling a dream from the previous night. At the time I was studying the psychological significance of a renaissance text and in the dream I had been puzzling over an actual image from this manuscript in which three birds are either fighting or dead within a flask – there was no reference or evident connection in the dream to this particular case. As the dream returned to consciousness I wondered how it might be tied to the present moment and observed my patient carefully, discerning a slightly glazed look about him. When asked about this, he sheepishly reported having "left the room." Treating this as a field phenomenon, I remarked that I had found myself reflecting on my own imagings prior to that moment and wondered what this diffuse state might be about. This reduced his felt shame and exposure, allowing him to go further into his "disappearance." We subsequently discovered an unconscious suicide attempt he had made as a child, falling into a pit and being rendered unconscious. This had occurred at a moment of abject loneliness but had never been consciously acknowledged as an internal assault or attempt to annihilate himself. It was as if "my" dream were being redreamt within the hour, amplifying the state of the field with the unconscious rage that was knocking out consciousness through dissociation. The shared use of this coincidence, though not made explicit, helped to shift the therapy into a new, more affectively charged phase.

This brings us to the place of emergent phenomena in the individuation process. Synchronicity theory when focused on rare or unique events, which was Jung's primary orientation, implies a corresponding heightened value for the uniqueness of the individual. The core of individuality was personified by the ancient Greeks in the figure of the *daemon* operating in a person's psychology, or what the ancient Latins called the *genius*, the tutelary deity responsible for one's being, begetting individuality yet operating at a collective, or familial level (for a study of this figure see Nitzsche 1975). Thus in articulating the synchronicity principle, Jung was also presenting a psychology of genius or of those sparks of genius, however great or small, that on occasion may burst forth upon the world. And this theory of his, like many other productions of genius, is itself a delicately blended balance of brilliant insight and irrationality, i.e. it is a theory at the edge of chaos and order. Because of the terrible tensions inherent in this residing in such a locale, it is a dangerous realm, at times leading to incredible breakthroughs in human thought and experience and at other times resulting in madness.

In "Synchronicity and emergence" (Cambray 2002) I began to explore this realm through the lives of two mathematicians: Georg Cantor, the nine-teenth-century creator of the field of the study of practical infinites with his explorations into "transfinite numbers" and the continuum hypothesis, who also constructed the first fractal (the Cantor Set) but struggled with repeated bouts of psychotic depression (Aczel 2000), and Nobel Laureate John Forbes Nash recently the subject of book, film and theatrical productions, see Nasar (1998), who suffered for 30 years with paranoid schizophrenia before going into remission. Both of these figures of genius successfully worked on prob-lems that they "solved" by extraordinarily novel approaches which entailed re-visioning previously insoluble dilemmas from the perspective of a higher order or dimension. Unfortunately these efforts strained their personalities to and beyond the breaking point multiple times. It would seem that much of this strain came from trying to remain at or near the font of their creativity, the glimpses that each had of higher order phenomena that resolved the insoluble problems and tension in the previous order of the lower level, i.e. they were in a sense addicted to emergent experiences without the psycho-logical capacity to tolerate such states of mind or to discern when they were getting lost in the higher order visions. Also, emergent phenomena are ephemeral: what is emergent at a particular moment can with repetitious attempts to fix or codify it result in the loss of the living quality.

To conclude, many features of synchronistic experience can be reconsidered in the light of contemporary science as a form of psychological emergence. Heralding the constellation of supraordinate self-organizing states, synchro-nicities offer valuable clues to the unfolding of the psyche or individuation but must be treated as value-neutral, i.e. in themselves they do not convey direction to consciousness. Instead this can only come from reflective, ethical struggles with meaning which we subjectively attribute to these occurrences.

Notes

1   Portions of this chapter were first published in *American Imago* (**59**(4), 2002) and aspects of the historical background section were presented at the *Journal of Analytical Psychology* conference "Science and the Symbolic World" in April 2003.
    As this is an advanced series publication, it is assumed the reader has basic familiarity with Jung's ideas. In addition to his monograph *Synchronicity: An Acausal Connecting Principle*, the reader wishing for more detailed background would profit from reading *Encountering Jung: Jung on Synchronicity and the Para-normal* selected and introduced by Roderick Main, and *C. G. Jung's Psychology of Religion and Synchronicity* by Robert Aziz. Both the latter volumes have critical, scholarly essays on the subject. For the specialist reader, an essential text is *Syn-chronicity and Intellectual Intuition in Kant, Swedenborg, and Jung* by Paul Bishop.
2   Jung borrowed the term "psychoid" from Hans Driesch (who coined it in 1929 as part of a movement in biology to conceptualize organisms in non-reductive *hol-istic* terms – see Harrington 1996:48–54) and expanded on the psychosomatic meaning his former chief, Eugen Bleuler, had given it. The editors of Jung's letters give a concise statement of his concept of the psychoid as belonging to "the

transconscious areas where psychic processes and their physical substrate touch" (Jung 1975:22, n. 5). In related passages Jung himself discusses the "irrepresentable" nature of the "archetypes *per se*" and synchronisitic phenomena as partaking of a psychoid factor which provides *a priori* meaning or "equivalence" [of physical and psychological aspects of an experience].

Ferenczi in his *Clinical Diary* was also beginning to approach the psychoid realm, as when he remarked "in human beings, given certain conditions, it can happen that the (organic, perhaps also the inorganic) substance recovers its psychic quality ... the capacity to be impelled by motives, that is, the psyche continues to exist potentially in substances as well" (Dupont 1988:5).

3   These concepts from contemporary math and science must be used with care and reflection; the three measures listed here are hallmarks of many self-organizing critical systems. Since this is not a science text, I will only make a few brief remarks about power laws: they are mathematical formulations in which one variable can be expressed in terms of an exponential power of another variable, most simply expressed as $N(s) = s^{-a}$, where N and s are the variables, say a total population N, which in our case would be the total number of synchronicities in a study of s individual synchronistic events of varying intensity. Taking the logarithm of each side: $\log N(s) = -a \log (s)$, so that a log–log plot will yield a straight line with slope $= -a$. The significance of this is that when a power law holds, the dynamics involved are scale-invariant or scale-free. Their relationship exhibits fractal properties (having geometrical features at all length scales) and if this manifests in time (rather than spatially), it often appears as what is termed 1/f noise (which some scientists claim is what give classical music its special qualities).

Some major technical difficulties that would face researchers attempting to implement a synchronicity study of this sort would be how to take measurements of intensities (psychophysical correlates might be explored) in conjunction with noting the frequency of such events (this could be addressed at the lower levels of intensity by studies on enactments and analytic reverie, which I postulate are low level synchronicities at core; see next section of text).

References

Aczel, A. (2000) *The Mystery of the Aleph: Mathematics, the Kabbalah, and the Human Mind*, New York: Pocket Books.

Aziz, R. (1990) *C.G. Jung's Psychology of Religion and Synchronicity*, Albany, NY: SUNY Press.

Bak, P. (1996) *How Nature Works*, New York: Copernicus Springer-Verlag New York.

Bishop, P. (2000) *Synchronicity and Intellectual Intuition in Kant, Swedenborg, and Jung*, Ceredigion, Wales: Edwin Mellen Press.

Bright, G. (1997) "Synchronicity as a basis of analytic attitude", *Journal of Analytical Psychology*, **42**(4), 613–635.

Cambray, J. (2001) "Enactments and amplification", *Journal of Analytical Psychology*, **46**(2), 275–303.

—— (2002) "Synchronicity and emergence", *American Imago*, **59**(4), 409–434.

—— (2003) "17th century precursors to synchronicity", delivered at the 3rd History Symposium, San Francisco, November 2003.

—— (submitted) "Ethics in supervision", in H. Solomon and J. Cambray (eds), *Ethics Matter*, London: Karnac.

Charet, F.X. (1993) *Spiritualism and the Foundations of C.G. Jung's Psychology*, Albany, NY: SUNY Press.

Chertok, L. and Stengers, I. (1992) *A Critique of Psychoanalytic Reason*, Stanford: Stanford University Press.

Devereux, G. (ed.) (1953) *Psychoanalysis and the Occult*, New York: International Universities Press.

Diaconis, P. and Mosteller, F. (1989) "Methods for studying coincidence", *Journal of the American Statistical Association*, **84**(408), 853–861.

Dupont, J. (ed.) (1988) *The Clinical Diary of Sandor Ferenczi*, Cambridge, MA: Harvard University Press.

Ellenberger, H.F. (1970) *The Discovery of the Unconscious*, New York: Basic Books.

Falzeder, E. (ed.) (2002) *The Complete Correspondence of Sigmund Freud and Karl Abraham 1907–1925, Completed Edition* (trans. C. Schwarzacher), London: Karnac.

Falzeder, E. and Haynal, A. (2003) "Ferenczi and Jung: some parallel lines?", *Journal of Analytical Psychology*, **44**(4), 467–478.

Fordham, M. (1957) *New Developments in Analytical Psychology*, London: Routledge and Kegan Paul.

Freud, S. (1919) "The 'uncanny' ", Standard Edition, 17, 219–256.

—— (1921/1941) "Psychoanalysis and telepathy", Standard Edition, 18, 177–193.

—— (1922) "Dreams and telepathy" Standard Edition, 18, 197–220.

Frey-Wehrlin, C.T. (1976) "Reflections on C.G. Jung's concept of synchronicity", *Journal of Analytical Psychology*, **21**(1): 37–49.

Gleick, J. (1987) *Chaos: Making a New Science*, New York: Viking Press.

Goodheart, W. (1984) "C.G. Jung's first 'patient': on the seminal emergence of Jung's thought", *Journal of Analytical Psychology*, **29**(1), 1–34.

Gordon, R. (1993) *Bridges: Psychic Structures, Functions, and Processes*, London: Karnac.

Harrington, A. (1996) *Reenchanted Science*, Princeton, NJ: Princeton University Press.

Hogenson, G. (2001) "The Baldwin effect: a neglected influence on C.G. Jung's evolutionary thinking", *Journal of Analytical Psychology*, **46**(4), 591–611.

Johnson, S. (2001) *Emergence: The Connected Lives of Ants, Brains, Cities, and Software*, New York: Scribner.

Jones, E. (1957) *The Life and Work of Sigmund Freud: Volume 3, The Last Phase 1919–1939*, New York: Basic Books.

Jung, C.G. (1902) "On the psychology and pathology of so-called occult phenomena", CW 1, Princeton, NJ: Princeton University Press.

—— (1930) "Richard Wilhelm: In Memoriam", CW 15.

—— (1947/1954) "On the nature of the psyche", CW 8.

—— (1951) *On Synchronicity*, CW 8.

—— (1952) *Synchronicity: An Acausal Connecting Principle*, CW 8.

—— (1963) *Memories, Dreams, Reflections*, New York: Vintage Books.

—— (1973) *Letters*, Vol. 1: 1906–1950 (eds G. Adler and A. Jaffe), London: Routledge & Kegan Paul.

—— (1975) *Letters*, Vol. 2: 1951–1961 (eds G. Adler and A. Jaffe), Princeton, NJ: Princeton University Press.

Kaufman, S. (1995) *At Home in the Universe*, Oxford: Oxford University Press.

Kim, J. (1998) *Mind in a Physical World*, Cambridge, MA: MIT Press.

Knox, J. (2003) *Archetype, Attachment, Analysis*, Hove: Brunner-Routledge.

Luckhurst, R. (2002) *The Invention of Telepathy*, Oxford: Oxford University Press.

Ludwig, K. (1995) "Why the difference between quantum and classical physics is irrelevant to the mind/body problem", *Psyche*, **2**(16) – online at: http://psyche.cs.monash.edu.au/v2/psyche-2-16-ludwig.html

McGuire, W. and Hull, R.F.C. (eds) (1977) *C.G. Jung Speaking*, Princeton, NJ: Princeton University Press.

Main, R. (ed.) (1997) *Jung on Synchronicity and the Paranormal*, Princeton, NJ: Princeton University Press.

Martindale, D. (2000) "Beetle to bee", *Scientific American*, **283**(1), July, 26.

Mayer, E.L. (1996a) Subjectivity and intersubjectivity of clinical facts, *International Journal of Psychoanalysis*, **77**, 709–738.

—— (1996b) "Changes in science and changing ideas about knowledge and authority in psychoanalysis", *Psychoanalytic Quarterly*, **65**, 158–200.

—— (2000) "Psychodynamic therapy: heading in new directions", in J. Shay and J. Wheelis (eds), *Odysseys in Psychotherapy*, New York: Ardent Media.

—— (2001) "On 'telepathic dreams?': an unpublished paper by R.J. Stoller, *Journal of the American Psychoanalytical Associates*, **49**, 629–658.

—— (2002a) "How the unconscious continues to surprise us", lecture given to the San Francisco Psychoanalytic Institute, 9 December; another version of this lecture was given at the JAP conference, "Science and the Symbolic World", held in Charleston, SC, May 2003.

—— (2002b) "Freud and Jung: the boundaried mind and the radically connected mind", *Journal of Analytical Psychology*, **47**(1), 91–99.

Meier, C.A. (1986) *Soul and Body*, San Francisco: Lapis Press.

Meier, C.A. (ed., with assistance of C.P. Enz and M. Fierz; trans. D. Roscoe; introductory essay by B. Zabriskie) (2001) *Atom and Archetype: The Pauli/Jung Letters, 1932–1958*, Princeton, NJ: Princeton University Press.

Morowitz, H. (2002) *The Emergence of Everything*, Oxford: Oxford University Press.

Nasar, S. (1998) *A Beautiful Mind*, New York: Touchstone.

Nitzsche, J.C. (1975) *The Genius Figure in Antiquity and the Middle Ages*, New York: Columbia University Press.

Ogden, T. (2001) *Conversations at the Frontier of Dreaming*, Northvale, NJ: Jason Aronson.

Palombo, S.R. (1999) *The Emergent Ego: Complexity and Coevolution in the Psychoanalytic Process*, Madison, CT: International Universities Press.

Prigogine, I. and Stengers, I. (1984) *Order Out of Chaos*, New York: Bantam Books.

Rieff, P. (ed.) (1963) *Studies in Parapsychology*, New York: Collier Books.

Saunders, P. and Skar, P. (2001) "Archetypes, complexes and self-organization", *Journal of Analytical Psychology*, **46**(2), 305–323.

Schneider, E. and Kay, J. (1994) "Complexity and thermodynamics: towards a new ecology", *Futures*, **24**(6), 626–647.

Shamdasani, S. (1998) "From Geneva to Zurich: Jung and French Switzerland", *Journal of Analytical Psychology*, **43**(1), 115–126.

Sole, R. and Goodwin, B. (2000) *Signs of Life: How Complexity Pervades Biology*, New York: Basic Books.

Taves, A. (1999) *Fits, Trances, & Visions*, Princeton, NJ: Princeton University Press.

Taylor, E. (1998) "Jung before Freud, not Freud before Jung: the reception of Jung's work in American psychoanalytic circles between 1904 and 1909", *Journal of Analytical Psychology*, **43**(1), 97–114.

Taylor, R.P. (2002) "Order in Pollock's chaos", *Scientific American*, **287**(6), 116–121.

Thurschwell, P. (2001) *Literature, Technology and Magical Thinking, 1880–1920*, Cambridge: Cambridge University Press.

Totton, N. (ed.) (2003) *Psychoanalysis and the Paranormal*, London: Karnac.

Tresan, D. (1996) "Jungian metapsychology and neurobiological theory", *Journal of Analytical Psychology*, **41**(3), 399–436.

Von Franz, M.L. (1992) *Psyche and Matter*, Boston: Shambhala.

Winnicott, D.W. (1949/1958) *Through Paediatrics to Psycho-Analysis*, New York: Basic Books.

Chapter 10

The ethical attitude in analytic training and practice

Archetypal and developmental perspectives and implications for continuing professional development

Hester McFarland Solomon

There has been a surge of interest recently in matters pertaining to ethical issues within the analytic and psychotherapeutic professions. No doubt this interest has been activated in part by increased calls for accountability in the helping professions from the general public, by steps taken towards voluntary and now towards statutory registration of psychotherapists, by ethical questions relating to genetic and foetal research that have raised awareness of ethical issues generally, and by an increasing number of ethics complaints brought against practitioners. But I suspect that these reasons alone do not account for what amounts to a radical change in focus and interest in ethics matters. The expectation that high ethical standards be consistently maintained in clinical practice has been a principle enshrined in the Constitution and Code of Ethics of the International Association for Analytical Psychology (IAAP). Recently, the IAAP has devoted considerable organisational time and energy to improving and updating its ethics provisions. But however much we require at the institutional level that ethics be taken as a core value, and rightly insist on the principle of high ethical standards for our profession, we have not really worked out a depth psychological understanding of this core value. There has been little attempt to locate and understand the ethical attitude as an intrinsic component of the self, or, indeed, to locate the ethical attitude as an intrinsic component of the analytic attitude, which seeks to protect the development of the self and of that so intimate of relationships, between patient and analyst. Indeed, rather curiously and with some notable exceptions, ethics does not receive much exposure, if any, in our training curricula, and even less do theories about the origins and functioning of an ethical capacity or attitude in human beings appear in analytic literature. This chapter will attempt to make a contribution to this needed enquiry.

Perhaps one reason for the dearth of theorising about the origins and dynamics of the ethical attitude in analytical and psychoanalytic literature belongs to a shadow aspect of our profession, a commonly held assumption that as long as the Code of Ethics has not been contravened, essentially it, and the principles underlying it, need not be thought about. It is as if thinking about ethical issues is an unwelcome disruption or intrusion into the real analytic task. It seems to me that where this attitude exists, there is an ethical deficit. Disclaimers or denials, conscious or unconscious, about the place of ethics in one's analytic practice or in an organisation constitute the tell-tale signs of the shadow side of professional ethics.

From where do the ethical principles derive that clinicians are eager to stress underlie their professional practice? Where does a capacity for ethical thinking and behaviour come from? Is the ethical attitude innate, or do we learn it? Are the ethical principles that form the professional basis of our clinical practice related to our depth psychological theories? Is a capacity for ethical thinking and behaviour an archetypal potential that awaits activation by the right circumstances, or do we learn it through socialising processes and the quality of our object relations? And why is there so little about the origins of the ethical attitude in analytic literature?

Historical perspectives

Freud and Jung, founders of the analytic tradition, shared common ground in their view of the psyche as suffused with the ubiquitous presence of unconscious conflict, of psychological processes and behaviours that are multi-determined and multi-motivated, of unconscious and subversive impulses and desires that can undermine conscious intent, and of the counterbalancing possibility within the psyche of conscious ego choice, moral energy and ethical struggle. To this shared view, Jung added a deep conviction regarding the overriding teleological nature of the self and its continued search to become itself, even in the face of dire internal resistance or malign external forces. These are the component elements of a profound view of the psyche that have a direct bearing on our understanding of the attainment of an ethical attitude.

Freud pointed to the development of two regulating systems relevant to moral behaviour that seem to reflect the operation of the talion law and the principle of agape respectively. They are: (i) the archaic superego, representing power and authority and capable of evoking in talionic ways such affects as shame, humiliation, the fear of revenge, and the desire for triumph; and (ii) the ego ideal, based on more agapaic emotions such as empathic guilt and the wish to preserve and identify with the internalised good parents. Later, Klein would elaborate the dual system of the paranoid/schizoid and depressive positions. Although she did not specify them in these terms, the paranoid/schizoid position may be thought of as operating according to talionic principles, and these may give way to the more agapaic responses of the depressive position through the capacity for concern and reparation.

Over and over in the *Collected Works*, Jung stressed the centrality of moral and ethical values as being deeply implicated in psychotherapeutic treatment.

He stressed the emotional value of ethical ideas and the fact that ethical issues require that affect and thought struggle together to reach ethical discernment (see, for example, Jung (1964):para. 855ff.).

For Jung, the understanding of the teleological unfolding of the self operating through the transcendent function over the stages of an entire life underpins a view of the self's ethical capacity. In particular, the recognition and integration of the shadow is crucial to the self's potential to develop and grow, to individuate and thereby to fulfil the self's ethical nature. As Murray Stein (1995) has said, "for Jung . . . ethics is the action of the whole person, the self".

Jung repeatedly acknowledged (for example, Jung (1959/1968):para. 14–16) that the shadow is a moral problem that challenges the whole of the personality, requiring considerable moral effort to overcome, and meeting considerable internal resistance in the process of gaining self-knowledge. The shadow, that portion of the self that the ego designates as bad and projects as unwanted, carries what is treacherous and subversive – what is unethical and immoral – within the self and hides it, relegating its contents to unconscious areas within the psyche where it can then be lived out in projection, using and abusing the other as a vehicle for holding the bad aspects of the self. To withdraw shadow projections can require tremendous struggle of an ethical nature, bringing to consciousness what is unconscious and projected. Beebe has emphasised the powerful negative forces activated in the struggle with the shadow that threaten integrity: anxiety, doubt, shame, painfulness, an absence of well-being, and the wish to repair the damaged relationship (Beebe 1992:38).

Philosophical perspectives

It is clearly not possible to review in this chapter the entire philosophical literature regarding ethics. It is truly vast and stretches across more than two thousand years of recorded philosophical enquiry. Here I wish to put forward three axioms or principles which underpin my approach to personal and professional ethics, and which gather together, in my view, the major strands of philosophical thinking about ethics relevant to this discussion.

1   The self is not called upon to be ethical in a vacuum. In order to fulfil its ethical function, the self must recognise the substantive reality and subjectivity of the other. The ways in which this is achieved have as much relevance for the work in the consulting room as they have for day-to-day ethical functioning as human beings.
2   The integrity of the self is called into question if parts of the self are unknown or eschewed, and projected outside the self, in particular its immoral and unethical parts. To the extent that the other is used as an object of projection, the self remains split and thereby diminished. The

teleological project of the self to achieve wholeness requires the withdrawal of shadow projections and the integration of their contents within
the personality.

3   Mature ethical thinking and behaviour belong to a noncontingent realm
of object relations. Following Kant's notion of the categorical impera-
tive, the contemporary moral philosopher Ziegmund Bauman (1993) has
pointed out that the self's ethical capacity is derived from a system of
value and meaning-making that belongs to a different, higher order and
unconditional realm of relating to the other. It is the unique and non-
reversible nature of my responsibility to another, *regardless* of whether
the other sees their duties in the same way towards me, that makes me an
ethical being.

So, we may ask, where does this value and meaning, this sense of unconditional
responsibility, come from? How do we account for the self's willingness to
tolerate the ethical burden, that real struggle involved in the withdrawal of
projections and integration of the shadow?

Neuroscientific perspectives

The internalisation of the experience of non-talionic relating nourishes
psychically, mentally and emotionally, as recent neuropsychological research
has indicated (Schore 1994). The young self develops through a good enough
holding environment, allowing the infant to experience being held and protected without undue fear of retaliatory responses or undue regard to placat-
ing another for its survival. This gives the young self the security and freedom
to express himself or herself as an authentic being. This total situation in turn
becomes the basis for the potential eventually to develop an ethical capacity.
When these conditions are not met, pathologies of the self arise, such as the
false self, the "as if" personality, and the various pathologies relating to
the defences of the self and the self-care systems as discussed by Solomon
(2004).

The new and burgeoning field of psychoneurobiology has shown that the
development *post partum* of the neural circuitry and structures of the infant's
brain which regulate the development of the higher human capacities (i.e.
cognitive and socioaffective) are dependent on the existence and quality of
the early interactions between infant and mother or caregiver. Allan Schore
(2003a, 2003b), Daniel Stern (1985), Jean Knox (2003) and Margaret Wilkinson (2003), among others, have made powerful contributions from different
but complementary approaches to this area. They have shown through different research perspectives that there is a direct link between the quality of
attunement of the infant and its mother and the development of the infant's
neural circuitry. Since the infant instinctively seeks to participate in activating
these mutual exchanges, we can infer that the infant, a proactive partner, is

participating directly in the development of its own neural circuitry, in its own neural growth. Moreover, the particular circuitry involved is that which determines cognitive and socioaffective activity, the cortical and subcortical limbic systems, which must eventually have bearing on and underpin the achievement of the higher psychological capacities, including the ethical capacity. This suggests that there are grounds for considering that the ethical capacity is, at least in part, innate, derived from the earliest, instinctually driven exchanges with the primary caregiver, including exchanges initiated by the baby; and, at least in part, is influenced by environmental factors, by the impact of that very caregiver's capacity to be responsive to and to initiate appropriate and meaningful interactions with the infant (see Solomon (2000a) for a fuller discussion).

Emergence of an ethical capacity

In considering these questions and perspectives, I wish to offer an image to highlight an archetypal potential for ethical capacity. In thinking about the possible origins of the ethical attitude, a primordial image emerges of a combined parental function. What I am combining is the maternal and paternal functions: combining, on the one hand, in Winnicott's (1964) evocative notion, the primary preoccupied mother, precursor of the ordinarily devoted mother; and, on the other hand, the notion of the discerning, discriminating thinking function which is often imaged symbolically in masculine, paternal terms. It is through the combination of these functions – of devotion and thinking – that the ethical attitude is maintained in the parental couple, and eventually internalised in the psyche. The idea of the ordinarily devoted mother, or caregiver, represents a deeply ethical mode in the instinctual and unconditional devotedness to another, the infant, as she works to overcome her narcissistic needs and frustrated rages, shadow projections, resisting by and large the impulse to skew her infant's development through undue acquiescence to her requirements. At an appropriate point will begin the processes of socialisation, so necessary a part of ethical development – the capacity to say, in different ways, "no", thereby establishing boundaries and expectations of self-regulation, particularly in relation to others. The activation of the archetypal potential for eventual ethical behaviour will be thus reinforced in ordinary good enough situations by caregivers capable of sharing acts of thoughtful devotedness and of empathic thinking about their infant. This combined archetypal–developmental view of the gradual achievement in stages of an ethical capacity has been discussed by Stein, referring to the work of Bachofen (Stein 1993:67).

I am conjecturing that the identification with and internalisation of the agapaic function of the parental figures in their empathic holding as well as their thinking and discriminating aspects trigger or catalyse a nascent ethical capacity in a young mind, the first steps of which include those primitive mental acts of discriminating good and bad which constitute the foundations of the psychic defences of splitting and projection. Early (as well as later) splitting and projecting may therefore be instances of primitive moral activity, what Samuels (1989) calls original morality – the expulsion from the self of what is unwanted and felt to be bad onto the other, where it is identified as bad and eschewed. Even in situations where the good is split and projected, it is in the service of maintaining a discriminating, but highly defensive, psychic structure. So we come full circle: the primitive acts of discriminating the bad, and splitting it off from the psyche by projection into the caretakers, constitute the very preconditions for the creation of the shadow which eventually will require a further ethical action of reintegration – a first, primordial or prototypical moral discernment prior to the state where there is sufficient ego strength for anything resembling proper moral or ethical behaviour to arise.

Fordham (1969/1994) placed Jung's notion of the self within a developmental framework by positing the self as a primary integrate, autonomous but very much in relation to another or others. So, too, we are alone as moral beings while at the same time finding our moral nature in relation to others. To truly find another represents a transcendence of narcissistic ways of relating in which the other is appropriated for use in the internal world, denying the other's subjective reality. To live with the implications of this – a capacity to recognise and relate to the truth of the other – is a step in the development of (and perhaps eventually beyond) the depressive position. The depressive position is usually considered to contain acts of reparation through guilt and fear that the object may have been damaged and therefore may be unable to go on caring for one's self (Hinshelwood 1989). As such, acts of reparation remain contingent on preserving the other for the benefit of the self. The ethical attitude envisaged here goes beyond this contingency and suggests a noncontingent realm of ethical behaviour. This situation has direct implications for what transpires in the consulting room between the analytic couple (see Solomon (2000b) for further discussion).

Emergence of an ethical capacity in the consulting room

Much of the work between patient and analyst concerns the vicissitudes in the modes of and capacity for *coniunctio* between them. Jung emphasised the importance of mutuality in the relationship between patient and doctor, and he was very aware of the psychological dangers and ethical pressures that arise from this, as aspects of what he called unconscious identity, or *participation mystique* (Jung 1964:para. 852), now usually conceptualised as projective identification, in which primitive levels of communication can lead to states of greatly reduced psychological differentiation between the two individuals within the relating pair. This is now thought of as the dynamic of the transference and countertransference relationship. However helpful such states may be in providing immediate conduits for unconscious communication, thus enhancing clinical understanding, the very real dangers are clear. Unconscious identification without the discriminating function of thinking and reflection can lead to the perversion of the ethical attitude. Boundaries may then be crossed, enactments remain unmetabolised, actings out become possibilities, and the safety of the container lost, curtailing thereby the psychological freedom necessary to carry out the analytic work (examples of which are set out in detail by Gabbard and Lester (1995)).

The "special act of ethical reflection", as Jung called it (Jung 1964:para. 852), as it appears in the consulting room, itself requires special conditions, in particular the maintenance and protection of boundaried space, the *vas bene clausum*, or in Langs' (1974) terms, the analytic frame. In the unequal analytic relationship, maintaining a boundaried space ensures that the analytic work may proceed safely and with the necessary analytical freedom so that regression and states of powerful deintegration and sometimes dramatic disintegration can occur. Inevitably, the analytic frame may be called into question, and Wiener (2001) has discussed some of the issues that may be involved, requiring the maintenance of what she has called "ethical space". This indicates the importance of ongoing supervision or consultation in analytic practice post-qualification. One implication of this for training is the need to revise a former primary training aim, which had been to prepare and assess that candidates are ready to work "independently". I will come back to this point shortly.

Freedom from appropriation for narcissistic use in another's intimate, internal world may precede the ability to relate ethically to an intimate other. This is a freedom which results from the rule of abstinence, whether familial between the generations, or professionally between patient and analyst, or supervisor and supervisee, who are also of two different (analytic) generations. In conditions where such freedom was not available, the self may have had to devise ways of protecting itself from such incursions, erecting defences of the self, and a loss of ethical capacity may have ensued. Much analytic work is then devoted to reinstating this freedom, through facing up to the inevitable forces of sabotage which seek to undermine the ethical attitude in the analytic work.

The unbalanced nature of the analytic dyad resembles the situation that I described earlier in which one person takes on unconditional ethical responsibilities towards another who is not obliged to reciprocate in an equal way; so, too, in the consulting room, where the analyst undertakes to maintain an ethical attitude which the patient is not called upon to adhere to in the same way. Of course, the patient abides by other rules, such as payment of fees and regular attendance (within certain parameters). It is by maintaining the analytic attitude that the psychopathology of the patient, including the sometimes unconscionable pressures that the patient brings to bear on the analytic relationship, may emerge and be tolerated in the service of eventual transformation. Kenneth Lambert (1981) has discussed the importance for the ongoing treatment that the analyst maintains an agapaic function in the face of the patient's and the analyst's own impulses to behave according to the talion law. If such pressure can be contained in the holding environment of the analytic attitude, as sustained by the analyst's capacity for *agape*, it is then that, as Jung stated, the transcendent function may be activated and a solution found.

Beyond the depressive position

If the attainment of an ethical attitude is a developmental achievement, then we could venture a view that the ethical attitude is a developmental position and depends on the *quality* of the relationship between self and other and the meaning of the relationship for each – an interior and exterior situation. In the following sections, I argue that the ethical attitude represents a developmental step beyond the Kleinian notion of the depressive position.

Jung stressed the teleological view of the self in which the innate capacity for the self to become itself through the process of individuation was a fundamental aspect. An ethically mature attitude is not predicated on the ethical behaviour of the other towards the self, but rather is founded on the earliest experience of the unconditional devotedness of another in relation to the self, regardless of the self's relation to the other. In Klein's view, on the other hand, the capacity for guilt, concern and the wish for reparation seen in the infant results from the self's capacity to imagine the damage it has caused the other and thus how the other's wish or capacity to go on loving and caring for the self may be diminished or disappear. It also represents the concern for and fear of the loss of the self's own internal good objects which are necessary in supporting the ongoing viability of the self and without which psychic dissolution may occur (see Klein 1935, 1940). Here is an internal accounting system at work which remains related in this way to the anxieties evoked by the talion law of the paranoid–schizoid position.

In speaking about the struggle with an ethical conflict which can leave the person feeling locked in a dilemma from which there seems to be no possible development or recourse, Jung states:

> The deciding factor . . . proceeds not from the traditional moral code but from the unconscious foundation of the personality. The decision is drawn from dark and deep waters . . . If one is sufficiently conscientious the conflict is endured to the end . . . The nature of the solution is in accord with the deepest foundations of the personality as well as with its wholeness; it embraces conscious and unconscious and therefore transcends the ego . . . a conflict of duty [finds] its solution through the creation of a third standpoint.
>
> (Jung 1964:para. 856–857)

Triangulation and the archetypal third

The importance of the third standpoint is a core concept within Jung's philosophical and clinical position and reaches back to 1916, when he wrote about the dialectics of the transcendent function (see Solomon (1994)). At that time, soon after the split with Freud, when he was suffering what might be described as a psychotic regression in the face of his loss of Freud who represented at one level the centrally organising psychic function of the father figure he had never had, Jung wrote two landmark papers that can appear to be diametrically opposite in content and form: "VII Sermones ad mortuos" ("Seven sermons to the dead") and "The transcendent function". The former was published at the time, but not in a separate English edition until 1982, whereas the latter was not published until 1957, only a few years before his death in 1961. Both reflect, in different ways, the immediacy of Jung's distressing and threatening psychic experiences that arose from his self-analysis, undertaken, as Freud's self-analysis, on his own. At the same time Jung continued to function as Clinical Director of the Burghölzli Hospital in Zurich and also fathered a growing family. If the tone of the "Seven sermons" was that of a chilling account of the horrifyingly vivid psychic experiences he endured at the time of his "confrontation with the unconscious" (Jung 1961:194), that of the "Transcendent function" was of a measured, scientific contribution to analytic theory-building concerning the dynamics of psychic movement, growth and change, which he compared to a "mathematical formula" (Jung 1960:para. 131). We could interpret it as a dispassionate exteriorisation of his highly emotive internal state at the time, a kind of self-supervision, in respect of his own disturbing and unbalanced reaction to the loss of his relationship with Freud a few years earlier. In this paper, Jung set out an archetypal, deep structural schema of triangulation in which he demonstrated that psychic change occurs through the emergence of a third position out of an original conflictual and polarised internal or external situation, the characteristics of which cannot be predicted alone by those of the original dyad. In relation to this idea, it is interesting to note that the philosopher and psychoanalyst, Marcia Cavell, who has recently put forward the idea of triangulation in a psychoanalytic context, refers to Polanyi's notion of "emergent properties" in much the same manner as that pertaining to the dialectical nature of the transcendent function, that is, as "properties that in a developmental process arise spontaneously from elements at the preceding levels and are not specifiable or predictable in terms of them" (Cavell 1998:461). The paradigm of "emergence" has recently been addressed in analytic theory-building by Cambray (2002) and Knox (2003).

Whether or not he consciously drew on its philosophical origins, Jung's notion of the transcendent function is based on the idea of the dialectical and deep structural nature of all change in the living world expounded by the nineteenth-century German philosopher, Hegel, in his great work, *The*

Phenomenology of the Spirit (see Solomon (1994)). Hegel posited a tripartite schema as fundamental to all change, including psychic change; a situation in which an original oppositional pair, a dyad, which he called thesis and antithesis, struggle together until, under the right conditions, a third position, a synthesis, is achieved. This third position heralds the transformation of the oppositional elements of the dyad into a position or state with new properties which could not have been known about before their encounter – the *tertium quid non datur* in Jung's terms. Hegel called this ubiquitous struggle dialectical, because it demonstrated how transformations in the natural world happen through the resolution of an oppositional struggle and can be understood to have meaning and purposefulness. This was a deep structural patterning of dynamic change that was archetypal in nature and developmental as a dynamic movement in time. Jung followed the dialectical language of Hegel – thesis, antithesis, synthesis.

This archetypal schema can also be thought of as the basis of the tripartite Oedipal situation, where transformation from out of a primordial pair, mother and child, can be achieved through the third position afforded by the paternal function, whether this be a real father or a capacity of mind in the mother or in the child. Recently, a number of psychoanalysts have made contributions regarding the important dynamic of the third standpoint (for example, Steiner, Britton, Ogden, Bollas, and Fonagy) which bear on the centrality of the archetypal third as evinced in the Oedipus complex that was the cornerstone of Freud's metapsychology. Peter Fonagy (1989) has developed a theory of mind which the child has achieved when he or she is aware that their thoughts and those of the other are separate and not available directly to each other (as assumed in states of fusion or identification), but only through reference to a third perspective. As Marcia Cavell states:

> the child needs not just one but two other persons, one of whom, at least in theory, might be only the child's idea of a third . . . the child must move from interacting with his mother to grasping the idea that both his perspective on the world and hers are *perspectives*; that there is a possible third point of view, more inclusive than theirs, from which both his mother's and his own can be seen and from which the interaction between them can be understood.
>
> (Cavell 1998:459–460)

It is in this sense that we might speak of the emergence of the child's identity, as separate from his or her mother, through the provision of a third perspective. For Jung, this would be thought of as the gradual emergence of the self, through successive states of transformation and individuation via the transcendent function.

Drawing on these perspectives, I wish to put forward the view that the provision of ongoing supervision, a third area of analytic discourse, offers the possibility that both patient and analyst are helped to emerge from out of the *massa confusa* of the analytic dyad and that, following Jung's dictum, both are helped to change as individuation progresses.

In psychoanalytic theory, the importance of the negotiation of the Oedipal threesome, that archetypal triad *par excellence*, constitutes much of the psychoanalytic understanding of developmental achievement. Freud first used the term "Oedipus complex" in 1910, following Jung's scientific researches on the complexes that he demonstrated through the word association test (WAT). At that time, both considered that the Oedipus complex was one of many organising complexes of the psyche, but it soon became the core psychoanalytic concept.

Britton sums up concisely the Oedipal situation:

> we notice in the two different sexes the same elements: a parental couple
> . . . a death wish towards the parent of the same sex; and a wish-fulfilling
> dream or myth of taking the place of one parent and marrying the other.
> (Britton 1998:30)

Britton evokes the notion of internal triangulation, which requires the toleration of an internal version of the Oedipal situation. He describes "triangular psychic space" as "a *third* position in mental space . . . from which the *subjective self* can be observed having a relationship with an idea" (ibid.:13). He concludes that "in all analyses the basic Oedipus situation exists whenever the analyst exercises his or her mind independently of the inter-subjective relationship of patient and analyst" (ibid.:44).

In my view, the external manifestation and facilitation of this internal triangular state is quintessentially present in the supervisory or consultative relationship. Here, two people, the analyst and the supervisor, are linked in relation to a third, the patient. Equally, in the consulting room, the analyst with the patient works with reference to the internalised third standpoint, i.e. the supervisor and the analytic attitude represented by the supervisor in his or her mind; and similarly, the patient in the presence of the analyst is aware more or less consciously of the analyst's relationship to his analytic attitude, i.e. of the analytic third.

Within psychoanalysis, the current debate about intersubjectivity, in which the analyst and patient are seen to be acting together within the treatment relationship (for example, Atwood and Stolorow (1993:47)), is akin to the close study made by Jung regarding the vicissitudes of the *coniunctio* (Jung 1966). The psychoanalyst Marcia Cavell's (1998) notion of "progressive triangulation" has relevance here: "in order to know our own minds, we require an interaction with another mind in relation to what would be termed objective reality" (Rose 2000:454, summarising Cavell). I hold that the provision of supervision, including the internal supervision that happens when the analyst thinks about aspects of the patient and the analytic relationship, is an important instance of "progressive triangulation" in that it allows for ongoing interaction with another mind in relation to a third, the patient, who can be thought about because differentiated from the dyadic relating of the patient–analyst couple.

Triangular space and supervision in analytic practice

The provision and function of supervision of analytic and psychotherapeutic work with individuals, children, couples, or families creates a triangular space essential to the care and maintenance – the ongoing hygiene – of the therapeutic relationship. I use the term "hygiene" in the sense that, through its provision, supervision keeps constantly activated the awareness of the analytic attitude, including its ethical component, in and through the presence of a third person (the supervisor), or a third position (the supervisory space), and that it acts as an aid in the restoration of the analytic and ethical attitudes when at times they might be lost in the maelstrom of clinical practice, which is rife with identificatory and projective dynamics, as any intense and intimate relationship would be. Supervision is itself the representation of that attitude through the provision of a third area of reflection. The treatment, at profound levels, of the psyche in distress always involves a regressive and/or narcissistic pull back into primitive modes of relating, those either/or, dichotomous states of mind that are liable to being dominated by archetypal forces and the resulting defences that are set up to protect the self and ensure its survival (Kalsched 1996; Solomon 1997). The provision of sustained triangular space via the supervisory situation creates the necessary opportunity for analytic reflection, where two people work together to think about a third, whether the third is an individual, a couple, a family, or an idea or aspect within the therapist or analyst, that is relevant to their clinical work. The provision of triangular space through internal or external supervision, or both, is essential to the maintenance of the analytic attitude in the face of the multitudinous forces and pressures at work within the analytic and therapeutic situation, arising from the conscious and unconscious dynamics within and between patient and analyst alike, and the consequently inevitable, often unconscious, intersubjective exchanges between them as a pair, which would seek, for defensive reasons, to undermine analytic achievements.

To the extent that this triangular space created by supervision is necessary to the hygiene of the analytic couple (just as the paternal, reflective principle is essential to the hygiene of the mother–infant dyad, providing the space for psychological growth to occur), supervision has an ethical as well as a clinical and didactic role to play in all analytic and therapeutic work, notwithstanding the years of experience of the practitioner. Whether supervision is provided in the same way as during training, with weekly meetings in a one-to-one situation with a senior practitioner, or in consultations with a senior practitioner at agreed intervals, or whether peer supervision in small groups is selected as the means of providing the triangular space, are questions that are up to each clinician to decide upon, according to personal need, inclination, and available resources.

In the case of the analysis and supervision of training candidates, where there are particular ongoing boundary issues and other pressures inherent in the training situation that do not usually pertain in work with non-training patients, such as the need to see a patient under regular supervision at a certain minimum intensity, over a certain minimum amount of time, supervision will help to identify and work under these constraints without forgoing the analytic attitude. This will in turn foster in the candidate their own ethical attitude, as they internalise the expectation that all analytic work, including the work of their own analyst and supervisors, is in turn supervised. The trainee will then know from the very outset of his or her training that there is always a third space created in which he or she as a patient or as a supervisee will be thought about by another supervisor-practitioner pair.

Fostering the ethical expectation of ongoing supervisory provision is more likely to engender a generationally based commitment to the analytic attitude within a training institution, as the tradition of good clinical practice is passed down across the analytic training generations. Currently, there is an assumption that the aim and goals of training can be summed up in the opposite way: that is, that the success of the candidate's progress through his or her training is assessed according to whether he or she is judged to be ready to "work independently". Of course, the assessment of the trainee's capacity for independent judgement and a sense of their own viable auton-omy is an important, indeed crucial, factor in the process of assessing whether someone is ready to qualify to practise as an analyst or therapist. I am arguing here that included in this assessment should be a judgement about the candidate's awareness of the need for and usefulness of the provi-sion of a triangular space in which to discuss their clinical practice, in order best to ensure against the risks inherent in working in such intimate and depth psychological ways, including the dangers of mutual identificatory states or the abuse of power.

My contention is that, as well as its obvious advantages, the expectation that the practitioner will ensure that they have ongoing supervision or con-sultation on their clinical practice is a sign of maturation, on the part of the practitioner as well as that of the training institution, as they assess their own and others' clinical competence. This is part of the assessment process, which results in the authorisation to practise as members of the training institution. There is the added dimension that some members go on to become eventual trainers, i.e. training analysts, supervisors, and clinical and theoretical seminar leaders, entrusted with the responsibility for training future generations of analysts. The expectation in the trainee of ongoing supervisory and consultative provision, modelled by the trainers, fosters the candidate's respect for and understanding of the conditions that create and sustain the analytic and ethical attitude. This includes attention to boundary issues that can arise within and through the intensity of the intersubjective dynamics within the analytic and therapeutic relationship (see Gabbard and Lester (1995) for a detailed discussion of boundary issues in analytic practice). These intersubjective dynamics are inevitably released by the inter-penetrative, projective, introjective and projective identificatory exchanges within the transference and countertransference.

The recommendation that (i) members of analytic training institutions seek to establish an ongoing supervisory ethos to discuss their work, even if the provision is not systematically maintained, and that (ii) all training ana-lysts and supervisors of the institutions have regular consultations regarding their training cases (including patients, supervisees, or training patients), represents a further development of those ubiquitous triads created by the training situation: the trainee–training analyst-supervisor; the trainee–training patient-supervisor; and the trainee–supervisor-training committee. The expectation of providing a space for reflection with another would bene-fit all parties concerned and at the same time increase clinical awareness. Without this benefit, we run the risk of identifying with those narcissistic and other pathological processes and pressures inevitable in analytic practice, as we are liable to treat those aspects in our patients that correspond and reson-ate with our own internal issues and personal histories. Hence the importance of clinical "hygiene", of creating the third space of supervision; this can help us to maintain our connection to genuine object relating and to staying alert to the pitfalls of intense dyadic relating.

Conclusion

In this chapter I have explored ways in which the self finds, defines, creates and struggles with ethical value. It seems to me that the concept of the ethical attitude can function as a pivotal concept in depth psychological work. It does so because it causes the clinician to stretch deeply into the bases of the developing psyche and includes commonly held, collective core values, thus providing an opportunity for the joint study of the sources and conditions for maintaining one of the deepest expressions of our higher and mental functioning. Furthermore, how pragmatic ethical issues are dealt with in the consulting room, in analytic organisations, and with colleagues is a common concern that all professionals need to address.

The more I have thought about the question of ethics in developmental and archetypal terms, the more I have realised that ethics is with us profes-sionally all the time in the consulting room, day by day, hour by hour. Even though we are not necessarily made consciously aware of our ethical attitude as we work, we are, as professionals, constantly living within an ethical dimension. Every action that we take in relation to our patients and supervisees and, I would add, our colleagues, has an ethical aspect which, if ignored, can have serious implications for our capacity to maintain the analytic attitude, the analytic frame, and to do our analytic work in an appropriately professional context.

I have also explored some aspects of the supervisory function in analytic practice in relation to developmental and archetypal perspectives. The provision through supervision of a triangular space in which clinical work with patients can be thought about creates the necessary dimensionality for psychological transformation to occur and has resonance with developmental reality and archetypal truth. The ethical aspect of supervisory provision and process is predicated on the notion that genuine object relating arises out of such dimensionality, in which one mind is aware of the subjective reality of another and chooses to take ethical responsibility towards the other, as the parent in relation to the child, and the analyst or therapist in relation to the patient. This is fostered in the supervisory setting, where the triangular relationship of supervisor–analyst–patient makes manifest in concrete form a universal, triangular and deep structural situation that is necessary if psychological development is to occur.

The emergence of an ethical capacity represents a development on from the depressive position, in that it seeks to provide for and protect a non-contingent space or place for reflection about another, be it a person, a relationship or an idea. Such reflection may result in decisions taken with respect to another, and may be followed by actions, which include the content, form, timing and other characteristics of interpretations as well as other, more subtle, modes of being in the presence of another, which will have a direct impact on the quality of their internal world. It is for this reason – because of the possibility of doing harm to the vulnerable interior reality of another – that the Hippocratic Oath was first established 2,500 years ago with its main premise, *nolo nocere*, "to do no harm", and why we, as practitioners, continue to seek to hone its ethos.

The ethical attitude is an essential and integral part of the analytical relationship, and is not just an addendum to the practitioner's work. If it is experienced by the analyst as an external problem, then analytic work may become no more than an intellectual exercise, and the Code of Ethics a mere checklist that may be forgotten as long as it is not transgressed. Analytic practice and the ethical attitude are intimately bound together; each permeates the other and defines and gives value to the other. This reflects the analytic relationship itself in which, as Jung stressed, both partners make themselves available to, and are liable to be changed by, the encounter with the other. This is the essence both of the analytic work and of the ethical attitude. Thus, we may say that the analytic attitude is in essence an ethical attitude, and therefore that our analytic and ethical attitude is embedded deeply within our humanness.

Acknowledgements

A draft of this chapter was delivered at a conference, "Ethics Matters", organised by the IAAP in Cambridge, UK in July 2003. An earlier version of this paper was given at a conference entitled "Diversity and its Limits: New Directions in Analytical Psychology and Psychoanalysis", organised by the *Journal of Analytical Psychology* in Prague in May 2001. This also appeared as the following: "The ethical self", in Christopher, E. and Solomon, H. (eds), *Jungian Thought in the Modern World*, Free Association Books, 2000; "Origins of the ethical attitude", *Journal of Analytical Psychology*, **46**(3), 2001; "The ethics of supervision: developmental and archetypal perspectives", in Christopher, E. and Solomon, H. (eds), *Contemporary Jungian Clinical Practice*, Karnac Books, 2003; "The ethical attitude: a bridge between psychoanalysis and analytical psychology", in Solomon, H. and Twyman, M. (eds), *The Ethical Attitude in Analytic Practice*, Free Association Books, 2003; "The ethics of supervision: developmental and archetypal perspectives", in Solomon, H. and Twyman, M. (eds), *The Ethical Attitude in Analytic Practice*. Free Association Books, 2003.

References

Atwood, G. and Stolorow, R. (1993) *Structures of Subjectivity*, Northvale, NJ: Analytic Press.

Bauman, Z. (1993) *Postmodern Ethics*, Oxford: Blackwell.

Beebe, J. (1992) *Integrity in Depth*, College Station, TX: A & M University Press.

Britton, R. (1998) *Belief and Imagination*, London: Routledge.

Cambray, J. (2002) "Synchronicity and emergence", *American Imago*, **59**(4), 409–434.

Cavell, M. (1998) "Triangulation, one's own mind and objectivity", *International Journal of Psychoanalysis*, **79**, 3.

Fonagy, P. (1989) "On tolerating mental states: theory of mind in borderline personality", Bulletin of the Anna Freud Centre, **12**, 91–95.

Fordham, M. (1969/1994) *Children as Individuals*, London: Free Association Books.

Freud, S. (1910) *Leonardo da Vinci and a memory of his childhood*. SE 9, London: Hogarth Press (1950/1974).

Gabbard, G. and Lester, E. (1995) *Boundaries and Boundary Violations in Psychoanalysis*, New York: Basic Books.

Hegel, G.W.F. (1807/1977) *The Phenomenology of Spirit* (trans. A.V. Miller), Oxford: Oxford University Press.

Hinshelwood, R.D. (1989) *A Dictionary of Kleinian Thought*, London: Free Association Books.

Jung, C.G. (1960) *The Structure and Dynamics of the Psyche*. CW 8, Princeton, NJ: Princeton University Press.

—— (1961) *Memories, Dreams, Reflections*, London: Collins.

—— (1959/1968) *Aion*, CW 9ii.

—— (1964) *Civilisation in Transition*, CW 10.

—— (1966) *The Practice of Psychotherapy*, CW 16.

Kalsched, D. (1996) *The Inner World of Trauma*, London: Routledge.

Klein, M. (1935) "A contribution to the psychogenesis of manic-depressive states", in R. Money-Kyrle (ed.), *The Writings of Melanie Klein*, Vol. 1, pp. 262–289. New York: Free Press.

—— (1940) "Mourning and its relation to manic-depressive states", in R. Money-Kyrle (ed.), *The Writings of Melanie Klein*, Vol. 1, pp. 344–369. New York: Free Press.

Knox, J. (2003) *Archetype, Attachment, Analysis. Jungian Psychology and Emergent Mind*, Hove and New York: Brunner-Routledge.

Lambert, K. (1981) *Analysis, Repair and Individuation*, London: Academic Press.

Langs, R. (1974) *The Technique of Psychoanalytic Psychotherapy*, Vol. II. New York: Jason Aronson.

Rose, J. (2000) "Symbols and their function in managing the anxiety of change: an intersubjective approach", *International Journal of Psychoanalysis*, **81**(3), 453–470.

Samuels, A. (1989) *The Plural Psyche*, London: Routledge.

Schore, A. (1994) *Affect Regulation and the Origin of the Self*, Hillsdale, NJ: Lawrence Erlbaum.

—— (2003a) *Affect Dysregulation and Disorders of the Self*, New York: W.W. Norton & Co.

—— (2003b) *Affect Regulation and the Repair of the Self*, New York: W.W. Norton & Co.

Solomon, H.M. (1994) "The transcendent function and Hegel's dialectical vision. *Journal of Analytical Psychology*, **39**, 1. Also in: Mattoon, M. (ed.), *Collected Papers from the 1992 IAAP Congress, The Transcendent Function*, Chicago.

—— (1997) "The not-so-silent couple in the individual", *Journal of Analytical Psychology*, **42**(3), 383–402. Also in *Bulletin of the Society of Psychoanalytic Marital Psychotherapists*, 1994, Bulletin 1, inaugural issue.

—— (2000a) "Recent developments in the neurosciences", in E. Christopher and H.M. Solomon (eds), *Jungian Thought in the Modern World*, London: Free Association Books.

—— (2000b) "The ethical self", in E. Christopher and H.M. Solomon (eds), *Jungian Thought in the Modern World*, London: Free Association Books.

—— (2004) "Self creation and the limitless void of dissociation: the 'as if' personality", *Journal of Analytical Pyschology*, **49**, 5.

Stein, M. (1993) *Solar Conscience, Lunar Conscience*, Wilmette, IL: Chiron.

—— (1995) *Jung on Evil*, London: Routledge.

Stern, D. (1985) *The Interpersonal World of the Infant*, New York: Basic Books.

Wiener, J. (2001) "Confidentiality and paradox: the location of ethical space", *Journal of Analytical Psychology*, **46**(3), 431–442.

Wilkinson, M. (2003) "Undoing trauma: contemporary neuroscience. A Jungian clinical perspective", *Journal of Analytical Psychology*, **48**(2), 235–253.

Winnicott, D.W. (1964) "Further thoughts on babies as persons", in *The Child, the Family and the Outside World*, London: Penguin Books.

Chapter 11

Endnotes
Whence and whither?

Beverley Zabriskie

Endnotes have a purpose that belies their name. Placed at the end of a text, they are, ostensibly, meant to review, recapitulate, and summarize, to wrap up the presented themes by suggesting how the matters covered have arrived at their current state.

But we bring to endnotes an expectation that they will demonstrate that the matters at hand are so relevant, worthy, and of such import as to require and deserve further attention. Endnotes place the material presented at a cutting edge. Hence, while they purport to "wrap up," endnotes are also to hint that for the sake of what is yet to come, there may be a reworking of what has just been discussed.

As a retrospective also anticipates a prospective, endnotes insinuate that if there is to be further advance, we may anticipate a redressing, a rebalancing, and indeed some unraveling of the current body of knowledge in the face of future information. There may even be a discarding of what is now understood and emphasized in the service of the still to be discovered and the yet to be known.

In this sense, endnotes are vectors in disguise. If they do their proper work, they search for the emergent in the disguise of the *status quo*.

Advancing the theory

Within a tradition or movement, it often takes some time before the later practitioners of a school catch up with the genius of the founder. At precisely such a moment, the advocates of a theory and practice simultaneously confirm and substantially add to inherited insights, and so both demonstrate and advance the process of understanding and engagement in a chosen field.

This volume illustrates that the tradition of analytical psychology is currently enjoying this phenomenon. Its authors know so well the complex process of human identity and experience, called psyche by the Swiss psychiatrist and depth analyst, C.G. Jung, that they can transmit its essences and insights for the reader. And through their own originality of mind, independent thought, and practice expertise, these analysts carry on the diverse efforts of earlier promulgators of analytical psychology – such as Marie Louise von Franz, Erich Neumann, Michael Fordham. They present contemporary templates and current contextualizations for Jungian and post-Jungian approaches to the nature of reality, the reality of the psyche, and the practice of a clinical discipline.

As a citizen of the world, one may engage this work for the many ways it augments perceptions of one's outer environment and one's temporal and spatial place in it. With its references to, and inclusions of, the symbolic and mythological, anthropological and philosophical, scientific and artistic, literary and cultural, its contents add to the appreciation of the multiple forces at work in our surrounds, and the manifold modes of our apprehension of them. The chapters follow Jung's dictums that every aspect of reality may be engaged and expressed by the human psyche, and thus the models discovered and invented in each realm of research and reflection may be adopted as analogies for further considerations.

As a private person, with curiosity about the inner environment – of brain and body, mind and imagination, emotion and instinct – one finds insights into the makings of human personality, and the dynamics of human experience and relations. We are moved by observations of the earliest resonances and imprints from the infant stages of human development, and impressed by the increasingly cogent mappings of the neurosciences.

For a clinician, this volume give entries into the intensities of analytic process between the analyst and analysand, the dynamics within any therapeutic endeavor, and the framing of the issues at work with individuals and with groups. It is particularly successful in linking the classical Jungian language – such as the *coniunctio* model Jung adopted from the philosophy of alchemy and the field phenomena to which he was sensitized through William James – with current formulations from infant observation, attachment theory, and the newer psychoanalytic awareness of the importance of "the third" in dyadic analytic relationship.

The discussion of Jungian models of psychological types enhances appreciation of the specific emphases and perspectives that comprise individual and relational experience. The studies of the collective, cultural dimensions alert one to their impact on both the practitioner and the patient. And finally, one is urged to alertness about the ethical considerations intrinsic to authentic relationship, especially within the empathic discipline necessary for depth analytic work

This would be sufficient fare for the most questing student and seeker. But in addition, we have far-reaching explorations linking phenomena beyond the individual and personal about which Jung speculated: those which Jung called archetypal are examined in connection with philosophy; those seemingly coincidental occurrences that he termed synchronistic are pursued through physics' complexity theory; models for internal associative process, interpersonal relations, and analytic conversation are put against the graphs of "scale-free networks."

The relation between analytical psychology and the possibilities of another dimension that transcends the possibility of knowing is seen through a study of the religious appetite or function of the psyche *vis-à-vis* a modernism that would deny the thrust toward meaning.

Jung in time

To grasp the spectrum of these studies, and appreciate the vast range covered by this volume, it is helpful to note the pivotal and transitional place of Jung and analytical psychology in the intellectual and clinical traditions prominent at the beginning and end of his era, i.e. to see his position in the history of events and of the intellect.

Jung's 86-year-long life, and the sweep of his interests, intuitions, and empirical pursuits, spanned philosophical, scientific, social and artistic eras.

When C.G. Jung was born in 1875, Franz-Joseph was monarch of the Austro-Hungarian Kingdoms, Germany was an empire, Victoria would have 26 years more on the English throne, and the American Civil War had ended only a decade before. Identity was based in Cartesian dualisms between being and thinking and a separation of self into mind vs body. From the onset of the enlightenment and statistical science, the experiments of alchemy to transmute matter had been dismissed as mad at best, and fraudulent at worst. Newton's mechanistic physics and classical ideas of linear time were dominant modes of understanding space and time.

By the time Jung died in 1961, he had seen the two "world wars," Europe was divided by the Berlin Wall, Kennedy was in the White House, Americans were in Vietnam, and the 1960s were beginning. Space-time had been introduced as relative rather than linear and absolute. Physics had moved away from the mechanistic toward the quantum. Reactors had changed the structure and energetics of matter, allowing the horrors of atomic explosions.

The evolution in Jung's thought is evident in his 60 years of writing – from his 1902 university dissertation, "On the psychology and pathology of so-called occult phenomena" to the 1961 essay "Approaching the unconscious," finished ten days before his death. Throughout, he demonstrates his central conviction: that to understand the microcosmic nature of the psyche and its relation to the macrocosm, any of its myriad expressions is worth pursuit as a form of psyche.

In viewing Jung through his own theory of psychological types, for the past two generations, analytical psychology has tended to focus on the introverted Jung of his inward mid-life and reflective old age, when he focused on his dreams, painted his pictures, worked with his stones, and built his tower. Following his image as the wise old man, Jung and the Jungians were perceived as focused only on the inner life of the individual.

A shift in this focus for analytical psychology became apparent to me as chair of the program for the 2004 Scientific Congress of the International Association of Analytical Psychology, in Barcelona. Many of the 250 proposals and presentations from analysts in all parts of the world were addressed to cultural and political issues and concerns. This is a return, I would argue, to Jung's wider, life-long concerns.

The historical Jung was on staff at Burghölzli at 25, at 30 on the medical faculty at Zurich University, at 34 received Clark University's honorary degree, at 35 became the first president of the International Psychoanalytic Association, and at 37 was lecturing at Fordham. Even after the break with Freud at 38, after his self-enforced withdrawal, after resigning his university post, Jung was a commandant of a First World War camp for interned English soldiers; he traveled to Algeria, Tunisia, Kenya, Uganda, the Nile, Egypt, Palestine, and India, and made several more journeys to the United States.

Jung earned a professorship at the ETH, the Swiss Polytechnic, and the chair of Medical Psychology was founded for him at the University of Basel. He lectured, accepted prizes and was awarded honorary doctorates from many universities: Harvard in 1936, Calcutta, Benares, Allahabad, and Oxford in 1938, Geneva in 1945, and the Swiss Polytechnic in 1955. Jung addressed the clinicians of London's Tavistock Clinic in 1935, gave the Terry Lectures at Yale in 1938, and, from 1933 to 1951, exchanged ideas with scholars from multiple disciplines at the Eranos Conferences in Ascona, Switzerland. And all the while, Jung researched his own and his patients' psychic material, and he wrote – all those books and essays, all those letters pressing his discourse with theologians, scientists, philosophers, graduate students – with delight when understood, and increasing distress when misinterpreted.

As Chapter 1 indicates, since the era after Jung's death, chapters of his life have been dissected and read as if bits of his entrails, amid conflict and dispute as to which readings were most true, most quintessential. In retrospect, the idealizations, the reminiscences and rivalries seem emblems of mourning, denials of Jung's death – or perhaps eruptions of a collective pre-separation, pre-individuation phase.

Fortunately, there has been much original work by analytical psychologists of different persuasions. The scholars and scientists who collaborated with Jung, such as Kerenyi, Quispel, and Pauli, added and acquired new dimensions in ongoing exchange. Others – Neumann, Fordham, von Franz and later Hillman – furthered or diverged from the corpus, in evolution or revolution.

Now it is 43 years since Jung's death – a chronologically short time, but psychologically a pivotal one. Soon, there will be no one who analyzed with Jung, or with someone whom Jung analyzed. Without his personal weight, what will ultimately matter is the relevance of his insights and ideas. Without a real or a reified Jung, his empirical observations will or will not be relevant in the ongoing process of humankind seeking to understand itself and its world.

As shown in Chapter 2, for Jung, all of the psyche's contents, all its attempts at utterance of what it understood or intimated – language, image, symbol; thesis, formula, belief; rite, ritual, creation, experiment – were appropriate to the depth psychologist's study. He thus summoned forth the narratives and images that the human mind has registered and produced, from the mythopoesis of the archaic past to the most current proofs of modern science.

As is indicated in Chapter 3, Jung conceived the healthy psyche as a dynamic vector that emerges out of dualisms and dissociations into more or less stable balance. Through their interplay, an effective attitude capable of both constancy and further inclusions – through essential regressions and ambiguous progressions, through dissociations and reintegrations – is established.

> After violent oscillations at the beginning the opposites equalize one another, and gradually a new attitude develops, the final stability of which is the greater in proportions to the magnitude of the initial differences . . . the further this range extends, the less chance is there of subsequent disturbances which might arise from friction . . . an attitude that has been formed out of a far reaching process of equalization is an especially lasting one.
>
> (Jung 1928:para. 49)

Especially in the chapters dealing with the current resonances with attachment theory, developmental models, and the personal contents of transference, this volume offers a healthy and necessary rebalancing of Jung's later emphasis of impersonal material as it appears in the personal psyche. But it also engages the psyche as a field of dynamic statements and interactions, in constant process between the personal consciousness and unconsciousness, between the conscious and the unconscious, the personal and collective, oneself and the other.

The ability to maintain this embracing and progressive stance will determine how well Jung's most emergent and essential views are articulated, received, and put into practice. This demands an avoidance of simplification and the temptation to emphasize one orientation to the detriment of the other, to preserve the multiple valences of Jung's thought. This also requires a taboo against fundamentalism, which would have us reify contents of experience as if they are assertions of transconscious truths rather than dynamic aspects of humankind's ongoing existence.

As all the authors have suggested, in many fields, Jung's speculations are proving to have currency. The psycho-physical premises of the word association test and the basic outlines of his typology, albeit reified, have been incorporated into the culture. While sometimes misunderstood, the terminology of archetype, and increasingly of synchronicity, is in common usage.

As we have read, his hypotheses about the mind are being confirmed by the demonstrable working of the brain. The informed and intuitive analogies for his inferences about the nature of reality seem increasingly plausible as the implicit orders of our existence are made increasingly explicit by the natural sciences.

This volume demonstrates that many contemporary practitioners of analytical psychology work from the synthesis of the clinical, developmental, and personal, from the alchemical sensibility of interactive process, as well as from a sense of the emergent archetypal and synchronistic. In my own practice, I have been guided by analogies from ancient myth (Zabriskie 2000) as well as from the modern sciences (Zabriskie 1997).

Jung out of time

More than in any other clinical tradition, analytical psychology places the psyche between a linear time- and place-bound personal ego, and the space-time relativity of the dream-time unconscious – between a knowing unknowing and an unknowing knowing.

In his last decade, Jung enlarged the early understanding of fields in ways that are consonant with the most forward vectors of modern science. The contributors to this volume are among those who are now catching up with the edges of Jung's thought, and adding their own knowledge and experience to create pathways toward new understanding.

Perhaps Jung shows his postmodern self most fully in his discussions of the psyche in relation to time. In an essay from *The New York Times* of 1 January 2004, the physicist Brian Greene, an exponent of superstring theory, writes thus of time:

> Today's scientists seeking to combine quantum mechanics with Einstein's theory of gravity (the general theory of relativity) are convinced that we are on the verge of another major upheaval, one that will pinpoint the more elemental concepts from which time and space emerge. Many believe this will involve a radically new formulation of natural law in which scientists will be compelled to trade the space-time matrix within which they have worked for centuries for a more basic "realm" that is itself devoid of time and space.
>
> (Greene 2004)

More than 50 years ago, in a letter of 1952, Jung allows himself to wonder:

> whether we can as hitherto go on thinking in terms of space and time, while modern physics begins to relinquish these terms in favor of a time-space continuum, in which space is no more space and time no more time. The question is, in short: shouldn't we give up the time-space categories altogether when we are dealing with psychic existence? It might

be that psyche should be understood as *unextended intensity*, not as a body moving with time. One might assume the psyche gradually rising from minute extensity to infinite intensity, transcending for instance the velocity of and thus irrealizing the body.

(Jung 1975:45)

Jung continues:

the brain might be a transformer station, in which the relatively infinite tension or intensity of the psyche proper is transformed into perceptible frequencies or "extensions". Conversely, the fading of introspective perception of the body explains itself as due to a gradual "psychification", i.e. intensification at the expense of extension. Psyche = highest intensity in the smallest space.

(Jung 1975:45)

This volume moves us, takes us, and advances us to such edges of consideration.

References

Greene, B. (2004) "The time we thought we knew", *The New York Times*, 1 January.
Jung, C.G. (1928) "On psychic energy", CW 8, Princeton, NJ: Princeton University Press.
—— (1975) *Letters*, Vol. 2; Adler, G. (ed.). Princeton, NJ: Princeton University Press.
Zabriskie, B. (1997) "Thawing the frozen accidents: the archetypal dimension of countertransference", *Journal of Analytical Psychology*, **42**(1), 25–40.
—— (2000) "Transference and dream in illness: waxing psyche, waning body", *Journal of Analytical Psychology*, **45**(1), 93–107.

Index

acting out 10, 169, 255; *see also* enactments
active imagination 2–3, 122, 126, 128–30, 140, 141; critics of Jung 212; as spiritual discipline 210; transference 159
Adams, Michael Vannoy 184
Adler, Gerhard 23, 85–6, 91, 210
aesthetic–teleological process 35
aesthetics 121
affect-ego 186, 196
agape 250, 253, 255–6
AJA *see* Association of Jungian Analysts
alchemy 8, 63, 158, 267, 268
Alex, Bill 102
Alexander, Samuel 229
Allen, Woody 110, 209
amplification 2–3, 12, 119, 123–8; analogical expansion 139–40; archetypes 51, 53; transference 159–60; unconscious communications 79
analysts: affective engagement 135–6; Jung's view on 62–3; narcissism of 167; negative spirituality 215–16; non-verbal communication 77, 79, 163–4; personality of 116, 159, 160–1, 168–70, 237; preconscious 122, 150; reflective function 79; *see also* analytic relationship; countertransference; therapeutic dyad
"analytic attitude" 242, 249, 259, 260–2, 263
analytic relationship: contents of the psyche 151; countertransference 161–2; ethical issues 254–6, 260–2, 263; interactive nature of 171; personality of analyst 169–70; religious function 205; therapeutic

focus 144; third position 258, 259, 260, 267; transference 149, 150, 158, 165–8; *see also* analysts; therapeutic dyad
analytic third 122, 239–40, 242, 258–9, 260, 267
analytical psychology 266–9, 271; central concepts of 56–63; classical school 23, 24, 124, 212–13; developmental aspects of 2, 56–82; developmental school 23, 24, 63, 212–13; history of 1–2, 5–31; origin of term 7; *see also* depth psychology
Analytical Psychology Clubs: London 22; Los Angeles 20; New York 15, 16; Paris 28; San Francisco 17–18; Zurich 9, 11, 20
anima 98, 103, 112, 180; definition of 112n4; eight types of 97; inferior function 102; shadow side 105, 107, 110; women's spirit 112n6
anthropology 33
anti-Semitism 25, 26, 185, 189, 192–7, 202n1
appraisal 71, 72, 76, 77, 78
Aquinas, Thomas 185
ARAS *see* Archive for Research in Archetypal Symbolism
archetypal school 24
archetypes 2, 9, 32–55, 58–9, 68–71, 267; amplification 123; archetypal image 43–4, 45–8, 51, 70, 211; archetype-as-such 43–4, 45–8, 52, 70; common usage of term 8, 270; complex theory 176, 180; cultural complexes 176, 187, 188, 189–92, 197; cultural unconscious 182, 183–4; destructive potential 214; development of Jung's theory 37–42; developmental school 63; dual nature